Learning Tableau 2020

Fourth Edition

Create effective data visualizations, build interactive
visual analytics, and transform your organization

Joshua N. Milligan

BIRMINGHAM - MUMBAI

Learning Tableau 2020
Fourth Edition

Producer: Tushar Gupta
Acquisition Editor – Peer Reviews: Suresh Jain
Content Development Editor: Edward Doxey
Technical Editor: Karan Sonawane
Project Editor: Carol Lewis
Copy Editor: Safis Editing
Proofreader: Safis Editing
Indexer: Manju Arasan
Presentation Designer: Sandip Tadge

First published: April 2015

Second edition: September 2016

Third edition: March 2019

Fourth edition: August 2020

Production reference: 2280820

Published by Packt Publishing Ltd.
Livery Place
35 Livery Street
Birmingham B3 2PB, UK.

ISBN 978-1-80020-036-4

www.packt.com

packt.com

Subscribe to our online digital library for full access to over 7,000 books and videos, as well as industry leading tools to help you plan your personal development and advance your career. For more information, please visit our website.

Why subscribe?

- Spend less time learning and more time coding with practical eBooks and Videos from over 4,000 industry professionals
- Learn better with Skill Plans built especially for you
- Get a free eBook or video every month
- Fully searchable for easy access to vital information
- Copy and paste, print, and bookmark content

Did you know that Packt offers eBook versions of every book published, with PDF and ePub files available? You can upgrade to the eBook version at www.Packt.com and as a print book customer, you are entitled to a discount on the eBook copy. Get in touch with us at customercare@packtpub.com for more details.

At www.Packt.com, you can also read a collection of free technical articles, sign up for a range of free newsletters, and receive exclusive discounts and offers on Packt books and eBooks.

Contributors

About the author

Joshua N. Milligan is a five-time Hall of Fame Tableau Zen Master. His passion is mentoring and helping people gain insights from their data using Tableau and Tableau Prep. As principal consultant at Teknion Data Solutions he has served clients in numerous industries since 2004 with expertise in software development, data modeling, and visual analytics.

Joshua has technically reviewed several Packt titles and authored each edition of *Learning Tableau*. He lives with his wife and four children in Tulsa.

Thank you first to all the wonderful individuals at Packt: Carol Lewis, Edward Doxey, and others who edited, reviewed, published, and publicized! Special thanks to Chris Love, Tableau Zen Master, who pointed out errors and areas needing clarity. Finally, thank you to my wife, Kara, who has supported me through this project as well as all of life!

About the reviewer

Chris Love is a Tableau and Alteryx expert working out of Nottingham, United Kingdom, where he works for Tableau Gold Partner, The Information Lab. Chris's experience in business information and analytics spans 20 years and he has been recognized as a Tableau Zen Master for 5 years, most recently in 2020. While we get to see his mastery in his work on Tableau Public, we also appreciate his focus on helping people who are new to Tableau, or those who just need to do the simplest thing possible to bring change in their organization. He uses his expertise to promote simplicity, not just advanced uses of Tableau.

Table of Contents

Preface

When Tableau was first introduced, it was a dramatic paradigm shift away from clunky reports and endless data integration projects that often produced results long after relevant decisions could have been made. Tableau disrupted the paradigm for visually interacting with data. It made it easy and intuitive (and fun!) to be hands-on with the data, to receive instant visual feedback with every action, and to ask questions and uncover insights in a natural flow of thought and interaction. The result is an ever-growing **#datafam**, a community that loves Tableau for its simplicity, beauty, and its ability to make working with data fun!

Tableau continues to expand and evolve in ways that make seeing and understanding data easier and more powerful. New features such as the Tableau Data Model, set and parameter actions, ever-growing geospatial support, animations, and new dashboard objects expand what's possible and make it easier than ever to gain and share insights from data.

The continued evolution of Tableau Prep brings the same intuitive instant feedback to data prep and cleansing that Tableau Desktop brought to data visualization, greatly extending the analytical platform of Tableau. We'll cover these new features (and more) in the chapters of this book!

We'll look at Tableau through the lens of understanding the underlying paradigm of how and why Tableau works, in the context of practical examples. Then, we'll build on this solid foundation of understanding so that you will have the tools and skills to tackle even the toughest data challenges!

Who this book is for

This book is for anyone who needs to see and understand their data! From the business user to the hardcore data analyst to the CEO, everyone needs to have the ability to ask and answer questions of data. Having a bit of background with data will definitely help, but you don't need to be confident with scripting, SQL, or database structures.

Whether you're new to Tableau, or have been using it for months or even years, with this book you'll gain a solid foundation of understanding Tableau, and the tools and skills required to build toward an advanced mastery of the tool.

What this book covers

Chapter 1, Taking Off with Tableau, introduces the foundational principles of Tableau. We'll walk through multiple examples in a logical progression that will introduce everything—from the interface, to connecting to data, to building your first visualization and even a dashboard. This chapter will give you a solid foundation for the terminology and concepts that will be used throughout the book.

Chapter 2, Connecting to Data in Tableau, using several practical examples, this chapter covers the foundational concepts involved in connecting to data. It covers the various types of connections, file types, cloud-based and on-premise databases, and how to work with metadata.

Chapter 3, Moving Beyond Basic Visualizations, builds on the basic visualization principles covered in the first chapter to explore variations and extended possibilities. You will learn when and how to use a wide variety of visualizations to analyze and communicate data.

Chapter 4, Starting an Adventure with Calculations and Parameters, introduces calculations and parameters, giving an overview of the major types of calculations, and then detailed examples of row-level and aggregate calculations. It combines conceptual knowledge with practical examples, and concludes with performance considerations.

Chapter 5, Leveraging Level of Detail Calculations, takes an in-depth look at level of detail expressions and how to use them to solve complex data challenges. It not only gives an overview, but dives into examples of FIXED, INCLUDE, and EXCLUDE variations.

Chapter 6, Diving Deep with Table Calculations, gives you a strong foundation for understanding and using table calculations to solve a wide range of data challenges. It covers the concepts of scope and direction, addressing and partitioning, and walks through several in-depth practical examples.

Chapter 7, Making Visualizations That Look Great and Work Well, covers how to extend and alter the default formatting applied to visualizations by Tableau, to customize options such as font, color, lines, shading, annotations, and tooltips to effectively communicate a data story.

Chapter 8, Telling a Data Story with Dashboards, builds on concepts that were introduced in the first chapter and expanded on throughout, walking through several practical examples of various kinds of dashboards to help you gain a solid understanding of what a dashboard is, how to build one and make it interactive, and how to use it to tell a compelling data story.

Chapter 9, Visual Analytics – Trends, Clustering, Distributions, and Forecasting, introduces the visual and statistical analytics capabilities built into Tableau and supplies you with practical examples of how and when to leverage these capabilities. This includes adding and modifying trend models, leveraging clustering capabilities, using and modifying forecast models, and visualizing the distribution of data. You will not only understand how to employ statistical models, but also evaluate their accuracy.

Chapter 10, Advanced Visualizations, builds upon the visualizations and techniques already covered, demonstrating how Tableau can be used to create any kind of visualization. A multitude examples demonstrate a wide variety of advanced visualizations, from bump charts to Marimekko charts to animated visualizations.

Chapter 11, Dynamic Dashboards, builds your dashboard skills by demonstrating various techniques to show, hide, and swap content on a dashboard. The result is a truly dynamic user experience that enhances your ability to communicate data.

Chapter 12, Exploring Mapping and Advanced Geospatial Features, demonstrates everything about maps and geospatial visualization, from map basics to geospatial functions, custom territories, and plotting data on custom background images.

Chapter 13, Understanding the Tableau Data Model, Joins, and Blends, explores the major ways of relating data in Tableau, including the new Data Model capabilities introduced in Tableau 2020.2. With practical examples and detailed descriptions, you will understand the difference between logical and physical layers and how to leverage relationships, joins, and blends to achieve great analytical results.

Chapter 14, Structuring Messy Data to Work Well in Tableau, acknowledges that real-world data is sometimes a mess and gives you a foundation for understanding well-structured data and a toolset for dealing with data that isn't structured well in Tableau.

Chapter 15, Taming Data with Tableau Prep, explores the Tableau Prep Builder tool, including the overall paradigm and specific features. You will work through an extended practical example to understand how to leverage Tableau Prep's amazing ability to clean and structure data.

Chapter 16, Sharing Your Data Story, concludes the book with a look at a wide range of options for sharing your story. From printing to sharing interactive dashboards to output PDFs and images—you'll be ready to share the stories contained in your data with those who need it most.

To get the most out of this book

This book does not assume specific database knowledge, but it will definitely help to have some basic familiarity with data itself. We'll cover the foundational principles first, and while it may be tempting to skip the first chapter, please don't! We'll lay a foundation of terminology and explore the paradigm that will be used throughout the remainder of the book.

You'll be able to follow along with many of the examples in the book using Tableau Desktop and Tableau Prep Builder (in *Chapter 15, Taming Data with Tableau Prep*).

Most examples can be completed with almost any recent version of Tableau, but to fully explore the new Data Model capabilities, you will need Tableau 2020.2 or later.

You may download and install the most recent versions from Tableau using these links:

Tableau Desktop: https://www.tableau.com/products/desktop/download

Tableau Prep Builder: https://www.tableau.com/products/prep/download

Please speak to a Tableau representative for specific licensing information. In most cases, you may install a 14-day trial of each product if you do not currently have a license.

Depending on the terms of your license, Tableau also typically allows you to use your license on two machines. This means you might have Tableau installed at the office (perhaps even an older version) but can also install the latest version on your home machine. Check your licensing agreement and speak to a Tableau representative to verify details in your case.

Download the example code files

You can download the example code files for this book from your account at
http://www.packtpub.com. If you purchased this book elsewhere, you can visit
http://www.packtpub.com/support and register to have the files emailed directly
to you.

You can download the code files by following these steps:

1. Log in or register at http://www.packtpub.com.
2. Select the **SUPPORT** tab.
3. Click on **Code Downloads & Errata**.
4. Enter the name of the book in the **Search** box and follow the on-screen
   instructions.

Once the file is downloaded, please make sure that you unzip or extract the folder
using the latest version of:

- WinRAR / 7-Zip for Windows
- Zipeg / iZip / UnRarX for Mac
- 7-Zip / PeaZip for Linux

The code bundle for the book is also hosted on GitHub at https://github.com/
PacktPublishing/Learning-Tableau-2020. We also have other code bundles
from our rich catalog of books and videos available at https://github.com/
PacktPublishing/. Check them out!

Download the color images

We also provide a PDF file that has color images of the screenshots/diagrams
used in this book. You can download it here: https://static.packt-cdn.com/
downloads/9781800200364_ColorImages.pdf.

Conventions used

There are a number of text conventions used throughout this book.

CodeInText: Indicates code words in text, database table names, folder names,
filenames, file extensions, pathnames, dummy URLs, user input, and Twitter
handles. For example; "Connect to Hospital Visits.xlsx and generate an extract."

A block of code is set as follows:

```
IF LEFT([Room], 1) = "1"
THEN "First Floor"
ELSEIF LEFT([Room], 1) = "2"
THEN "Second Floor"
END
```

Bold: Indicates a new term, an important word, or words that you see on the screen, for example, in menus or dialog boxes, also appear in the text like this. For example: "Select **Table Layout** | **Advanced** from the **Analysis** menu."

Warnings or important notes appear like this.

Tips and tricks appear like this.

Get in touch

Feedback from our readers is always welcome.

General feedback: Email feedback@packtpub.com, and mention the book's title in the subject of your message. If you have questions about any aspect of this book, please email us at questions@packtpub.com.

Errata: Although we have taken every care to ensure the accuracy of our content, mistakes do happen. If you have found a mistake in this book we would be grateful if you would report this to us. Please visit, http://www.packtpub.com/submit-errata, selecting your book, clicking on the Errata Submission Form link, and entering the details.

Piracy: If you come across any illegal copies of our works in any form on the Internet, we would be grateful if you would provide us with the location address or website name. Please contact us at copyright@packtpub.com with a link to the material.

If you are interested in becoming an author: If there is a topic that you have expertise in and you are interested in either writing or contributing to a book, please visit http://authors.packtpub.com.

Reviews

Please leave a review. Once you have read and used this book, why not leave a review on the site that you purchased it from? Potential readers can then see and use your unbiased opinion to make purchase decisions, we at Packt can understand what you think about our products, and our authors can see your feedback on their book. Thank you!

For more information about Packt, please visit packtpub.com.

1
Taking Off with Tableau

Tableau is an amazing platform for seeing, understanding, and making key decisions based on your data! With it, you will be able to carry out incredible data discovery, analysis, and storytelling. You'll accomplish these tasks and goals visually using an interface that is designed for a natural and seamless flow of thought and work.

You don't need to write complex scripts or queries to leverage the power of Tableau. Instead, you will be interacting with your data in a visual environment where everything that you drag and drop will be translated into the necessary queries for you and then displayed visually. You'll be working in real time, so you will see results immediately, get answers as quickly as you can ask questions, and be able to iterate through potentially dozens of ways to visualize the data in order to find a key insight or tell a piece of the story.

This chapter introduces the foundational principles of Tableau. We'll go through a series of examples that will introduce you to the basics of connecting to data, exploring and analyzing data visually, and finally putting it all together in a fully interactive dashboard. These concepts will be developed far more extensively in subsequent chapters. However, *don't skip this chapter*, as it introduces key terminology and concepts, including the following:

- Connecting to data
- Foundations for building visualizations
- Creating bar charts
- Creating line charts

- Creating geographic visualizations
- Using Show Me
- Bringing everything together in a dashboard

Let's begin by looking at how you can connect Tableau to your data.

Connecting to data

Tableau connects to data stored in a wide variety of files and databases. This includes flat files, such as Excel documents, spatial files, and text files; relational databases, such as SQL Server and Oracle; cloud-based data sources, such as Snowflake and Amazon Redshift; and **Online Analytical Processing (OLAP)** data sources, such as Microsoft SQL Server Analysis Services. With very few exceptions, the process of analysis and creating visualizations will be the same, no matter what data source you use.

We'll cover data connections and related topics more extensively throughout the book. For example, we'll cover the following:

- Connecting to a wide variety of different types of data sources in *Chapter 2, Connecting to Data in Tableau.*

- Using joins, blends, and object model connections in *Chapter 13, Understanding the Tableau Data Models, Joins, and Blends.*

- Understanding the data structures that work well and how to deal with messy data in *Chapter 14, Structuring Messy Data to Work Well in Tableau.*

- Leveraging the power and flexibility of Tableau Prep to cleanse and shape data for deeper analysis in *Chapter 15, Taming Data with Tableau Prep.*

In this chapter, we'll connect to a text file derived from one of the sample datasets that ships with Tableau: Superstore.csv. **Superstore** is a fictional retail chain that sells various products to customers across the United States and the file contains a record for every line item of every order with details on the customer, location, item, sales amount, and revenue.

 Please use the supplied Superstore.csv data file instead of the Tableau sample data, as there are differences that will change the results.

The Chapter 1 workbooks, included with the code files bundle, already have connections to the file; however, for this example, we'll walk through the steps of creating a connection in a new workbook:

1. Open Tableau. You should see the home screen with a list of connection options on the left and, if applicable, thumbnail previews of recently edited workbooks in the center, along with sample workbooks at the bottom.

2. Under **Connect** and **To a File**, click on **Text File**.

3. In the **Open** dialog box, navigate to the \Learning Tableau\Chapter 01 directory and select the Superstore.csv file.

You will now see the data connection screen, which allows you to visually create connections to data sources. We'll examine the features of this screen in detail in the *Connecting to data* section of *Chapter 2, Connecting to Data in Tableau*. For now, Tableau has already added and given a preview of the file for the connection:

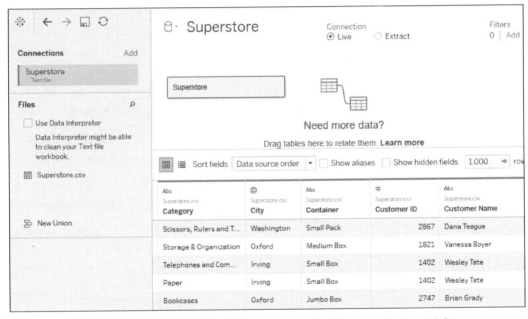

Figure 1.1: The data connection screen allows you to build a connection to your data

For this connection, no other configuration is required, so simply click on the **Sheet 1** tab at the bottom to start visualizing the data! You should now see the main work area within Tableau, which looks like this:

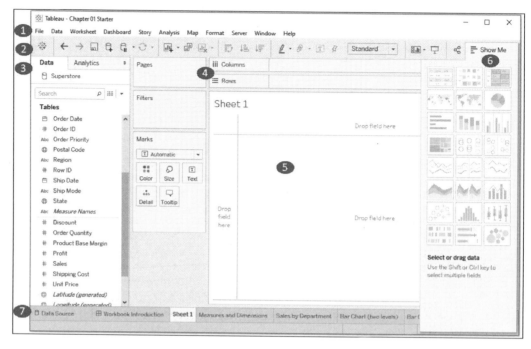

Figure 1.2: Elements of Tableau's primary interface, numbered with descriptions below

We'll refer to elements of the interface throughout the book using specific terminology, so take a moment to familiarize yourself with the terms used for various components numbered in the preceding screenshot:

1. The **menu** contains various menu items for performing a wide range of functions.

2. The **toolbar** allows common functions such as undo, redo, save, add a data source, and so on.

3. The **Data** pane is active when the **Data** tab is selected and lists all tables and fields of the selected data source. The **Analytics** pane is active when the **Analytics** tab is selected and gives options for supplementing visualizations with visual analytics.

4. Various shelves such as **Pages**, **Columns**, **Rows**, and **Filters** serve as areas to drag and drop fields from the data pane. The **Marks** card contains additional shelves such as **Color**, **Size**, **Text**, **Detail**, and **Tooltip**. Tableau will visualize data based on the fields you drop onto the shelves.

Data fields in the **Data** pane are available to add to a view. Fields that have been dropped onto a shelf are called *in the view* or *active fields* because they play an active role in the way Tableau draws the visualization.

5. The **canvas** or **view** is where Tableau will draw the data visualization. In addition to dropping fields on shelves, you may also drop fields directly on to the view. A **title** is located at the top of the canvas. By default, the title displays the name of the sheet, but it can be edited or hidden.

6. **Show Me** is a feature that allows you to quickly iterate through various types of visualizations based on data fields of interest. We'll look at **Show Me** toward the end of the chapter.

7. The tabs at the bottom of the window give you options for editing the data source, as well as navigating between and adding any number of sheets, dashboards, or stories. Often, any tab (whether it is a sheet, a dashboard, or a story) is referred to generically as a **sheet**.

A Tableau workbook is a collection of data sources, sheets, dashboards, and stories. All of this is saved as a single Tableau workbook file (`.twb` or `.twbx`). A workbook is organized into a collection of tabs of various types:

- A sheet is a single data visualization, such as a bar chart or a line graph. Since sheet is also a generic term for any tab, we'll often refer to a sheet as a **view** because it is a single view of the data.

- A **dashboard** is a presentation of any number of related views and other elements (such as text or images) arranged together as a cohesive whole to communicate a message to an audience. Dashboards are often designed to be interactive.

- A **story** is a collection of dashboards or single views that have been arranged to communicate a narrative from the data. Stories may also be interactive.

Along the bottom of the screen, you'll notice a few other items. As you work, a **status bar** at the bottom left will display important information and details about the view, selections, and the user. Various controls at the bottom right allow you to navigate between sheets, dashboards, and stories, as well as to view the tabs with **Show Filmstrip** or switch to a sheet sorter showing an interactive thumbnail of all sheets in the workbook.

Now that you have connected to the data in the text file, we'll explore some examples that lay the foundation for data visualization and then move on to building some foundational visualization types. To prepare for this, please do the following:

1. From the menu, select **File | Exit**.

2. When prompted to save changes, select **No**.

3. From the \learning Tableau\Chapter 01 directory, open the file Chapter 01 Starter.twbx. This file contains a connection to the Superstore data file and is designed to help you walk through the examples in this chapter.

 The files for each chapter include a Starter workbook that allows you to work through the examples given in this book. If, at any time, you'd like to see the completed examples, open the Complete workbook for the chapter.

Having made a connection to the data, you are ready to start visualizing and analyzing it. As you begin to do so, you will take on the role of an analyst at the retail chain. You'll ask questions of the data, build visualizations to answer those questions, and ultimately design a dashboard to share the results. Let's start by laying some foundations for understanding how Tableau visualizes data.

Foundations for building visualizations

When you first connect to a data source such as the Superstore file, Tableau will display the data connection and the fields in the **Data** pane. Fields can be dragged from the data pane onto the canvas area or onto various shelves such as **Rows**, **Columns**, **Color**, or **Size**. As we'll see, the placement of the fields will result in different encodings of the data based on the type of field.

Measures and dimensions

The fields from the data source are visible in the **Data** pane and are divided into **Measures** and **Dimensions**. In older versions of Tableau, these are separate sections in the **Data** pane. In newer versions, each table will have **Measures** and **Dimensions** separated by a line:

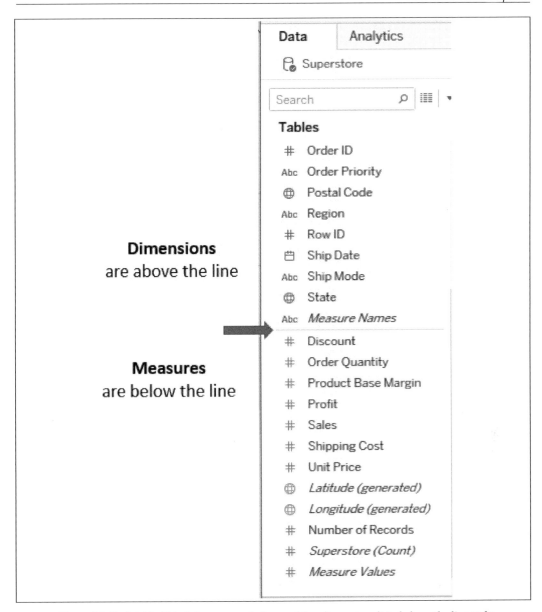

Figure 1.3: Each table (this data source only has one) has dimensions listed above the line and measures listed below the line

The difference between **Measures** and **Dimensions** is a fundamental concept to understand when using Tableau:

- **Measures** are values that are aggregated. For example, they are summed, averaged, counted, or the result is the minimum or maximum value.
- **Dimensions** are values that determine the level of detail at which measures are aggregated. You can think of them as slicing the measures or creating groups into which the measures fit. The combination of dimensions used in the view defines the view's basic level of detail.

As an example (which you can view in the Chapter 01 Starter workbook on the **Measures and Dimensions** sheet), consider a view created using the Region and Sales fields from the Superstore connection:

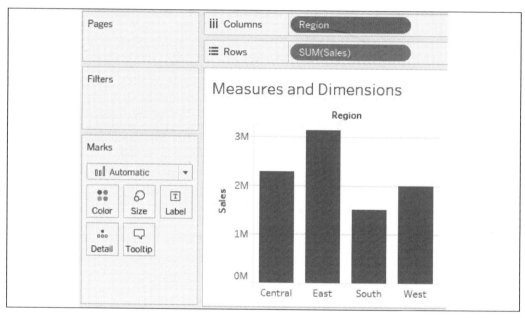

Figure 1.4: A bar chart demonstrating the use of Measures and Dimensions

The Sales field is used as a measure in this view. Specifically, it is being aggregated as a sum. When you use a field as a measure in the view, the type aggregation (for example, SUM, MIN, MAX, and AVG) will be shown on the active field. Note that, in the preceding example, the active field on **Rows** clearly indicates the sum aggregation of Sales: SUM(Sales).

The Region field is a dimension with one of four values for each record of data: **Central**, **East**, **South**, or **West**. When the field is used as a dimension in the view, it slices the measure. So, instead of an overall sum of sales, the preceding view shows the sum of sales for each region.

Discrete and continuous fields

Another important distinction to make with fields is whether a field is being used as **discrete** or **continuous.** Whether a field is discrete or continuous determines how Tableau visualizes it based on where it is used in the view. Tableau will give a visual indication of the default value for a field (the color of the icon in the **Data** pane) and how it is being used in the view (the color of the active field on a shelf). Discrete fields, such as `Region` in the previous example, are blue. Continuous fields, such as `Sales`, are green.

> In the screenshots in the printed version of this book, you should be able to distinguish a slight difference in shade between the **discrete** (blue) and the **continuous** (green) fields, but pay special attention to the interface as you follow along using Tableau. You may also wish to download the color image pack from Packt Publishing, available at `https://static.packt-cdn.com/downloads/9781800200364_ColorImages.pdf`.

Discrete fields

Discrete (blue) fields have values that are shown as distinct and separate from one another. Discrete values can be reordered and still make sense. For example, you could easily rearrange the values of `Region` to be `East`, `South`, `West`, and `Central`, instead of the default order in *Figure 1.4*.

When a discrete field is used on the **Rows** or **Columns** shelves, the field defines headers. Here, the discrete field `Region` defines the column headers:

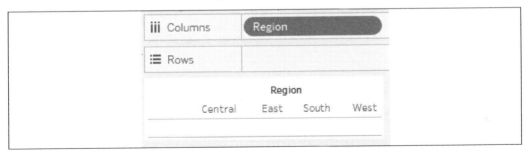

Figure 1.5: The discrete field on Columns defines column headers

Here, it defines the row headers:

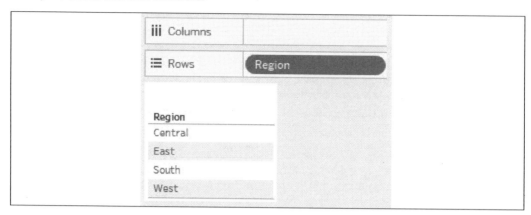

Figure 1.6: The discrete field on Rows defines row headers

When used for **Color**, a discrete field defines a discrete color palette in which each color aligns with a distinct value of the field:

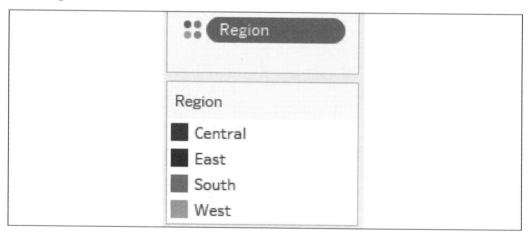

Figure 1.7: The discrete field on Color defines a discrete color palette

Continuous fields

Continuous (green) fields have values that flow from first to last as a continuum. Numeric and date fields are often (though, not always) used as continuous fields in the view. The values of these fields have an order that it would make little sense to change.

When used on **Rows** or **Columns**, a continuous field defines an axis:

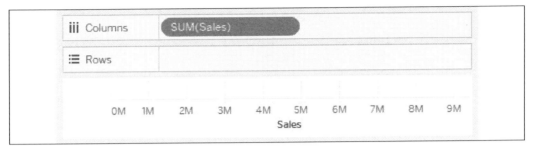

Figure 1.8: The continuous field on Columns (or Rows) defines an axis

When used for **color**, a continuous field defines a gradient:

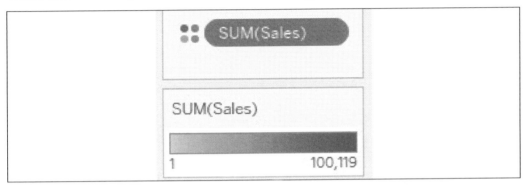

Figure 1.9: The continuous field on Color defines a gradient color palette

It is very important to note that continuous and discrete are different concepts from measure and dimension. While most dimensions are discrete by default, and most measures are continuous by default, it is possible to use any measure as a discrete field and some dimensions as continuous fields in the view, as shown here:

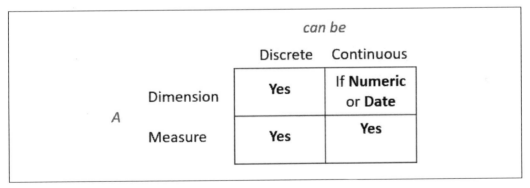

Figure 1.10: Measures and Dimensions can be discrete or continuous

To change the default of a field, right-click on the field in the **Data** pane and select **Convert to Discrete** or **Convert to Continuous**.

To change how a field is used in the view, right-click on the field in the view and select **Discrete** or **Continuous**. Alternatively, you can drag and drop the fields between **Dimensions** and **Measures** in the **Data** pane.

In general, you can think of the differences between the types of fields as follows:

- Choosing between a dimension and measure tells Tableau *how to slice or aggregate* the data.
- Choosing between discrete and continuous tells Tableau *how to display* the data with a header or an axis and defines individual colors or a gradient.

As you work through the examples in this book, pay attention to the fields you are using to create the visualizations, whether they are dimensions or measures, and whether they are discrete or continuous. Experiment with changing fields in the view from continuous to discrete, and vice versa, to gain an understanding of the differences in the visualization. We'll put this understanding into practice as we turn our attention to visualizing data.

Visualizing data

A new connection to a data source is an invitation to explore and discover! At times, you may come to the data with very well-defined questions and a strong sense of what you expect to find. Other times, you will come to the data with general questions and very little idea of what you will find. The visual analytics capabilities of Tableau empower you to rapidly and iteratively explore the data, ask new questions, and make new discoveries.

The following visualization examples cover a few of the most foundational visualization types. As you work through the examples, keep in mind that the goal is not simply to learn how to create a specific chart. Rather, the examples are designed to help you think through the process of asking questions of the data and getting answers through iterations of visualization. Tableau is designed to make that process intuitive, rapid, and transparent.

Something that is far more important than memorizing the steps to create a specific chart type is understanding how and why to use Tableau to create a chart and being able to adjust your visualization to gain new insights as you ask new questions.

Bar charts

Bar charts visually represent data in a way that makes the comparison of values across different categories easy. The length of the bar is the primary means by which you will visually understand the data. You may also incorporate color, size, stacking, and order to communicate additional attributes and values.

Creating bar charts in Tableau is very easy. Simply drag and drop the measure you want to see on to either the **Rows** or **Columns** shelf and the dimension that defines the categories on to the opposing **Rows** or **Columns** shelf.

As an analyst for **Superstore**, you are ready to begin a discovery process focused on sales (especially the dollar value of sales). As you follow the examples, work your way through the sheets in the Chapter 01 Starter workbook. The Chapter 01 Complete workbook contains the complete examples so that you can compare your results at any time:

1. Click on the **Sales by Department** tab to view that sheet.

2. Drag and drop the Sales field from **Measures** in the **Data** pane on to the **Columns** shelf. You now have a bar chart with a single bar representing the sum of sales for all of the data in the data source.

3. Drag and drop the Department field from **Dimensions** in the **Data** pane to the **Rows** shelf. This slices the data to give you three bars, each having a length that corresponds to the sum of sales for each department:

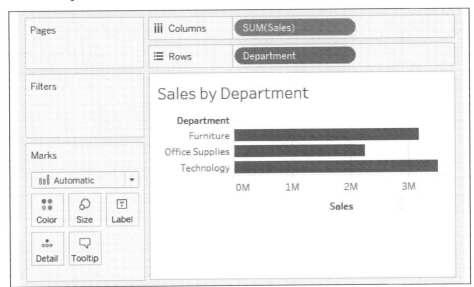

Figure 1.11: The view Sales by Department should look like this when you have completed the preceding steps

You now have a horizontal bar chart. This makes comparing the sales between the departments easy. The **type** drop-down menu on the **Marks** card is set to **Automatic** and indicates that Tableau has determined that bars are the best visualization given the fields you have placed in the view. As a dimension, Department slices the data. Being discrete, it defines row headers for each department in the data. As a measure, the Sales field is aggregated. Being continuous, it defines an axis. The mark type of bar causes individual bars for each department to be drawn from 0 to the value of the sum of sales for that department.

 Typically, Tableau draws a mark (such as a bar, a circle, or a square) for every combination of dimensional values in the view. In this simple case, Tableau is drawing a single bar mark for each dimensional value (Furniture, Office Supplies, and Technology) of Department. The type of mark is indicated and can be changed in the drop-down menu on the **Marks** card. The number of marks drawn in the view can be observed on the lower-left status bar.

Tableau draws different marks in different ways; for example, bars are drawn from 0 (or the end of the previous bar, if stacked) along the axis. Circles and other shapes are drawn at locations defined by the value(s) of the field that is defining the axis. Take a moment to experiment with selecting different mark types from the drop-down menu on the **Marks** card. A solid grasp of how Tableau draws different mark types will help you to master the tool.

Iterations of bar charts for deeper analysis

Using the preceding bar chart, you can easily see that the **Technology** department has more total sales than either the **Furniture** or **Office Supplies** departments. What if you want to further understand sales amounts for departments across various regions? Follow these two steps:

1. Navigate to the **Bar Chart (two levels)** sheet, where you will find an initial view that is identical to the one you created earlier.

2. Drag the Region field from **Dimensions** in the **Data** pane to the **Rows** shelf and drop it to the left of the Department field already in view.

You should now have a view that looks like this:

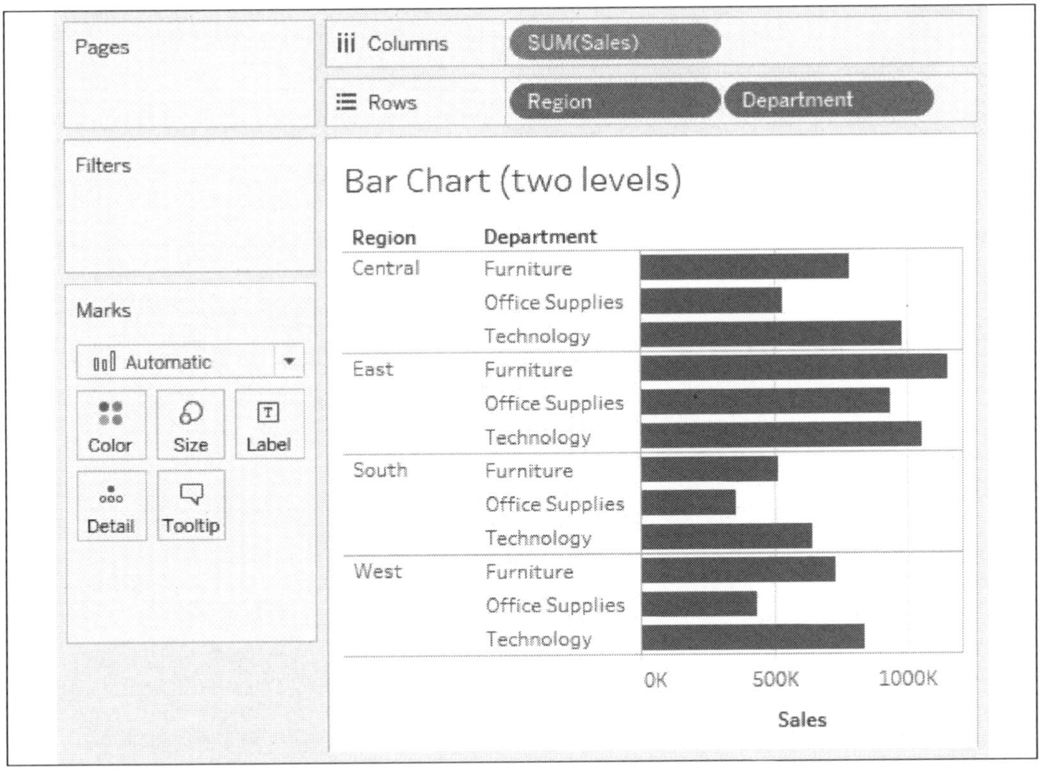

Figure 1.12: The view Bar Chart (two levels) should look like this when you have completed the preceding steps

You still have a horizontal bar chart, but now you've introduced Region as another dimension that changes the level of detail in the view and further slices the aggregate of the sum of sales. By placing Region before Department, you can easily compare the sales of each department within a given region.

Now you are starting to make some discoveries. For example, the **Technology** department has the most sales in every region, except in the **East**, where **Furniture** had higher sales. **Office Supplies** never has the highest sales in any region.

Consider an alternate view, using the same fields arranged differently:

1. Navigate to the **Bar Chart (stacked)** sheet, where you will find a view that is identical to the original bar chart.

2. Drag the Region field from the **Rows** shelf and drop it on to the **Color** shelf:

Figure 1.13: The view Bar Chart (stacked) should look like this

Instead of a **side-by-side bar chart**, you now have a **stacked bar chart**. Each segment of the bar is color-coded by the Region field. Additionally, a color legend has been added to the workspace. You haven't changed the level of detail in the view, so sales are still summed for every combination of Region and Department:

The **view level of detail** is a key concept when working with Tableau. In most basic visualizations, the combination of values of all dimensions in the view defines the lowest level of detail for that view. All measures will be aggregated or sliced by the lowest level of detail. In the case of most simple views, the number of marks (indicated in the lower-left status bar) corresponds to the number of unique combinations of dimensional values. That is, there will be one mark for each combination of dimension values.

*   If Department is the only field used as a dimension, you will have a view at the department level of detail, and all measures in the view will be aggregated per department.

- If Region is the only field used as a dimension, you will have a view at the region level of detail, and all measures in the view will be aggregated per region.

- If you use both Department and Region as dimensions in the view, you will have a view at the level of department and region. All measures will be aggregated per unique combination of department and region, and there will be one mark for each combination of department and region.

Stacked bars can be useful when you want to understand part-to-whole relationships. It is now easier to see what portion of the total sales of each department is made in each region. However, it is very difficult to compare sales for most of the regions across departments. For example, can you easily tell which department had the highest sales in the **East** region? It is difficult because, with the exception of the **West** region, every segment of the bar has a different starting place.

Now take some time to experiment with the bar chart to see what variations you can create:

1. Navigate to the **Bar Chart (experimentation)** sheet.

2. Try dragging the Region field from **Color** to the other various shelves on the **Marks** card, such as **Size**, **Label**, and **Detail**. Observe that in each case the bars remain stacked but are redrawn based on the visual encoding defined by the Region field.

3. Use the **Swap** button on the toolbar to swap fields on **Rows** and **Columns**. This allows you to very easily change from a horizontal bar chart to a vertical bar chart (and vice versa):

Figure 1.14: Swap Rows and Columns button

4. Drag and drop Sales from the **Measures** section of the **Data** pane on top of the Region field on the **Marks** card to replace it. Drag the Sales field to **Color** if necessary, and notice how the color legend is a gradient for the continuous field.

5. Experiment further by dragging and dropping other fields on to various shelves. Note the behavior of Tableau for each action you take.

6. From the **File** menu, select **Save**.

 If your OS, machine, or Tableau stops unexpectedly, then the **Autosave** feature should protect your work. The next time you open Tableau, you will be prompted to recover any previously open workbooks that had not been manually saved. You should still develop a habit of saving your work early and often, though, and maintaining appropriate backups.

As you continue to explore various iterations, you'll gain confidence with the flexibility available to visualize your data.

Line charts

Line charts connect related marks in a visualization to show movement or a relationship between those connected marks. The position of the marks and the lines that connect them are the primary means of communicating the data. Additionally, you can use size and color to communicate additional information.

The most common kind of line chart is a **time series**. A time series shows the movement of values over time. Creating one in Tableau requires only a date and a measure.

Continue your analysis of Superstore sales using the Chapter 01 Starter workbook you just saved:

1. Navigate to the **Sales over time** sheet.

2. Drag the Sales field from **Measures** to **Rows**. This gives you a single, vertical bar representing the sum of all sales in the data source.

3. To turn this into a time series, you must introduce a date. Drag the Order Date field from **Dimensions** in the **Data** pane on the left and drop it into **Columns**. Tableau has a built-in date hierarchy, and the default level of Year has given you a line chart connecting four years. Notice that you can clearly see an increase in sales year after year:

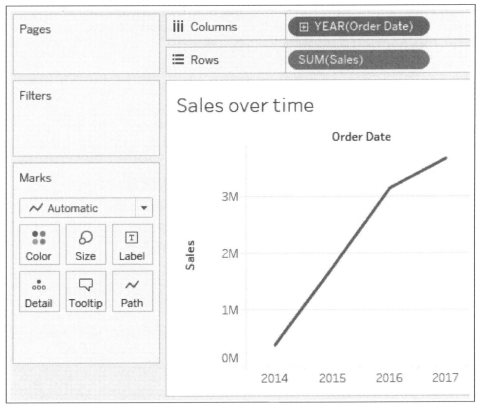

Figure 1.15: An interim step in creating the final line chart; this shows the sum of sales by year

4. Use the drop-down menu on the YEAR(Order Date) field on **Columns** (or right-click on the field) and switch the date field to use **Quarter**. You may notice that **Quarter** is listed twice in the drop-down menu. We'll explore the various options for date parts, values, and hierarchies in the *Visualizing Dates and Times* section of *Chapter 3, Moving Beyond Basic Visualizations*. For now, select the second option:

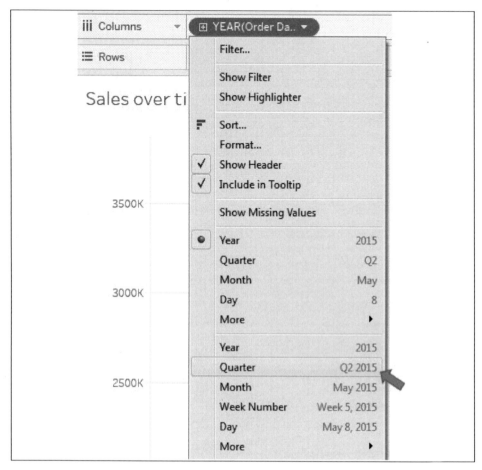

Figure 1.16: Select the second Quarter option in the drop-down menu.

Notice that the cyclical pattern is quite evident when looking at sales by quarter:

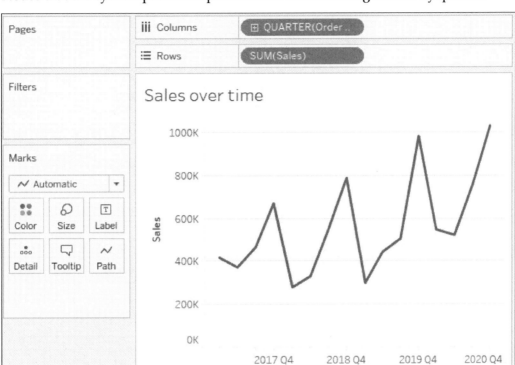

Figure 1.17: Your final view shows sales over each quarter for the last several years.

Let's consider some variations of line charts that allow you to ask and answer even deeper questions.

Iterations of line charts for deeper analysis

Right now, you are looking at the overall sales over time. Let's do some analysis at a slightly deeper level:

1. Navigate to the **Sales over time (overlapping lines)** sheet, where you will find a view that is identical to the one you just created.

2. Drag the Region field from **Dimensions** to **Color**. Now you have a line per region, with each line a different color, and a legend indicating which color is used for which region. As with the bars, adding a dimension to **color** splits the marks. However, unlike the bars, where the segments were stacked, the lines are not stacked. Instead, the lines are drawn at the exact value for the sum of sales for each region and quarter. This allows easy and accurate comparison. It is interesting to note that the cyclical pattern can be observed for each region:

Figure 1.18: This line chart shows sum of sales by quarter with different colored lines for each region

With only four regions, it's relatively easy to keep the lines separate. But what about dimensions that have even more distinct values? Let's consider that case in the following example:

1. Navigate to the **Sales over time (multiple rows)** sheet, where you will find a view that is identical to the one you just created.

2. Drag the Category field from **Dimensions** and drop it directly on top of the Region field currently on the **Marks** card. This replaces the Region field with Category. You now have 17 overlapping lines. Often, you'll want to avoid more than two or three overlapping lines. But you might also consider using color or size to showcase an important line in the context of the others. Also, note that clicking on an item in the **Color** legend will highlight the associated line in the view. Highlighting is an effective way to pick out a single item and compare it to all the others.

3. Drag the Category field from **Color** on the **Marks** card and drop it into **Rows**. You now have a line chart for each category. Now you have a way of comparing each product over time without an overwhelming overlap, and you can still compare trends and patterns over time. This is the start of a spark-lines visualization that will be developed more fully in *Chapter 10, Advanced Visualizations*:

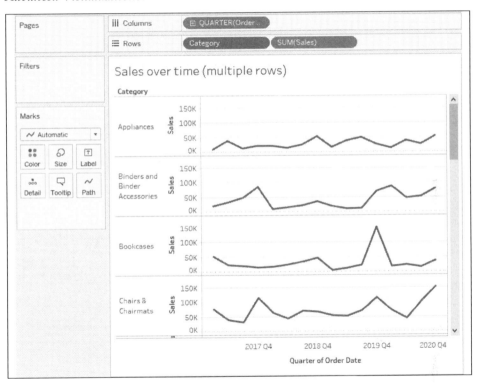

Figure 1.19: Your final view should be a series of line charts for each Category

The variations in lines for each Category allow you to notice variations in the trends, extremes, and the rate of change.

Geographic visualizations

In Tableau, the built-in geographic database recognizes geographic roles for fields such as Country, State, City, Airport, Congressional District, or Zip Code. Even if your data does not contain latitude and longitude values, you can simply use geographic fields to plot locations on a map. If your data does contain latitude and longitude fields, you may use those instead of the generated values.

> Tableau will automatically assign geographic roles to some fields based on a field name and a sampling of values in the data. You can assign or reassign geographic roles to any field by right-clicking on the field in the **Data** pane and using the **Geographic Role** option. This is also a good way to see what built-in geographic roles are available.

Geographic visualization is incredibly valuable when you need to understand where things happen and whether there are any spatial relationships within the data. Tableau offers several types of geographic visualization:

- Filled maps
- Symbol maps
- Density maps

Additionally, Tableau can read spatial files and geometries from some databases and render spatial objects, polygons, and more. We'll take a look at these and other geospatial capabilities in *Chapter 12, Exploring Mapping and Advanced Geospatial Features*. For now, we'll consider some foundational principles for geographic visualization.

Filled maps

Filled maps fill areas such as countries, states, or ZIP codes to show a location. The color that fills the area can be used to communicate measures such as average sales or population as well as dimensions such as region. These maps are also called **choropleth maps**.

Let's say you want to understand sales for Superstore and see whether there are any patterns geographically.

Note: If your regional settings are not US, you may need to use the **Edit Locations** option to set the country to the **United States**.

You might take an approach like the following:

1. Navigate to the **Sales by State** sheet.
2. Double-click on the State field in the **Data** pane. Tableau automatically creates a geographic visualization using the Latitude (generated), Longitude (generated), and State fields.
3. Drag the Sales field from the **Data** pane and drop it on the **Color** shelf on the **Marks** card. Based on the fields and shelves you've used, Tableau has switched the automatic mark type to **Map**:

Figure 1.20: A filled map showing the sum of sales per state

The filled map fills each state with a single color to indicate the relative sum of sales for that state. The color legend, now visible in the view, gives the range of values and indicates that the state with the least sales had a total of **3,543** and the state with the most sales had a total of **1,090,616**.

When you look at the number of marks displayed in the bottom status bar, you'll see that it is **49**. Careful examination reveals that the marks consist of the lower 48 states and Washington DC; Hawaii and Alaska are not shown. Tableau will only draw a geographic mark, such as a filled state, if it exists in the data and is not excluded by a filter.

Observe that the map does display Canada, Mexico, and other locations not included in the data. These are part of a background image retrieved from an online map service. The state marks are then drawn on top of the background image. We'll look at how you can customize the map and even use other map services in the *Mapping Techniques* section of *Chapter 12, Exploring Mapping and Advanced Geospatial Features.*

Filled maps can work well in interactive dashboards and have quite a bit of aesthetic value. However, certain kinds of analyses are very difficult with filled maps. Unlike other visualization types, where size can be used to communicate facets of the data, the size of a filled geographic region only relates to the geographic size and can make comparisons difficult. For example, which state has the highest sales? You might be tempted to say Texas or California because the larger size influences your perception, but would you have guessed Massachusetts? Some locations may be small enough that they won't even show up compared to larger areas. Use filled maps with caution and consider pairing them with other visualizations on dashboards for clear communication.

Symbol maps

With symbol maps, marks on the map are not drawn as filled regions; rather, marks are shapes or symbols placed at specific geographic locations. The size, color, and shape may also be used to encode additional dimensions and measures.

Continue your analysis of Superstore sales by following these steps:

1. Navigate to the **Sales by Postal Code** sheet.
2. Double-click on Postal Code under **Dimensions**. Tableau automatically adds Postal Code to the **Detail** of the **Marks** card and Longitude (generated) and Latitude (generated) to **Columns** and **Rows**. The mark type is set to a circle by default, and a single circle is drawn for each postal code at the correct latitude and longitude.
3. Drag Sales from **Measures** to the **Size** shelf on the **Marks** card. This causes each circle to be sized according to the sum of sales for that postal code.

4. Drag `Profit` from **Measures** to the **Color** shelf on the **Marks** card. This encodes the mark color to correspond to the sum of profit. You can now see the geographic location of profit and sales at the same time. This is useful because you will see some locations with high sales and low profit, which may require some action.

The final view should look like this, after making some fine-tuned adjustments to the size and color:

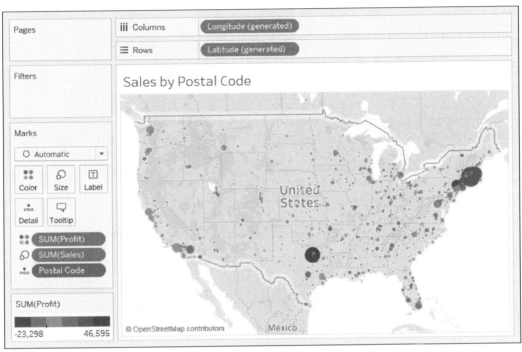

Figure 1.21: A symbol map showing the sum of profit (encoded with color) and the sum of sales (encoded with size) per Postal Code

Sometimes, you'll want to adjust the marks on a symbol map to make them more visible. Some options include the following:

- If the marks are overlapping, click on the **Color** shelf and set the transparency to somewhere between **50%** and **75%**. Additionally, add a dark border. This makes the marks stand out, and you can often better discern any overlapping marks.

- If marks are too small, click on the **Size** shelf and adjust the slider. You may also double-click on the **size** legend and edit the details of how Tableau assigns size.

- If the marks are too faint, double-click on the **Color** legend and edit the details of how Tableau assigns color. This is especially useful when you are using a continuous field that defines a color gradient.

A combination of tweaking the size and using **Stepped Color** and **Use Full Color Range**, as shown here, produced the result for this example:

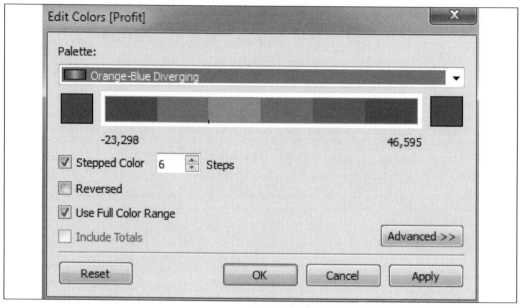

Figure 1.22: The Edit Colors dialog includes options for changing the number of steps, reversing, using the full color range, including totals, and advanced options for adjusting the range and center point

Unlike filled maps, symbol maps allow you to use size to visually encode aspects of the data. Symbol maps also allow greater precision. In fact, if you have latitude and longitude in your data, you can very precisely plot marks at a street address-level of detail. This type of visualization also allows you to map locations that do not have clearly defined boundaries.

Sometimes, when you manually select **Map** in the **Marks** card drop-down menu, you will get an error message indicating that filled maps are not supported at the level of detail in the view. In those cases, Tableau is rendering a geographic location that does not have built-in shapes.

Other than cases where filled maps are not possible, you will need to decide which type best meets your needs. We'll also consider the possibility of combining filled maps and symbol maps in a single view in later chapters.

Density maps

Density maps show the spread and concentration of values within a geographic area. Instead of individual points or symbols, the marks blend together, showing greater intensity in areas with a high concentration. You can control the **Color, Size**, and **Intensity**.

Let's say you want to understand the geographic concentration of orders. You might create a density map using the following steps:

1. Navigate to the **Density of Orders** sheet.
2. Double-click on the Postal Code field in the **Data** pane. Just as before, Tableau automatically creates a symbol map geographic visualization using the Latitude (generated), Longitude (generated), and State fields.
3. Using the drop-down menu on the **Marks** card, change the mark type to **Density**. The individual circles now blend together showing concentrations:

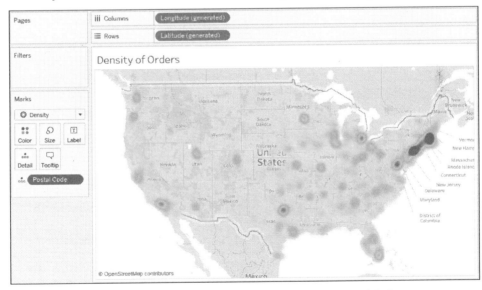

Figure 1.23: A density map showing concentration by Postal Code

Try experimenting with the **Color** and **Size** options. Clicking on **Color**, for example, reveals some options specific to the **Density** mark type:

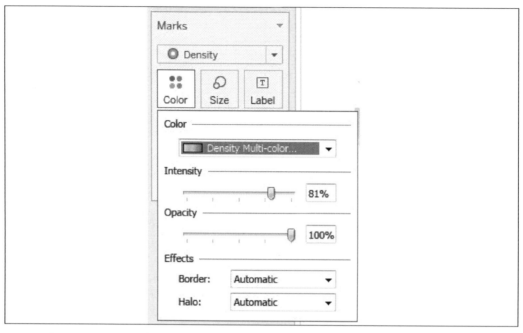

Figure 1.24: Options for adjusting the Color, Intensity, Opacity, and Effects for Density marks

Several color palettes are available that work well for density marks (the default ones work well with light color backgrounds, but there are others designed to work with dark color backgrounds). The **Intensity** slider allows you to determine how intensely the marks should be drawn based on concentrations. The **Opacity** slider lets you decide how transparent the marks should be.

This density map displays a high concentration of orders from the east coast. Sometimes, you'll see patterns that merely reflect population density. In such cases, your analysis may not be particularly meaningful. In this case, the concentration on the east coast compared to the lack of density on the west coast is intriguing.

Using Show Me

Show Me is a powerful component of Tableau that arranges selected and active fields into the places required for the selected visualization type. The **Show Me** toolbar displays small thumbnail images of different types of visualizations, allowing you to create visualizations with a single click. Based on the fields you select in the **Data** pane and the fields that are already in view, **Show Me** will enable possible visualizations and highlight a recommended visualization.

Explore the features of **Show Me** by following these steps:

1. Navigate to the **Show Me** sheet.

2. If the **Show Me** pane is not expanded, click on the **Show Me** button in the upper right of the toolbar to expand the pane.

3. Press and hold the *Ctrl* key while clicking on the Postal Code, State, and Profit fields in the **Data** pane to select each of those fields. With those fields highlighted, **Show Me** should look like this:

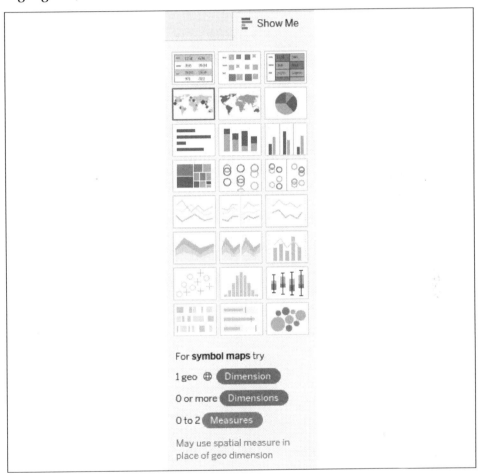

Figure 1.25: The Show Me interface

Notice that the **Show Me** window has enabled certain visualization types such as **text tables, heat maps, symbol maps, filled maps**, and **bar charts**. These are the visualizations that are possible given the fields already in the view, in addition to any selected in the **Data** pane. Show Me highlights the recommended visualization for the selected fields and gives a description of what fields are required as you hover over each visualization type. Symbol maps, for example, require one geographic dimension and 0 to 2 measures.

Other visualizations are grayed out, such as **lines**, **area charts**, and **histograms**. Show Me will not create these visualization types with the fields that are currently in the view and are selected in the **Data** pane. Hover over the grayed out line charts option in Show Me. It indicates that line charts require one or more measures (which you have selected) but also require a date field (which you have not selected).

Tableau will draw line charts with fields other than dates. Show Me gives you options for what is typically considered good practice for visualizations. However, there may be times when you know that a line chart would represent your data better. Understanding how Tableau renders visualizations based on fields and shelves instead of always relying on Show Me will give you much greater flexibility in your visualizations and will allow you to rearrange things when Show Me doesn't give you the exact results you want. At the same time, you will need to cultivate an awareness of good visualization practices.

Show Me can be a powerful way in which to quickly iterate through different visualization types as you search for insights into the data. But as a data explorer, analyst, and storyteller, you should consider Show Me as a helpful guide that gives suggestions. You may know that a certain visualization type will answer your questions more effectively than the suggestions of Show Me. You also may have a plan for a visualization type that will work well as part of a dashboard but isn't even included in Show Me.

You will be well on your way to learning and mastering Tableau when you can use Show Me effectively but feel just as comfortable building visualizations without it. Show Me is powerful for quickly iterating through visualizations as you look for insights and raise new questions. It is useful for starting with a standard visualization that you will further customize. It is wonderful as a teaching and learning tool.

However, be careful to not use it as a crutch without understanding how visualizations are actually built from the data. Take the time to evaluate why certain visualizations are or are not possible. Pause to see what fields and shelves were used when you selected a certain visualization type.

End the example by experimenting with Show Me by clicking on various visualization types, looking for insights into the data that may be more or less obvious based on the visualization type. **Circle views** and **box-and-whisker plots** show the distribution of postal codes for each state. Bar charts easily expose several postal codes with negative profit.

Now that you have become familiar with creating individual views of the data, let's turn our attention to putting it all together in a dashboard.

Putting everything together in a dashboard

Often, you'll need more than a single visualization to communicate the full story of the data. In these cases, Tableau makes it very easy for you to use multiple visualizations together on a dashboard. In Tableau, a **dashboard** is a collection of views, filters, parameters, images, and other objects that work together to communicate a data story. Dashboards are often interactive and allow end users to explore different facets of the data.

Dashboards serve a wide variety of purposes and can be tailored to suit a wide variety of audiences. Consider the following possible dashboards:

- A summary-level view of profit and sales to allow executives to take a quick glimpse at the current status of the company
- An interactive dashboard, allowing sales managers to drill into sales territories to identify threats or opportunities
- A dashboard allowing doctors to track patient readmissions, diagnoses, and procedures to make better decisions about patient care
- A dashboard allowing executives of a real-estate company to identify trends and make decisions for various apartment complexes
- An interactive dashboard for loan officers to make lending decisions based on portfolios broken down by credit ratings and geographic location

Considerations for different audiences and advanced techniques will be covered in detail in *Chapter 8, Telling a Data Story with Dashboards*.

The dashboard interface

When you create a new dashboard, the interface will be slightly different than it is when designing a single view. We'll start designing your first dashboard after a brief look at the interface. You might navigate to the **Superstore Sales** sheet and take a quick look at it yourself.

The dashboard window consists of several key components. Techniques for using these objects will be detailed in *Chapter 8, Telling a Data Story with Dashboards*. For now, focus on gaining some familiarity with the options that are available. One thing you'll notice is that the left sidebar has been replaced with dashboard-specific content:

Figure 1.26: The sidebar for dashboards

The left sidebar contains two tabs:

- A **Dashboard** tab, for sizing options and adding sheets and objects to the dashboard.
- A **Layout** tab, for adjusting the layout of various objects on the dashboard.

The **Dashboard** pane contains options for previewing based on the target device along with several sections:

- A **Size** section, for dashboard sizing options.
- A **Sheets** section, containing all sheets (views) available to place on the dashboard.
- An **Objects** section with additional objects that can be added to the dashboard.

You can add sheets and objects to a dashboard by dragging and dropping. As you drag the view, a light-gray shading will indicate the location of the sheet in the dashboard once it is dropped. You can also double-click on any sheet and it will be added automatically.

In addition to adding sheets, the following objects may be added to the dashboard:

- **Horizontal** and **Vertical** layout containers will give you finer control over the layout.
- **Text** allows you to add text labels and titles.
- An **Image** and even embedded **Web Page** content can be added.
- A **Blank** object allows you to preserve blank space in a dashboard, or it can serve as a placeholder until additional content is designed.
- A **Navigation** object allows the user to navigate between dashboards.
- An **Export** button allows end users to export the dashboard as a PowerPoint, PDF, or image.
- An **Extension** gives you the ability to add controls and objects that you or a third party have developed for interacting with the dashboard and providing extended functionality.

Using the toggle, you can select whether new objects will be added as **Tiled** or **Floating**. **Tiled** objects will snap into a tiled layout next to other tiled objects or within layout containers. **Floating** objects will float on top of the dashboard in successive layers.

When a worksheet is first added to a dashboard, any legends, filters, or parameters that were visible in the worksheet view will be added to the dashboard. If you wish to add them at a later point, select the sheet in the dashboard and click on the little drop-down caret on the upper-right side. Nearly every object has the drop-down caret, providing many options for fine-tuning the appearance of the object and controlling behavior.

Take note of the various controls that become visible for selected objects on the dashboard:

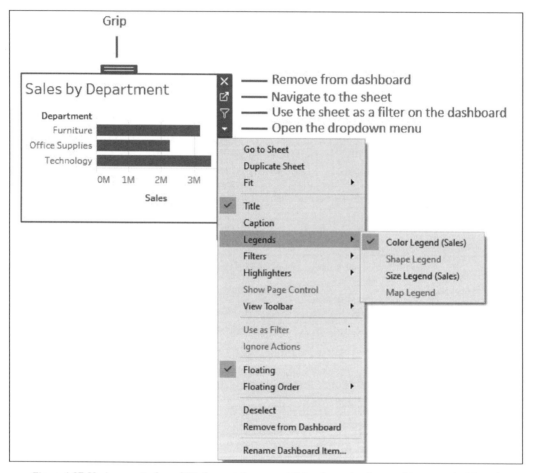

Figure 1.27: Various controls and UI elements become visible when selecting an object on a dashboard

You can resize an object on the dashboard using the border. The **Grip**, labelled in *Figure 1.27*, allows you to move the object once it has been placed. We'll consider other options as we go.

Building your dashboard

With an overview of the interface, you are now ready to build a dashboard by following these steps:

1. Navigate to the **Superstore Sales** sheet. You should see a blank dashboard.

2. Successively double-click on each of the following sheets listed in the **Dashboard** section on the left: **Sales by Department, Sales over time**, and **Sales by Postal Code**. Notice that double-clicking on the object adds it to the layout of the dashboard.

3. Add a title to the dashboard by checking **Show Dashboard title** at the lower left of the sidebar.

4. Select the **Sales by Department** sheet in the dashboard and click on the drop-down arrow to show the menu.

5. Select **Fit | Entire View**. The **Fit** options describe how the visualization should fill any available space.

Be careful when using various fit options. If you are using a dashboard with a size that has not been fixed, or if your view dynamically changes the number of items displayed based on interactivity, then what might have once looked good might not fit the view nearly as well.

6. Select the **Sales** size legend by clicking on it. Use the **X** option to remove the legend from the dashboard:

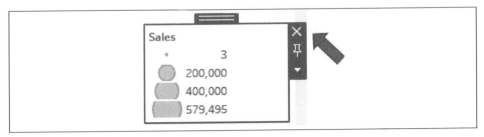

Figure 1.28: Select the legend by clicking on it, then click the X to remove it from the dashboard

7. Select the **Profit** color legend by clicking on it. Use the **Grip** to drag it and drop it under the map.

8. For each view (**Sales by Department**, **Sales by Postal Code**, and **Sales over time**), select the view by clicking on an empty area in the view. Then, click on the **Use as Filter** option to make that view an interactive filter for the dashboard:

Figure 1.29: Click on the Use as Filter button to use a view as a filter in a dashboard

Your dashboard should look like this:

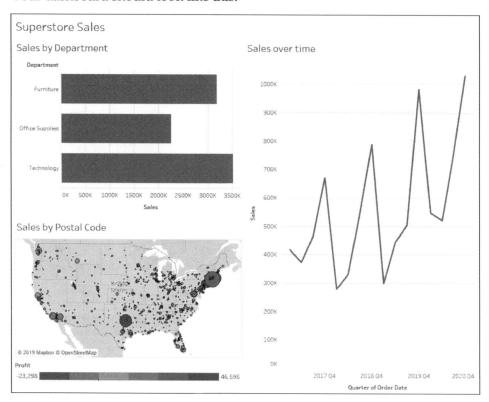

Figure 1.30: The final dashboard consisting of three views

9. Take a moment to interact with your dashboard. Click on various marks, such as the bars, states, and points of the line. Notice that each selection filters the rest of the dashboard. Clicking on a selected mark will deselect it and clear the filter. Also, notice that selecting marks in multiple views causes filters to work together. For example, selecting the bar for **Furniture** in **Sales by Department** and the **2019 Q4** in **Sales over time** allows you to see all the ZIP codes that had furniture sales in the fourth quarter of 2019.

Congratulations! You have now created a dashboard that allows you to carry out interactive analysis!

As an analyst for the Superstore chain, your visualizations allowed you to explore and analyze the data. The dashboard you created can be shared with members of management, and it can be used as a tool to help them see and understand the data to make better decisions. When a manager selects the furniture department, it immediately becomes obvious that there are locations where sales are quite high, but the profit is actually very low. This may lead to decisions such as a change in marketing or a new sales focus for that location. Most likely, this will require additional analysis to determine the best course of action. In this case, Tableau will empower you to continue the cycle of discovery, analysis, and storytelling.

Summary

Tableau's visual environment allows a rapid and iterative process of exploring and analyzing data visually. You've taken your first steps toward understanding how to use the platform. You connected to data and then explored and analyzed the data using some key visualization types such as bar charts, line charts, and geographic visualizations. Along the way, you focused on learning the techniques and understanding key concepts such as the difference between measures and dimensions, and discrete and continuous fields. Finally, you put all of the pieces together to create a fully functional dashboard that allows an end user to understand your analysis and make discoveries of their own.

In the next chapter, we'll explore how Tableau works with data. You will be exposed to fundamental concepts and practical examples of how to connect to various data sources. Combined with the key concepts you just learned about building visualizations, you will be well equipped to move on to more advanced visualizations, deeper analysis, and telling fully interactive data stories.

2
Connecting to Data in Tableau

Tableau offers the ability to connect to nearly any data source. It does this with a unique paradigm that leverages the power and efficiency of existing database engines or alternately extracts the data locally. We'll look at joins, blends, unions, and the brand new object model in *Chapter 13, Understanding the Tableau Data Model, Joins, and Blends*. In this chapter, we'll focus on essential concepts of how Tableau connects to and works with data. We'll cover the following topics:

- The Tableau paradigm
- Connecting to data
- Managing data source metadata
- Working with extracts instead of live connections
- Filtering data

We'll start by gaining an understanding of the underlying paradigm of how Tableau works with data.

The Tableau paradigm

The unique and exciting experience of working with data in Tableau is a result of **VizQL (Visual Query Language)**.

VizQL was developed as a Stanford University research project, focusing on the natural ways that humans visually perceive the world and how that could be applied to data visualization. We naturally perceive differences in size, shape, spatial location, and color. VizQL allows Tableau to translate your actions, as you drag and drop fields of data in a visual environment, into a query language that defines how the data encodes those visual elements. You will never need to read, write, or debug VizQL. As you drag and drop fields onto various shelves defining size, color, shape, and spatial location, Tableau will generate the VizQL behind the scenes. This allows you to focus on visualizing data, not writing code!

One of the benefits of VizQL is that it provides a common way of describing how the arrangement of various fields in a view defines a query related to the data. This common baseline can then be translated into numerous flavors of SQL, MDX, and **Tableau Query Language (TQL**, used for extracted data). Tableau will automatically perform the translation of VizQL into a native query to be run by the source data engine.

In its simplest form, the Tableau paradigm of working with data looks like the following diagram:

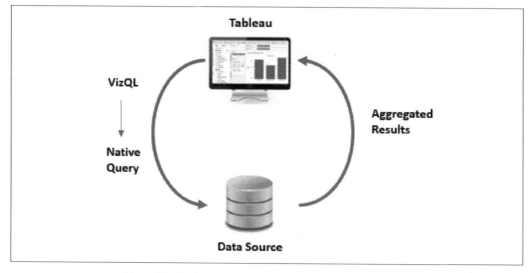

Figure 2.1: The basic Tableau paradigm for working with data

Let's look at how this paradigm works in a practical example.

A simple example

Open the `Chapter 02 Starter.twbx` workbook located in the `\Learning Tableau\ Chapter 02` directory and navigate to the `Tableau Paradigm` sheet. That view was created by dropping the **Region** dimension on **Columns** and the **Sales** measure on **Rows**. Here is a screenshot:

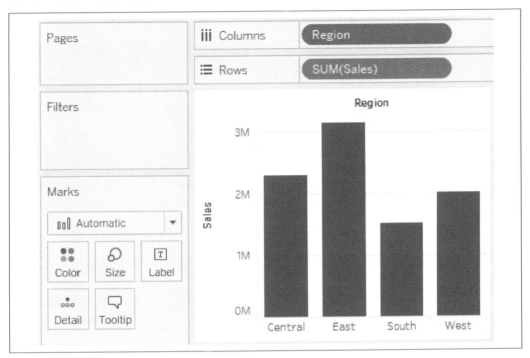

Figure 2.2: This bar chart is the result of a query that returned four aggregate rows of data

The view is defined by two fields. **Region** is the only dimension, which means it defines the level of detail in the view and slices the measure so that there will be a bar per region. **Sales** is used as a measure aggregated by summing each sale within each region. (Notice also that **Region** is discrete, resulting in column **headers** while **Sales** is continuous, resulting in an **axis**.)

For the purpose of this example (although the principle is applicable to any data source), let's say you were connected live to a SQL Server database with the Superstore data stored in a table. When you first create the preceding screenshot, Tableau generates a VizQL script, which is translated into an SQL script and sent to the SQL Server. The SQL Server database engine evaluates the query and returns aggregated results to Tableau, which are then rendered visually.

The entire process would look something like the following diagram in Tableau's paradigm:

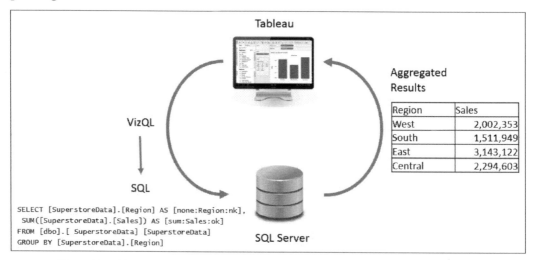

Figure 2.3: Tableau generated the bar chart in the previous image using a paradigm like this

There may have been hundreds, thousands, or even millions of rows of sales data in SQL Server. However, when SQL Server processes the query, it returns aggregate results. In this case, SQL Server returns only four aggregate rows of data to Tableau—one row for each region.

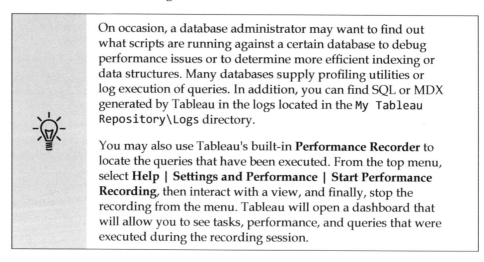

On occasion, a database administrator may want to find out what scripts are running against a certain database to debug performance issues or to determine more efficient indexing or data structures. Many databases supply profiling utilities or log execution of queries. In addition, you can find SQL or MDX generated by Tableau in the logs located in the My Tableau Repository\Logs directory.

You may also use Tableau's built-in **Performance Recorder** to locate the queries that have been executed. From the top menu, select **Help | Settings and Performance | Start Performance Recording**, then interact with a view, and finally, stop the recording from the menu. Tableau will open a dashboard that will allow you to see tasks, performance, and queries that were executed during the recording session.

To see the aggregate data that Tableau used to draw the view, press *Ctrl + A* to select all the bars, and then right-click one of them and select **View Data**.

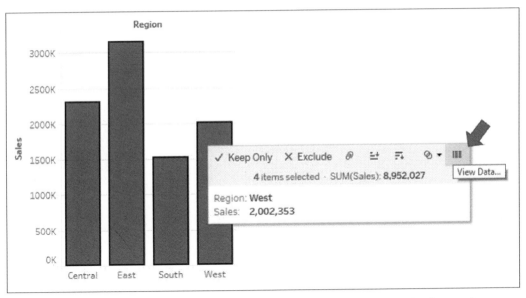

Figure 2.4: Use the View Data tooltip option to see a summary or underlying data for a mark

This will reveal a **View Data** window:

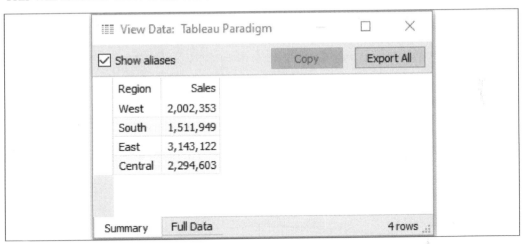

Figure 2.5: The Summary tab displays the aggregate data Tableau used to render each mark in the view

The **View Data** screen allows you to observe the data in the view. The **Summary** tab displays the aggregate-level data that was used to render the view. The **Sales** values here are the sum of sales for each region. When you click the **Full Data** (previously named **Underlying**) tab, Tableau will query the data source to retrieve all the records that make up the aggregate records. In this case, there are **9,426** underlying records, as indicated on the status bar in the lower-right corner of the following screenshot:

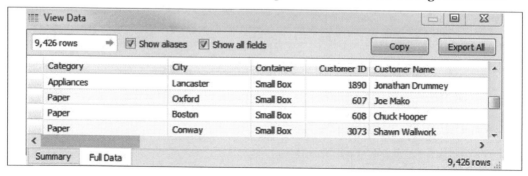

Figure 2.6: The Full Data tab reveals the row-level data in the database

Tableau did not need **9,426** records to draw the view and did not request them from the data source until the **Full Data** data tab was clicked.

Database engines are optimized to perform aggregations on data. Typically, these database engines are also located on powerful servers. Tableau leverages the optimization and power of the underlying data source. In this way, Tableau can visualize massive datasets with relatively little local processing of the data.

Additionally, Tableau will only query the data source when you make changes requiring a new query or a view refresh. Otherwise, it will use the aggregate results stored in a local cache, as illustrated here:

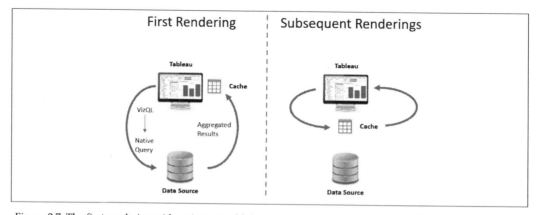

Figure 2.7: The first rendering with a given set of fields queries the data source directly. Subsequent renderings will query the cache, even if the same fields are re-arranged in the view

In the preceding example, the query with **Region** as a dimension and the sum of **Sales** as a measure will only be issued once to the data source. When the four rows of aggregated results are returned, they are stored in the cache. After the initial rendering, if you were to move **Region** to another visual encoding shelf, such as color, or **Sales** to a different visual encoding shelf, such as size, then Tableau will retrieve the aggregated rows from the cache and simply re-render the view.

 You can force Tableau to bypass the cache and refresh the data from a data source by pressing *F5* or selecting your data source from the **Data** menu and selecting **Refresh**. Do this any time you want a view to reflect the most recent changes in a live data source.

If you were to introduce new fields into the view that did not have cached results, Tableau would send a new query to the data source, retrieve the aggregated results, and add those results to the cache.

Connecting to data

There is virtually no limit to the data that Tableau can visualize! Almost every new version of Tableau adds new native connectors. Tableau continues to add native connectors for cloud-based data. The **web data connector** allows you to write a connector for any online data you wish to retrieve. The **Tableau Hyper API** allows you to programmatically read and write extracts of data, enabling you to access data from any source and write it to a native Tableau format. Additionally, for any database without a built-in connection, Tableau gives you the ability to use a generic **ODBC** connection.

You may have multiple data sources in the same workbook. Each source will show up under the **Data** tab on the left sidebar.

 Although the terms are often used interchangeably, it is helpful to make a distinction. A **connection** technically refers to the connection made to data in a single location, such as tables in a single database, or files of the same type in the same directory structure. A **data source** may contain more than one connection that can be joined together, such as a table in SQL Server joined to tables in a Snowflake database that are joined to an Excel table. You can think about it this way: a Tableau workbook may contain one or more data sources and each data source may contain one or more connections. We'll maintain this distinction throughout the book.

This section will focus on a few practical examples of connecting to various data sources. There's no way to cover every possible type of connection but we will cover several that are representative of others. You may or may not have access to some of the data sources in the following examples. Don't worry if you aren't able to follow each example. Merely observe the differences.

Connecting to data in a file

File-based data includes all sources of data where the data is stored in a file. File-based data sources include the following:

- **Extracts**: A .hyper or .tde file containing data that was extracted from an original source.

- **Microsoft Access**: An .mdb or .accdb database file created in Access.

- **Microsoft Excel:** An .xls, .xlsx, or .xlsm spreadsheet created in Excel. Multiple Excel sheets or sub-tables may be joined or unioned together in a single connection.

- **Text file**: A delimited text file, most commonly .txt, .csv, or .tab. Multiple text files in a single directory may be joined or unioned together in a single connection.

- **Local cube file**: A .cub file that contains multi-dimensional data. These files are typically exported from OLAP databases.

- **Adobe PDF**: A .pdf file that may contain tables of data that can be parsed by Tableau.

- **Spatial file**: A wide variety of spatial formats are supported such as .kml, .shp, .tab, .mif, spatial JSON, and ESRI database files. These formats contain spatial objects that can be rendered by Tableau.

- **Statistical file**: A .sav, .sas7bdat, .rda, or .rdata file generated by statistical tools, such as SAS or R.

- **JSON file**: A .json file that contains data in JSON format.

In addition to those mentioned previously, you can connect to Tableau files to import connections that you have saved in another Tableau workbook (.twb or .twbx). The connection will be imported, and changes will only affect the current workbook.

Follow this example to see a connection to an Excel file:

1. Navigate to the **Connect to Excel** sheet in the Chapter 02 Starter.twbx workbook.

2. From the menu, select **Data | New Data Source** and select **Microsoft Excel** from the list of possible connections.

3. In the open dialogue, open the `Superstore.xlsx` file from the `\Learning Tableau\Chapter 02` directory. Tableau will open the **Data Source** screen. You should see the two sheets of the Excel document listed on the left.

4. Double-click the **Orders** sheet and then the **Returns** sheet. Tableau will prompt you with an **Edit Relationship** dialog. We'll cover relationships in depth in *Chapter 13, Understanding the Tableau Data Model, Joins, and Blends*. For now, accept the defaults by closing the dialog.

Your data source screen should look similar to the following screenshot:

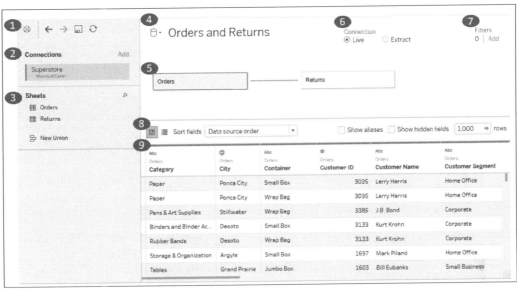

Figure 2.8: The data source screen with two objects (Orders and Returns)

Take some time to familiarize yourself with the **Data Source** screen interface, which has the following features (numbered in the preceding screenshot):

*   **Toolbar**: The toolbar has a few of the familiar controls, including undo, redo, and save. It also includes the option to refresh the current data source.

*   **Connections**: All the connections in the current data source. Click **Add** to add a new connection to the current data source. This allows you to join data across different connection types. Each connection will be color-coded so that you can distinguish what data is coming from which connection.

*   **Sheets (or Tables)**: This lists all the tables of data available for a given connection. This includes sheets, sub-tables, and named ranges for Excel; tables, views, and stored procedures for relational databases; and other connection-dependent options, such as **New Union** or **Custom SQL**.

- **Data Source Name**: This is the name of the currently selected data source. You may select a different data source using the drop-down arrow next to the database icon. You may click the name of the data source to edit it.

- **Object / Data Model Canvas**: Drop sheets and tables from the left into this area to make them part of the connection. You may add additional tables by dragging and dropping or double-clicking them. Each will be added as an object to the object model. You may also add tables as unions or double-click an object to edit the underlying tables and joins. We'll cover the details extensively in *Chapter 13, Understanding the Tableau Data Model, Joins, and Blends*. For now, simply note that Orders and Returns are related together by the Order ID.

- **Live or Extract Options**: For many data sources, you may choose whether you would like to have a live connection or an extracted connection. We'll look at these in further detail later in the chapter.

- **Data Source Filters**: You may add filters to the data source. These will be applied at the data-source level, and thus to all views of the data using this data source in the workbook.

- **Preview Pane Options**: These options allow you to specify whether you'd like to see a preview of the data or a list of metadata, and how you would like to preview the data (examples include alias values, hidden fields shown, and how many rows you'd like to preview).

- **Preview Pane/Metadata View**: Depending on your selection in the options, this space either displays a preview of data or a list of all fields with additional metadata. Notice that these views give you a wide array of options, such as changing data types, hiding or renaming fields, and applying various data transformation functions. We'll consider some of these options in this and later chapters.

 Once you have created and configured your data source, you may click any sheet to start using it.

Conclude this exercise with the following steps:

1. Click the data source name to edit the text and rename the data source to Orders and Returns.

2. Navigate to the **Connect to Excel** sheet and, using the Orders and Returns data source, create a time series showing **Returns (Count)** by **Return Reason**. Your view should look like the following screenshot:

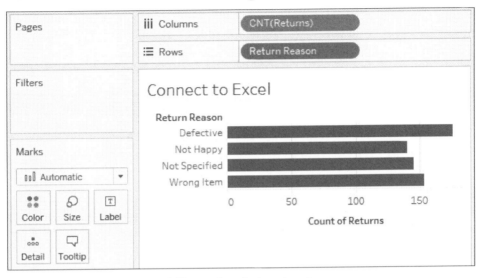

Figure 2.9: The number of returns by return reason

If you need to edit the connection at any time, select **Data** from the menu, locate your connection, and then select **Edit Data Source...**. Alternately, you may right-click any data source under the **Data** tab on the left sidebar and select **Edit Data Source...**, or click the **Data Source** tab in the lower-left corner. You may access the data source screen at any time by clicking the **Data Source** tab in the lower-left corner of Tableau Desktop.

Connecting to data on a server

Database servers, such as SQL Server, Snowflake, Vertica, and Oracle, host data on one or more server machines and use powerful database engines to store, aggregate, sort, and serve data based on queries from client applications. Tableau can leverage the capabilities of these servers to retrieve data for visualization and analysis. Alternately, data can be extracted from these sources and stored in an extract.

As an example of connecting to a server data source, we'll demonstrate connecting to SQL Server. If you have access to a server-based data source, you may wish to create a new data source and explore the details. However, this specific example is not included in the workbook in this chapter.

As soon as the Microsoft SQL Server connection is selected, the interface displays options for some initial configuration as follows:

Microsoft SQL Server

Ser̲ver: `TDS-W541-JM\AGAPE|`

D̲atabase: `Optional`

Enter information to sign in to the database:

⦿ Use W̲indows Authentication (preferred)

◯ Us̲e a specific username and password:

U̲sername: `_____`

P̲assword: `_____`

☐ Require SS̲L
☐ Read uncommitted dat̲a

Initial SQL…   Sign In

Figure 2.10: The connection editor for Microsoft SQL Server

A connection to SQL Server requires the **Server** name, as well as authentication information.

A database administrator can configure SQL Server to **Use Windows Authentication** or a SQL Server username and password. With SQL Server, you can also optionally allow reading uncommitted data. This can potentially improve performance but may also lead to unpredictable results if data is being inserted, updated, or deleted at the same time as Tableau is querying. Additionally, you may specify SQL to be run at connect time using the **Initial SQL...** link in the lower-left corner.

In order to maintain high standards of security, Tableau will not save a password as part of a data source connection. This means that if you share a workbook using a live connection with someone else, they will need to have credentials to access the data. This also means that when you first open the workbook, you will need to re-enter your password for any connections requiring a password.

Once you click the orange **Sign In** button, you will see a screen that is very similar to the connection screen you saw for Excel. The main difference is on the left, where you have an option for selecting a **Database**, as shown in the following screenshot:

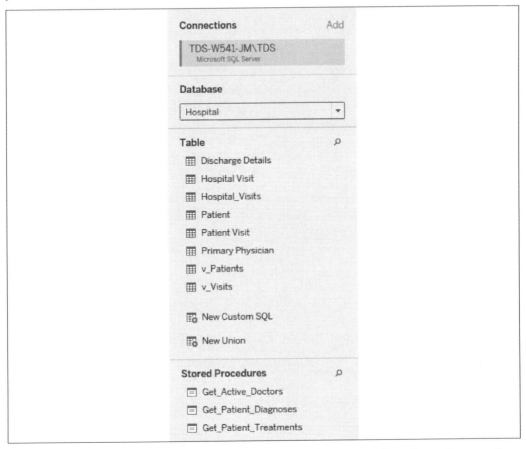

Figure 2.11: Once connected to a database, Tableau will display tables, views, and stored procedures as options to add to the object model

Once you've selected a database, you will see the following:

- **Table**: This shows any data tables or views contained in the selected database.

- **New Custom SQL**: You may write your own custom SQL scripts and add them as tables. You may join these as you would any other table or view.

- **New Union**: You may union together tables in the database. Tableau will match fields based on name and data type, and you may additionally merge fields as needed.

- **Stored Procedures**: You may use a stored procedure that returns a table of data. You will be given the option of setting values for stored procedure parameters or using or creating a Tableau parameter to pass values.

Once you have finished configuring the connection, click a tab for any sheet to begin visualizing the data.

Using extracts

Any data source that is using an extract will have a distinctive icon that indicates the data has been pulled from an original source into an extract, as shown in the following screenshot:

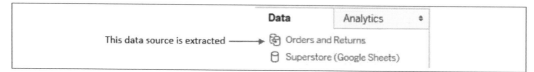

Figure 2.12: The icon next to a data source indicates whether it is extracted or not

The first data connection in the preceding data pane is extracted, while the second is not. After an extract has been created, you may choose to use the extract or not. When you right-click a data source (or **Data** from the menu and then the data source), you will see the following menu options:

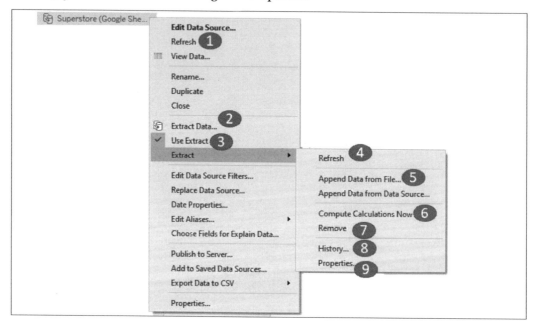

Figure 2.13: The context menu for a data connection in the Data pane with Extract options numbered

Let's cover them in more detail:

1. **Refresh**: The **Refresh** option under the data source simply tells Tableau to refresh the local cache of data. With a live data source, this would re-query the underlying data. With an extracted source, the cache is cleared and the extract is required, but this **Refresh** option does not update the extract from the original source. To do that, use **Refresh** under the **Extract** sub-menu (see number 4 in this list).

2. **Extract Data...**: This creates a new extract from the data source (replacing an existing extract if it exists).

3. **Use Extract**: This option is enabled if there is an extract for a given data source. Unchecking the option will tell Tableau to use a live connection instead of the extract. The extract will not be removed and may be used again by checking this option at any time. If the original data source is not available to this workbook, Tableau will ask where to find it.

4. **Refresh**: This **Refresh** option refreshes the extract with data from the original source. It does not optimize the extract for some changes you make (such as hiding fields or creating new calculations).

5. **Append Data from File...** or **Append Data from Data Source....**:These options allow you to append additional files or data sources to an existing extract, provided they have the same exact data structure as the original source. This adds rows to your existing extract; it will not add new columns.

6. **Compute Calculations Now**: This will restructure the extract, based on changes you've made since originally creating the extract, to make it as efficient as possible. Certain calculated fields may be *materialized* (that is, calculated once so that the resulting value can be stored) and newly hidden columns or deleted calculations will be removed from the extract.

7. **Remove**: This removes the definition of the extract, optionally deletes the extract file, and resumes a live connection to the original data source.

8. **History**: This allows you to view the history of the extract and refreshes.

9. **Properties**: This enables you to view the properties of the extract, such as the location, underlying source, filters, and row limits.

Let's next consider the performance ramifications of using extracts.

Connecting to data in the cloud

Certain data connections are made to data that is hosted in the cloud. These include **Amazon RDS, Google BigQuery, Microsoft SQL Azure, Snowflake, Salesforce, Google Sheets**, and many others. It is beyond the scope of this book to cover each connection in depth, but as an example of a cloud data source, we'll consider connecting to Google Sheets.

Google Sheets allows users to create and maintain spreadsheets of data online. Sheets may be shared and collaborated on by many different users. Here, we'll walk through an example of connecting to a sheet that is shared via a link.

To follow the example, you'll need a free Google account. With your credentials, follow these steps:

1. Click the **Add new data source** button on the toolbar, as shown here:

Figure 2.14: The Add Data button

2. Select **Google Sheets** from the list of possible data sources. You may use the search box to quickly narrow the list.

3. On the next screen, sign in to your Google account and allow Tableau Desktop the appropriate permissions. You will then be presented with a list of all your Google Sheets, along with preview and search capabilities, as shown in the following screenshot:

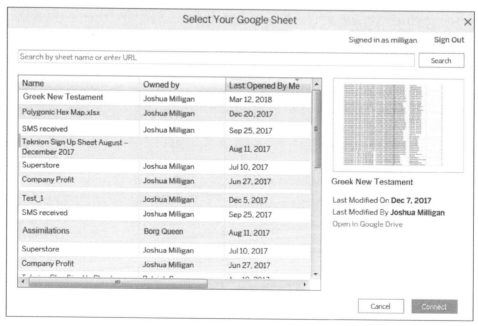

Figure 2.15: You may select any Google Sheet you have permissions to view
or you may enter the URL for a shared sheet

4. Enter the following URL (for convenience, it is included in the `Chapter 02 Starter` workbook in the **Connect to Google Sheets** tab, and may be copied and pasted) into the search box and click the **Search** button: `https://docs.google.com/spreadsheets/d/1fWMGkPt0o7sdbW50tG4QLSZDwkjNO9X0mCkw-LKYu1A/edit?usp=sharing`:

5. Select the resulting `Superstore` sheet in the list and then click the **Connect** button. You should now see the **Data Source** screen.

6. Click the **Data Source** name to rename it to `Superstore (Google Sheets)`:

Figure 2.16: Renaming a Data Source

7. For the purpose of this example, switch the connection option from **Live** to **Extract**. When connecting to your own Google Sheets data, you may choose either **Live** or **Extract**:

Figure 2.17: Switch between Live and Extract, Edit extract options, and Add Filters

8. Click the tab for the **Connect to Google Sheets** sheet. You will be prompted for a location to save the extract. Accept the default name and save it in the `Learning Tableau\Chapter 02` directory (selecting **Yes** to overwrite the existing file if needed). The data should be extracted within a few seconds.

9. Create a filled map of **Profit** by **State**, with **Profit** defining the **Color** and **Label**:

Figure 2.18: The filled map demonstrates the ability to connect to a
cloud-based data source

If your location is outside the United States, you may need to
change your regional settings for Tableau to properly show the
states in the map. Use the menu and select **File | Workbook
Locale | More** and select **English (United States)**.

Now that we've seen a few specific examples of connecting to data, let's consider
some shortcuts and how to manage our data sources.

Shortcuts for connecting to data

You can make certain connections very quickly. These options will allow you to
begin analyzing more quickly:

- Paste data from the clipboard. If you have copied data in your system's
  clipboard from any source (for example, a spreadsheet, a table on a web
  page, or a text file), you can then paste the data directly into Tableau. This
  can be done using *Ctrl + V*, or **Data | Paste Data** from the menu. The data
  will be stored as a file and you will be alerted to its location when you save
  the workbook.

- Select **File | Open** from the menu. This will allow you to open any data file that
  Tableau supports, such as text files, Excel files, Access files (not available on
  macOS), spatial files, statistical files, JSON, and even offline cube (.cub) files.

- Drag and drop a file from Windows Explorer or Finder onto the Tableau workspace. Any valid file-based data source can be dropped onto the Tableau workspace or even the Tableau shortcut on your desktop or taskbar.

- Duplicate an existing data source. You can duplicate an existing data source by right-clicking and selecting **Duplicate**.

These shortcuts provide a quick way for analyzing the data you need. Let's turn our attention to managing the data sources.

Managing data source metadata

Data sources in Tableau store information about the connection(s). In addition to the connection itself (for example, database server name, database, and/or filenames), the data source also contains information about all the fields available (such as field name, data type, default format, comments, and aliases). Often, this *data about the data* is referred to as **metadata**.

Right-clicking a field in the data pane reveals a menu of metadata options. Some of these options will be demonstrated in a later exercise; others will be explained throughout the book. These are some of the options available via right-clicking:

- Renaming the field
- Hiding the field
- Changing aliases for values of a non-date dimension
- Creating calculated fields, groups, sets, bins, or parameters
- Splitting the field
- Changing the default use of a date or numeric field to either discrete or continuous
- Redefining the field as a dimension or a measure
- Changing the data type of the field
- Assigning a geographic role to the field
- Changing defaults for how a field is displayed in a visualization, such as the default colors and shapes, number or date format, sort order (for dimensions), or type of aggregation (for measures)
- Adding a default comment for a field (which will be shown as a tooltip when hovering over a field in the data pane, or shown as part of the description when **Describe...** is selected from the menu)
- Adding or removing the field from a hierarchy

Metadata options that relate to the visual display of the field, such as default sort order or default number format, define the overall default for a field. However, you can override the defaults in any individual view by right-clicking the active field on the shelf and selecting the desired options.

To see how this works, use the filled map view of Profit by State that you created in the **Connect to Google Sheets** view. If you did not create this view, you may use the **Orders and Returns** data source, though the resulting view will be slightly different. With the filled map in front of you, follow these steps:

1. Right-click the **Profit** field in the data pane and select **Default Properties | Number Format...**. The resulting dialog gives you many options for numeric format.

2. Set the number format to **Currency (Custom)** with 0 **Decimal places** and the **Display Units** in Thousands (K). After clicking **OK**, you should notice that the labels on the map have updated to include currency notation:

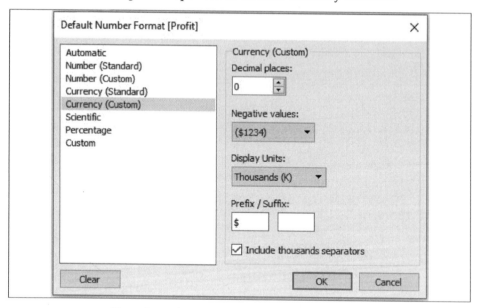

Figure 2.19: Editing the default number format of a field

3. Right-click the **Profit** field again and select **Default properties | Color...**. The resulting dialog gives you an option to select and customize the default color encoding of the **Profit** field. Experiment with various palettes and settings. Notice that every time you click the **Apply** button, the visualization updates.

Diverging palettes (palettes that blend from one color to another) work particularly well for fields such as **Profit**, which can have negative and positive values. The default center of 0 allows you to easily tell what values are positive or negative based on the color shown.

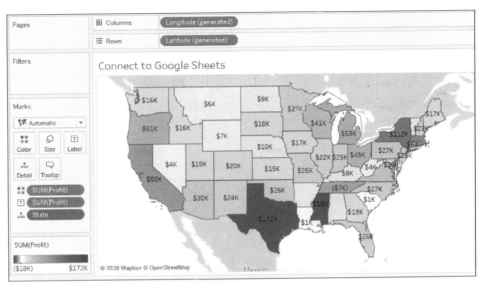

Figure 2.20: Customizing color

Because you have set the default format for the field at the data-source level, any additional views you create using **Profit** will include the default formatting you specified.

Consider using color blind-safe colors in your visualizations. Orange and blue are usually considered a color blind-safe alternative to red and green. Tableau also includes a discrete color blind-safe palette. Additionally, consider adjusting the intensity of the colors, using labels, or different visualizations to make your visualizations more accessible.

Working with extracts instead of live connections

Nearly all data sources allow the option of either connecting live or extracting the data. A few cloud-based data sources require an extract. Conversely, OLAP data sources cannot be extracted and require live connections.

Extracts extend the way in which Tableau works with data. Consider the following diagram:

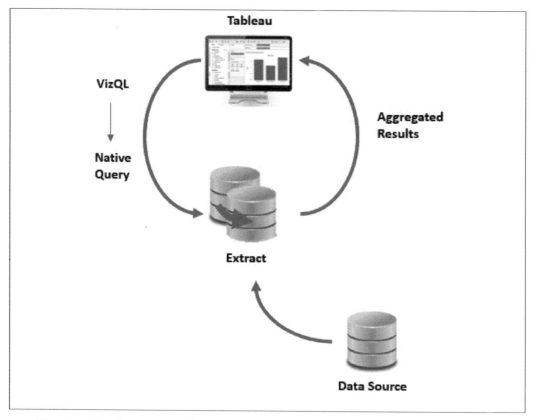

Figure 2.21: Data from the original Data Source is extracted into a self-contained snapshot of the data

When using a live connection, Tableau issues queries directly to the data source (or uses data in the cache, if possible). When you extract the data, Tableau pulls some or all of the data from the original source and stores it in an extract file. Prior to version 10.5, Tableau used a Tableau Data Extract (.tde) file. Starting with version 10.5, Tableau uses Hyper extracts (.hyper) and will convert .tde files to .hyper as you update older workbooks.

The fundamental paradigm of how Tableau works with data does not change, but you'll notice that Tableau is now querying and getting results from the extract. Data can be retrieved from the source again to refresh the extract. Thus, each extract is a snapshot of the data source at the time of the latest refresh. Extracts offer the benefit of being portable and extremely efficient.

Creating extracts

Extracts can be created in multiple ways, as follows:

- Select **Extract** on the **Data Source** screen as follows. The **Edit...** link will allow you to configure the extract:

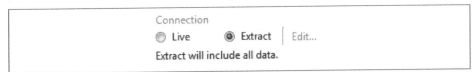

Figure 2.22: Select either Live or Extract for a connection and configure options for the extract by clicking Edit.

- Select the data source from the **Data** menu, or right-click the data source on the data pane and select **Extract data**. You will be given a chance to set configuration options for the extract, as demonstrated in the following screenshot:

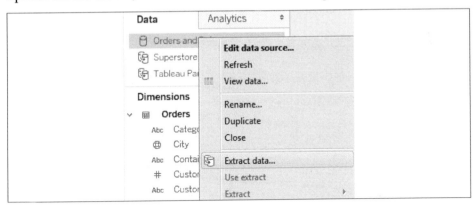

Figure 2.23: The Extract data… option

- Developers may create an extract using the Tableau Hyper API. This API allows you to use Python, Java, C++, or C#/.NET to programmatically read and write Hyper extracts. The details of this approach are beyond the scope of this book, but documentation is readily available on Tableau's website at `https://help.tableau.com/current/api/hyper_api/en-us/index.html`.

- Certain tools, such as `Alteryx` or `Tableau Prep`, can output Tableau extracts.

You'll have quite a few options for configuring an extract. To edit these options, select **Extract** and then **Edit...** on the **Data Source** screen or **Extract data...** from the context menu of a connection in the **Data** pane. When you configure an extract, you will be prompted to select certain options, as shown here:

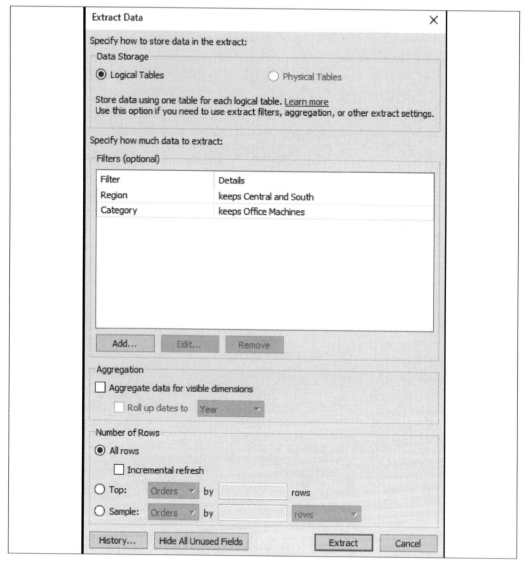

Figure 2.24: The Extract Data dialog gives quite a few options for how to configure the extract

You have a great deal of control when configuring an extract. Here are the various options, and the impact your choices will make on performance and flexibility:

- Depending on the data source and object model you've created, you may select between **Logical Tables** and **Physical Tables**. We'll explore the details in *Chapter 13, Understanding the Tableau Data Model, Joins, and Blends*.

- You may optionally add extract **Filters**, which limit the extract to a subset of the original source. In this example only, records where **Region** is **Central** or **South** and where **Category** is **Office Machines** will be included in the extract.

- You may aggregate an extract by checking the box. This means that data will be rolled up to the level of visible dimensions and, optionally, to a specified date level, such as year or month.

> **Visible fields** are those that are shown in the data pane. You may hide a field from the Data Source screen or from the data pane by right-clicking a field and selecting **Hide**. This option will be disabled if the field is used in any view in the workbook. Hidden fields are not available to be used in a view. Hidden fields are not included in an extract as long as they are hidden prior to creating or optimizing the extract.

In the preceding example, if only the **Region** and **Category** dimensions were visible, the resulting extract would only contain two rows of data (one row for **Central** and another for **South**). Additionally, any measures would be aggregated at the **Region/Category** level and would be done with respect to the **Extract** filters. For example, **Sales** would be rolled up to the sum of sales in **Central/Office Machines** and **South/Office Machines**. All measures are aggregated according to their default aggregation.

You may adjust the number of rows in the extract by including all rows or a sampling of the top *n* rows in the dataset. If you select all rows, you can indicate an incremental refresh. If your source data incrementally adds records, and you have a field such as an identity column or date field that can be used reliably to identify new records as they are added, then an incremental extract can allow you to add those records to the extract without recreating the entire extract. In the preceding example, any new rows where **Row ID** is higher than the highest value of the previous extract refresh would be included in the next incremental refresh.

> Incremental refreshes can be a great way to deal with large volumes of data that grow over time. However, use incremental refreshes with care, because the incremental refresh will only add new rows of data based on the field you specify. You won't get changes to existing rows, nor will rows be removed if they were deleted at the source. You will also miss any new rows if the value for the incremental field is less than the maximum value in the existing extract.

Now that we've considered how to create and configure extracts, let's turn our attention to using them.

Performance

There are two types of extracts in Tableau:

- Tableau Data Extracts (.tde files): prior to Tableau 10.5, these were the only type of extract available.

- Hyper (.hyper files) are available in Tableau 10.5 or later.

Depending on scale and volume, both .hyper and .tde extracts may perform faster than most traditional live database connections. For the most part, Tableau will default to creating Hyper extracts. Unless you are using older versions of Tableau, there is little reason to use the older .tde. The incredible performance of Tableau extracts is based on several factors, including the following:

- Hyper extracts make use of a hybrid of OLTP and OLAP models and the engine determines the optimal query. Tableau Data Extracts are columnar and very efficient to query.

- Extracts are structured so they can be loaded quickly into memory without additional processing and moved between memory and disk storage, so the size is not limited to the amount of RAM available, but RAM is efficiently used to boost performance.

- Many calculated fields are materialized in the extract. The pre-calculated value stored in the extract can often be read faster than executing the calculation every time the query is executed. Hyper extracts extend this by potentially materializing many aggregations.

You may choose to use extracts to increase performance over traditional databases. To maximize your performance gain, consider the following actions:

- Prior to creating the extract, hide unused fields. If you have created all desired visualizations, you can click the **Hide Unused Fields** button on the **Extract** dialog to hide all fields not used in any view or calculation.

- If possible, use a subset of data from the original source. For example, if you have historical data for the last 10 years but only need the last two years for analysis, then filter the extract by the Date field.

- Optimize an extract after creating or editing calculated fields or deleting or hiding fields.
- Store extracts on solid-state drives.

Although performance is one major reason to consider using extracts, there are other factors to consider, which we will do next.

Portability and security

Let's say that your data is hosted on a database server accessible only from inside your office network. Normally, you'd have to be onsite or using a VPN to work with the data. Even cloud-based data sources require an internet connection. With an extract, you can take the data with you and work offline.

An extract file contains data extracted from the source. When you save a workbook, you may save it as a Tableau workbook (.twb) file or a Tableau Packaged Workbook (.twbx) file. Let's consider the difference:

- A Tableau workbook (.twb) contains definitions for all the connections, fields, visualizations, and dashboards, but does not contain any data or external files, such as images. A Tableau workbook can be edited in Tableau Desktop and published to Tableau Server.
- A Tableau packaged workbook (.twbx) contains everything in a (.twb) file but also includes extracts and external files that are packaged together in a single file with the workbook. A packaged workbook using extracts can be opened with Tableau Desktop, Tableau Reader, and published to Tableau Public or Tableau Online.

 A packaged workbook file (.twbx) is really just a compressed .zip file. If you rename the extension from .twbx to .zip, you can access the contents as you would any other .zip file.

There are a couple of security considerations to keep in mind when using an extract. First, any security layers that limit which data can be accessed according to the credentials used will not be effective after the extract is created. An extract does not require a username or password. All data in an extract can be read by anyone. Second, any data for visible (non-hidden) fields contained in an extract file (.hyper or .tde), or an extract contained in a packaged workbook (.twbx), can be accessed even if the data is not shown in the visualization. Be very careful to limit access to extracts or packaged workbooks containing sensitive or proprietary data.

When to use an extract

You should consider various factors when determining whether to use an extract. In some cases, you won't have an option (for example, OLAP requires a live connection and some cloud-based data sources require an extract). In other cases, you'll want to evaluate your options.

In general, use an extract when:

- You need better performance than you can get with the live connection.

- You need the data to be portable.

- You need to use functions that are not supported by the database data engine (for example, MEDIAN is not supported with a live connection to SQL Server).

- You want to share a packaged workbook. This is especially true if you want to share a packaged workbook with someone who uses the free Tableau Reader, which can only read packaged workbooks with data extracted.

In general, do not use an extract when you have any of the following use cases:

- You have sensitive data that should not be accessible by certain users, or you have no control over who will be able to access the extract. However, you may hide sensitive fields prior to creating the extract, in which case they are no longer part of the extract.

- You need to manage security based on login credentials. (However, if you are using Tableau Server, you may still use extracted connections hosted on Tableau Server that are secured by a login. We'll consider sharing your work with Tableau Server in *Chapter 16, Sharing Your Data Story*).

- You need to see changes in the source data updated in real time.

- The volume of data makes the time required to build the extract impractical. The number of records that can be extracted in a reasonable amount of time will depend on factors such as the data types of fields, the number of fields, the speed of the data source, and network bandwidth. The Hyper engine typically builds .hyper extracts much faster than the older .tde files were built.

With an understanding of how to create, manage, and use extracts (and when not to use them), we'll turn our attention to various ways of filtering data in Tableau.

Filtering data

Often, you will want to filter data in Tableau in order to perform an analysis on a subset of data, narrow your focus, or drill into details. Tableau offers multiple ways to filter data.

If you want to limit the scope of your analysis to a subset of data, you can filter the data at the source using one of the following techniques:

- **Data Source Filters** are applied before all other filters and are useful when you want to limit your analysis to a subset of data. These filters are applied before any other filters.

- **Extract Filters** limit the data that is stored in an extract (.tde or .hyper). Data source filters are often converted into extract filters if they are present when you extract the data.

- **Custom SQL Filters** can be accomplished using a live connection with custom SQL, which has a Tableau parameter in the WHERE clause. We'll examine parameters in *Chapter 4, Starting an Adventure with Calculations and Parameters.*

Additionally, you can apply filters to one or more views using one of the following techniques:

- Drag and drop fields from the data pane to the **Filters** shelf.

- Select one or more marks or headers in a view and then select **Keep Only** or **Exclude**, as shown here:

Figure 2.25: Based on the mark selection, you may Keep Only
values that match or Exclude such values.

- Right-click any field in the data pane or in the view and select **Show Filter**. The filter will be shown as a control (examples include a drop-down list and checkbox) to allow the end user of the view or dashboard the ability to change the filter.

- Use an action filter. We'll look more at filters and action filters in the context of dashboards.

Each of these options adds one or more fields to the **Filters** shelf of a view. When you drop a field on the **Filters** shelf, you will be prompted with options to define the filter. The filter options will differ most noticeably based on whether the field is discrete or continuous. Whether a field is filtered as a dimension or as a measure will greatly impact how the filter is applied and the results.

Filtering discrete (blue) fields

When you filter using a discrete field, you will be given options for selecting individual values to keep or exclude. For example, when you drop the discrete **Department** dimension onto the **Filters** shelf, Tableau will give you the following options:

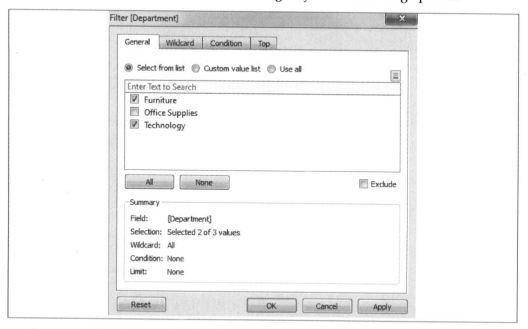

Figure 2.26: A filter for a discrete field will show options for including or excluding individual values

The **Filter** options include **General**, **Wildcard**, **Condition**, and **Top** tabs. Your filter can include options from each tab. The **Summary** section on the **General** tab will show all options selected:

- The **General** tab allows you to select items from a list (you can use the custom list to add items manually if the dimension contains a large number of values that take a long time to load). You may use the **Exclude** option to exclude the selected items.

- The **Wildcard** tab allows you to match string values that contain, start with, end with, or exactly match a given value.

- The **Condition** tab allows you to specify conditions based on aggregations of other fields that meet conditions (for example, a condition to keep any **Department** where the sum of sales was greater than $1,000,000). Additionally, you can write a custom calculation to form complex conditions. We'll cover calculations more in *Chapter 4, Starting an Adventure with Calculations and Parameters*, and *Chapter 6, Diving Deep with Table Calculations*.

- The **Top** tab allows you to limit the filter to only the top or bottom items. For example, you might decide to keep only the top five items by the sum of sales.

 Discrete measures (except for calculated fields using table calculations) cannot be added to the **Filters** shelf. If the field holds a date or numeric value, you can convert it to a continuous field before filtering. Other data types will require the creation of a calculated field to convert values you wish to filter into continuous numeric values.

Let's next consider how continuous filters are filtered.

Filtering continuous (green) fields

If you drop a continuous dimension onto the **Filters** shelf, you'll get a different set of options. Often, you will first be prompted as to how you want to filter the field, as follows:

Figure 2.27: For numeric values, you'll often see options for aggregating the value as part of the filter

The options here are divided into two major categories:

- **All values**: The filter will be based on each individual value of the field, *row by row*. For example, an **All values** filter keeping only sales above $100 will evaluate each record of underlying data and keep only individual sales above $100.

- **Aggregation**: The filter will be based on the aggregation specified (for example, **Sum, Average, Minimum, Maximum, Standard deviation**, and **Variance**) and the aggregation will be performed at the level of detail of the view. For example, a filter keeping only the sum of sales above $100,000 on a view at the level of category will keep only categories that had at least $100,000 in total sales.

Once you've made a selection (or if the selection wasn't applicable for the field selected), you will be given another interface for setting the actual filter, as follows:

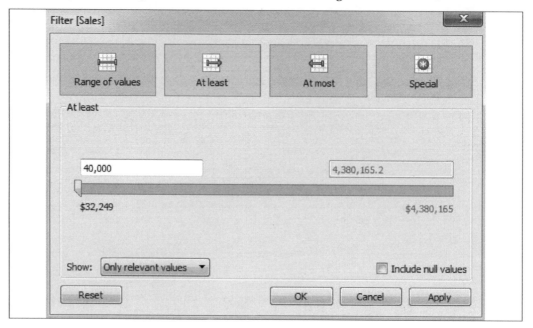

Figure 2.28: Filter options for Sales (as a SUM)

Here, you'll see options for filtering continuous values based on a range with a start, end, or both. The **Special** tab gives options for showing all values, NULL values, or non-NULL values.

From a user-interface perspective, the most dramatic difference in filtering options comes from whether a field is discrete or continuous. However, you should always think about whether you are using the field as a **Dimension Filter** or a **Measure Filter** to understand what kind of results you will get based on the order of operations, which is discussed in the *Appendix*.

- Dimension filters will filter *detail rows of data*. For example, filtering out the Central Region will eliminate all rows for that region. You will not see any states for that region and your aggregate results, such as SUM(Sales), will not include any values from that region.

- Measure filters will filter *aggregate rows of data* at the level of detail defined by the dimensions included in your view. For example, if you filtered to include only where SUM(Sales) was greater than $100,000 and your view included Region and Month, then the resulting view would include only values where the Region had more than $100,000 in sales for the given month.

Other than filtering discrete and continuous fields, you'll also notice some different options for filtering dates, which we'll consider next.

Filtering dates

We'll take a look at the special way Tableau handles dates in the *Visualizing dates and times* section of *Chapter 3, Moving Beyond Basic Visualizations*. For now, consider the options available when you drop an **Order Date** field onto the **Filters** shelf, as follows:

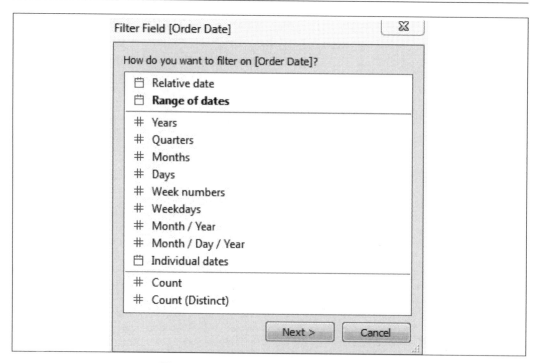

Figure 2.29: Initial filter options for a date field

The options here include the following:

- **Relative date**: This option allows you to filter a date based on a specific date (for example, keeping the last three weeks from today, or the last six months from January 1).

- **Range of dates**: This option allows you to filter a date based on a range with a starting date, ending date, or both.

- **Date Part**: This option allows you to filter based on discrete parts of dates, such as **Years, Months, Days**, or combinations of parts, such as **Month/Year**. Based on your selection, you will have various options for filtering and have the option of defaulting to the latest value in the data.

- **Individual dates**: This option allows you to filter based on each individual value of the date field in the data.

- **Count** or **Count (Distinct)**: This option allows you to filter based on the count, or distinct count, of date values in the data.

Depending on your selection, you will be given additional options for filtering.

Other filtering options

You will also want to be aware of the following options when it comes to filtering:

- You may display a filter control for nearly any field by right-clicking it and selecting **Show Filter**. The type of control depends on the type of field, whether it is discrete or continuous, and may be customized by using the little drop-down arrow at the upper-right of the filter control.

- **Filters** may be added to the **context**. Context is described in detail in the *Appendix* and we'll see why it's important in various examples throughout the book. For now, just note the option. This option is available via the drop-down menu on the filter control or the field on the **Filters** shelf.

- **Filters** may be set to show all values in the database, all values in the context, all values in a hierarchy, or only values that are relevant based on other filters. These options are available via the drop-down menu on the **Filter** control or the field on the **Filters** shelf.

- When using Tableau Server, you may define user filters that allow you to provide row-level security by filtering based on user credentials.

- By default, any field placed on the **Filters** shelf defines a filter that is specific to the current view. However, you may specify the scope by using the menu for the field on the **Filters** shelf. Select **Apply to** and choose one of the following options:

    - **All related data sources**: All data sources will be filtered by the value(s) specified. The relationships of fields are the same as blending (that is, the default by name and type match, or customized through the **Data | Edit Relationships...** menu option). All views using any of the related data sources will be affected by the filter. This option is sometimes referred to as **cross-data source filtering**.

    - **Current data source**: The data source for that field will be filtered. Any views using that data source will be affected by the filter.

    - **Selected worksheets**: Any worksheets selected that use the data source of the field will be affected by the filter.

    - **Current worksheet**: Only the current view will be affected by the filter.

We'll see plenty of practical examples of filtering data throughout the book, many of which will make use of some of these options.

Summary

This chapter covered key concepts of how Tableau works with data. Although you will not usually be concerned with what queries Tableau generates to query underlying data engines, having a solid understanding of Tableau's paradigm will greatly aid you as you analyze data.

We looked at multiple examples of different connections to different data sources, considered the benefits and potential drawbacks of using data extracts, considered how to manage metadata, and considered options for filtering data.

Working with data is fundamental to everything you do in Tableau. Understanding how to connect to various data sources, when to work with extracts, and how to customize metadata will be key as you begin deeper analysis and more complex visualizations, such as those covered in *Chapter 3, Moving Beyond Basic Visualizations*.

3

Moving Beyond Basic Visualizations

You are now ready to set out on your adventure of creating more advanced visualizations! *Advanced* does not necessarily mean *difficult* since Tableau makes many visualizations easy to create. *Advanced* also does not necessarily mean *complex*. The goal is to communicate the data, not to obscure it in needless complexity.

Instead, these visualizations are advanced in the sense that you will need to understand when they should be used, why they are useful, and how to leverage the capabilities of Tableau to create them. Additionally, many of the examples we will look at will introduce some advanced techniques, such as calculations, to extend the usefulness of foundational visualizations. Many of these techniques will be developed fully in future chapters, so don't worry about trying to absorb every detail right now.

Most of the examples in this chapter are designed so that you can follow along. However, don't simply memorize a set of instructions. Instead, take the time to understand how the combinations of different field types you place on different shelves change the way headers, axes, and marks are rendered. Experiment and even deviate from the instructions from time to time, just to see what else is possible. You can always use Tableau's back button to follow the example again!

In this chapter, visualizations will fall under the following major categories:

- Comparison
- Dates and times
- Relating parts of the data to the whole
- Distributions
- Multiple axes

You may have noticed the lack of a spatial location or geographic category in the preceding list. Mapping was introduced in *Chapter 1, Taking Off with Tableau,* and we'll get to some advanced geographic capabilities in *Chapter 12, Exploring Mapping and Advanced Geospatial Features.*

You may recreate the examples that are found in this chapter by using the Chapter 03 Starter.twbx workbook, or even start from scratch by using a blank workbook and connecting to the Hospital Visits.csv file that's located in the Learning Tableau/Chapter 03 folder. The completed examples may be found in the Chapter 03 Complete.twbx workbook.

We will begin by assessing which types of visualizations are effective for quantitative comparisons.

Comparing values

Often, you will want to compare the differences between measured values across different categories. You might find yourself asking the following questions:

- How many customers did each store serve?
- How much energy did each wind farm produce?
- How many patients did each doctor see?

In each case, you are looking to make a comparison (among stores, wind farms, or doctors) in terms of some quantitative measurement (number of customers, megawatts of electricity, and patients).

Let's take a look at some examples of visualizations that help answer these types of questions.

Bar charts

Here is a simple bar chart, similar to the one we built in *Chapter 1, Taking Off with Tableau*:

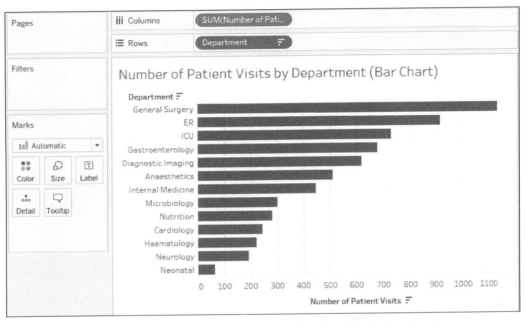

Figure 3.1: A bar chart showing the number of patient visits by department

This bar chart makes it easy to compare the number of patient visits between various departments in the hospital. As a dimension, **Department** slices the data according to each distinct value, such as **ER**, **ICU**, or **Cardiology**. It creates a header for these values because it is discrete (blue). As a measure, **Number of Patient Visits** gives the sum of patient visits for each department. Because it is a continuous (green) field, it defines an axis, and bars are rendered to visualize the value.

Notice that the bar chart is sorted by the department having the highest sum of patient visits at the top and the lowest at the bottom. Sorting a bar chart often adds a lot of value to the analysis because it makes it easier to make comparisons and see rank order. For example, it is easy to see that the **Microbiology** department has had more patient visits than the **Nutrition** department. If the chart wasn't sorted, this may not have been as obvious.

You can sort a view in multiple ways, as follows:

- Click one of the sort icons on the toolbar: This results in an automatic sort of the dimension based on the measure that defined the axis. Changes in data or filtering that result in a new order will be reflected in the view:

Figure 3.2: Toolbar sort icons

- Click the sort icon on the axis: The option icon will become visible when you hover over the axis and will then remain in place when you enable the sort. This will also result in automatic sorting:

0	200	400	600	800	1000

Number of Patient Visits ⊐

Figure 3.3: Axis sort icon

- Use the drop-down on the active dimension field and select **Sort** to view and edit the sorting options. You can also select **Clear Sort** to remove any sorting:

Figure 3.4: Sorting using the drop-down menu

- Use the drop-down on the field label for rows and select the desired sorting option:

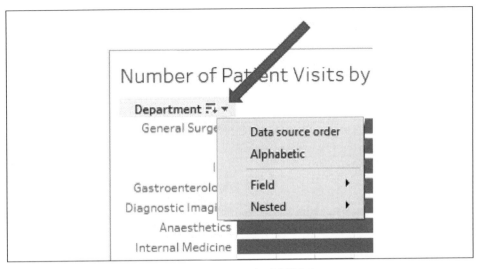

Figure 3.5: Sorting by field label

- Drag and drop row headers to manually rearrange them. This results in a manual sort that does not get updated with data refreshes.

All of these sorting methods are specific to the view and will override any default sort you defined in the metadata.

Bar chart variations

A basic bar chart can be extended in many ways to accomplish various objectives. Consider the following variations:

- Bullet chart to show progress towards a goal, target, or threshold
- Bar-in-bar chart to show progress toward a target or compare two specific values within a category
- Highlighting categories of interest

Bullet chart

A **bullet graph** (sometimes also called a **bullet chart**) is a great way to visually compare a measure with a goal, target, or threshold. The bar indicates the measure value, while the line indicates the target. Tableau also defaults to shading to indicate **60%** and **80%** of the distance to the goal or threshold. The line and the shading are reference lines that can be adjusted (we'll explore how in detail in future chapters):

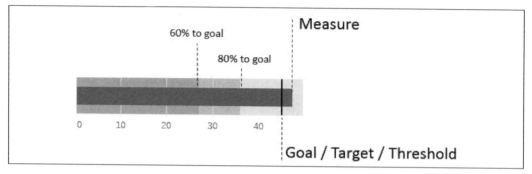

Figure 3.6: Parts of a bullet graph

In this scenario, we'll consider how the hospital operated with respect to revenue goals. Hospital administration set the following revenue goals for 2019 and now wants to understand how each department actually performed:

Department	Goal
Anaesthetics	$300,000
Cardiology	$5,000,000
Diagnostic Imaging	$500,000
ER	$6,000,000
Gastroenterology	$900,000
General Surgery	$8,000,000
Haematology	$800,000
ICU	$3,800,000
Internal Medicine	$200,000
Microbiology	$50,000
Neonatal	$10,000
Neurology	$3,000,000
Nutrition	$10,000

Figure 3.7: Department Goals are stored in a spreadsheet as shown here

The patient visit and revenue data is contained in `Hospital Visits.csv` and the revenue goals are in `Hospital Goals.csv`. These two data connections are related together in a **Data Model** in both the `Starter` and `Complete` workbooks. We'll look more at the data model in *Chapter 13, Understanding the Tableau Data Model, Joins, and Blends*. For now, simply use the `Hospital Visits & Revenue` data source to complete the examples in this chapter.

We'll build a bullet graph using the `Chapter 3` workbook, which contains the `Hospital Visits` and the `Hospital Goals` spreadsheet data sources. We'll use these two data sources to visualize the relationship between actual and target minutes to service as you follow these steps:

1. Navigate to the **Average Minutes to Service (Bullet Chart)** sheet.

2. Create a basic bar chart of the total **Revenue** per **Department**.

3. Sort **Department** from highest to lowest.

4. Filter **Date of Admit** by **Year** and keep only 2019 data. At this point, your view should look like this:

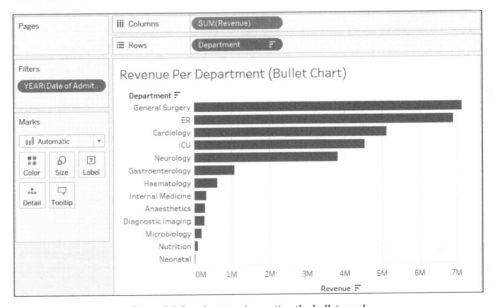

Figure 3.8: Interim steps in creating the bullet graph

5. In the **Data** pane, select the **Goal** field under the `Hospital Goals.csv` table.

6. Open **Show Me** and select the bullet graph. At this point, Tableau will have created a bullet graph using the fields already in the view and the `Goal` field you selected in the data pane.

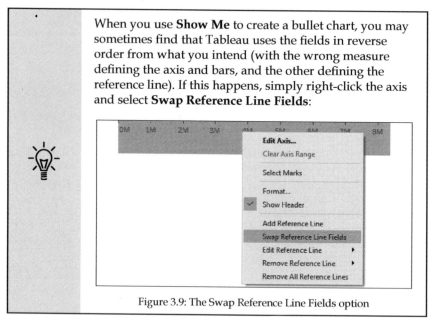

> When you use **Show Me** to create a bullet chart, you may sometimes find that Tableau uses the fields in reverse order from what you intend (with the wrong measure defining the axis and bars, and the other defining the reference line). If this happens, simply right-click the axis and select **Swap Reference Line Fields**:

Figure 3.9: The Swap Reference Line Fields option

The completed bullet chart should look like the following:

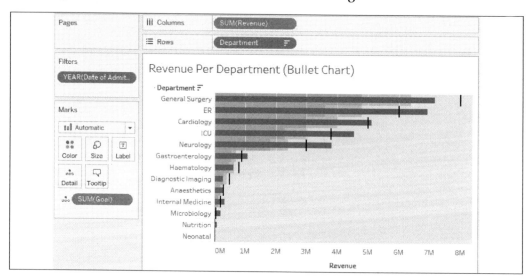

Figure 3.10: The complete bullet graph

The completed bullet graph allows us to see which departments have met their goals and which are behind. Next, let's consider how we can highlight this even more.

Calling out thresholds

With bullet charts, it can be helpful to visually call out the bars that fail to meet or exceed the threshold. We'll look at calculations in depth in the next chapter, but for now, you can complete this example with the following steps:

1. Use the drop-down arrow in the **Data** pane and select **Create Calculated Field...**:

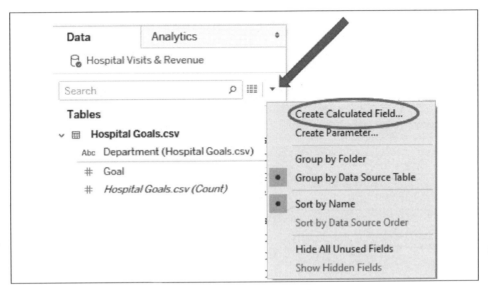

Figure 3.11: Creating a calculated field

2. Name the calculated field named Goal Met? with the following code:

   ```
   SUM([Revenue]) >= SUM([Goal])
   ```

3. Click **OK** and drag the new Goal Met? field from the data pane and drop it on **Color**.

The calculation returns `true` when the `Revenue` value for a department is greater than the goal value, and `false` otherwise. With the calculated field on **Color**, it becomes very easy to see which departments have met the 2019 goals:

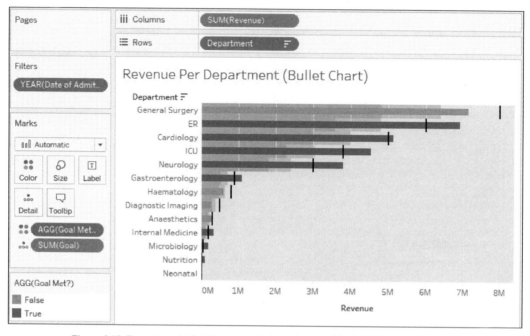

Figure 3.12: Departments that have met their goal are highlighted in this bullet chart

Color is one of the strongest ways to get attention with your visualizations. Use color with intent. Decide whether you want to highlight good or poor performance.

Bar-in-bar chart

Another possibility for showing relationships between two values for each category is a bar-in-bar chart. Like the bullet chart, the bar-in-bar chart can show progress toward a goal. It can also be used to compare any two values. For example, you might compare revenue to a target, or you might compare the revenue for the current year to the previous year:

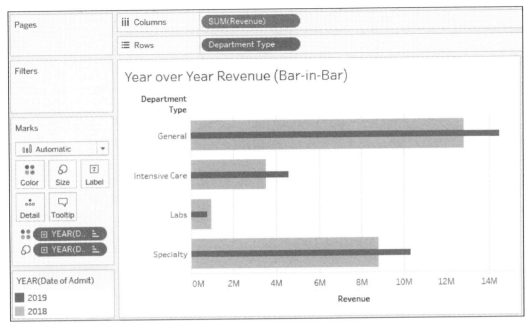

Figure 3.13: Bar-in-bar chart

To create this view, continue in the same workbook and follow these steps:

1. Navigate to the **Year over Year Revenue (Bar-in-Bar)** sheet.

2. Drag and drop **Revenue** onto the horizontal axis in the view (which gives the same results as dropping it onto the **Columns** shelf).

3. Drag and drop **Department Type** onto **Rows**.

4. Drag and drop **Date of Admit** onto **Color**. We'll discuss dates in more detail in the next section, but you'll notice that Tableau uses the year of the date to give you a stacked bar chart that looks like this:

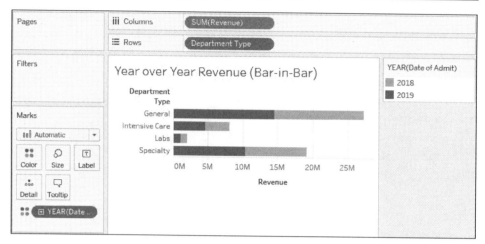

Figure 3.14: Interim steps in creating the bar-in-bar chart

5. For a bar-in-bar chart, we do not want the marks to be stacked. To turn off stacking, use the main menu to select **Analysis | Stack Marks | Off**.

6. All the bar segments now begin at 0 and some bars may completely obscure others. To see each bar, we'll need to adjust another visual element. In this case, hold down the *Ctrl* key while dragging the **YEAR(Date of Admit)** field that is currently on **Color** in the **Marks** card to **Size**.

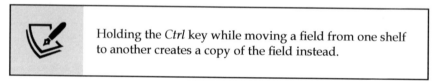

Holding the *Ctrl* key while moving a field from one shelf to another creates a copy of the field instead.

After completing the previous step, a size legend should appear. The bars will be sized based on the year and we will be able to see all of the segments that are available, even if they overlap.

7. We want **2019** to be in front and **2018** to be in the background, so drag and drop **2019** within the **Size** legend to reorder the values so that **2018** comes after **2019**:

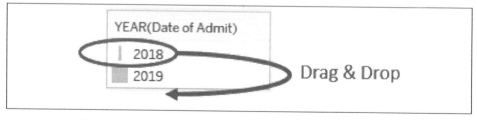

Figure 3.15: You can drag and drop items in legends to reorder them

8. Double-click the **Color** legend to edit the colors so that **2019** is emphasized. A darker orange or blue for **2019** with a light gray for **2018** would serve this purpose well (though you may find other color combinations that you prefer!).

At this point, your view should look like the bar-in-bar chart that was shown in *Figure 3.13* at the beginning of this section. You may wish to further enhance the visualization by doing the following:

- Adding a border to the bars. Accomplish this by clicking the **Color** shelf and using the **Border** option.

- Adjusting the size range to reduce the difference between the large and small extremes. Accomplish this by double-clicking the **Size** legend (or using the caret drop-down and selecting **Edit** from the menu).

- Adjusting the sizing of the view. Accomplish this by hovering over the canvas, just over the bottom border, until the mouse cursor changes to a sizing cursor, and then click and drag to resize the view. You may also want to adjust how the view fills the space. Use the drop-down on the toolbar and experiment with the options:

Figure 3.16: This drop-down determines how the current view is sized

- Hiding the size legend. You may decide that the size legend does not add anything to this particular view as size was only used to allow overlapping bars to be seen. To hide any legend, use the drop-down arrow on the legend and select **Hide Card**:

Figure 3.17: The Hide Card option for legends

The bar-in-bar chart gives you another way to compare values. Next, we'll consider a variation that allows us to highlight areas of interest.

Highlighting categories of interest

Let's say one of your primary responsibilities at the hospital is to monitor the number of patient visits for the **ICU** and **Neonatal** departments. You don't necessarily care about the details of other departments, but you do want to keep track of how your two departments compare with others. You might design something like this:

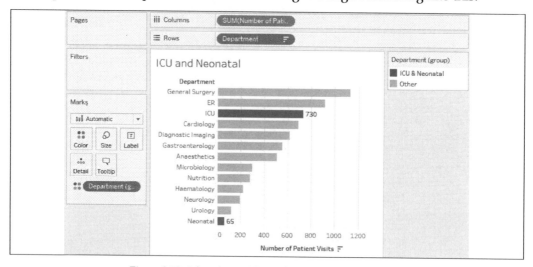

Figure 3.18: A bar chart with two bars highlighted via color

Now, as the data is refreshed over time, you will be able to immediately see how the two departments of interest to you compared to other departments. To create this view, follow these steps:

1. Navigate to the **ICU and Neonatal** sheet.

2. Place **Department** on **Rows** and **Number of Patient Visits** on **Columns**. Sort the bar chart in descending order.

3. Click on the bar in the view for **ICU** and, while holding down the *Ctrl* key, click the bar for **Neonatal**.

4. Hover the cursor over one of the selected bars for a few seconds and, from the menu that appears, click the **Create Group** button (which looks like a paperclip):

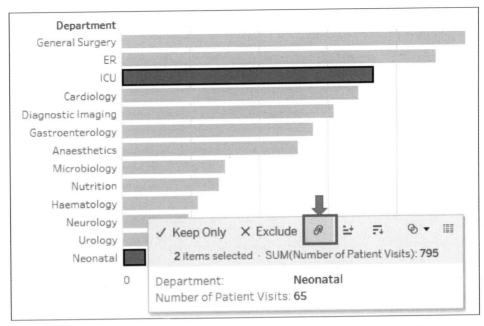

Figure 3.19: After Ctrl + clicking the two bars, use the paperclip icon to group them

This will create a group, which results in a new dimension, named **Department (group)**, in the left-hand data pane. Tableau automatically assigns this field to **Color**.

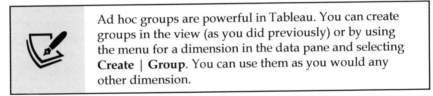

Ad hoc groups are powerful in Tableau. You can create groups in the view (as you did previously) or by using the menu for a dimension in the data pane and selecting **Create | Group**. You can use them as you would any other dimension.

5. To add a label only to the bars for those two departments, right-click each bar and select **Mark label | Always show**. The label for the mark will always be shown, even if other labels are turned off for the view or the label overlaps marks or other labels.

The color will continue to make monitoring easy. The label will only show for the two departments you selected and will update with the changing data.

Now that we've considered how bar charts can be used to compare values and have walked through several examples of variations, let's turn our attention to visualizing dates and times.

Visualizing dates and times

In your analysis, you will often want to understand when something happened. You'll ask questions like the following:

- When did we gain the most new customers?

- Is profit trending up or down?

- What times of day have the highest call volume?

- What kinds of seasonal trends do we see in sales?

Fortunately, Tableau makes this kind of visual discovery and analysis easy. In this section, we'll look at how Tableau works with dates and some various ways you might visualize time.

Date parts, date values, and exact dates

When you are connected to a flat file, relational, or extracted data source, Tableau provides a robust built-in date hierarchy for any date field.

 Cubes/OLAP connections do not allow Tableau hierarchies. You will want to ensure that all date hierarchies and date values you need are defined in the cube.

To see this in action, continue with the Chapter 3 workbook, navigate to the Built-in Date Hierarchy sheet, and create a view similar to the one that was shown by dragging and dropping **Number of Patient Visits** to **Rows** and **Date of Admit** to **Columns**. The **YEAR(Date of Admit)** field on **Columns** will have a plus sign indicator, like this:

Figure 3.20: The field representing the Year part of the date hierarchy

You'll also find a plus or minus indicator as you hover over headers, like this:

Figure 3.21: A plus icon on the column headers that could be used to expand the hierarchy

When you click it, the hierarchy expands by adding **QUARTER(Date of Admit)** to the right of the **YEAR(Date of Admit)** on **Columns**, and the view is expanded to the new level of the hierarchy:

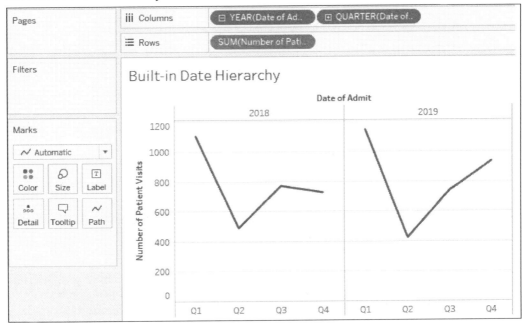

Figure 3.22: The expanded hierarchy with the year and quarter shown

The **YEAR(Date of Admit)** field now has a minus sign indicator that allows you to collapse the hierarchy back to the year level. The **QUARTER** field also has a plus sign, indicating that you can expand the hierarchy further. Starting with **Year**, the hierarchy flows as follows: **Year | Quarter | Month | Day**. When the field is a date and time, you can further drill down into **Hour | Minute | Second**. Any of the parts of the hierarchy can be moved within the view or removed from the view completely.

The hierarchy is made up of **Date Parts**, which is one of the three ways a date field can be used. When you right-click the date field in the view or by using the drop-down menu, you'll see multiple date options, as follows:

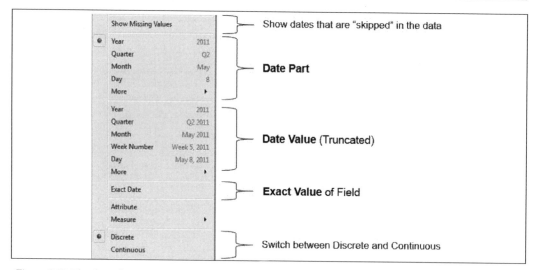

Figure 3.23: The drop-down menu on an active date field demonstrates the various aspects of dates in Tableau

The three major date types are evident, though not explicitly labeled, in the menu:

- **Date part**: This field will represent a specific part of the date, such as the quarter or month. The part of the date is used by itself and without reference to any other part of the date. This means that a date of November 8, 1980, when used as a month date part, is simply **November** in the view. The **November** that's selected in the view here represents all of the Novembers in the dataset, while the number of patient visits is the total for both 2018 and 2019:

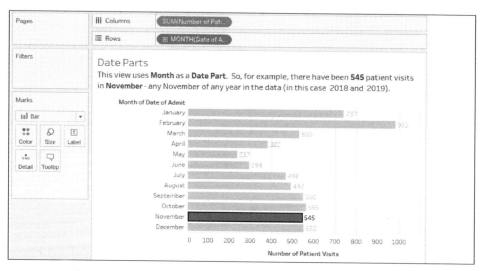

Figure 3.24: This view uses Month as a date part. The number of patient visits is the total for the month, without regard to the year

- **Date value**: This field will represent a date value, but rolled up or truncated to the level you select. For example, if you select a date value of **Month**, then November 8, 2019 gets truncated to the month and year, and is **November 2019**. You'll notice that **November 2018** and **November 2019** each have a separate value in the header and a distinct bar:

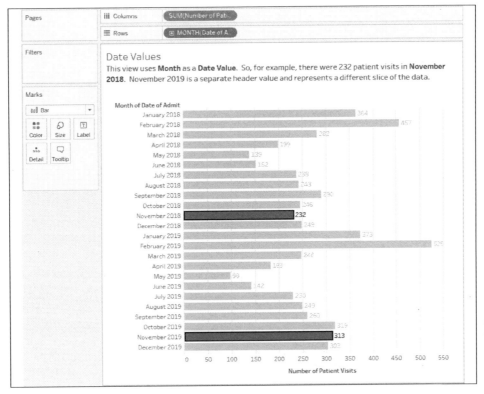

Figure 3.25: This view uses Month as a date value. The number of patient visits
is the total for the month with regard to the year

- **Exact date**: This field represents the exact date value (including time, if applicable) in the data. This means that November 8, 1980, 2:01 am is treated as distinct from November 8, 1980, 3:08 pm.

It is important to note that nearly any of these options can be used as discrete or continuous fields. Date parts are discrete by default. Date values and exact dates are continuous by default. However, you can switch between discrete and continuous as required to allow flexibility in the visualization.

For example, you must have an axis (requiring a continuous field) to create a reference line. Also, Tableau will only connect lines at the lowest level of row or column headers. Using a continuous date value instead of multiple discrete date parts will allow you to connect lines across multiple years, quarters, and months.

 As a shortcut, you can right-click and then drag and drop a date field into the view to get a menu of options for how the date field should be used prior to the view being drawn.

Let's next consider some various ways we might visualize dates and times.

Variations of date and time visualizations

The ability to use various parts and values of dates and even mix and match them gives you a lot of flexibility in creating unique and useful visualizations.

For example, using the month date part for columns and the year date part for color gives a time series that makes a visual year-over-year comparison quite easy. The year date part has been copied to the label so that the lines can be labeled:

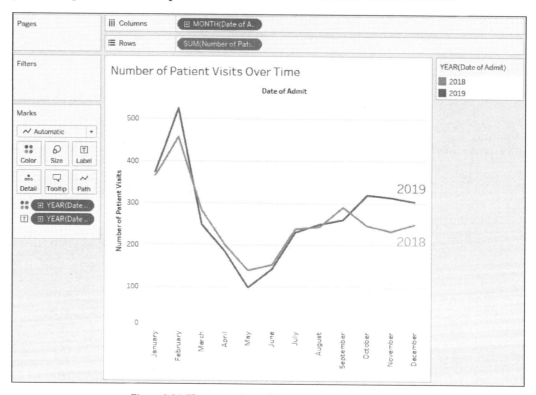

Figure 3.26: The comparison of two years, month-by-month

This kind of view allows for easy year-over-year comparison.

 Clicking on any of the shelves on the **Marks** card will give you a menu of options. Here, **Label** has been clicked, and the label was adjusted to show only at the end of each line.

The following heat map is another example of using date parts on different shelves to achieve useful analysis. This kind of visualization can be quite useful when looking at patterns across different parts of time, such as hours in a day, or weeks in a month. Here, we are looking at how many patients were admitted by month and day:

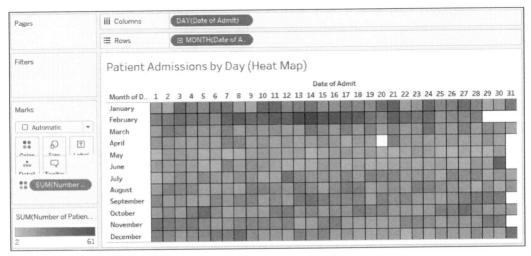

Figure 3.27: A heat map showing the intensity of patient visits by day and month

The year has not been included in the view, so this is an analysis of all years in the data and allows us to see whether there are any seasonal patterns or hotspots. We might notice patterns related to epidemics, doctors' schedules, or the timing of insurance benefits. Perhaps the increased intensity of patient admissions in February corresponds to the flu season.

Observe that placing a continuous field on the **Color** shelf resulted in Tableau completely filling each intersection of **Row** and **Column** with the shade of color that encoded the sum of patient visits. Clicking on the **Color** shelf gives us some fine-tuning options, including the option to add borders to marks. In this view, a black border has been added to help distinguish each cell.

Gantt charts

Gantt charts can be incredibly useful for understanding any series of events with a duration, especially if those events have some kind of relationship. Visually, they are very useful for determining whether certain events overlap, have dependency, or take more or less time than other events.

As an example (not included in the workbook), the following Gantt chart shows a series of processes that run when an application is started. Some of these processes run in parallel, and some are clearly dependent on others. The Gantt chart makes these dependencies clear:

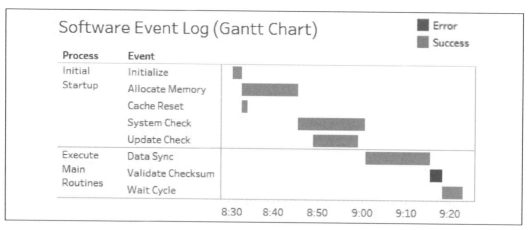

Figure 3.28: A Gantt chart showing the time each process started and how long each took

Gantt charts use the **Gantt mark** type on the **Marks** card drop-down. A Gantt bar mark starts at the value that was specified by the field on **Rows** that defines the axis. The length of the Gantt bar is then determined by the field on the size card, with positive values stretching to the right and negative values to the left.

At the hospital, you might want to see each patient visit to the **ER** in 2019 and understand how long each visit lasted, whether any patients returned to the hospital, and how much time there was between visits. The following steps give an example of how you might create a Gantt chart with steps like these:

1. Place **Department** on **Filters** and keep only **ER**.

2. Place **Date of Admit** on **Filters**, select **Years** as the option for filtering, and keep only **2019**.

3. Place **Date of Admit** on **Columns** as a continuous **Exact Date** or as a **Day** value (not **Day part**). Notice that Tableau's automatic default for the mark type is Gantt bars:

Figure 3.29: In this case, Gantt bars are the automatic mark type.

4. Place **Doctor** and **Patient Name** on **Rows**. The result is a row for each patient grouped by each doctor. A Gantt bar represents a stay in the hospital.

> In most cases, we'd also want to add a unique identifier to the view, such as Patient ID, to ensure that patients who happen to share the same name are distinguished in the visualization. This is not necessary with this dataset, as all names happen to be unique, but it may be vitally important when you work with your data.

5. The length of the Gantt bar is set by placing a field with a value of duration on the **Size** shelf. There is no such field in this dataset. However, we have the **Date of Discharge**, and we can create a calculated field for the duration. We'll cover calculations in more detail in the next chapter. For now, select **Analysis** from the menu and click **Create Calculated Field....** Name the field **Days in the Hospital** and enter the following code:

```
DATEDIFF('day', [Date of Admit], [Date of Discharge])
```

6. The new calculated field will appear under **Measures** in the data pane. Drag and drop the field onto the **Size** shelf. You now have a Gantt chart showing when patients were admitted and how long each visit lasted.

> Consider sorting the **Patient Name** dimension in the view. For example, sorting by field and selecting **Date of Admit** as minimum would enable you to see patients who were admitted earlier towards the top and patients who were admitted later towards the bottom. It is based on the earliest (minimum) date of admission for the patient, even if they were admitted multiple times. Sorting can be a very useful technique for seeing patterns in the Gantt chart.

Your final view should look something like this:

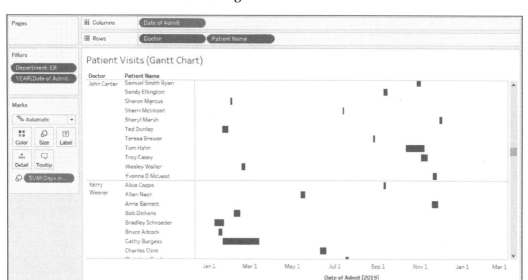

Figure 3.30: The final Gantt chart, showing each patient, when they were admitted, how long they stayed, and whether they ever returned

This type of chart can be very useful in seeing patterns and relationships between entities over time.

When plotted on a date axis, the field defining the length of Gantt bars always needs to be in terms of days. If you want to visualize events with durations that are measured in hours or seconds, avoid using the day argument for DATEDIFF because it computes whole days and loses precision in terms of hours and seconds.

Instead, calculate the difference in hours or seconds and then convert back to days. The following code converts the number of seconds between a start and end date, and then divides by 86,400 to convert the result into days, including fractional parts of the day: DATEDIFF('second', [Start Date], [End Date]) / 86400.

With a good understanding of how Tableau works with dates and times, we've considered some different options for visualization. Let's turn next to focus on how to visualize parts-to-whole relationships.

Relating parts of the data to the whole

As you explore and analyze data, you'll often want to understand how various parts add up to a whole. For example, you'll ask questions such as the following:

- How much does each electric generation method (wind, solar, coal, and nuclear) contribute to the total amount of energy produced?
- What percentage of total profit is made in each state?
- How much space does each file, subdirectory, and directory occupy on my hard disk?

These types of questions are asking about the relationship between the part (production method, state, file/directory) and the whole (total energy, national sales, and hard disk). There are several types of visualizations and variations that can aid you in your analysis.

Let's now look at some visualization examples that will aid us as we consider how to show part-to-whole relationships.

Stacked bars

We took a look at stacked bars in *Chapter 1, Taking Off with Tableau*, where we noted one significant drawback: it is difficult to compare values across most categories. Except for the leftmost (or bottom-most) bars, the other bar segments have different starting points, so lengths are much more difficult to compare. It doesn't mean stacked bars should never be used, but caution should be exercised to ensure clarity of communication.

Here, we are using stacked bars to visualize the makeup of the whole. We are less concerned with visually comparing across categories and more concerned with seeing the parts that make up a category.

For example, at the hospital, we might want to know what the patient population looks like within each type of department. Perhaps each patient was assigned a risk profile on admission.

We can visualize the number of visits broken down by risk profile as a stacked bar, like this:

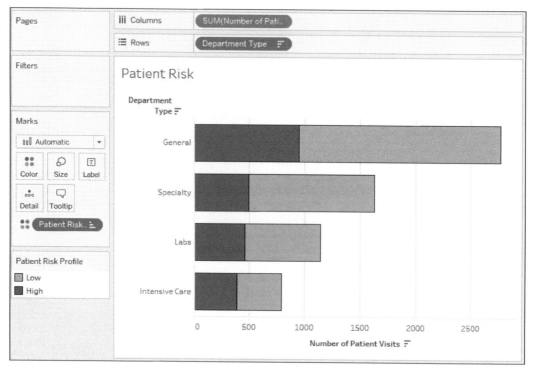

Figure 3.31: A stacked bar chart showing the total number of patients per department and the breakdown of low and high risk

This gives a decent view of the visits for each department type. We can tell that more people visit the general departments and that the number of high-risk patients for both **Specialty** and **Labs** are about the same. **Intensive Care** sees fewer high-risk patients and fewer patients overall. But this is only part of the story.

Consider a stacked bar that doesn't give the absolute value, but gives percentages for each type of department:

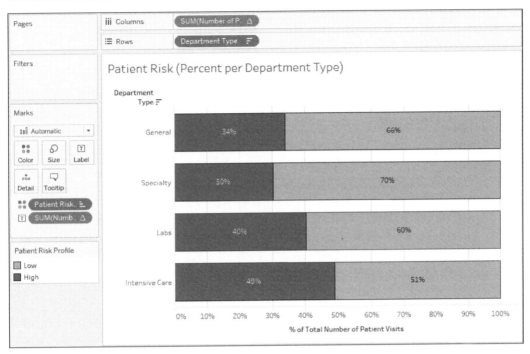

Figure 3.32: A stacked bar chart showing the relative number of high-risk and low-risk patients per department

Compare the previous two stacked bar charts. The fact that nearly 50% of patients in **Intensive Care** are considered **High** risk is evident in both charts. However, the second chart makes this immediately obvious.

None of the data has changed between the two charts, but the bars in the second chart represent the percent of the total for each type of department. You can no longer compare the absolute values but comparing the relative breakdown of each department type has been made much easier. Although there are fewer patients in **Intensive Care**, a much higher percentage of them are in a high-risk category.

Let's consider how the preceding charts can be created and even combined into a single visualization in Tableau. We'll use a quick table calculation. We'll cover table calculations much more in *Chapter 6, Diving Deep with Table Calculations*. Here, simply follow these steps:

1. Create a stacked bar chart by placing **Department Type** on **Rows**, **Number of Patient Visits** on **Columns**, and **Patient Risk Profile** on **Color**. You'll now have a single stacked bar chart.

2. Sort the bar chart in descending order.

3. Duplicate the **Number of Patient Visits** field on **Columns** by holding down *Ctrl* while dragging the **Number of Patient Visits** field in the view to a new spot on **Columns**, immediately to the right of its current location. Alternatively, you can drag and drop the field from the data pane to **Columns**. At this point, you have two **Number of Patient Visits** axes which, in effect, duplicate the stacked bar chart:

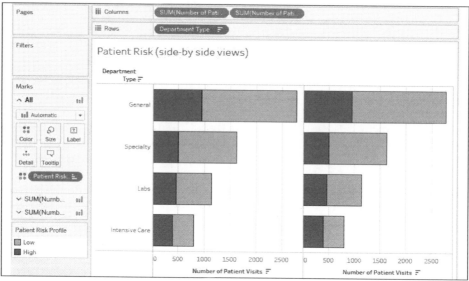

Figure 3.33: An interim step in creating the stacked bars

4. Using the drop-down menu of the second **Number of Patient Visits** field, select **Quick Table Calculation | Percent of Total**. This table calculation runs a secondary calculation on the values that were returned from the data source to compute a percentage of the total. Here, you will need to further specify how that total should be computed.

5. Using the same drop-down menu, select **Compute Using | Patient Risk Profile**. This tells Tableau to calculate the percent of each **Patient Risk Profile** within a given department. This means that the values will add up to 100% for each department.

6. Turn on labels by clicking the **T** button on the top toolbar. This turns on default labels for each mark:

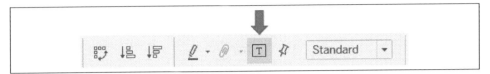

Figure 3.34: This toolbar option toggles labels on/off

After following the preceding steps, your completed stacked bar charts should appear as follows:

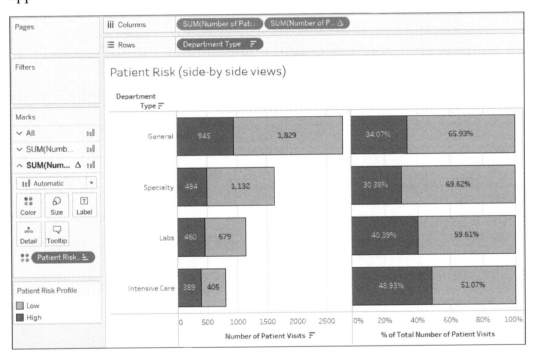

Figure 3.35: The final stacked bar view with absolute and relative values

Using both the absolute values and percentages in a single view can reveal significant aspects and details that might be obscured with only one of the charts.

Treemaps

Treemaps use a series of nested rectangles to display parts of the whole, especially within hierarchical relationships. Treemaps are particularly useful when you have hierarchies and dimensions with **high cardinality** (a high number of distinct values).

Here is an example of a treemap that shows the number of days spent in the hospital by patients. The largest rectangle sections show **Department Type**. Within those are departments and patients:

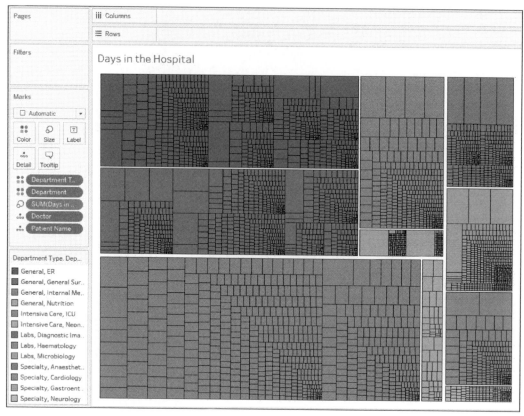

Figure 3.36: A treemap showing part-to-whole relationship of Department Types / Departments / Doctors / Patients

To create a treemap, you simply need to place a measure on the **Size** shelf and a dimension on the **Detail** shelf. You can add additional dimensions to the level of detail to increase the detail of the view. Tableau will add borders of varying thickness to separate the levels of detail that are created by multiple dimensions. Note that in the preceding view, you can easily see the division of department types, then departments, then doctors, and finally individual patients. You can adjust the border of the lowest level by clicking the **Color** shelf.

The order of the dimensions on the **Marks** card defines the way the treemap groups the rectangles. Additionally, you can add dimensions to rows or columns to slice the treemap into multiple treemaps. The result is effectively a bar chart of treemaps:

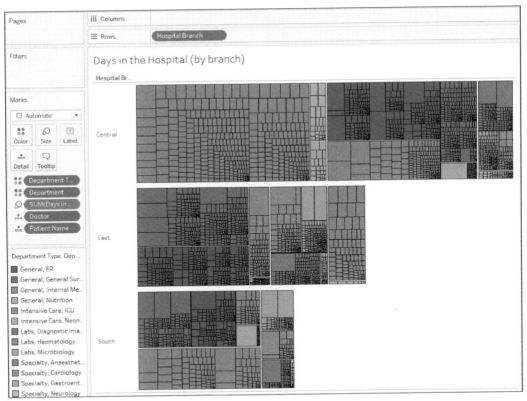

Figure 3.37: Adding a dimension to Rows has effectively made a bar chart of treemaps

The preceding treemap not only demonstrates the ability to have multiple rows (or columns) of treemaps—it also demonstrates the technique of placing multiple fields on the **Color** shelf. This can only be done with discrete fields. You can assign two or more colors by holding down the *Shift* key while dropping the second field on color. Alternatively, the icon or space to the left of each field on the **Marks** card can be clicked to change which shelf is used for the field:

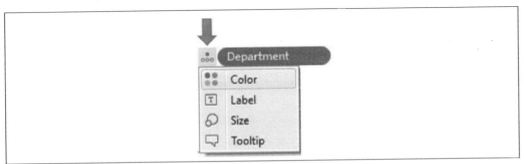

Figure 3.38: Clicking the icon next to a field on the Marks card allows you to change which shelf is used

Treemaps, along with packed bubbles, word clouds, and a few other chart types, are called **non-Cartesian** chart types. This means that they are drawn without an *x* or *y* axis, and do not even require row or column headers. To create any of these chart types, do the following:

- Make sure that no continuous fields are used on Rows or Columns.

- Use any field as a measure on **Size**.

- Change the mark type based on the desired chart type: square for treemap, circle for packed bubbles, or text for word cloud (with the desired field on **Label**).

Area charts

Take a line chart and then fill in the area beneath the line. If there are multiple lines, then stack the filled areas on top of each other. That's how you might think of an area chart.

In fact, in Tableau, you may find it easy to create a line chart, like you've done previously, and then change the mark type on the **Marks** card to **Area**. Any dimensions on the **Color**, **Label**, or **Detail** shelves will create slices of area that will be stacked on top of each other. The **Size** shelf is not applicable to an area chart.

As an example, consider a visualization of patient visits over time, segmented by hospital branch:

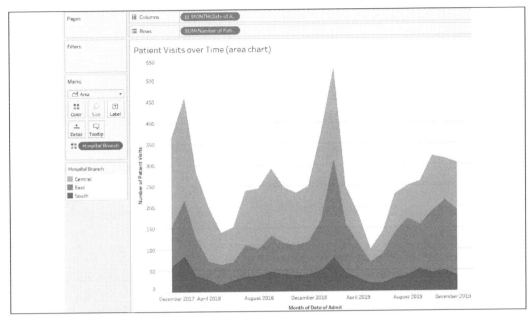

Figure 3.39: An area chart showing patient visits over time by hospital branch

Each band represents a different hospital branch location. In many ways, the view is aesthetically pleasing and it does highlight some patterns in the data. However, it suffers from some of the same weaknesses as the stacked bar chart. Only the bottom band (**South**) can be read in terms of the values on the axis.

The other bands are stacked on top and it becomes very difficult to compare. For example, it is obvious that there is a spike around February of each year. But is it at each branch? Or is one of the lower bands pushing the higher bands up? Which band has the most significant spike?

Now, consider the following view:

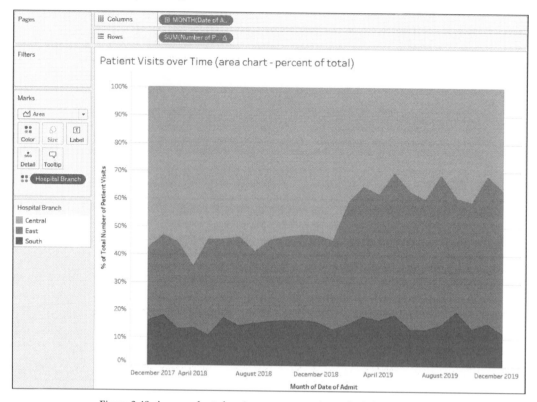

Figure 3.40: An area chart showing percentages instead of absolute values

This view uses a quick table calculation, like the stacked bars example. It is no longer possible to see the spikes, as in the first chart. However, it is much easier to see that there was a dramatic increase in the percentage of patients seen by the **East** branch (the middle band) around February 2019, and that the branch continued to see a significant number of patients through the end of the year.

It is important to understand what facets of the data story are emphasized (or hidden) by selecting a different chart type. You might even experiment in the Chapter 3 workbook by changing the first area chart to a line chart. You may notice that you can see the spikes as well as the absolute increase and decrease in patient visits per branch. Each chart type contributes to a certain aspect of the data story.

You can define the order in which the areas are stacked by changing the sort order of the dimensions on the shelves of the **Marks** card. Additionally, you can rearrange them by dragging and dropping them within **Color Legend** to further adjust the order.

Pie charts

Pie charts can also be used to show part-to-whole relationships. To create a pie chart in Tableau, change the mark type to **Pie**. This will give you an **Angle** shelf, which you can use to encode a measure. Whatever dimension(s) you place on the **Marks** card (typically on the **Color** shelf) will define the slices of the pie:

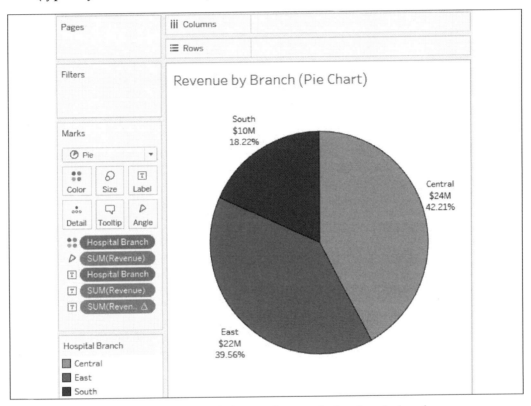

Figure 3.41: A pie chart showing total revenue broken down by branch

Observe that the preceding pie chart uses the sum of revenue to define the angle of each slice; the higher the sum, the wider the slice. The **Hospital Branch** dimension is slicing the measure and defining slices of the pie. This view also demonstrates the ability to place multiple fields on the **Label** shelf. The second **SUM(Revenue)** field is the percentage of the total table calculation you saw previously. This allows you to see the absolute values of revenue, as well as the percentage of the whole.

Pie charts can work well with a few slices. In most cases, more than two or three become very difficult to see and understand. Also, as a good practice, sort the slices by sorting the dimension that defines the slices. In the preceding example, the **Hospital Branch** dimension was sorted by the SUM of revenue descending. This was done by using the drop-down menu option. This causes slices to be ordered from largest to smallest and allows anyone reading the chart the ability to easily see which slices are larger, even when the size and angles are nearly identical.

With a good understanding of some techniques for visualizing part-to-whole relationships, let's move on to visualizing distributions.

Visualizing distributions

Often, simply understanding totals, sums, and even the breakdown of part-to-whole only gives a piece of the overall picture. Most of the time, you'll want to understand where individual items fall within a distribution of all similar items.

You might find yourself asking questions such as the following:

- How much does each customer spend at our stores and how does that compare to all other customers?

- How long do most of our patients stay in the hospital? Which patients fall outside the normal range?

- What's the average life expectancy for components in a machine and which last more than average? Are there any components with extremely long or extremely short lives?

- How far above or below passing were students' test scores?

These questions all have similarities. In each case, you seek an understanding of how individuals (customers, patients, components, students) relate to the group. In each case, you most likely have a relatively high number of individuals. In data terms, you have a dimension (customer, patient, component, and student) representing a relatively large population of individuals and some measure (amount spent, length of stay, life expectancy, test score) you'd like to compare. Using one or more of the following visualizations might be a good way to do this.

Circle charts

Circle charts are one way to visualize a distribution. Consider the following view, which shows how each doctor compares to other doctors within the same type of department in terms of the average days their patients stay in the hospital:

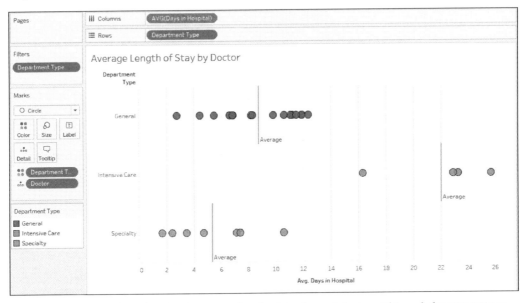

Figure 3.42: A circle chart showing the average length of stay for each doctor within each department type

Here you can see which doctors have patients that stay in the hospital longer or shorter on average. It is also interesting to note that certain types of departments have longer average lengths of stay versus others. This makes sense as each type of department has patients with different needs. It's probably not surprising that patients in **Intensive Care** tend to stay longer. Certain departments may have different goals or requirements. Being able to evaluate doctors within their type of department makes comparisons far more meaningful.

To create the preceding circle chart, you need to place the fields on the shelves that are shown and then simply change the mark type from **Automatic** (which was a bar mark) to **Circle**. **Department Type** defines the rows, and each circle is drawn at the level of **Doctor**, which is in the level of **Detail** on the **Marks** card. Finally, to add the average lines, simply switch to the **Analytics** tab of the left pane and drag **Average Line** to the view, specifically dropping it on the **Cell** option:

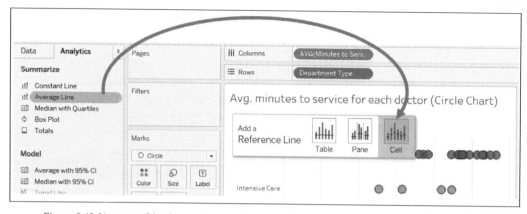

Figure 3.43: You can add reference lines and more by dragging from the Analytics tab to the view

You may also click one of the resulting average lines and select **Edit** to find fine-tuning options, such as labeling.

Jittering

When using views like circle plots or other similar visualization types, you'll often see that marks overlap, which can lead to obscuring part of the true story. Do you know for certain, just by looking, how many doctors there are in **Intensive Care** who are above average? How many are below? Or could there be two or more circles exactly overlapping? One way of minimizing this is to click the **Color** shelf and add some transparency and a border to each circle. Another approach is a technique called **jittering**.

Jittering is a common technique in data visualization that involves adding a bit of intentional noise to a visualization to avoid overlap without harming the integrity of what is communicated. Alan Eldridge and Steve Wexler are among those who pioneered techniques for jittering in Tableau.

Various jittering techniques, such as using Index() or Random() functions, can be found by searching for *jittering* on the Tableau forums or *Tableau jittering* using a search engine.

Here is one approach that uses the Index() function, computed along **Doctor**, as a continuous field on **Rows**. Since **INDEX()** is continuous (green), it defines an axis and causes the circles to spread out vertically. Now, you can more clearly see each individual mark and have higher confidence that the overlap is not obscuring the true picture of the data:

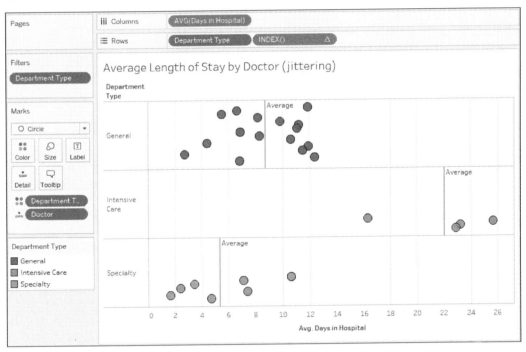

Figure 3.44: Here INDEX() has been added as a continuous field on Rows (the table calculation is computed along Doctor)

In the preceding view, the vertical axis that was created by the **Index** field is hidden. You can hide an axis or header by using the drop-down menu of the field defining the axis or header and unchecking **Show Header**. Alternatively, you can right-click any axis or header in the view and select the same option.

You can use jittering techniques on many kinds of visualizations that involve plotting fixed points that could theoretically overlap, such as dot plots and scatterplots. Next, we will move onto another useful distribution visualization technique: box and whisker plots.

Box and whisker plots

Box and whisker plots (sometimes just called **box plots**) add additional statistical context to distributions. To understand a box and whisker plot, consider the following diagram:

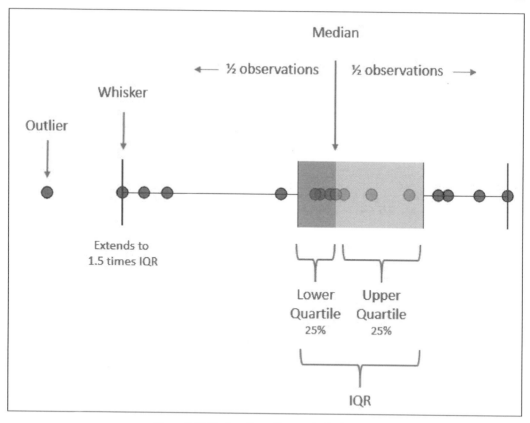

Figure 3.45: Explanation of box and whisker plot

Here, the box plot has been added to a circle graph. The box is divided by the median, meaning that half of the values are above, and half are below. The box also indicates the lower and upper quartiles, which each contain a quarter of the values. The span of the box makes up what is known as the **Interquartile Range (IQR)**. The whiskers extend to 1.5 times the IQR value (or the maximum extent of the data). Any marks beyond the whiskers are outliers.

To add box and whisker plots, use the **Analytics** tab on the left sidebar and drag **Box Plot** to the view. Doing this to the circle chart we considered in *Figure 3.42* yields the following chart:

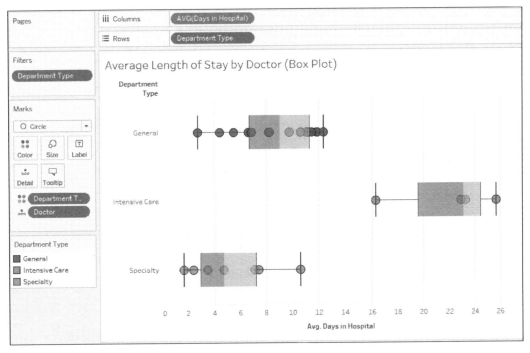

Figure 3.46: A box plot applied to the previous circle chart

The box plots help us to see and compare the medians, the ranges of data, the concentration of values, and any outliers. You may edit box plots by clicking or right-clicking the box or whisker and selecting **Edit**. This will reveal multiple options, including how whiskers should be drawn, whether only outliers should be displayed, and other formatting possibilities.

Histograms

Another possibility for showing distributions is to use a histogram. A histogram looks similar to a bar chart, but the bars show a count of occurrences of a value. For example, standardized test auditors looking for evidence of grade tampering might construct a histogram of student test scores. Typically, a distribution might look like the following example (not included in the workbook):

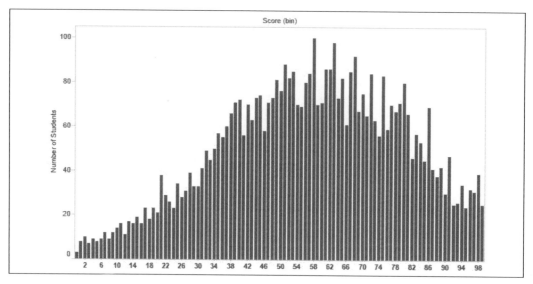

Figure 3.47: A histogram of test scores

The test scores are shown on the *x* axis and the height of each bar shows the number of students that made that particular score. A typical distribution often has a recognizable bell curve. In this case, some students are doing poorly and some are doing extremely well, but most have scores somewhere in the middle.

What if auditors saw something like this?

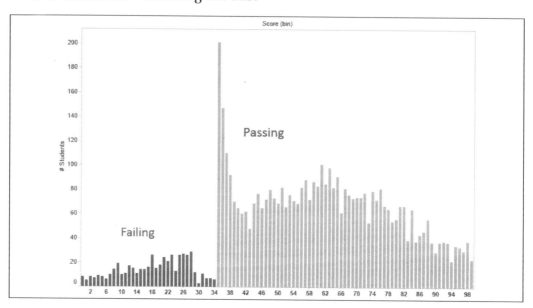

Figure 3.48: A histogram that does not have a typical bell curve, raising some questions

Something is clearly wrong. Perhaps graders have bumped up students who were just shy of passing to barely passing. It's also possible this may indicate bias in subjective grading instead of blatant tampering. We shouldn't jump to conclusions, but the pattern is not normal and requires investigation. Histograms are very useful in catching anomalies like this.

Now that we've seen an example of histograms, let's shift our focus back to the hospital data and work through an example. What if you want to visualize the time it takes to begin patient treatment so that you can observe the patterns for different patient populations. You might start with a blank view follow steps like these:

1. Click to select the **Minutes to Service** field under **Measures** in the data pane.

2. Expand **Show Me** if necessary and select the histogram.

Upon selecting the histogram, Tableau builds the chart by creating a new dimension, **Minutes to Service (bin)**, which is used in the view, along with a COUNT of **Minutes to Service** to render the view:

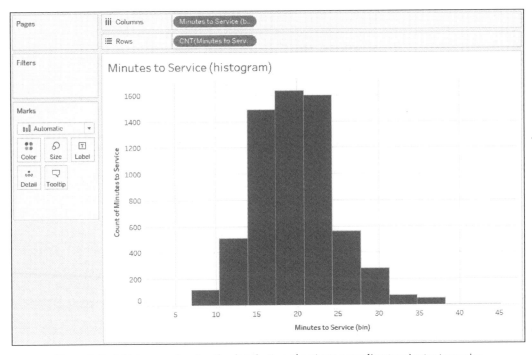

Figure 3.49: A histogram showing the distribution of patients according to minutes to service

Bins are ranges of measure values that can be used as dimensions to slice the data. You can think of bins as buckets. For example, you might look at test scores by 0-5%, 5-10%, and so on, or people's ages by 0-10, 10-20, and so on. You can set the size, or range, of the bin when it is created and edit it at any point. Tableau will also suggest a size for the bin based on an algorithm that looks at the values that are present in the data. Tableau will use uniform bin sizes for all bins.

For this view, Tableau automatically set the bin size to **3.47** minutes, which is not very intuitive. Experiment with different values by right-clicking or using the drop-down on the **Minutes to Service (bin)** field in the data pane and selecting **Edit**. The resulting window gives some information and allows you to adjust the size of the bins:

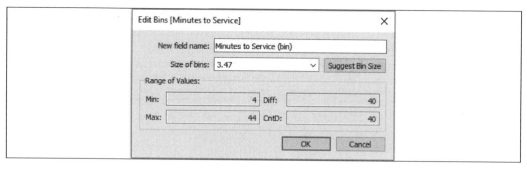

Figure 3.50: Options for editing a bin

Here, for example, is the same histogram with each bin sized to 2 minutes:

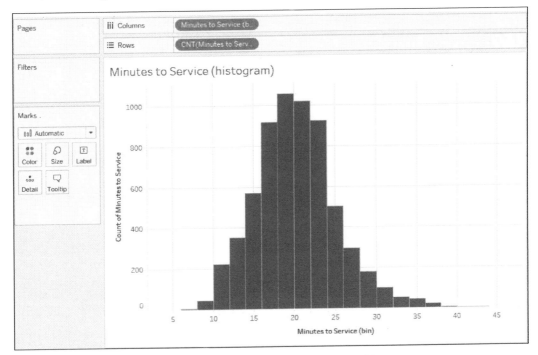

Figure 3.51: A histogram with a bin size of 2

You can see the curve, which peaks at just under **20** minutes and then tapers off with a few patients having to wait as long as **40** minutes. You might pursue additional analysis, such as seeing how wait times vary for the majority of patients based on their risk profile, such as in this view:

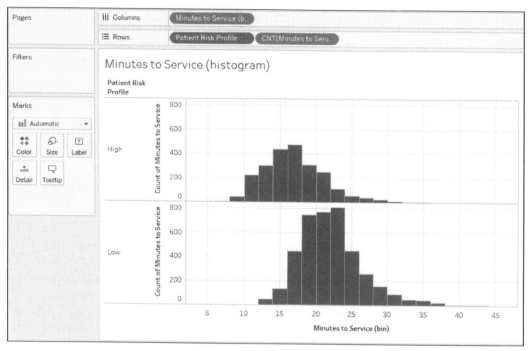

Figure 3.52: Patient risk profile creates two rows of histograms, showing that most high-risk patients receive faster care (as we would hope)

 You can create new bins on your own by right-clicking a numeric field and selecting **Create | Bins**. You may edit the size of bins by selecting the **Edit** option for the bin field.

You'll also want to consider what you want to count for each bin and place that on **Rows**. When you used **Show Me**, Tableau placed the COUNT of **Minutes to Service** on **Rows**, which is just a count of every record where the value was not null. In this case, that's equivalent to a count of patient visits because the data set contains one record per visit. However, if you wanted to count the number of unique patients, you might consider replacing the field in the view with COUNTD([Patient ID]).

Just like dates, when the bin field in the view is discrete, the drop-down menu includes an option for **Show Missing Values**. If you use a discrete bin field, you may wish to use this option to avoid distorting the visualization and to identify what values don't occur in the data.

We've seen how to visualize distributions with circle plots, histograms, and box plots. Let's turn our attention to using multiple axes to compare different measures.

Visualizing multiple axes to compare different measures

Often, you'll need to use more than one axis to compare different measures, understand correlation, or analyze the same measure at different levels of detail. In these cases, you'll use visualizations with more than one axis.

Scatterplot

A scatterplot is an essential visualization type for understanding the relationship between two measures. Consider a scatterplot when you find yourself asking questions like the following:

- Does how much I spend on marketing really make a difference on sales?
- How much does power consumption go up with each degree of heating/cooling?
- Is there any correlation between hours of study and test performance?

Each of these questions seeks to understand the correlation (if any) between two measures. Scatterplots help you understand these relationships and see any outliers.

Consider the following scatterplot, which looks for a relationship between the total revenue for a department and the number of patient visits:

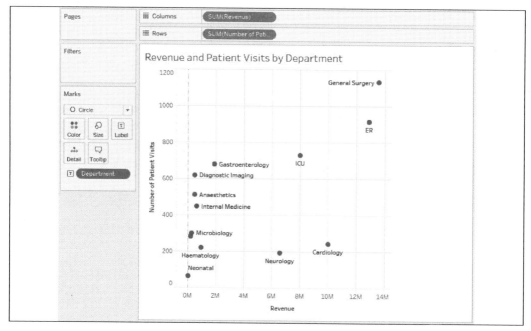

Figure 3.53: A scatterplot showing the correlation between Revenue and Number of Patient Visits

The **Department** dimension is on **Text** and defines the view level of detail. Each mark in the view represents the total **Revenue** and total **Number of Patient Visits** for the department.

As you would expect, most departments have higher revenue with a higher volume of patients. **Neurology** and **Cardiology** stand out as having high revenue despite a lower volume of patients.

 Look for ways to use **Size** and **Color** to encode additional data in scatterplots. For example, we might add **Department Type** to **Color** to see if departments of the same type show similar correlations. We might encode **Size** with average length of stay to see if higher revenues can also be explained by patients who stay longer.

Let's consider a few other types of charts that use multiple axes.

Dual-axis and combination charts

One very important feature in Tableau is the ability to use a dual axis. Scatterplots use two axes, but they are X and Y. You also observed in the stacked bar example that placing multiple continuous (green) fields next to each other on **Rows** or **Columns** results in multiple side-by-side axes. Dual axis, on the other hand, means that a view is using two axes that are opposite each other with a common pane.

Here is an example (not included in the workbook) using a dual axis for **Sales** and **Profit**:

Figure 3.54: A dual-axis chart with an indication of which field defines which axis

There are several key features of the view, which are as follows:

- The **Sales** and **Profit** fields on **Rows** indicate that they have a dual axis by sharing a flattened side.

- The axes defined by **Sales** and **Profit** are on opposing sides of the view. Also, note that they are not synchronized, which, in many cases, can give a distorted view of the data. It would be great if profit was that close to total sales! But it's not. To synchronize the axes, right-click the right axis and select **Synchronize Axis**. If that option is grayed out, it is likely that one of the values is a whole number type and the other is a decimal type. You can change the data type of one of the fields by right-clicking it in the data pane and selecting **Change Data Type | Number (Whole)** or **Number (Decimal)**.

- The **Marks** card is now an accordion-like control with an **All** section and a section for **Sales** and **Profit**. You can use this to customize marks for all measures or specifically customize marks for either **Sales** or **Profit**.

To create a dual axis, drag and drop two continuous (green) fields next to each other on **Rows** or **Columns**, then use the drop-down menu on the second, and select **Dual Axis**. Alternatively, you can drop the second field onto the canvas, opposite the existing axis.

> Dual axes can be used with any continuous field that defines an axis. This includes numeric fields, date fields, and latitude or longitude fields that define a geographic visualization. In the case of latitude or longitude, simply copy one of the fields and place it immediately next to itself on the **Rows** or **Columns** shelf. Then, select **Dual Axis** by using the drop-down menu.

A **combination chart** extends the use of dual axes to overlay different mark types. This is possible because the **Marks** card will give options for editing all marks or customizing marks for each individual axis.

> Multiple mark types are available any time two or more continuous fields are located beside each other on **Rows** or **Columns**.

As an example of a **combination chart**, consider the following visualization:

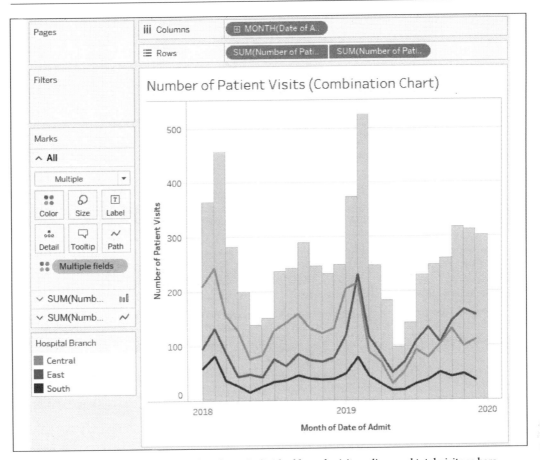

Figure 3.55: A combination chart that shows individual branch visits as lines and total visits as bars.

This chart uses a combination of bars and lines to show the total number of patient visits over time (the bars) and the breakdown of patient visits by hospital branch over time (the lines). This kind of visualization can be quite effective at giving additional context to detail.

There are several things to note about this view:

- The field on the **Color** shelf is listed as **Multiple Fields** and is gray on the **Marks** card. This indicates that different fields have been used for **Color** for each axis on **Marks**.

- The view demonstrates the ability to mix levels of detail in the same view. The bars are drawn at the highest level (patient visits for each month), while the lines have been drawn at a lower level (patient visits for each branch for each month).

- The view demonstrates the ability to use the same field (**Patient Visits**, in this case) multiple times on the same shelf (**Rows**, in this case).

- The second axis (the **Patient Visits** field on the right) has the header hidden to remove redundancy from the view. You can do this by unchecking **Show Header** from the drop-down menu on the field in the view or right-clicking the axis or header you wish to hide.

Dual axis and combination charts open a wide range of possibilities for mixing mark types and levels of detail and are very useful for generating unique insights. We'll see a few more examples of these throughout the rest of this book. Be sure to experiment with this feature and let your imagination run wild with all that can be done.

Summary

We've covered quite a bit of ground in this chapter! You should now have a good grasp of when to use certain types of visualizations. The types of questions you ask about data will often lead you to a certain type of view. You've explored how to create these various types and how to extend basic visualizations using a variety of advanced techniques, such as calculated fields, jittering, multiple mark types, and dual axis. Along the way, we've also covered some details on how dates work in Tableau.

Hopefully, the examples of using calculations in this chapter have whet your appetite for learning more about creating calculated fields. The ability to create calculations in Tableau opens endless possibilities for extending analysis of data, calculating results, customizing visualizations, and creating rich user interactivity. We'll dive deep into calculations in the next two chapters to see how they work and what amazing things they can do.

4

Starting an Adventure with Calculations and Parameters

We have already seen what amazing discovery, analysis, and data storytelling is possible in Tableau by simply connecting to data and dragging and dropping fields. Now, we'll set off on an adventure with calculations.

Calculations significantly extend the possibilities for analysis, design, and interactivity in Tableau. In this chapter, we'll see how calculations can be used in a wide variety of ways. We'll see how calculations can be used to address common issues with data, extend data by adding new dimensions and measures, and provide additional flexibility in interactivity.

At the same time, while calculations provide incredible power and flexibility, they introduce a level of complexity and sophistication. As you work through this chapter, try to understand the key concepts behind how calculations work in Tableau. As usual, follow along with the examples, but feel free to explore and experiment. The goal is not to merely have a list of calculations you can copy, but to gain knowledge of how calculations can be used to solve problems and add creative functionality to your visualizations and dashboards.

The first half of this chapter focuses on laying a foundation, while the second half provides quite a few practical examples. The topics we will study here are as follows:

- Overview of the four main types of calculations
- Creating and editing calculations
- Row-level calculation examples

- Aggregate calculation examples
- Parameters
- Practical examples
- Performance considerations

We'll start with an introduction to the types of calculations in Tableau and then delve into some examples.

Introduction to calculations

A calculation is often referred to as a **Calculated Field** in Tableau because, in most cases, when you create a calculation, it will show up as either a new measure or dimension in the data pane. Calculations consist of code that's made up of functions, operations, and references to other fields, parameters, constants, groups, or sets. This code returns a value. Sometimes, this result is per row of data, and sometimes it is done at an aggregate level. We'll consider the difference between Tableau's major calculation types next.

The four main types of calculations

The most fundamental way to understand calculations in Tableau is to think of four major types of calculations:

- **Row-level calculations**: These calculations are performed for every row of underlying data.

- **Aggregate calculations**: These calculations are performed at an aggregate level, which is usually defined by the dimensions used in the view.

- **Level of detail calculations**: These special calculations are aggregations that are performed at a specified level of detail, with the results available at the row level.

- **Table calculations**: These calculations are performed on the table of aggregate data that has been returned by the data source to Tableau.

Understanding and recognizing the four main types of calculations will enable you to leverage the power and potential of calculations in Tableau.

In this chapter, we'll take a close look at two of the four main types of calculations in Tableau: row-level and aggregate calculations. We'll consider the final two types in *Chapter 5, Leveraging Level of Detail Calculations*, and *Chapter 6, Diving Deep with Table Calculations*.

As you think through using a calculation to solve a problem, always consider the type of calculation you might need. Look for tips throughout this chapter and the next two that will help you consider *why* a certain type of calculation was used.

Now we have examined the major calculation types in Tableau, we will see how they are created and edited.

Creating and editing calculations

There are multiple ways to create a calculated field in Tableau:

1. Select **Analysis | Create Calculated Field...** from the menu.
2. Use the drop-down menu next to **Dimensions** in the **Data** pane:

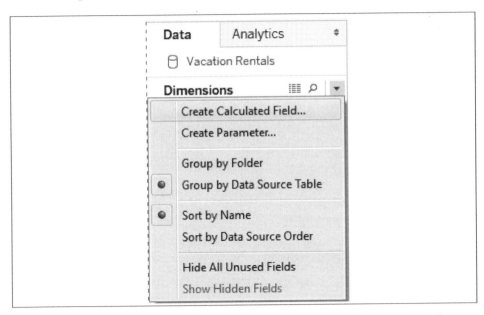

Figure 4.1: The Create Calculated Field... option

3. Right-click an empty area in the **Data** pane and select **Create Calculated Field...**.
4. Use the drop-down menu on a field, set, or parameter in the data pane and select **Create | Calculated Field...**. The calculation will begin as a reference to the field you selected.

5. Double-click an empty area on the **Rows**, **Columns**, or **Measure Values** shelves, or in the empty area on the **Marks** card to create an ad hoc calculation (though this will not show the full calculation editor).

6. When you create a calculated field, it will be part of the data source that is currently selected at the time you create it. You can edit an existing calculated field in the data pane by using the drop-down menu and selecting **Edit...**.

The interface for creating and editing calculations looks like this:

Figure 4.2: The creating and editing calculations interface

This window has several key features:

- **Calculated field name**: Enter the name of the calculated field here. Once created, the calculated field will show up as a field in the data pane with the name you entered in this text box.

- **Code editor**: Enter code in this text area to perform the calculation. The editor includes autocomplete for recognized fields and functions. Additionally, you may drag and drop fields and text snippets to and from the code editor and the data pane and view.

- An **indicator** at the bottom of the editor will alert you to errors in your code. Additionally, if the calculation is used in views or other calculated fields, you will see a drop-down indicator that will let you see the dependencies. Click the **Apply** button to apply changes to the calculation throughout the workbook while leaving the calculation editor open. The **OK** button will save the code changes and close the editor. If you wish to discard any changes you've made, click the **X** button in the upper-right corner to cancel the changes.

- The **functions list** contains all the functions that you can use in your code. Many of these functions will be used in examples or discussed in this chapter. Tableau groups various functions according to their overall use:

- **Number**: Mathematical functions, such as rounding, absolute value, trig functions, square roots, and exponents.

- **String**: Functions that are useful for string manipulation, such as getting a substring, finding a match within a string, replacing parts of a string, and converting a string value to uppercase or lowercase.

- **Date**: Functions that are useful for working with dates, such as finding the difference between two dates, adding an interval to a date, getting the current date, and transforming strings with non-standard formats into dates.

- **Type Conversion**: Functions that are useful for converting one type of field to another, such as converting strings into integers, integers into floating-point decimals, or strings into dates. We'll cover the major Tableau data types in the next section.

- **Logical**: Decision-making functions, such as `if then else` logic or `case` statements.

- **Aggregate**: Functions that are used for aggregating such as summing, getting the minimum or maximum values, or calculating standard deviations or variances.

- **Pass Through** (only available when connected live to certain databases, such as SQL Server): These functions allow you to pass through raw SQL code to the underlying database and retrieve a returned value at either a row level or aggregate level.

- **User**: Functions that are used to obtain usernames and check whether the current user is a member of a group. These functions are often used in combination with logical functions to customize the user's experience or to implement user-based security when publishing to Tableau Server or Tableau Online.

- **Table calculation**: These functions are different from the others. They operate on the aggregated data *after* it is returned from the underlying data source and just prior to the rendering of the view.

- **Spatial**: These functions allow you to perform calculations with spatial data.

- Selecting a function in the list or clicking a field, parameter, or function in the code will reveal details about the selection on the right. This is helpful when nesting other calculated fields in your code, when you want to see the code for that particular calculated field, or when you want to understand the syntax for a function.

With a good understanding of the interface, let's briefly look at some foundational concepts for calculations.

Data types

Fundamental to the concept of calculations are **data types**, which describe the kind of information stored by a field, parameter, or returned by a function. Tableau distinguishes six types of data:

- **Number (decimal)**: These are numeric values that include places after the decimal. Values such as 0.02, 100.377, or 3.14159 are decimal values.

- **Number (whole)**: These are integer or whole numbers with no fractional values or places after the decimal. Values such as 5, 157, and 1,455,982 are whole numbers.

- **Date and Time**: These are dates along with times. Values such as November 8, 1980 12:04:33 PM are date and time types.

- **Date**: These are dates without times. Values such as July 17, 1979 are date types.

- **String**: These are a series of characters. A string may consist of a mixture of alphabetic characters, numeric characters, symbols, or special characters. They may even be blank (empty). Values such as Hello World, password123, and %$@*! are all strings. In code, strings will be surrounded by single or double quotes.

- **Boolean**: This is a true or false value. The values TRUE, FALSE, and the expressions 1=1 (which evaluates as true) and 1=2 (which evaluates as false) are all Boolean types.

- **Spatial:** A complex value that describes a location, line or shape as it relates to a spatial area.

Every field in Tableau has one of these data types and every function in Tableau returns one of these data types. Some functions expect input that matches some of these types and you'll receive errors if you try to pass in the wrong type.

Some types can be converted to other types. For example, using some of the type conversion functions mentioned above, you could convert the string "2.81" to the decimal value 2.81. You could convert that decimal value to a whole number, but in that case, you'd lose the places after the decimal value and the whole number would simply be 2.

A data type is different from the format displayed. For example, you may choose to format a decimal as a percentage (for example, 0.2 could be shown as 20%), as currency (for example, 144.56 could be formatted as $144.56), or even as a number with 0 decimals (for example, 2.81 would be rounded to 3).

Pay attention to the data types of fields and functions as we continue.

Additional functions and operators

Tableau supports numerous functions and operators. In addition to the functions that are listed on the calculation screen, Tableau supports the following operators, keywords, and syntax conventions:

Operator / Keyword	Description
AND	Logical *and* between two Boolean (true/false) values or statements
OR	Logical *or* between two Boolean values or statements
NOT	Logical *not* to negate a Boolean value or statement
= or ==	Logical *equals to* to test the equality of two statements or values (single or double equal signs are equivalent in Tableau's syntax)
+	Addition of numeric or date values or the concatenation of strings
-	Subtraction of numeric or date values
*	Multiplication of numeric values
/	Division of numeric values
^	Raise to a power with numeric values
( )	Parentheses to define the order of operations or enclose function arguments
[ ]	Square brackets to enclose field names
{ }	Curly braces to enclose the level of detail calculations
//	Double slash to start a comment

Field names that are a single word may optionally be enclosed in brackets when used in calculations. Field names with spaces, special characters, or from secondary data sources must be enclosed in brackets.

You'll see these operators and functions throughout the next few chapters, so familiarize yourself with their uses. Now, let's consider the data that will guide us through some practical examples.

Example data

Before we get started with some examples, let's consider a sample dataset that will be used for the examples in this chapter. It's simple and small, which means we will be able to easily see how the calculations are being done.

This dataset is included as `Vacation Rentals.csv` in the `\Learning Tableau\Chapter 04` directory of this book's resources, and is also included in the `Chapter 4` workbook as a data source named `Vacation Rentals`:

Rental Property	First	Last	Start	End	Discount	Rent	Tax per Night
112-Asbury Atoll	Mary	Slessor	Dec 2	Dec 9	150	1,500	15
112-Asbury Atoll	Amy	Carmichael	Dec 9	Dec 15	0	1,500	15
155-Beach Breeze	Charles	Ryrie	Dec 2	Dec 9	260	1,300	10
155-Beach Breeze	Dwight	Pentecost	Dec 16	Dec 23	280	1,400	10
207-Beach Breeze	Lewis	Chafer	Dec 9	Dec 23	280	2,800	10
207-Beach Breeze	John	Walvoord	Dec 2	Dec 9	60	1,500	10

The dataset describes several vacation rental properties, the renters, the start and end dates of the rental period, the discount, rent, and tax per night. We'll use it throughout the rest of the chapter as we see some examples of calculations. Let's start with row-level calculations.

Row-level calculations

We'll walk through several examples of row-level calculations in this section. You'll find the completed calculations in the `Complete` workbook, but you might prefer to start from scratch in the `Starter` workbook. We won't necessarily cover creating a visualization for every example, but try building some of your own as you work through the examples.

Simple example

We'll start with a very simple example and then build up in complexity. In the `Chapter 04` workbook, create a new calculated field called `Full Name` with the following code:

```
[First] + " " + [Last]
```

This code concatenates the strings of First and Last with a space in-between them. Your calculation editor should look something like the following:

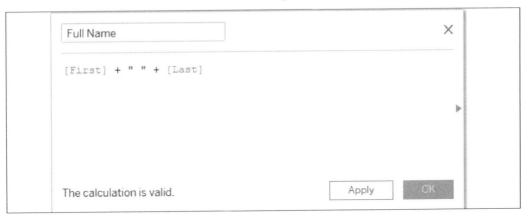

Figure 4.3: Creating the Full Name calculation in the editor

After clicking **OK**, you should notice a new **Full Name** field in the data pane. The value for that field is calculated per row of data. That is, every row of data contains the full name of the renter.

More complex examples

Note that the Rental Property field contains values such as 112-Asbury Atoll or 207-Beach Breeze. Let's assume that the naming convention of the rental unit in the vacation rental data gives us the room number and the name of the building separated by a dash. For example, the unit named 207-Beach Breeze is room 207 of the Beach Breeze building.

Name the first Room with the following code:

```
SPLIT([Rental Property], "-", 1)
```

Then, create another calculated field named Building with the following code:

```
SPLIT([Rental Property], "-", 2)
```

Both of these functions use the Split() function, which splits a string into multiple values and keeps one of those values. This function takes three arguments: the **string**, the **delimiter** (a character or set of characters that separate values), and the **token number** (which value to keep from the split, that is, first, second, third, and so on.) Using the - (dash) as the delimiter, Room is the first value and Building is the second.

Using the two calculated fields, create a bar chart of **Rent per Building & Room**, like this:

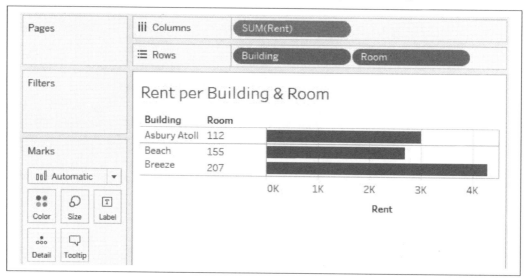

Figure 4.4: Using your calculated fields to build a view

The **Building** and **Room** fields show up in the data pane as dimensions. The calculated dimensions can be used just like any other dimension. They can slice the data, define the level of detail, and group measures.

Row-level calculations are calculated at the row level, but you can choose to aggregate the results. For example, you could aggregate to find the highest **Room** number (MAX) or count the distinct number of **Buildings** (COUNTD). In fact, if the result of a row-level calculation is numeric, Tableau will often place the resulting field as a measure by default. But as we've seen, you can use a row-level field as either a dimension or measure in the view.

Note that Tableau adds a small equals sign to the icon of the fields in the data pane to indicate that they are calculated fields:

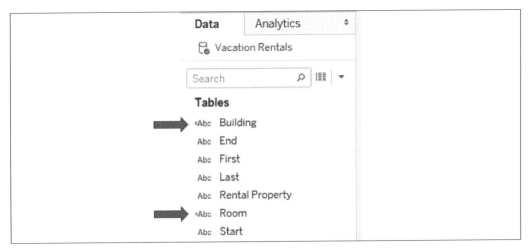

Figure 4.5: The small = sign indicates a field is a calculation

The code for both calculated fields is executed for every row of data and returns a row-level value. We can verify that the code is operating on the row level by examining the source data. Simply click on the **View Data** icon next to dimensions to see the row-level detail (it's next to the magnifying glass icon in the preceding screenshot). Here, the new fields of **Building** and **Unit**, along with the row-level values, can be clearly seen:

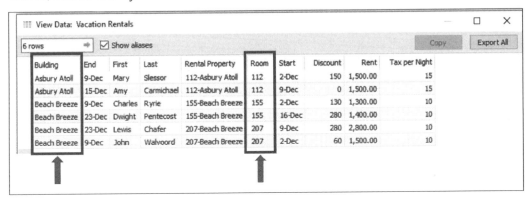

Figure 4.6: Viewing the underlying data shows us the calculation is done per row of data

Tableau provides a shortcut for splitting a field. You can use the drop-down menu on a field in the data pane and select **Transform | Split** or **Transform | Custom Split** (if you have a non-standard delimiter). The results are calculated fields similar to those you created previously, but with some additional logic around determining data types. Transform functionality, such as split, is also available for fields in the **Preview** or **Metadata** views on the **Data** source screen.

Extending the example

We'll extend the example a bit more and assume you know that the floor of a room is indicated by its number. Rooms 100 through 199 are on the first floor, and 200 through 299 are on the second. You'd like to have that information available for analysis.

We could potentially add this attribute to the source data, but there are times when this may not be an option or may not be feasible. You may not have permission to change the source data or the source might be a spreadsheet that is automatically generated every day, and any changes would be overwritten.

Instead, you can create a row-level calculation in Tableau to extend the data. To do so, create a calculated field named Floor with the following code:

```
IF LEFT([Room], 1) = "1"
THEN "First Floor"
ELSEIF LEFT([Room], 1) = "2"
THEN "Second Floor"

END
```

This code uses the LEFT() function to return the leftmost character of the room. Thus, 112 gives a result of 1; 207 gives a result of 2. The IF THEN END logic allows us to assign a result (either First Floor or Second Floor), depending on which case is true. Notice that you used the Room field in the calculation, which, in turn, was another calculation.

Using a reference to a calculated field within another calculation is referred to as **nesting**. The calculations that use other calculated fields are called **nested calculations**. There's no theoretical limit to how many levels of nesting you can use, but it may become hard to untangle the logic if you use too many levels of nesting.

Planning for data variations

As you write calculations, consider whether your calculation covers variations in the data that are not currently present.

 A few good questions to ask yourself whenever you write a calculation in Tableau are: *What happens if the data changes? Does the calculation handle unexpected or invalid values? Have I covered every case?*

For example, the preceding floor calculation only works if all the rooms are either 100- or 200-level rooms. What if there is a room, 306, on the third floor, or a room, 822, on the eighth floor?

To account for additional cases, we might simplify our calculation to the following:

```
LEFT([Room], 1)
```

This code simply returns the leftmost character of the room number. We'll get 3 for 306 and 8 for 822. But what if we have room numbers such as 1056 on the tenth floor, and 1617 on the sixteenth? We'd have to consider other options, such as the following:

```
MID([Room], 0, LEN([Room]) - 2)
```

Although this is more complicated, the string functions return a substring that starts at the beginning of the string and ends just before the last two characters. That gives us floor 10 for 1025, and floor 18 for 1856.

We've now considered some row-level calculation examples. Let's move on to the next major type of calculation in Tableau: aggregate-level calculations.

Aggregate calculations

We've already considered aggregations such as sum, min, and max in Tableau. Often, you'll use fields as simple aggregations in the view. But sometimes, you'll want to use aggregations in more complex calculations.

For example, you might be curious to explore the percentage of the rent that was discounted. There is no such field in the data. It could not really be stored in the source, because the value changes based on the level of detail present in the view (for example, the percent discounted for an individual unit will be different to the percent discounted per floor or per building). Rather, it must be calculated as an aggregate and recalculated as the level of detail changes.

Let's create a calculation named `Discount %` with the following code:

```
SUM([Discount]) / SUM([Rent])
```

This code indicates that the sum of `Discount` should be divided by the sum of `Rent`. This means that all the values of `Discount` will be added, and all the values of `Rent` will be added. Only after the sums are calculated will the division occur.

 Once you've created the calculation, you'll notice that Tableau treats the new field as a **Measure** in the data pane. Tableau will treat any calculation with a numeric result as a measure by default, but you can change *row-level calculations* to dimensions if desired. In this case, though, you are not even able to redefine the new field as a dimension. The reason for this is that Tableau will treat every *aggregate calculation* as a measure, no matter what data type is returned. This is because an aggregate calculation depends on dimensions to define the level of detail at which the calculation is performed. So, an aggregate calculation cannot be a dimension itself.

As the value of your calculation is a percentage, you will also likely want to define the format as a percentage. To do this, right-click the `Discount %` field, select **Default Properties | Number Format**, and select **Percentage**. You may adjust the number of decimal places that are displayed if desired.

Now, create a couple of views to see how the calculation returns different results, depending on the level of detail in the view. First, we'll build a view to look at each individual rental period:

1. Place **Building, Room, Full Name, Start,** and **End** on **Rows**.
2. In the data pane, under **Measures**, double-click each of the following fields: **Rent, Discount,** and **Discount %**. Tableau will place each of these measures in the view by using **Measure Names** and **Measure Values**.

3. Rearrange the fields on the **Measure Values** shelf so that the order is **Rent**, **Discount**, and **Discount** %:

Figure 4.7: Illustrates the Discount % calculated at the level of
Building, Room, Full Name, Start, and End

You can see the percentage given by way of discount for each rental period. However, notice how the values change when you remove all fields except **Building** and **Room**:

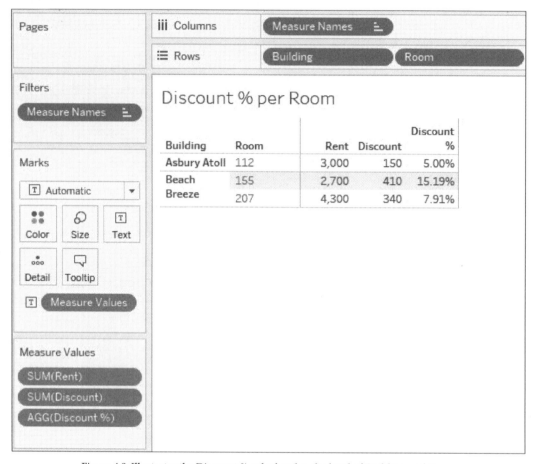

Figure 4.8: Illustrates the Discount % calculated at the level of Building and Room

Why did the values change? Because aggregations depend on what dimensions are defining the level of detail of the view. In the first case, **Building** and **Room**, **Full Name**, **Start**, and **End** defined the level of detail in the view. So, the calculation added up all the rent for each rental period and all the discounts for the rental period and then divided them. In the second case, **Building** and **Room** redefine the level of detail. So, the calculation added up all the prices for each building and room and all the discounts for each building and room and then divided them.

 You may have noticed that as you double-clicked each measure, it was added to the pane of the view in a special way. **Measure Names** and **Measure Values** are special fields that appear in every data connection (toward the bottom of the **Data** pane). These serve as placeholders for multiple measures that share the same space in the view.

In the view you just created, for example, three measures all shared space in the pane. **Measure Values** on **Text** indicated that all values of measures on the **Measure Values** shelf should be displayed as text. The **Measure Names** field on **Columns** created a column for each measure, with the value of the name of that measure.

Notice that the values change again, as expected, if you look at the overall dataset without slicing by any dimensions:

Figure 4.9: Illustrates the Discount % calculated at the highest possible level: the entire dataset

An easy way to get Tableau to implement **Measure Names /
Measure Values** is to remember that they are used whenever you
want to use *two or more measures in the same space* in a view. So, if
you want to use two or more measures in the pane, drag the first
to the pane and then the second. If you want to use two or more
measures on the same axis, drag the first to the axis, and then drag
and drop the second on the same spot.

Now that you have a basic understanding of row-level and aggregate calculations,
let's consider why the distinction is important.

Why the row level versus aggregate difference matters

Let's say you created a Discount % (row level) calculation with the following code:

```
[Discount]/[Rent]
```

The code differs from the aggregate calculation you created previously, which had
the following code:

```
SUM([Discount])/SUM([Rent]) .
```

Here is the dramatic difference in results:

Figure 4.10: Illustrates the Discount % calculated as a row-level value and as an aggregate

Why is there such a difference in the results? It's a result of the way the calculations were performed.

Notice that Discount % (row level) appears on the **Measure Values** shelf as a SUM. That's because the calculation is a row-level calculation, so it gets calculated row by row and then aggregated as a measure after all row-level values have been determined. The 54.00% value you see is actually a sum of percentages that were calculated in each record of underlying data.

In fact, the row-level calculation and the final aggregation is performed like this:

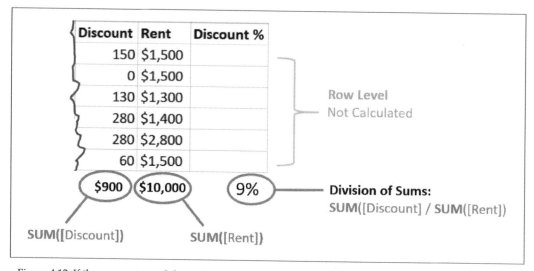

Rental Property	First	Discount	Rent	Discount %
112-Asbury Atoll	Mary	150	$1,500	10%
112-Asbury Atoll	Amy	0	$1,500	0%
155-Beach Breeze	Charles	130	$1,300	10%
155-Beach Breeze	Dwight	280	$1,400	20%
207-Beach Breeze	Lewis	280	$2,800	10%
207-Beach Breeze	John	60	$1,500	4%

Row Level
[Discount] / [Rent]
Results calculated for each row

54% — **Final Aggregation**
Sum of row level results

Figure 4.11: If each Discount % result is calculated at a row level and then aggregated, the result is wrong

Contrast that with the way the aggregate calculation is performed. Notice that the aggregation that's listed in the active field on the **Measure Values** shelf in the view is AGG, and not SUM. This indicates that you have defined the aggregation in the calculation. Tableau is not aggregating the results further. Here is how the aggregate calculation is performed:

Discount	Rent	Discount %
150	$1,500	
0	$1,500	
130	$1,300	
280	$1,400	
280	$2,800	
60	$1,500	

Row Level
Not Calculated

$900 $10,000 9% — **Division of Sums:**
SUM([Discount] / SUM([Rent])

SUM([Discount])   SUM([Rent])

Figure 4.12: If the numerator and denominator are aggregated first, then the Discount % calculation is correct

It is vital to understand the difference between row-level and aggregate calculations to ensure you are getting the results you expect and need. In general, use row-level calculations when you are certain that you will use either the value as a dimension or that an aggregation of the row-level values will make sense. Use aggregate calculations if aggregations must be performed prior to other operations.

One of the most common error messages that's encountered while writing Tableau calculations is *Cannot mix aggregate and non-aggregate arguments with this function*. When you encounter this message, check your code to make sure you are not improperly mixing row-level fields and calculations with aggregate fields and calculations. For example, you cannot have something like [Discount] / SUM([Rent]).

This mixture of a row-level value (Discount) and the aggregation (SUM of Rent) is invalid.

With the distinction between row-level and aggregate calculations clear, let's take an interlude and discuss parameters before building additional examples.

Parameters

Before moving to some additional examples of row-level and aggregate calculations, let's take a little side trip to examine parameters, given that they can be used in incredible ways in calculations.

A **parameter** in Tableau is a placeholder for a single, global value such as a number, date, or string. Parameters may be shown as controls (such as sliders, drop-down lists, or type-in text boxes) to end users of dashboards or views, giving them the ability to change the current value of the parameter. Parameter values may even be changed with actions, as you'll see in *Chapter 8*, *Telling a Data Story with Dashboards*.

The value of a parameter is global so that if the value is changed, every view and calculation in the workbook that references the parameter will use the new value. Parameters provide another way to provide rich interactivity to the end users of your dashboards and visualizations.

Parameters can be used to allow anyone interacting with your view or dashboard to dynamically do many things, including the following:

- Alter the results of a calculation
- Change the size of bins
- Change the number of top or bottom items in a top *n* filter or top *n* set
- Set the value of a reference line or band
- Change the size of bins
- Pass values to a custom SQL statement that's used in a data source

Some of these are options we'll consider in later chapters.

Since parameters can be used in calculations, and since calculated fields can be used to define any aspect of a visualization (from filters to colors to rows and columns), the change in a parameter value can have dramatic results. We'll see some examples of this in the following sections.

Creating parameters

Creating a parameter is similar to creating a calculated field.

There are multiple ways to create a parameter in Tableau:

- Use the drop-down menu next to **Dimensions** in the data pane and select **Create Parameter**.

- Right-click an empty area in the data pane and select **Create Parameter**.

- Use the drop-down menu on a field, set, or parameter already in the data pane and select **Create | Parameter...**.

In the last case, Tableau will create a parameter with a list of potential values based on the **domain** (distinct values) of the field. For fields in the data pane that are **discrete** (blue) by default, Tableau will create a parameter with a list of values matching the discrete values of the field. For fields in the data pane that are **continuous** (green), Tableau will create a parameter with a range set to the minimum and maximum values of the field that's present in the data.

When you first create a parameter (or subsequently edit an existing parameter), Tableau will present an interface like this:

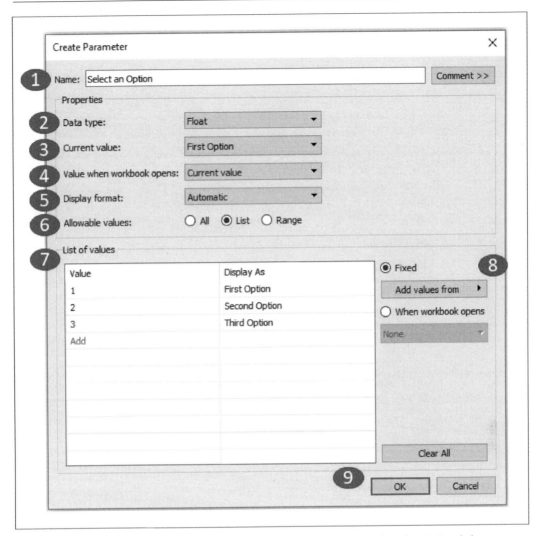

Figure 4.13: The Create Parameter interface numbered with corresponding descriptions below

The interface contains the following features:

1. **Name** will show as the default title for parameter controls and will also be the reference in calculations. You can also add a **Comment** to describe the use of the parameter.

2. **Data type** defines what type of data is allowed for the value of the parameter. Options include integer, float (floating-point decimal), string, Boolean, date, or date with time.

3. **Current value** defines what the initial default value of the parameter will be. Changing this value on this screen or on a dashboard or visualization where the parameter control is shown will change the current value.

4. **Value when workbook opens** allows you to optionally change the default value of the parameter when the workbook opens based on a calculated value.

5. **Display format** defines how the values will be displayed. For example, you might want to show an integer value as a dollar amount, a decimal as a percentage, or display a date in a specific format.

6. The **Allowable values** option gives us the ability to restrict the scope of values that are permissible. There are three options for **Allowable values**:

   - **All** allows any input from the user that matches the data type of the parameter.

   - **List** allows us to define a list of values from which the user must select a single option. The list can be entered manually, pasted from the clipboard, or loaded from a dimension of the same data type.

   - **Range** allows us to define a range of possible values, including an optional upper and lower limit, as well as a step size. This can also be set from a field or another parameter.

7. In the example of the preceding screenshot, since we've selected **List** for **Allowable values**, we are given options to enter the list of possible values. In this example, a list of three items has been entered. Notice that the value must match the data type, but the display value can be any string value. You can drag and drop values in the list to reorder the list. If **Range** had been selected, the screen would instead show options for setting the **Minimum**, **Maximum**, and **Step Size** for the range.

8. Also specific to **List** are a couple of additional options for populating the list:

   - **Fixed**: You may manually enter the values, paste from the clipboard, or set them from the existing values of a field in the data. In any case, the list will be a static list and will not change even if the data is updated.

   - **When the workbook opens** allows you to specify a field that will dynamically update the list based on the available values for that field when the workbook is first opened.

Click **OK** to save changes to the parameter or **Cancel** to revert.

When the parameter is created, it appears in the data pane in the **Parameters** section. The drop-down menu for a parameter reveals an option, **Show Parameter Control**, which adds the parameter control to the view. The little drop-down caret in the upper right of the parameter control reveals a menu for customizing the appearance and behavior of the parameter control. Here is the parameter control, shown as a single value list, for the parameter we created earlier:

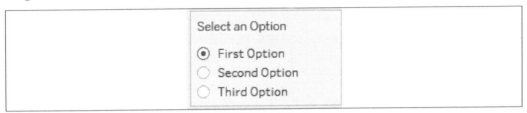

Figure 4.14: The parameter control shown as a single select radio button list

This control can be shown on any sheet or dashboard and allows the end user to select a single value. When the value is changed, any calculations, filters, sets, or bins that use the parameter will be re-evaluated, and any views that are affected will be redrawn.

Next, we'll consider some practical examples that use parameters in calculations.

Practical examples of calculations and parameters

Let's turn our attention to some practical examples of row-level and aggregate calculations. The goal is to learn and understand some of what is possible with calculations. You will be able to build on these examples as you embark on your analysis and visualization journey.

 A great place to find help and suggestions for calculations is the official Tableau forums at https://community.tableau.com/s/explore-forums.

Fixing data issues

Often, data is not entirely clean. That is, it has problems that need to be corrected before meaningful analysis can be accomplished. For example, dates may be incorrectly formatted, or fields may contain a mix of numeric values and character codes that need to be separated into multiple fields. Calculated fields can often be used to fix these kinds of issues.

 We'll consider using Tableau Prep—a tool designed to shape and cleanse data—in *Chapter 14, Structuring Messy Data to Work Well in Tableau*. Tableau Prep's calculation syntax is nearly identical, so many of the examples in this chapter will also be applicable in that context. Knowing how to address data issues in either Tableau Desktop or Tableau Prep will help you greatly.

We'll continue working with the Vacation Rentals data. You'll recall that the start and end dates looked something like this:

Start	End
Dec 2	Dec 9
Dec 9	Dec 15
Dec 16	Dec 23

Without the year, Tableau does not recognize the Start or End fields as *dates*. Instead, Tableau recognizes them as *strings*. You might try using the drop-down menu on the fields in the data pane to change the data type to date, but without the year, Tableau will almost certainly parse them incorrectly, or at least incompletely. This is a case where we'll need to use a calculation to fix the issue.

Assuming, in this case, that you are confident the year should always be 2020, you might create calculated fields named Start Date and End Date.

Here is the code for getting the start date:

```
DATE([Start] + ", 2020")
```

And here is the code for getting the end date:

```
DATE([End] + ", 2020")
```

What these calculated fields do is concatenate the month and day with the year and then use the DATE() function to convert the string into a date value. Indeed, Tableau recognizes the resulting fields as dates (with all the features of a date field, such as built-in hierarchies). A quick check in Tableau reveals the expected results:

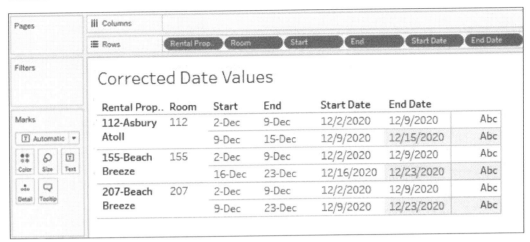

Figure 4.15: The corrected dates appear next to the string versions. All fields are discrete dimensions on Rows (the dates are exact dates)

Not only are we able to fix problems in the data, but we can also extend the data and our analysis using calculations. We'll consider this next.

Extending the data

Often, there will be dimensions or measures you'd like to have in your data, but which are not present in the source. Many times, you will be able to extend your dataset using calculated fields. We already considered an example of creating a field for the full name of the guest where we only had first and last name fields.

Another piece of data that might unlock some truly interesting analysis would be the length of each rental. We have the start and end dates, but not the length of time between those two dates. Fortunately, this is easy to calculate.

Create a calculated field named Nights Rented with the following code:

```
DATEDIFF('day', [Start Date], [End Date])
```

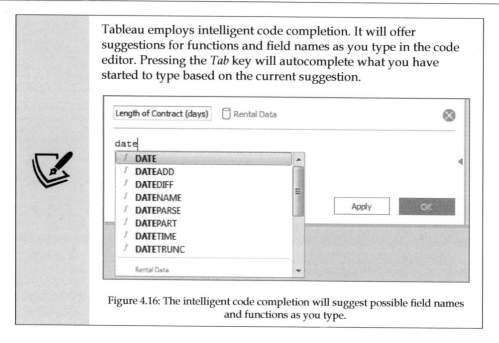

Tableau employs intelligent code completion. It will offer suggestions for functions and field names as you type in the code editor. Pressing the *Tab* key will autocomplete what you have started to type based on the current suggestion.

Figure 4.16: The intelligent code completion will suggest possible field names and functions as you type.

The DATEDIFF() function takes a date part description, a start and an end date, and returns a numeric value for the difference between the two dates. We now have a new measure, which wasn't available previously. We can use this new measure in our visualizations, such as the Gantt chart of rentals, as follows:

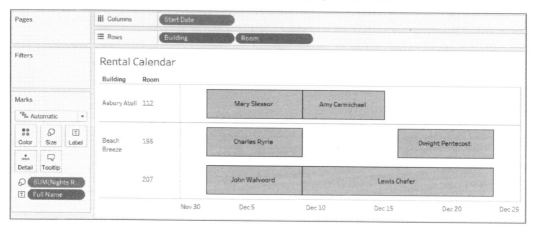

Figure 4.17: The calculated field allows us to create the Gantt chart

You'll find many ways to extend your data with calculations as you continue your journey in Tableau. And that will enable you to accomplish some amazing analysis and visualizations. We'll consider some examples next.

Enhancing user experience, analysis, and visualizations

Calculations and parameters can greatly enhance the user experience, the analysis, and the visualizations.

Let's say we want to give the vacation condo manager the ability to do some what-if analysis. Every year, she offers a free night during the month of December. She wants to be able to see which renters would have received the free night, depending on which night she chooses.

To accomplish this, follow these steps:

1. If you have not done so, create a Gantt chart similar to what was shown earlier (following the field placement of the screenshot).

2. Create a parameter called **Free Night** with a data type of **Date** and a starting value of 12/12/2020. This will allow the manager to set and adjust the starting date for the promotional month. Show the parameter control by selecting **Show Parameter Control** from the drop-down menu on the **Free Night** parameter in the data pane.

3. Now, add a reference line to the view to show the free night. Do this by switching to the **Analytics** tab in the left sidebar. Drag **Reference Line** to the view and drop it on **Table**:

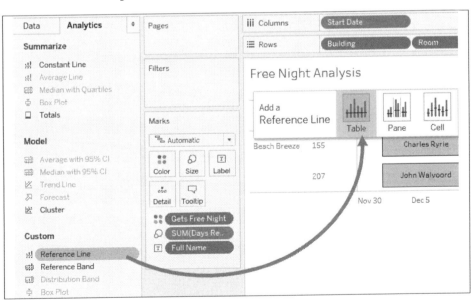

Figure 4.18: Add a reference line by switching to the Analytics pane
and dragging the reference line onto the canvas

4. In the resulting dialog box, set **Line** Value to **Free Night**. You may wish to set the **Label** to **None**, or **Custom** with the text Free Night. You may also wish to adjust the formatting of the line:

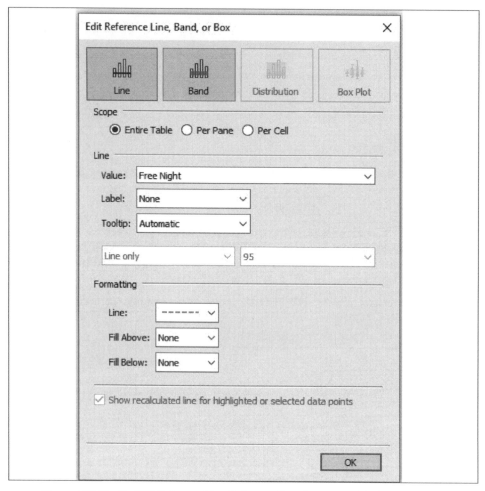

Figure 4.19: Use the Edit Reference Line dialog to adjust formatting, labels, and tooltips

5. Create a calculated field called **Gets Free Night** that returns a true or false value, depending on whether the free night falls within the rental period:

    ```
    [Free Night] >= [Start Date]
    AND
    [Free Night] <= [End Date]
    ```

6. Place this new calculated field on the **Color** shelf.

We now have a view that allows the apartment manager to change the date and see a dynamically changing view that makes it obvious which renters would have fallen within a given promotional period. Experiment by changing the value of the **Free Night** parameter to see how the view updates:

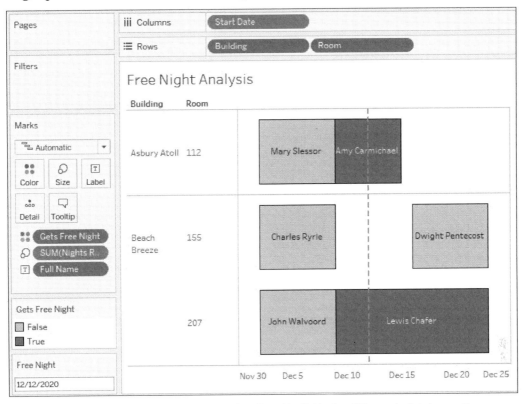

Figure 4.20: The reference line will move, and the affected individuals will be recalculated every time you change the Free Night parameter value

The preceding view shows the proposed free night as a dashed line and highlights which rental periods would receive a free night. The line and colors will change as the apartment manager adjusts the **Free Night** parameter value.

In addition to extending your analysis, visualization, and user experience, you might also use calculations to add required business logic. We'll consider that next.

Meeting business requirements

Sometimes, data doesn't exactly match what your organization wants. For example, the measures in the data may not be the exact metrics required to make key business decisions. Or dimension values may need to be grouped according to a certain set of rules. Although this kind of business logic is often applied as data is transformed or modeled prior to connecting to it with Tableau, you may find cases where you need to implement business logic on the fly.

In this example, consider that the measure Rent is simply the base rent and does not include the discount or taxes. Those are separate fields in the data. If you needed to analyze the total Revenue, you'd need to calculate it. That calculation might look something like this:

```
[Rent] - [Discount] + ([Tax per Night] * [Nights Rented])
```

This formula takes the base Rent, subtracts the Discount, and then adds the Tax per Night multiplied by the Nights Rented. The parentheses aid readability but are not required because the multiplication operator, *, has higher precedence and is evaluated before the addition, +.

Up until now, we've created calculated fields that extend the data source. Sometimes you just need a quick calculation to help in a single view. We'll conclude by looking at these quick ad hoc calculations.

Ad hoc calculations

Ad hoc calculations allow you to add calculated fields to shelves in a single view without adding fields to the data pane.

Let's say you have a simple view that shows the **Revenue per Guest**, like this:

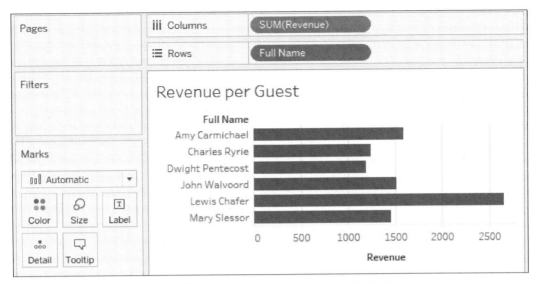

Figure 4.21: The revenue generated from each individual's stay

What if you wanted to quickly highlight any renters who had paid less than $1,500? One option would be to create an ad hoc calculation. To do so, simply double-click on an empty area of the **Columns**, **Rows**, or **Measure Values** cards, or on the empty space of the **Marks** shelf, and then start typing the code for a calculation. In this example, we've double-clicked the empty space on the **Marks** shelf:

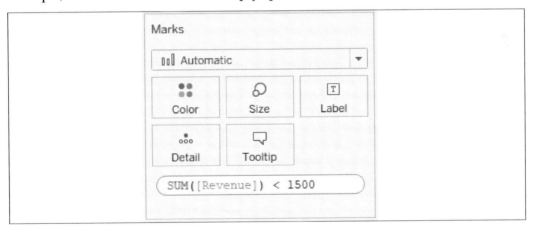

Figure 4.22: Creating an ad hoc calculation on the Marks card

Here, we've entered code that will return True if the sum of Rent is less than $1,500 and False otherwise. Pressing *Enter* or clicking outside the text box will reveal a new ad hoc field that can be dragged and dropped anywhere within the view. Here, we've moved it to the **Color** shelf:

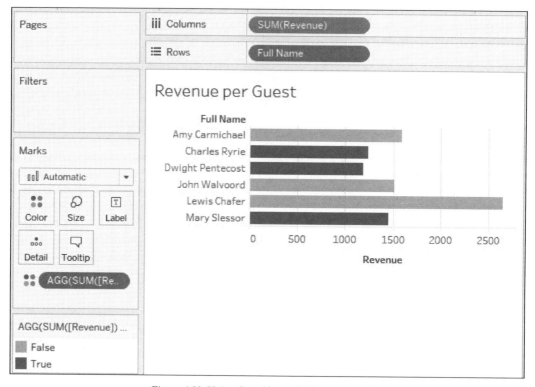

Figure 4.23: Using the ad hoc calculation on Color

The ad hoc field is only available within the view and does not show up in the data pane. You can double-click the field to edit the code.

 Dragging and dropping an ad hoc field into the data pane transforms it into a regular calculated field that will be available for other views that are using that data source.

Having seen a number of practical examples, let's conclude by considering some ways to ensure good performance when using calculations.

Performance considerations

When working with a small dataset and an efficient database, you often won't notice inefficient calculations. With larger datasets, the efficiency of your calculations can start to make a difference to the speed at which a view is rendered.

Here are some tips for making your calculations as efficient as possible:

- Boolean and numeric calculations are much faster than string calculations. If possible, avoid string manipulation and use aliasing or formatting to provide user-friendly labels. For example, don't write the following code: `IF [value] == 1 THEN "Yes" ELSE "No" END`. Instead, simply write `[value] == 1`, and then edit the aliases of the field and set `True` to `Yes` and `False` to `No`.

- Look for ways to increase the efficiency of a calculation. If you find yourself writing a long `IF ELSEIF` statement with lots of conditions, see whether there are one or two conditions that you can check first to eliminate the checks of all the other conditions. For example, let's consider simplifying the following code:

```
//This is potentially less efficient...
IF [Type] = "Dog" AND [Age] < 1 THEN "Puppy"
ELSEIF [Type] = "Cat" AND [Age] < 1 THEN "Kitten"
END

//...than this code:
IF [Age] < 1 THEN
    IF [Type] = "Dog" THEN "Puppy"
    ELSEIF [Type] = "Cat" THEN "Kitten"
    END
END
```

Notice how the check of type doesn't have to be done for any records where the age was less than 1. That could be a very high percentage of records in the dataset.

- Row-level calculations have to be performed for every row of data. Try to minimize the complexity of row-level calculations. However, if that is not possible or doesn't solve a performance issue, consider the final option.

- When you create a data extract, certain row-level calculations are materialized. This means that the calculation is performed once when the extract is created, and the results are then stored in the extract. This means that the data engine does not have to execute the calculation over and over. Instead, the value is simply read from the extract. Calculations that use any user functions, parameters, or TODAY() or NOW(), will not be materialized in an extract as the value necessarily changes according to the current user, parameter selection, and system time. Tableau's optimizer may also determine whether to materialize certain calculations that are more efficiently performed in memory rather than having to read the stored value.

When you use an extract to materialize row-level calculations, only the calculations that were created at the time of the extract are materialized. If you edit calculated fields or create new ones after creating the extract, you will need to optimize the extract (use the drop-down menu on the data source or select it from the **Data** menu and then select **Extract | Optimize** or **Extract | Compute Calculations Now**).

As you continue to work with calculations, pay special attention to situations where you notice performance issues, and consider whether you can optimize your calculations for better results.

Summary

Calculations open amazing possibilities in Tableau. You are no longer confined to the fields in the source data. With calculations, you can extend the data by adding new dimensions and measures, fix bad or poorly formatted data, and enhance the user experience with parameters for user input and calculations that enhance the visualizations.

The key to using calculated fields is understanding the four main types of calculations in Tableau. Row-level calculations are performed for every row of source data. These calculated fields can be used as dimensions or they can be aggregated as measures. Aggregate calculations are performed at the level of detail that's defined by the dimensions that are present in a view. They are especially helpful, and even necessary, when you must first aggregate components of the calculation before performing additional operations.

In the next chapter, we'll explore the third of the four main types of calculations: **Level of Detail calculations**. This will greatly extend your ability to work with data and solve all kinds of interesting problems.

5
Leveraging Level of Detail Calculations

Having considered row-level and aggregate calculations, it's time to turn our attention to the third of the four main types of calculations: **level of detail calculations**.

Level of detail calculations (sometimes referred to as **LOD calcs** or **LOD expressions**) allow you to perform aggregations at a specified level of detail, which may be different from the level of detail that is defined in the view. You can leverage this capability to perform a wide variety of analyses that would otherwise be quite difficult.

In this chapter, we'll cover the following:

- Overview of level of detail
- Level of detail calculation syntax and variations
- Examples of FIXED level of detail calculations
- Examples of INCLUDE level of detail calculations
- Examples of EXCLUDE level of detail calculations

Overview of level of detail

What does the term **level of detail** mean? A lot depends on the context in which the term is used. Within Tableau, we'll distinguish several levels of detail, each of which is vitally important to understand in order to properly analyze data:

- **Data level of detail**: Sometimes referred to as the **grain** of the data, this is the level of detail defined by a single record of the data set. When you can articulate what one record of the data represents (for example, "Every record represents a single order" or "There is one record for every customer"), then you have a good understanding of the data level of detail. *Row-level calculations operate at this level.*

- **View level of detail**: We've previously discussed that the combination of fields used as dimensions in the view defines the view level of detail. Normally in a view, Tableau draws a single mark for each distinct combination of values present in the data for all the dimensions in the view. For example, if **Customer** and **Year** are the two dimensions in your view, Tableau will draw a mark (such as a bar or circle) for each **Customer/Year** combination present in the data (that is not excluded by a filter). *Aggregate calculations operate at this level.*

- **Calculated level of detail**: This is a separate level of detail defined by a calculation. As we'll see, you may use any number of dimensions to define the level of detail. *Level of detail calculations are used to define this level.*

Consider the following data set, with a **data level of detail** of one record per customer:

Customer	State	Membership Date	Membership Level	Orders
Neil	Kansas	2009-05-05	Silver	1
Jeane	Kansas	2012-03-17	Gold	5
George	Oklahoma	2016-02-01	Gold	10
Wilma	Texas	2018-09-17	Silver	4

In this case, each record defines a single unique customer. If we were to perform a row-level calculation, such as DATEDIFF('year', [Membership Date], TODAY()) to determine the number of years each customer has been a member, then the result would be calculated per record.

Now consider a view created from the data with a **view level of detail** of state:

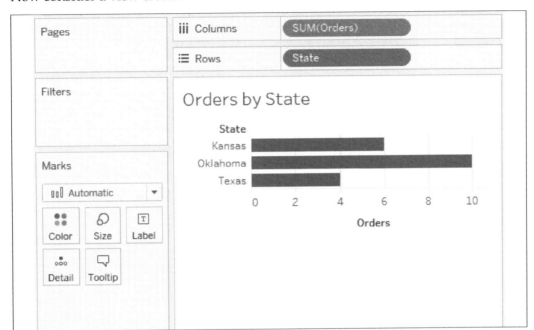

Figure 5.1: The view level of detail of state

As the only dimension in the view, **State** defines the view level of detail. There is one mark per state, and calculations and fields used as aggregates, such as **SUM(Orders)**, will be performed per state.

Based on that particular view, we might want to enhance our understanding by asking additional questions, such as the following:

- Which customer was the first member of each state in the view?
- How does the number of orders per state compare to the average number of orders for all states?
- Which membership level had the highest or lowest number of orders per state?

In each case, the question involves a level of detail that is different from the view (the minimum membership date per state compared to each individual customer, the average orders overall compared to orders per state, and the minimum or maximum number of orders per membership level per state). In some cases, it might make sense to build a new view to answer these questions. But sometimes we want to supplement an existing view or compare different levels of detail in the same view. Level of detail calculations provide a solution!

Level of detail calculations

Before getting into practical examples of using level of detail calculations, let's take a moment to understand the syntax and types of level of detail calculations.

Level of detail syntax

Level of detail calculations follow this basic pattern of syntax:

```
{FIXED|INCLUDE|EXCLUDE [Dim 1],[Dim 2] : AGG([Field])}
```

The definitions of the preceding declaration are as follows:

- FIXED, INCLUDE, and EXCLUDE are keywords that indicate the type of level of detail calculation. We'll consider the differences in detail in the following section.
- Dim 1, Dim 2 (and as many dimensions that are needed) is a comma-separated list of dimension fields that defines the level of detail at which the calculation will be performed.
- AGG is the aggregate function you wish to perform (such as SUM, AVG, MIN, and MAX).
- Field is the value that will be aggregated as specified by the aggregation you choose.

Level of detail types

Three types of level of detail calculations are used in Tableau: **FIXED, INCLUDE,** and **EXCLUDE**.

FIXED

Fixed level of detail expressions work at the level of detail that's specified by the list of dimensions in the code, regardless of what dimensions are in the view. For example, the following code returns the average orders per state, regardless of what other dimensions are in the view:

```
{FIXED [State] : AVG([Orders])}
```

You may include as many dimensions as needed or none at all. The following code represents a fixed calculation of the average orders for the entire set of data from the data source:

```
{FIXED : AVG([Orders])}
```

Alternately, you might write the calculation in the following way with identical results:

```
{AVG([Orders])}
```

 A fixed level of detail expression with no dimensions specified is sometimes referred to as a *table-scoped fixed level of detail expression*, because the aggregation defined in the calculation will be for the entire table.

INCLUDE

Include level of detail expressions aggregate at the level of detail that's determined by the dimensions in the view, *along with* the dimensions listed in the code. For example, the following code calculates the average orders at the level of detail that's defined by dimensions in the view, but includes the dimension Membership Level, even if Membership Level is not in the view:

```
{INCLUDE [Membership Level] : AVG([Orders])}
```

EXCLUDE

Exclude level of detail expressions aggregate at the level of detail determined by the dimensions in the view, *excluding* any listed in the code. For example, the following code calculates the average number of orders at the level of detail defined in the view, but does not include the Customer dimension as part of the level of detail, even if Customer is in the view:

```
{EXCLUDE [Customer] : AVG([Orders])}
```

An illustration of the difference level of detail can make

As you analyze data, one thing you might often wonder is how slices of data relate to the overall picture. For example, you might wonder how the number of orders for each state in the view above relates to the overall average number of orders. One quick and easy option is to add an **Average Line** to the view from the **Analytics** tab, by dragging and dropping like this:

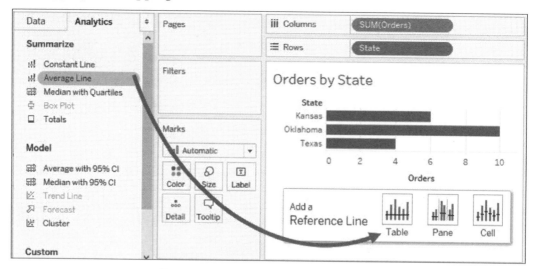

Figure 5.2: Adding an average line to the view

You'll end up with an average line that looks like this:

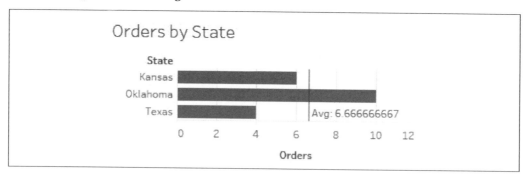

Figure 5.3: The overall average is reported as 6.66667. This is the average per state

But is 6.66667 truly the average number of orders overall? It turns out that it's not. It's actually the average of the sum of the number of orders for each state: (6 + 10 + 4) / 3. Many times, that average line (that is, the average of the total number of orders per state) is exactly what we want to compare when using aggregate numbers.

But sometimes, we might want to calculate the true overall average. To get the average number of orders present in the entire data set, we might consider creating a calculation named Overall Average Number of Orders and using a fixed level of detail calculation like this:

```
{FIXED : AVG([Orders])}
```

Adding that calculated field to the **Detail** part of the **Marks** card and editing the reference line to use that field instead gives us a different result:

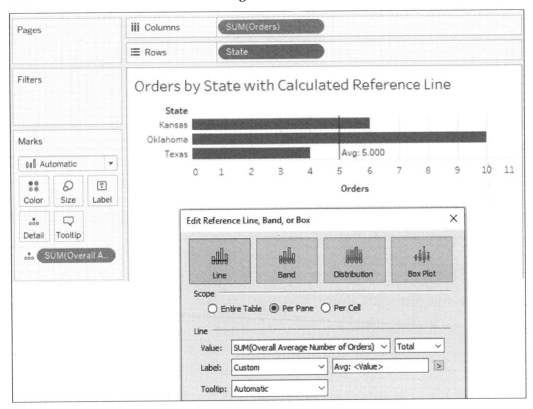

Figure 5.4: The true overall average number of orders per customer is 5

You'll recall that the original data set had four records, and a quick check validates the result:

```
(1 + 5 + 10 + 4) / 4 = 5
```

Now we have examined how level of detail calculations make a real difference; let's look at some practical examples.

Examples of fixed level of detail calculations

As we turn our attention to some practical examples of level of detail calculations, we'll use the `Chapter 05 Loans` data set contained in the `Chapter 05` workbook. The true data set contains many more records, but here is an example of the kinds of data it contains:

Date	Portfolio	Loan Type	Balance	Open Date	Member Name	Credit Score	Age	State
3/1/2020	Auto	New Auto	15987	9/29/2018	Samuel	678	37	California
7/1/2020	Mortgage	1st Mortgage	96364	8/7/2013	Lloyd	768	62	Ohio
3/1/2020	Mortgage	HELOC	15123	4/2/2013	Inez	751	66	Illinois
3/1/2020	Mortgage	1st Mortgage	418635	9/30/2015	Patrick	766	60	Ohio
5/1/2020	Auto	Used Auto	1151	10/22/2018	Eric	660	44	Pennsylvania
...	...	...	...	...	...	...	...	...
...	...	...	...	...	...	...	...	...

The data set represents historical data for loans for members at a bank, credit union, or similar financial institution. Each record is a monthly snapshot of a loan and contains the date of the snapshot along with fields that describe the loan (**Portfolio**, **Loan Type**, **Balance**, and **Open Date**) and fields for the member (**Name**, **Credit Score**, **Age**, and **State**).

As in previous chapters, the goal is to understand key concepts and some key patterns. The following are only a few examples of all the possibilities presented by level of detail calculations.

Was a member ever at risk?

Let's say branch management has determined that any member who has ever had a credit score of less than 550 is considered to be at risk and eligible for special assistance. Consider the history for the following three individuals:

Member ID	Member Name	Loan Type	Date	Balance	Credit Score	
158	Vicki Modzelewski	Used Auto	1/1/2020	10,615	712	
			2/1/2020	10,441	712	
			3/1/2020	10,285	699	
			4/1/2020	10,108	699	
			5/1/2020	9,891	699	
			6/1/2020	9,736	717	
			7/1/2020	9,556	717	
479	Thomas Villareal	Used Auto	2/1/2020	7,407	526	←
			3/1/2020	7,191	526	←
			4/1/2020	6,984	563	
			5/1/2020	6,771	563	
			6/1/2020	6,551	563	
			7/1/2020	6,334	591	
			8/1/2020	6,115	591	
576	Charles Reeves	Used Auto	1/1/2020	28,145	610	
			2/1/2020	27,187	610	
			3/1/2020	26,226	535	←
			4/1/2020	25,267	535	←
			5/1/2020	24,302	535	←
			6/1/2020	23,337	530	←
			7/1/2020	22,366	530	←

Figure 5.5: Credit scores for three individuals with scores under the 550 threshold indicated via arrows

Every month, a new snapshot of history is recorded. Loan balances often change along with the member's credit score. Some members have never been at risk. The first member, Vicki, has 699 as her lowest recorded score and has never been at risk. However, both Charles and Thomas had periods in the history where their credit scores fell below the threshold (indicated with arrows in the preceding screenshot).

A simple row-level calculation, such as [Credit Score] < 550, could identify each record where the monthly snapshot of credit score indicated a risk. But members whose scores fluctuated *below* and *above* the threshold would have records that were alternately TRUE or FALSE.

We want every record for a given member to be TRUE if *any* of the records for that member are below the threshold and FALSE if *none* of the records are below the threshold.

One solution is to use a level of detail calculation, which we'll name Member Ever at Risk?, with the code:

```
{FIXED [Member ID] : MIN([Credit Score])} < 550
```

This calculation determines the lowest credit score for each member and compares it to the risk threshold of 550. The result is the same for each record for a given member, as you can see here:

FIXED Example 1: Member Ever at Risk?

Member ID	Member Name	Loan Type	Date	Member Ever at Risk?	Balance	Credit Score
158	Vicki Modzelewski	Used Auto	1/1/2020	False	10,615	712
			2/1/2020	False	10,441	712
			3/1/2020	False	10,285	699
			4/1/2020	False	10,108	699
			5/1/2020	False	9,891	699
			6/1/2020	False	9,736	717
			7/1/2020	False	9,556	717
479	Thomas Villareal	Used Auto	2/1/2020	True	7,407	526
			3/1/2020	True	7,191	526
			4/1/2020	True	6,984	563
			5/1/2020	True	6,771	563
			6/1/2020	True	6,551	563
			7/1/2020	True	6,334	591
			8/1/2020	True	6,115	591
576	Charles Reeves	Used Auto	1/1/2020	True	28,145	610
			2/1/2020	True	27,187	610
			3/1/2020	True	26,226	535
			4/1/2020	True	25,267	535
			5/1/2020	True	24,302	535
			6/1/2020	True	23,337	530
			7/1/2020	True	22,366	530

Figure 5.6: The Member Ever at Risk? field is True or False for all records of a given member

Notice that every record contains the result for the relevant member. This illustrates one key concept for fixed level of detail calculations: *while the calculation is an aggregation at a defined level of detail, the results are at the row level.* That is, the TRUE or FALSE value is calculated at the member level, but the results are available as row-level values for every record for that member.

This enables all kinds of analysis possibilities, such as:

- Filtering to include only at-risk members but retaining all records for their history. If you instead filtered based on individual credit score, you'd lose all records for parts of the history where the credit score was above the threshold. Those records might be critical for your analysis.

- Correctly counting members as either at risk or not while avoiding counting them for both cases if the history fluctuated.

- Comparing members who were or were not at risk at other levels of detail. For example, this view shows the number of members who were at risk or not at risk by portfolio:

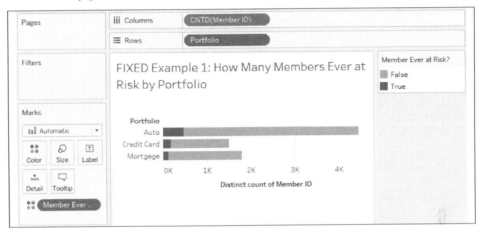

Figure 5.7: We can implement some brushing to show what proportion
of members has ever been at risk

 Fixed level of detail calculations are context sensitive. That is, they operate within a context, which is either 1) the entire data set, or 2) defined by **context filters** (filters where the drop-down **Add to Context** option has been selected). In this example, that means the values calculated for each member will not change if you don't use context filters. Consider Thomas, who will always be considered at risk, even if you applied a normal filter that kept only dates after March 2020. That is because the fixed level of detail calculation would work across the entire data set and find at-risk values in January and February. If you were to add such a filter to context, the result could change. This behavior of fixed level of detail calculations can be leveraged to aid your analysis but can also cause unexpected behavior if not understood.

This is a single example of the kinds of analysis made simple with level of detail calculations. There's so much more we can do and we'll see another example next!

Latest balance for a member

Many data sets contain a series of events or a history of transactions. You may find yourself asking questions such as:

- What diagnoses are common for a patient's first visit to the hospital?
- What was the last reported status of each computer on the network?
- How much did each customer spend on their last order?
- How much did the first trade of the week make compared to the last?

None of these questions is simply asking when the earliest or latest event happened. A simple MIN or MAX aggregation of the date would provide that answer. But with these questions, there is the added complexity of asking for additional detail about what happened on the earliest or latest dates. For these kinds of questions, level of detail calculations provide a way to arrive at answers.

Consider the following three members' data contained in the Chapter 05 Loans data set:

Member ID	Member Name	Loan Number	Loan Type	Date	
14827	Kelly Wooldridge	1	New Auto Plus	1/1/2020	21,684
				2/1/2020	21,348
				3/1/2020	21,001
				4/1/2020	21,001
				5/1/2020	20,327
				6/1/2020	19,987
				7/1/2020	19,646
16024	Joseph Clark	1	Used Auto	2/1/2020	19,043
				3/1/2020	18,656
				4/1/2020	18,263
				5/1/2020	17,873
				6/1/2020	17,479
				7/1/2020	17,087
				8/1/2020	16,691
16070	Gerald Quinney	1	1st Mortgage	3/1/2020	144,138
				4/1/2020	140,943
				5/1/2020	137,737
				6/1/2020	134,520
				7/1/2020	131,293
		2	Used Auto	3/1/2020	6,809
				4/1/2020	6,636
				5/1/2020	6,460
				6/1/2020	6,285
				7/1/2020	6,107
				8/1/2020	5,929
				9/1/2020	5,749

Figure 5.8: The data for three selected members in the Loans data set

Each has a history of balances for each of their loans. However, the most recent date of history differs for each loan. Kelly's most recent balance is given for July. Joseph's latest balance is for August. Gerald has two loans: the first has the most recent balance for July and the second has the most recent balance for September.

What if you want to identify only the records that represent the latest known balance for a member? You might consider using a fixed level of detail calculation called `Latest Date per Member/Loan` with code such as this:

```
{FIXED [Member ID],[Loan Number] : MAX([Date])} = [Date]
```

This determines the maximum date per member per loan and compares the result to each row-level date, returning TRUE for matches and FALSE otherwise.

Two dimensions have been used to define the level of detail in the previous calculation because a single member can have more than one loan. If you had a truly unique identifier for each loan, you could alternatively use that as the single dimension defining the level of detail. You will need to have a good understanding of your data to accurately leverage level of detail calculations.

You can see the results of the calculation here:

Member ID	Member Name	Loan Number	Loan Type	Date	Latest Date per Member/ Loan	
FIXED Example 2: Most Recent Balance						
14827	Kelly Wooldridge	1	New Auto Plus	1/1/2020	False	21,684
				2/1/2020	False	21,348
				3/1/2020	False	21,001
				4/1/2020	False	21,001
				5/1/2020	False	20,327
				6/1/2020	False	19,987
				7/1/2020	True	19,646
16024	Joseph Clark	1	Used Auto	2/1/2020	False	19,043
				3/1/2020	False	18,656
				4/1/2020	False	18,263
				5/1/2020	False	17,873
				6/1/2020	False	17,479
				7/1/2020	False	17,087
				8/1/2020	True	16,691
16070	Gerald Quinney	1	1st Mortgage	3/1/2020	False	144,138
				4/1/2020	False	140,943
				5/1/2020	False	137,737
				6/1/2020	False	134,520
				7/1/2020	True	131,293
		2	Used Auto	3/1/2020	False	6,809
				4/1/2020	False	6,636
				5/1/2020	False	6,460
				6/1/2020	False	6,285
				7/1/2020	False	6,107
				8/1/2020	False	5,929
				9/1/2020	True	5,749

Figure 5.9: The latest date per loan per person is indicated by a True value for the calculation

If you had wanted to determine the first record for each loan, you would have simply changed MAX to MIN in the code. You can use the level of detail calculation's row-level TRUE / FALSE result as a filter to keep only the latest records, or even as part of other calculations to accomplish an analysis, such as comparing, starting, and ending balances.

The technique demonstrated by this calculation has many applications. In cases where data *trickles in*, you can identify the most recent records. In cases where you have duplication of records, you can filter to keep only the first or last. You can identify a customer's first or last purchase. You can compare historic balances to the original balance and much, much more!

We've just seen how fixed level of detail calculations can be leveraged to answer some complex questions. Let's continue by examining include level of detail expressions.

Example of include level of detail expressions

Include level of detail calculations can be very useful when you need to perform certain calculations at levels of detail that are lower (more detailed) than the view level of detail. Let's take a look at an example.

Average loans per member

Some members have a single loan. Some have two or three or possibly more. What if we wanted to see how many loans the average member has on a state by state basis? Let's consider how we might go about that.

We'll start with a sheet where the view level of detail is **State**:

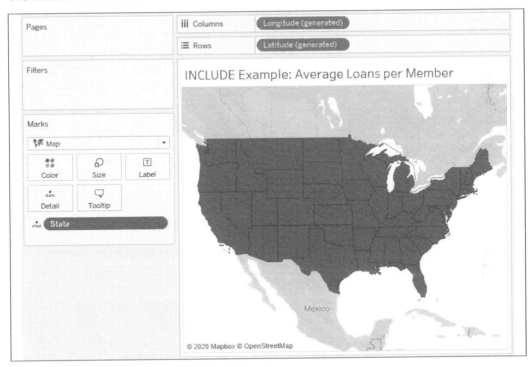

Figure 5.10: The starting place for the example—a filled map by state

It would be relatively easy to visualize the average credit score or average balance per state. But what if we want to visualize the average number of loans per member for each state? While there are several possible approaches to solving this kind of problem, here we'll consider using the following level of detail expression named `Number of Loans per Member`:

```
{INCLUDE [Member ID] : COUNTD([Loan Number])}
```

This code returns a distinct count of loan numbers at a level of detail that includes the member ID along with all dimensions that defined the view level of detail (state, in this case). When we add the calculation to the view, we'll need to decide how to aggregate it. In this case, we want the average number of loans per member, so we'll select **Measure | Average** from the dropdown on the field, revealing an interesting geographic pattern:

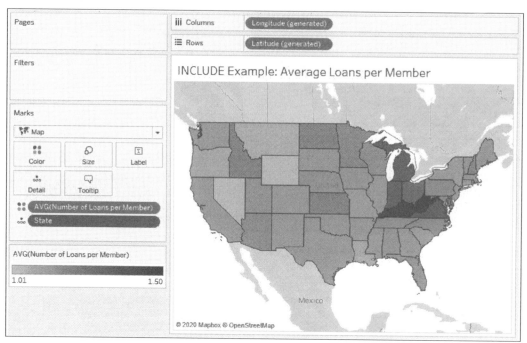

Figure 5.11: Using the Include level of detail calculation to create a gradient of color to show average loans per member

As you think through how include level of detail calculations work, you might want to construct a crosstab at the level of detail:

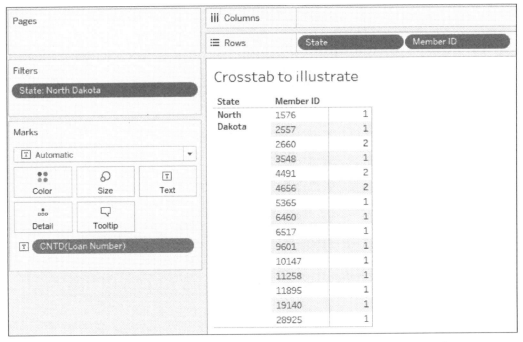

Figure 5.12: A crosstab helps illustrate how the distinct count of loans can be used as a basis for an average

State, the first dimension on **Rows**, comes from the view level of detail. **Member ID** has been included in the crosstab to simulate the dimension included in the level of detail expression. COUNTD(Loan Number) gives the number of loans per member. Averaging the values for all the members in the state gives the state average. A quick check for **North Dakota** gives us an average of 1.2 loans per member, which matches the map visualization exactly.

In this case, the include level of detail expression gives us a useful solution. There are some alternative ways to solve and it is helpful to consider some of these as you think through how you might solve similar issues. We'll consider those next.

Alternative approaches

It's worth noting that the above dataset actually allows you to use
MAX([Loan Number]) instead of COUNTD([Loan Number]) as the number simply
increments for each member based on how many loans they have. The highest
number is identical to the number of loans for that member. In a significantly large
data set, the MAX calculation should perform better.

There are also a few other approaches to solving this problem, such as the
calculation. For example, you could write the following code:

```
COUNTD(STR([Member ID]) + "_" + STR([Loan Number]))
/
COUNTD([Member ID])
```

This code takes the distinct count of loans and divides it by the distinct count of
members. In order to count the distinct number of loans, the code creates a unique
key by concatenating a string of a member ID and a loan number.

 The aggregate calculation alternative has the advantage of working
at any level of detail in your view. You may find either the level
of detail or aggregate calculation to be easier to understand, and
you will need to decide which best helps you to maintain a flow of
thought as you tackle the problem at hand.

Another approach would be to use a fixed level of detail expression, such as:

```
{FIXED [State],[Member ID] : COUNTD([Loan Number])}
```

This calculation results in the same level of detail as the include expression and
uses the same distinct count of loan number. It turns out that in this data set, each
member belongs to only a single state, so state wouldn't necessarily have to be
included in the fixed level of detail expression. However, if you wanted to change
the level of detail you'd need to adjust the calculation, whereas, with the include
expression, you'd only have to add or remove dimensions to the view.

With the include example along with some alternatives in mind, let's turn our
attention to an example of exclude level of detail calculations.

Example of exclude level of detail calculations

Exclude level of detail calculations are useful when you want to perform certain calculations at higher (less detailed) levels than the view level of detail. The following example will demonstrate how we can leverage this functionality.

Average credit score per loan type

In this example, we'll answer the following question: how does the average credit score for a given loan type compare to the overall average for the entire portfolio?

Take the following view, which shows the average credit score per loan type (where loan types are grouped into portfolios):

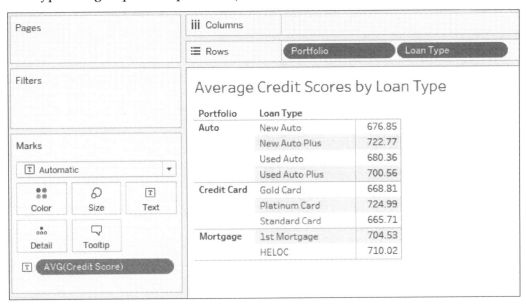

Figure 5.13: This crosstab shows the average credit score per loan type

What if we wanted to compare the average credit score of each loan type with the overall average credit score for the entire portfolio? We could accomplish this with an exclude level of detail calculation that looks like this:

```
{EXCLUDE [Loan Type] : AVG([Credit Score])}
```

This removes **Loan Type** from the level of detail and the average is calculated only per portfolio. This gives us results like the following:

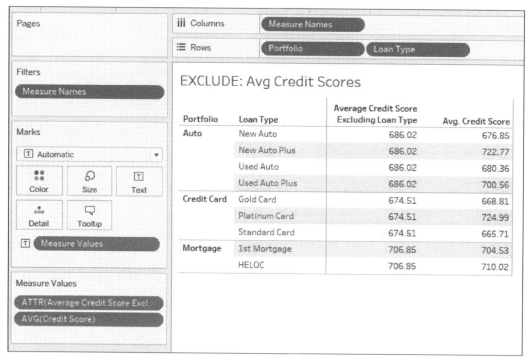

Figure 5.14: The exclude level of detail expression removes Loan Type so the average is only at the portfolio level

You'll notice that the same value for the average excluding loan type is repeated for each loan type. This is expected because the overall average is at the portfolio level and is not affected by the loan type. As is, this is perhaps not the most useful view. But we can extend the calculation a bit to give us the difference between the overall portfolio average and the average of each loan type. The code would look like this:

```
AVG([Credit Score]) - AVG([Average Credit Score Excluding Loan Type])
```

This takes the average at the view level of detail (loan type and portfolio) and subtracts the average at the portfolio level to give us the difference between each loan type average and the overall portfolio average. We might rearrange the view to see the results visually, like this:

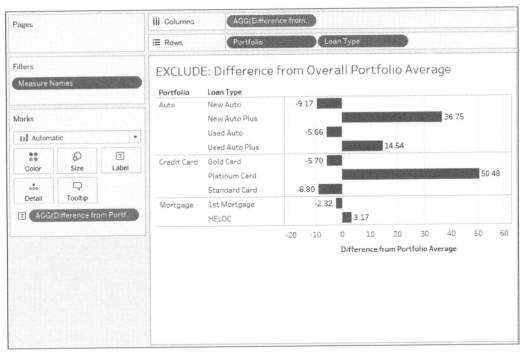

Figure 5.15: The final view shows the difference between the loan type average credit score and the overall portfolio average

Exclude level of detail expressions give us the ability to analyze differences between the view level of detail and higher levels of detail.

Summary

Level of detail expressions greatly extend what you can accomplish with calculations. You now have a toolset for working with data at different levels of detail. With fixed level of detail calculations, you can identify the first or last event in a series or whether a condition is ever true across entire subsets of data. With include expressions, you can work at lower levels of detail and then summarize those results in a view. With exclude expressions, you can work at higher levels of detail, greatly expanding analysis possibilities.

In the next chapter, we'll explore the final main type of calculations: **table calculations**. These are some of the most powerful calculations in terms of their ability to solve problems, and they open up incredible possibilities for in-depth analysis. In practice, they range from very easy to exceptionally complex.

6
Diving Deep with Table Calculations

Table calculations are one of the most powerful features in Tableau. They enable solutions that really couldn't be achieved any other way (short of writing a custom application or complex custom SQL scripts!). The features include the following:

- They make it possible to use data that isn't structured well and still get quick results without waiting for someone to fix the data at the source.
- They make it possible to compare and perform calculations on aggregate values across rows of the resulting table.
- They open incredible possibilities for analysis and creative approaches to solving problems, highlighting insights, or improving the user experience.

Table calculations range in complexity, from incredibly easy to create (a couple of clicks) to extremely complex (requiring an understanding of **addressing**, **partitioning**, and **data densification**, for example). We'll start off simple and move toward complexity in this chapter. The goal is to gain a solid foundation in creating and using table calculations, understanding how they work, and looking at some examples of how they can be used. We'll consider these topics:

- An overview of table calculations
- Quick table calculations
- Scope and direction
- Addressing and partitioning

- Custom table calculations
- Practical examples

The examples in this chapter will return to the sample Superstore data that we used in the first chapter. To follow along with the examples, use the Chapter 06 Starter. twbx workbook.

An overview of table calculations

Table calculations are different from all other calculations in Tableau. Row-level, aggregate calculations, and LOD expressions, which we explored in the previous chapters, are performed as part of the query to the data source. If you were to examine the queries sent to the data source by Tableau, you'd find the code for your calculations translated into whatever implementation of SQL the data source used.

Table calculations, on the other hand, are performed after the initial query. Here's a diagram that demonstrates how aggregated results are stored in Tableau's cache:

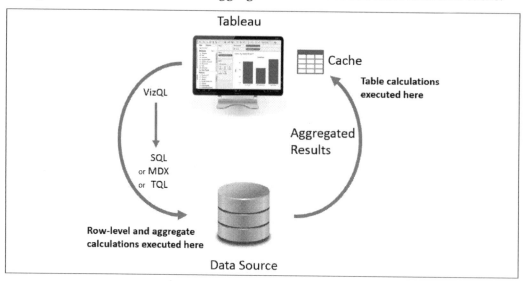

Figure 6.1: Table calculations are computed in Tableau's cache of aggregated data

Table calculations are performed on the aggregate table of data in Tableau's cache right before the data visualization is rendered. As we'll see, this is important to understand for multiple reasons, including the following:

- **Aggregation**: Table calculations operate on aggregate data. You cannot reference a field in a table calculation without referencing the field as an aggregate.

- **Filtering**: Regular filters will be applied before table calculations. This means that table calculations will only be applied to data returned from the source to the cache. You'll need to avoid filtering any data necessary for the table calculation.

- **Table calculation filtering** (sometimes called **late filtering**): Table calculations used as filters will be applied after the aggregate results are returned from the data source. The order is important: row-level and aggregate filters are applied first, the aggregate data is returned to the cache, and then the table calculation is applied as a filter that effectively hides data from the view. This allows some creative approaches to solving certain kinds of problems that we'll consider in some of the examples later in the chapter.

- **Performance**: If you are using a live connection to an enterprise database server, then row-level and aggregate-level calculations will be taking advantage of enterprise-level hardware. Table calculations are performed in the cache, which means they will be performed on whatever machine is running Tableau. You will not likely need to be concerned if your table calculations are operating on a dozen or even hundreds of rows of aggregate data, or if you anticipate publishing to a powerful Tableau server. However, if you are getting back hundreds of thousands of rows of aggregate data on your local machine, then you'll need to consider the performance of your table calculations. At the same time, there are cases where table calculations might be used to avoid an expensive filter or calculation at the source.

With this overview of table calculations in mind, let's jump into understanding some options for creating table calculations.

Creating and editing table calculations

There are several ways to create table calculations in Tableau, including:

- Using the drop-down menu for any active field used as a numeric aggregate in the view, select **Quick Table Calculation** and then the desired calculation type.

- Using the drop-down menu for any active field that is used as a numeric aggregate in the view, select **Add Table Calculation**, then select the calculation type, and adjust any desired settings.

- Creating a calculated field and using one or more table calculation functions to write your own custom table calculations.

The first two options create a quick table calculation, which can be edited or removed using the drop-down menu on the field and selecting **Edit Table Calculation...** or **Clear Table Calculation**. The third option creates a calculated field, which can be edited or deleted like any other calculated field.

A field on a shelf in the view that is using a table calculation, or which is a calculated field using table calculation functions, will have a delta symbol icon (Δ) visible, as follows.

Following is a snippet of an active field without a table calculation:

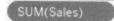

Figure 6.2: An active field without a table calculation applied

Following is the active field with a table calculation:

Figure 6.3: An active field with a table calculation applied includes the delta symbol

Most of the examples in this chapter will utilize text tables/cross tab reports as these most closely match the actual aggregate table in the cache. This makes it easier to see how the table calculations are working.

 Table calculations can be used in any type of visualization. However, when building a view that uses table calculations, especially more complex ones, try using a table with all dimensions on the **Rows** shelf and then adding table calculations as discrete values on **Rows** to the right of the dimensions. Once you have all the table calculations working as desired, you can rearrange the fields in the view to give you the appropriate visualization.

We'll now move from the concept of creating table calculations to some examples.

Quick table calculations

Quick table calculations are predefined table calculations that can be applied to fields used as measures in the view. These calculations include common and useful calculations such as **Running Total, Difference, Percent Difference, Percent of Total, Rank, Percentile, Moving Average, YTD Total** (year-to-date total), **Compound Growth Rate, Year over Year Growth**, and **YTD Growth**. You'll find applicable options on the drop-down list on a field used as a measure in the view, as shown in the following screenshot:

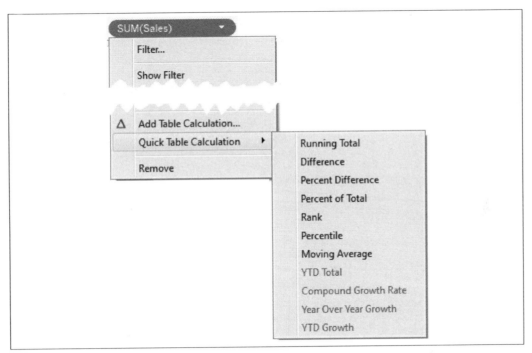

Figure 6.4: Using the dropdown, you can create a quick table calculation from an aggregate field in the view

Consider the following example using the sample Superstore Sales data:

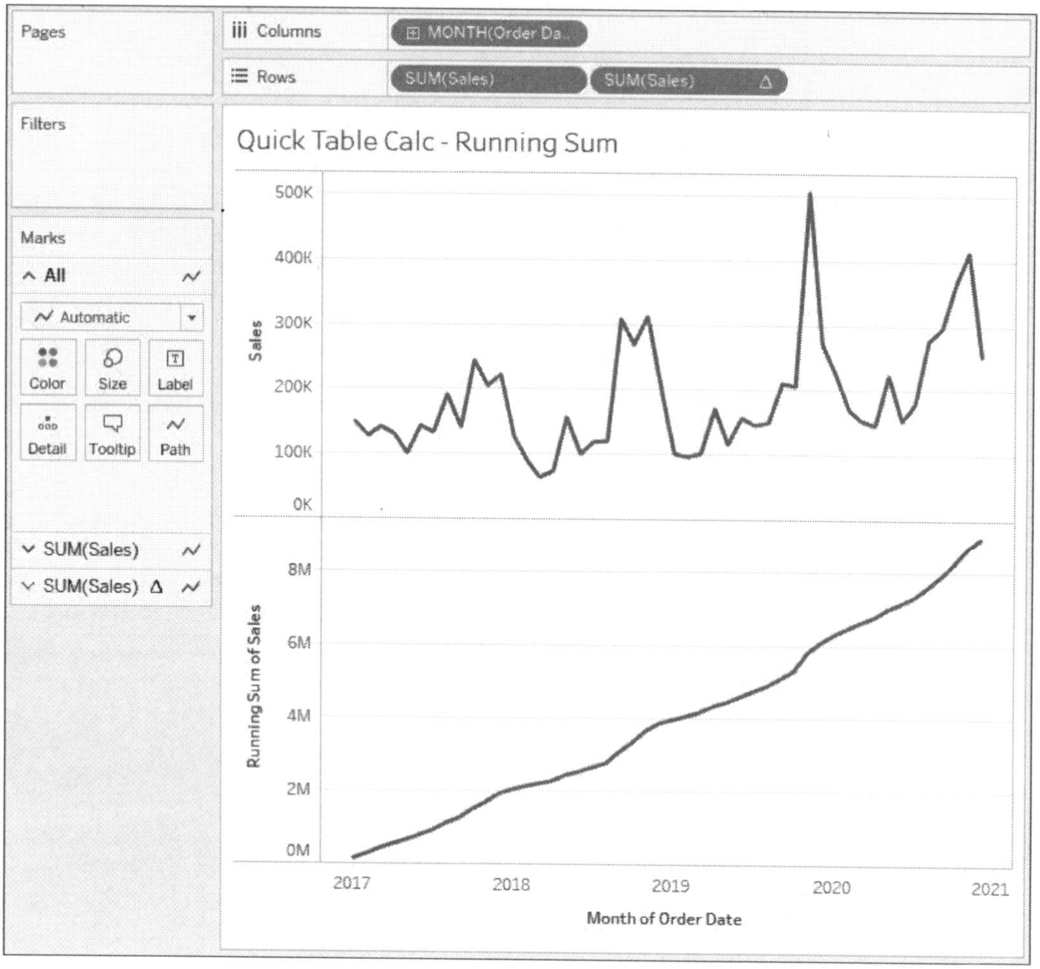

Figure 6.5: The first SUM(Sales) field is a normal aggregate.
The second has a quick table calculation of Running Total applied

Here, **Sales** over time is shown. **Sales** has been placed on the **Rows** shelf twice and the second **SUM(Sales)** field has had the **running total** quick table calculation applied. Using the quick table calculation meant it was unnecessary to write any code.

You can actually see the code that the quick table calculations uses by double-clicking the table calculation field in the view. This turns it into an ad hoc calculation. You can also drag an active field with a quick table calculation applied to the data pane, which will turn it into a calculated field that can be reused in other views.

The following table demonstrates some of the quick table calculations:

Some examples of Quick Table Calcs					
Year of Order Date	Quarter of Order Date	Sales	Running Sum of Sales along Table (Down)	Difference in Sales from the Previous along Table (Down)	Rank of Sales along Table (Down)
2017	Q1	417,555	417,555		12
	Q2	372,289	789,844	-45,266	13
	Q3	464,319	1,254,163	92,030	10
	Q4	670,182	1,924,345	205,863	5
2018	Q1	279,148	2,203,493	-391,034	16
	Q2	330,269	2,533,762	51,121	14
	Q3	546,875	3,080,637	216,606	7
	Q4	788,255	3,868,892	241,380	3
2019	Q1	298,848	4,167,740	-489,407	15
	Q2	443,764	4,611,504	144,916	11
	Q3	505,453	5,116,957	61,689	9
	Q4	982,675	6,099,632	477,222	2
2020	Q1	547,656	6,647,288	-435,019	6
	Q2	521,650	7,168,938	-26,006	8
	Q3	752,933	7,921,871	231,283	4
	Q4	1,030,156	8,952,027	277,223	1

Figure 6.6: Sales in the first column is simply the SUM(Sales). The three additional columns show various table calculations applied (Running Sum, Difference, Rank)

Although it is quite easy to create quick table calculations, it is essential to understand some fundamental concepts. We'll take a look at these next, starting with the difference between relative and fixed table calculations.

Relative versus fixed

We'll look at the details shortly, but first it is important to understand that table calculations may be computed in one of the two following ways:

- **Relative**: The table calculation will be computed relative to the layout of the table. They might move across or down the table. Rearranging dimensions in a way that changes the table will change the table calculation results. As we'll see, the key for relative table calculations is **scope** and **direction**. When you set a table calculation to use a relative computation, it will continue to use the same relative scope and direction, even if you rearrange the view. (The term here is different from **Relative To** that appears in the UI for some quick table calculations.)

- **Fixed**: The table calculation will be computed using one or more dimensions. Rearranging those dimensions in the view will not change the computation of the table calculation. Here, the scope and direction remain fixed to one or more dimensions, no matter where they are moved within the view. When we talk about fixed table calculations, we'll focus on the concepts of **partitioning** and **addressing**.

You can see these concepts in the user interface. The following is the **Table Calculation** editor that appears when you select **Edit Table Calculation** from the menu of a table calculation field:

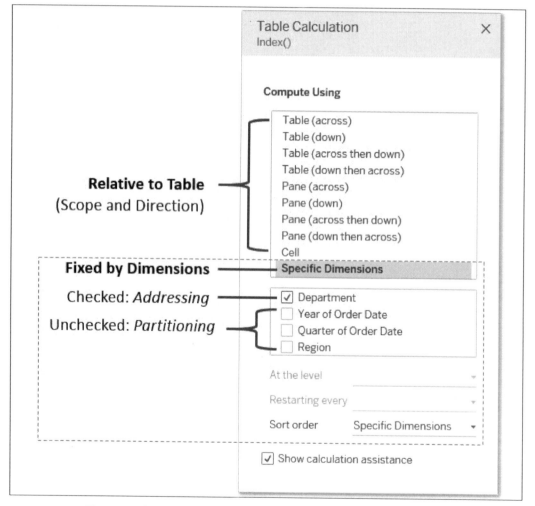

Figure 6.7: The Edit Table Calculation UI demonstrates the difference between Relative and Fixed table calculations

We'll explore the options and terms in more detail, but for now, notice the options that relate to specifying a table calculation that is computed relative to rows and columns, and options that specify a table calculation that is computed fixed to certain dimensions in the view.

Next, we'll look at **scope** and **direction**, which describe how relative table calculations operate.

Scope and direction

Scope and **direction** are terms that describe how a table calculation is computed relative to the table. Specifically, scope and direction refer to the following:

- **Scope**: The scope defines the boundaries within which a given table calculation can reference other values.
- **Direction**: The direction defines how the table calculation moves within the scope.

You've already seen table calculations being calculated **Table (across)** (the running sum of sales over time in *Figure 6.5*) and **Table (down)** (in *Figure 6.6*). In these cases, the scope was the entire table and the direction was either across or down. For example, the running total calculation ran across the entire table, adding subsequent values as it moved from left to right.

To define scope and direction for a table calculation, use the drop-down menu for the field in the view and select **Compute Using**. You will get a list of options that vary slightly depending on the location of dimensions in the view. The first of the options listed allows you to define the scope and direction relative to the table. After the option for cell, you will see a list of dimensions present in the view. We'll look at those in the next section.

The options for scope and direction relative to the table are as follows:

- **Scope options**: Table, pane, and cells
- **Direction options**: Down, across, down then across, across then down

In order to understand these options, consider the following example:

			Furniture	Office Supplies	Technology	Furniture	Office Supplies	Technology	
2017	Q1		103,094	21,517	47,770	41,391	6,221	24,258	Table
	Q2		50,254	77,176	35,663	44,256	5,275	30,549	
	Q3		33,016	34,014	30,213	32,794	30,200	119,668	
	Q4		72,409	124,765	108,417	43,313	35,524	26,782	
2018	Q1		55,241	26,176	19,534	20,296	9,793	28,652	Pane
	Q2		47,499	29,320	41,988	22,534	19,487	31,268	
	Q3		102,001	44,762	81,264	46,923	15,995	74,876	
	Q4		63,724	75,442	110,800	41,742	39,343	101,173	Cell
2019	Q1		33,938	20,638	23,858	14,296	17,108	13,947	
	Q2		47,778	51,273	73,519	37,173	36,998	35,092	
	Q3		83,456	59,039	32,302	34,504	16,305	76,077	
	Q4		124,363	65,704	86,405	171,909	51,372	62,808	
2020	Q1		51,050	74,600	83,149	53,471	24,272	33,619	
	Q2		57,299	83,749	52,066	22,994	19,818	42,868	
	Q3		92,243	51,459	70,612	56,791	62,900	66,427	
	Q4		132,884	98,473	157,206	42,129	45,894	71,268	

Figure 6.8: The difference between table, pane, and cell in the view

When it comes to the scope of table calculations, Tableau makes the following distinctions:

- The **table** is the entire set of aggregate data.
- The **pane** is a smaller section of the entire table. Technically, it is defined by the penultimate level of the table; that is, the next-to-last dimension on the **Rows** and/or **Columns** shelf defines the pane. In the preceding image, you can see that the intersection of **Year** on rows and **Region** on columns defines the panes (one of eight is highlighted in the view).
- The **cell** is defined by the lowest level of the table. In this view, the intersection of one **Department** within a **Region** and one **Quarter** within a **Year** is a single cell (one of 96 is highlighted in the view).

The bounded areas in the preceding screenshot are defined by the scope. Scope (and as we'll see, also partition) defines windows within the data that contain various table calculations. Window functions, such as WINDOW_SUM() in particular, work within the scope of these windows.

Working with scope and direction

In order to see how scope and direction work together, let's work through a few examples. We'll start by creating our own custom table calculations. Create a new calculated field named Index with the code Index().

Index() is a table calculation function that starts with a value of 1 and increments by one as it moves in a given direction and within a given scope. There are many practical uses for Index(), but we'll use it here because it is easy to see how it is moving for a given scope and direction.

Create the table as shown in *Figure 6.8*, with **YEAR(Order Date)** and **QUARTER(Order Date)** on **Rows** and **Region** and **Department** on **Columns**. Instead of placing **Sales** in the view, add the newly created **Index** field to the **Text** shelf. Then experiment, using the drop-down menu on the **Index** field and select **Compute Using** to cycle through various scope and direction combinations. In the following examples, we've only kept the **East** and **West** regions and two years, **2015** and **2016**:

- **Table (across)**: This is Tableau's default when there are columns in the table. Notice in the following how **Index** increments across the entire table:

		East			West		
			Office			Office	
		Furniture	Supplies	Technolo..	Furniture	Supplies	Technolo..
2015	Q1	1	2	3	4	5	6
	Q2	1	2	3	4	5	6
	Q3	1	2	3	4	5	6
	Q4	1	2	3	4	5	6
2016	Q1	1	2	3	4	5	6
	Q2	1	2	3	4	5	6
	Q3	1	2	3	4	5	6
	Q4	1	2	3	4	5	6

Figure 6.9: Table (across)

- **Table (down)**: When using `table (down)`, **Index** increments down the entire table:

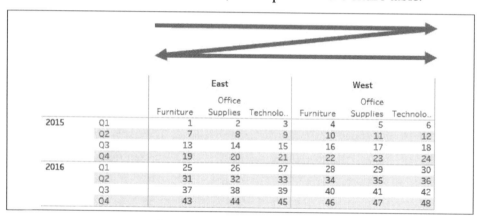

		East			West		
			Office			Office	
		Furniture	Supplies	Technolo..	Furniture	Supplies	Technolo..
2015	Q1	1	1	1	1	1	1
	Q2	2	2	2	2	2	2
	Q3	3	3	3	3	3	3
	Q4	4	4	4	4	4	4
2016	Q1	5	5	5	5	5	5
	Q2	6	6	6	6	6	6
	Q3	7	7	7	7	7	7
	Q4	8	8	8	8	8	8

Figure 6.10: Table (down)

- **Table (across then down)**: This increments **Index** across the table, then steps down, continues to increment across, and repeats for the entire table:

		East			West		
			Office			Office	
		Furniture	Supplies	Technolo..	Furniture	Supplies	Technolo..
2015	Q1	1	2	3	4	5	6
	Q2	7	8	9	10	11	12
	Q3	13	14	15	16	17	18
	Q4	19	20	21	22	23	24
2016	Q1	25	26	27	28	29	30
	Q2	31	32	33	34	35	36
	Q3	37	38	39	40	41	42
	Q4	43	44	45	46	47	48

Figure 6.11: Table (across then down)

- **Pane (across)**: This defines a boundary for **Index** and causes it to increment across until it reaches the pane boundary, at which point the indexing restarts:

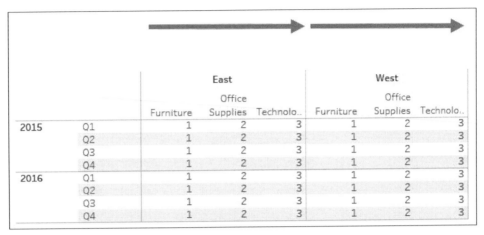

		East			West		
			Office			Office	
		Furniture	Supplies	Technolo..	Furniture	Supplies	Technolo..
2015	Q1	1	2	3	1	2	3
	Q2	1	2	3	1	2	3
	Q3	1	2	3	1	2	3
	Q4	1	2	3	1	2	3
2016	Q1	1	2	3	1	2	3
	Q2	1	2	3	1	2	3
	Q3	1	2	3	1	2	3
	Q4	1	2	3	1	2	3

Figure 6.12: Pane (across)

- **Pane (down)**: This defines a boundary for **Index** and causes it to increment down until it reaches the pane boundary, at which point the indexing restarts:

		East			West		
			Office			Office	
		Furniture	Supplies	Technolo..	Furniture	Supplies	Technolo..
2015	Q1	1	1	1	1	1	1
	Q2	2	2	2	2	2	2
	Q3	3	3	3	3	3	3
	Q4	4	4	4	4	4	4
2016	Q1	1	1	1	1	1	1
	Q2	2	2	2	2	2	2
	Q3	3	3	3	3	3	3
	Q4	4	4	4	4	4	4

Figure 6.13: Pane (down)

- **Pane (across then down)**: This allows **Index** to increment across the pane and continue by stepping down. The pane defines the boundary here:

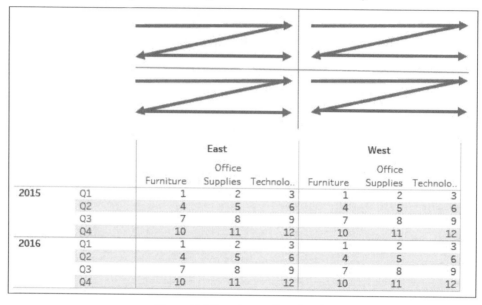

		East			West		
			Office			Office	
		Furniture	Supplies	Technolo..	Furniture	Supplies	Technolo..
2015	Q1	1	2	3	1	2	3
	Q2	4	5	6	4	5	6
	Q3	7	8	9	7	8	9
	Q4	10	11	12	10	11	12
2016	Q1	1	2	3	1	2	3
	Q2	4	5	6	4	5	6
	Q3	7	8	9	7	8	9
	Q4	10	11	12	10	11	12

Figure 6.14: Pane (across then down)

You may use scope and direction with any table calculation. Consider how a running total or percentage difference would be calculated using the same movement and boundaries shown here. Keep experimenting with different options until you feel comfortable with how scope and direction work.

Scope and direction operate relative to the table, so you can rearrange fields, and the calculation will continue to work in the same scope and direction. For example, you could swap **Year of Order Date** with **Department** and still see **Index** calculated according to the scope and direction you defined.

Next, we'll take a look at the corresponding concept for table calculations that are fixed to certain dimensions.

Addressing and partitioning

Addressing and **partitioning** are very similar to scope and direction but are most often used to describe how table calculations are computed with absolute reference to certain fields in the view. With addressing and partitioning, you define which dimensions in the view define the addressing (direction) and all others define the partitioning (scope).

Using addressing and partitioning gives you much finer control because your table calculations are no longer relative to the table layout, and you have many more options for fine-tuning the scope, direction, and order of the calculations.

To begin to understand how this works, let's consider a simple example. Using the preceding view, select **Edit table calculation** from the drop-down menu of the **Index** field on **Text**. In the resulting dialog box, check **Department** under **Specific Dimensions**.

The result of selecting **Department** is as follows:

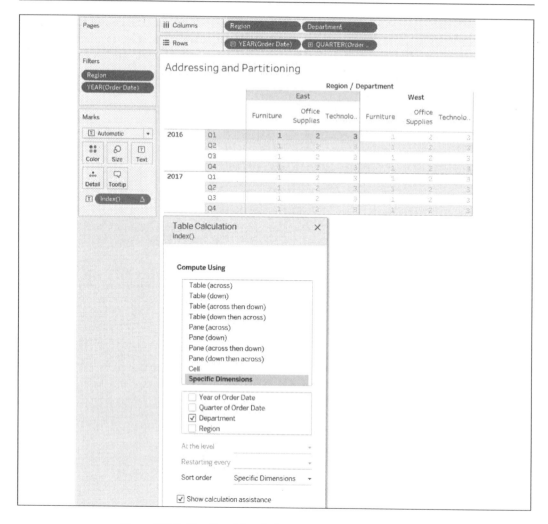

Figure 6.15: Setting the table calculation to Compute Using Specific
Dimensions uses addressing and partitioning

You'll notice that Tableau is computing **Index** along (in the direction of) the checked dimension, **Department**. In other words, you have used **Department** for addressing, so each new department increments the index. All other unchecked dimensions in the view are implicitly used for partitioning; that is, they define the scope or boundaries at which the index function must restart. As we saw with scope, these boundaries are sometimes referred to as a window.

The preceding view looks identical to what you would see if you set **Index** to compute using **Pane (across)**. However, there is a major difference. When you use **Pane (across)**, **Index** is always computed across the pane, even if you rearrange the dimensions in the view, remove some, or add others.

But when you compute using a dimension for addressing, the table calculation will always compute using that dimension. Removing that dimension will break the table calculation (the field will turn red with an exclamation mark) and you'll need to edit the table calculation via the drop-down menu to adjust the settings. If you rearrange dimensions in the view, **Index** will continue to be computed along the **Department** dimension.

Here, for example, is the result of clicking the **Swap Rows and Columns** button in the toolbar:

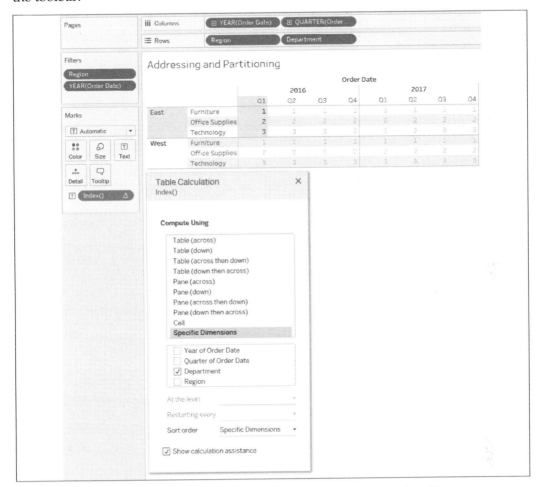

Figure 6.16: Swapping Rows and Columns does not change how this table
calculation was computed as it is fixed to the dimensions rather than the table layout

Notice that **Index** continues to be computed along **Department** even though the entire orientation of the table has changed. To complete the following examples, we'll undo the swap of rows and columns to return our table to its original orientation.

Working with addressing and partitioning

Let's consider a few other examples of what happens when you add additional dimensions. For example, if you check **Quarter of Order Date**, you'll see Tableau highlight a partition defined by **Region** and **Year of Order Date**, with **Index** incrementing by the addressing fields of **Quarter of Order Date** and then **Department**:

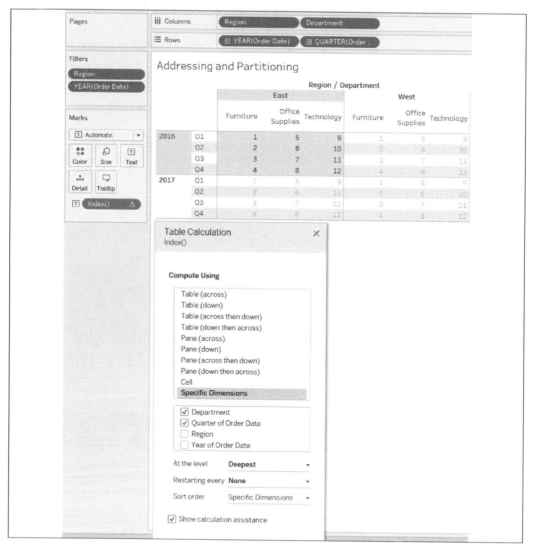

Figure 6.17: Adding dimensions alters the table calculation's behavior.
One of the resulting partitions is highlighted

If you were to select **Department** and **Year of Order Date** as the addressing of **Index**, you'd see a single partition defined by **Region** and **Quarter**, like this:

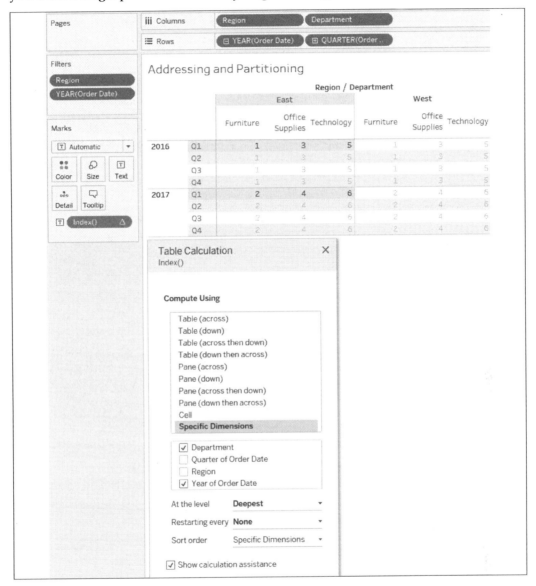

Figure 6.18: Changing the checked dimensions alters the table calculation's behavior. One of the resulting partitions is highlighted

You'll notice, in this view, that **Index** increments for every combination of **Year** and **Department** within the partition of **Quarter** and **Region**.

These are a few of the other things to consider when working with addressing and partitioning:

- You can specify the sort order. For example, if you wanted **Index** to increment according to the value of the sum of sales, you could use the drop-down list at the bottom of the table calculation editor to define a custom sort.

- The **At the Level** option in the edit table calculation dialog box allows you to specify a level at which the table calculations are performed. Most of the time, you'll leave this set at **Deepest** (which is the same as setting it to the bottom-most dimension), but occasionally, you might want to set it at a different level if you need to keep certain dimensions from defining the partition but need the table calculation to be applied at a higher level. You can also reorder the dimensions by dragging and dropping within the checkbox list of **Specific Dimensions**.

- The **Restarting Every...** option effectively makes the selected field, and all dimensions in the addressing above that selected field, part of the partition, but allows you to maintain the fine-tuning of the ordering.

- Dimensions are the only kinds of fields that can be used in addressing; however, a discrete (blue) measure can be used to partition table calculations. To enable this, use the drop-down menu on the field and uncheck **Ignore in Table Calculations**.

Take some time to experiment with various options and become comfortable with how addressing and partitioning works. Next, we'll look at how to write our own custom table calculations.

Custom table calculations

Before we move on to some practical examples, let's briefly discuss how to write your own table calculations, instead of using quick table calculations. You can see a list of available table calculation functions by creating a new calculation and selecting **Table Calculation** from the drop-down list under **Functions**.

For each of the examples, we'll set **Compute Using | Category**. This means **Department** will be the partition.

You can think of table calculations broken down into several categories. The following table calculations can be combined and even nested just like other functions.

Meta table functions

These are the functions that give you information about the partitioning and addressing. These functions also include **Index**, **First**, **Last**, and **Size**:

- **Index** gives an increment as it moves along the addressing within the partition.

- **First** gives the offset from the first row in the partition, so the first row in each partition is **0**, the next row is **-1**, then **-2**, and so on.

- **Last** gives the offset to the last row in the partition, so the last row in each partition is **0**, the next-to-last row is **1**, then **2** and so on.

- **Size** gives the size of the partition.

The following image illustrates the various functions:

Meta Table Calculations

Department	Category	Index along Category	First along Category	Last along Category	Size along Category
Furniture	Bookcases	1	0	3	4
	Chairs & Chairmats	2	-1	2	4
	Office Furnishings	3	-2	1	4
	Tables	4	-3	0	4
Office Supplies	Appliances	1	0	8	9
	Binders and Binder Accessories	2	-1	7	9
	Envelopes	3	-2	6	9
	Labels	4	-3	5	9
	Paper	5	-4	4	9
	Pens & Art Supplies	6	-5	3	9
	Rubber Bands	7	-6	2	9
	Scissors, Rulers and Trimmers	8	-7	1	9
	Storage & Organization	9	-8	0	9
Technology	Computer Peripherals	1	0	3	4
	Copiers and Fax	2	-1	2	4
	Office Machines	3	-2	1	4
	Telephones and Communication	4	-3	0	4

Figure 6.19: Meta table calculations

Index, **First**, and **Last** are all affected by scope/partition and direction/addressing, while **Size** will give the same result at each address of the partition, no matter what direction is specified.

Lookup and previous value

The first of these two functions gives you the ability to reference values in other rows, while the second gives you the ability to carry forward values. Notice from the following screenshot that direction is very important for these two functions:

Departme..	Category	Lookup	Previous Value
Furniture	Bookcases	Null	,Bookcases
	Chairs & Chairmats	Bookcases	,Bookcases,Chairs & Chairmats
	Office Furnishings	Chairs & Chairmats	,Bookcases,Chairs & Chairmats,Office Furnishings
	Tables	Office Furnishings	,Bookcases,Chairs & Chairmats,Office Furnishings,Tables
Office Supplies	Appliances	Null	,Appliances
	Binders and Binder Accessor..	Appliances	,Appliances,Binders and Binder Accessories
	Envelopes	Binders and Binder Acc..	,Appliances,Binders and Binder Accessories,Envelopes
	Labels	Envelopes	,Appliances,Binders and Binder Accessories,Envelopes,Labels
	Paper	Labels	,Appliances,Binders and Binder Accessories,Envelopes,Labels,Paper
	Pens & Art Supplies	Paper	,Appliances,Binders and Binder Accessories,Envelopes,Labels,Paper,Pens & Art Supplies
	Rubber Bands	Pens & Art Supplies	,Appliances,Binders and Binder Accessories,Envelopes,Labels,Paper,Pens & Art Supplies,Rubber Bands
	Scissors, Rulers and Trimmers	Rubber Bands	,Appliances,Binders and Binder Accessories,Envelopes,Labels,Paper,Pens & Art Supplies,Rubber Bands,Scissors,
	Storage & Organization	Scissors, Rulers and ..	,Appliances,Binders and Binder Accessories,Envelopes,Labels,Paper,Pens & Art Supplies,Rubber Bands,Scissors,
Technology	Computer Peripherals	Null	,Computer Peripherals
	Copiers and Fax	Computer Peripherals	,Computer Peripherals,Copiers and Fax
	Office Machines	Copiers and Fax	,Computer Peripherals,Copiers and Fax,Office Machines
	Telephones and Communication	Office Machines	,Computer Peripherals,Copiers and Fax,Office Machines,Telephones and Communication

Lookup and Previous Value

Figure 6.20: Lookup and Previous_Value functions (though Previous_Value includes some additional logic described below)

Both calculations are computed using an addressing of **Category** (so **Department** is the partition).

Here, we've used the code Lookup(ATTR([Category]), -1), which looks up the value of the category in the row offset by -1 from the current one. The first row in each partition gets a NULL result from the lookup (because there isn't a row before it).

For `Previous_Value`, we used this code:

```
Previous_Value("") + "," + ATTR([Category])
```

Notice that in the first row of each partition, there is no previous value, so `Previous_Value()` simply returned what we specified as the default: an empty string. This was then concatenated together with a comma and the category in that row, giving us the value **Bookcases**.

In the second row, **Bookcases** is the previous value, which gets concatenated with a comma and the category in that row, giving us the value **Bookcases, Chairs & Chairmats**, which becomes the previous value in the next row. The pattern continues throughout the partition and then restarts in the partition defined by the department **Office Supplies**.

Running functions

These functions run along direction/addressing and include `Running_Avg()`, `Running_Count()`, `Running_Sum()`, `Running_Min()`, and `Running_Max()`, as follows:

Running Functions

Department	Category	Sales	Running Sum of Sales along Category	Running Min of Sales along Category
Furniture	Bookcases	507,496	507,496	507,496
	Chairs & Chairmats	1,164,586	1,672,082	507,496
	Office Furnishings	444,634	2,116,716	444,634
	Tables	1,061,922	3,178,638	444,634
Office Supplies	Appliances	456,736	456,736	456,736
	Binders and Binder ..	638,583	1,095,319	456,736
	Envelopes	147,915	1,243,234	147,915
	Labels	23,446	1,266,680	23,446
	Paper	253,620	1,520,300	23,446
	Pens & Art Supplies	103,265	1,623,565	23,446
	Rubber Bands	8,670	1,632,235	8,670
	Scissors, Rulers and ..	40,432	1,672,667	8,670
	Storage & Organizat..	585,717	2,258,384	8,670
Technology	Computer Periphera..	490,851	490,851	490,851
	Copiers and Fax	661,215	1,152,066	490,851
	Office Machines	1,218,655	2,370,721	490,851
	Telephones and Com..	1,144,284	3,515,005	490,851

Figure 6.21: Running Functions

Notice that `Running_Sum(SUM[Sales]))` continues to add the sum of sales to a running total for every row in the partition. `Running_Min(SUM[Sales]))` keeps the value of the sum of sales if it is the smallest value it has encountered so far as it moves along the rows of the partition.

Window functions

These functions operate across all rows in the partition at once and essentially aggregate the aggregates. They include `Window_Sum`, `Window_Avg`, `Window_Max`, and `Window_Min`, among others, as shown in the following screenshot:

Window Functions

Department	Category	Sales	Window Sum along Category	Window Max along Category
Furniture	Bookcases	507,496	3,178,638	1,164,586
	Chairs & Chairmats	1,164,586	3,178,638	1,164,586
	Office Furnishings	444,634	3,178,638	1,164,586
	Tables	1,061,922	3,178,638	1,164,586
Office Supplies	Appliances	456,736	2,258,384	638,583
	Binders and Binder..	638,583	2,258,384	638,583
	Envelopes	147,915	2,258,384	638,583
	Labels	23,446	2,258,384	638,583
	Paper	253,620	2,258,384	638,583
	Pens & Art Supplies	103,265	2,258,384	638,583
	Rubber Bands	8,670	2,258,384	638,583
	Scissors, Rulers and..	40,432	2,258,384	638,583
	Storage & Organizat..	585,717	2,258,384	638,583
Technology	Computer Periphera..	490,851	3,515,005	1,218,655
	Copiers and Fax	661,215	3,515,005	1,218,655
	Office Machines	1,218,655	3,515,005	1,218,655
	Telephones and Com..	1,144,284	3,515,005	1,218,655

Figure 6.22: Examples of Window functions

`Window_Sum(SUM([Sales])` adds up the sums of sales within the entire window (in this case, for all categories within the department). `Window_Max(SUM([Sales])` returns the maximum sum of sales within the window.

You may pass optional parameters to window functions to further limit the scope of the window. The window will always be limited to, at most, the partition.

Rank functions

These functions provide various ways to rank based on aggregate values. There are multiple variations of rank, which allow you to decide how to deal with ties and how dense the ranking should be, as shown in the following screenshot:

Rank Functions

Department	Category	Sales	Rank along Category
Furniture	Bookcases	507,496	3
	Chairs & Chairmats	1,164,586	1
	Office Furnishings	444,634	4
	Tables	1,061,922	2
Office Supplies	Appliances	456,736	3
	Binders and Binder ..	638,583	1
	Envelopes	147,915	5
	Labels	23,446	8
	Paper	253,620	4
	Pens & Art Supplies	103,265	6
	Rubber Bands	8,670	9
	Scissors, Rulers and ..	40,432	7
	Storage & Organizat..	585,717	2
Technology	Computer Periphera..	490,851	4
	Copiers and Fax	661,215	3
	Office Machines	1,218,655	1
	Telephones and Com..	1,144,284	2

Figure 6.23: Examples of rank functions

The Rank(SUM([Sales])) calculation returns the rank of the sum of sales for categories within the department.

Script functions

These functions allow integration with the R analytics platform or Python, either of which can incorporate simple or complex scripts for everything from advanced statistics to predictive modeling. It's beyond the scope of this book to dive into all that is possible, but documentation and examples are readily available on Tableau's website and from various members of the Tableau community.

 Bora Beran, for example, has an excellent post here: `https://www.tableau.com/about/blog/2016/11/leverage-power-python-tableau-tabpy-62077`

The Total function

The `Total` function deserves its own category because it functions a little differently from the others. Unlike the other functions that work on the aggregate table in the cache, `Total` will re-query the underlying source for all the source data rows that make up a given partition. In most cases, this will yield the same result as a window function.

For example, `Total(SUM([Sales]))` gives the same result as `Window_Sum(SUM([Sales]))`, but `Total(AVG([Sales]))` will possibly give a different result from `Window_AVG(SUM([Sales]))` because `Total` is giving you the actual average of underlying rows, while the `Window` function is averaging the sums.

In this section, we have looked at a number of table calculation functions. These will give you the building blocks to solve all kinds of practical problems and answer a great many questions. From ranking to year-over-year comparisons, you now have a foundation for success. Let's now move on to some practical examples.

Practical examples

Having looked at some of the essential concepts of table calculations, let's consider some practical examples. We'll look at several examples, although the practical use of table calculations is nearly endless. You can do everything from running sums and analyzing year-over-year growth to viewing percentage differences between categories, and much more.

Year over year growth

Often, you may want to compare year over year values. How much has our customer base grown over the last year? How did sales in each quarter compare to sales in the same quarter last year? These types of question can be answered using **Year over Year Growth**.

Tableau exposes **Year over Year Growth** as one option in the quick table calculations. Here, for example, is a view that demonstrates **Sales** by **Quarter**, along with the percentage difference in sales for a quarter compared with the previous year:

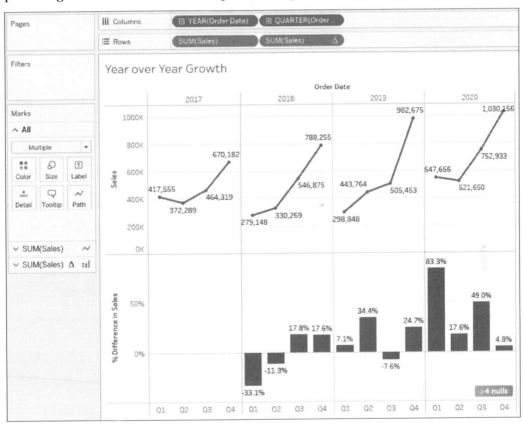

Figure 6.24: Year over year growth of Sales

The second **Sum(Sales)** field has had the **Year over Year Growth** quick table calculation applied (and the **Mark** type changed to bar). You'll notice the **>4 nulls** indicator in the lower right, alerting you to the fact that there are at least four null values (which makes sense as there is no 2016 with which to compare quarters in 2017).

If you filtered out 2017, the nulls would appear in 2018 as table calculations can only operate on values present in the aggregated data in the cache. Any regular filters applied to the data are applied at the source and the excluded data never makes it to the cache.

As easy as it is to build a view like this example, take care, because Tableau assumes each year in the view has the same number of quarters. For example, if the data for **Q1** in 2017 was not present or filtered out, then the resulting view would not necessarily represent what you want. Consider the following, for example:

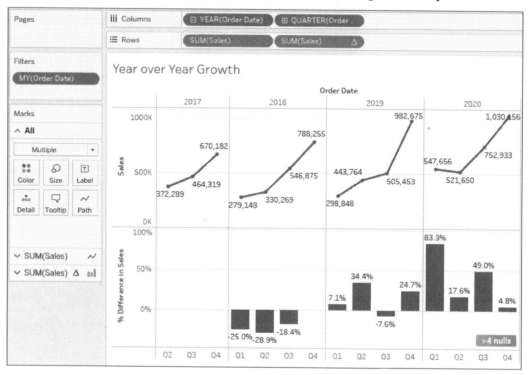

Figure 6.25: Year over year growth of Sales—but it doesn't work with Q1 missing in the first year

The problem here is that Tableau is calculating the quick table calculation using an addressing of **Year** and **Quarter** and an *At the Level* of value of **Year of Order Date**. This works assuming all quarters are present. However, here, the first quarter in **2018** is matched with the first quarter present in **2017**, which is really **Q2**. To solve this, you would need to edit the table calculation to only use **Year** for addressing. **Quarter** then becomes the partition and thus comparisons are done for the correct quarter.

An additional issue arises for consideration: what if you don't want to show 2017 in the view? Filtering it out will cause issues for 2018. In this case, we'll look at **table calculation filtering**, or **late filtering**, later in this section. Another potential way to remove 2017 but keep access to its data values is to right-click the 2017 header in the view and select **Hide**.

Hide is a special command that simply keeps Tableau from rendering data, even when it is present in the cache. If you later decide you want to show 2017 after hiding it, you can use the menu for the **YEAR(Order Date)** field and select **Show Hidden Data**. Alternately, you can use the menu to select **Analysis | Reveal Hidden Data**.

You may also wish to hide the null indicator in the view. You can do this by right-clicking the indicator and selecting **Hide Indicator**. Clicking the indicator will reveal options to filter the data or display it as a default value (typically, 0).

Year over year growth (or any period over another) is a common analytical question which table calculations allow you to answer. Next, let's consider another example of table calculations in practice.

Dynamic titles with totals

You've likely noticed the titles that are displayed for every view. There are also captions that are not shown unless you specifically turn them on (to do this, select **Worksheet | Show Caption** from the menu).

By default, the title displays the sheet name and captions are hidden, but you can show and modify them. At times, you might want to display totals that help your end users understand the broad context or immediately grasp the magnitude.

Here, for example, is a view that allows the user to select one or more **Regions** and then see **Sales per State** in each **Region**:

Figure 6.26: Sales per State for two regions

It might be useful to show a changing number of states as the user selects different regions. You might first think to use an aggregation on **State**, such as Count Distinct. However, if you try showing that in the title, you will always see the value 1. Why? Because the view level of detail is **State** and the distinct count of states per state is 1!

But there are some options with table calculations that let you further aggregate aggregates. Or, you might think of determining the number of values in the table based on the size of the window. In fact, here are several possibilities:

- To get the total distinct count: TOTAL(COUNTD([State]))
- To get the sum within the window: WINDOW_SUM(SUM(1))
- To get the size of the window: SIZE()

You may recall that a window is defined as the boundaries determined by scope or partition. Whichever we choose, we want to define the window as the entire table. Either a relative computation of Table (down) or a fixed computation using all of the dimensions would accomplish this. Here is a view that illustrates a dynamic title and all three options in the caption:

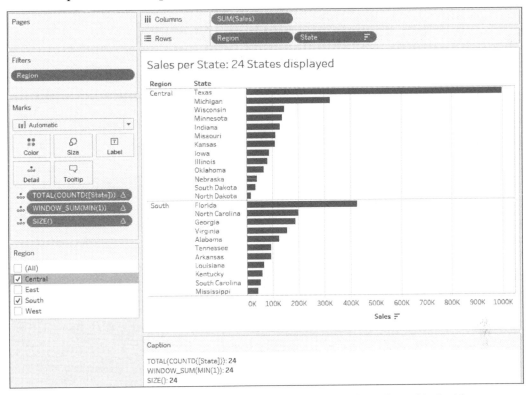

Figure 6.27: Various table calculations could be employed to achieve the total in the title

This example illustrated how you might use various table calculations to work at higher levels of detail, specifically counting all the states in the view. This technique will enable you to solve various analytical questions as you use Tableau. Let's now turn our attention to another technique that helps solve quite a few problems.

Table calculation filtering (late filtering)

Let's say you've built a view that allows you to see the percentage of total sales for each department. You have already used a quick table calculation on the **Sales** field to give you the percent of the total. You've also used **Department** as a filter. But this presents a problem.

Since table calculations are performed after the aggregate data is returned to the cache, the filter on department has already been evaluated at the data source and the aggregate rows don't include any departments excluded by the filter. Thus, the percent of the total will always add up to 100%; that is, it is the percentage of the filtered total, as shown in the following screenshot:

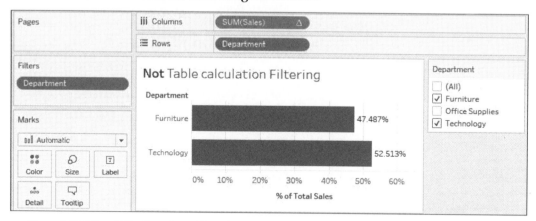

Figure 6.28: When Office Supplies is filtered out, the percentage table calculation adds up to 100% for the departments remaining in the view

What if you wanted to see the percentage of the total sales for all departments, even if you want to exclude some from the display? One option is to use a table calculation as a filter.

You might create a calculated field called Department (table calc filter) with the code LOOKUP(ATTR([Department]), 0). The Lookup() function makes this a table calculation, while ATTR() treats **Department** as an aggregation (further explanation is provided at the end of this section). The second argument, 0, tells the lookup function not to look backward or forward. Thus, the calculation returns all values for **Department**, but as a table calculation result.

When you place that table calculation on the **Filters** shelf instead of the **Department** dimension, then the filter is not applied at the source. Instead, all the aggregate data is still stored in the cache and the table calculation filter merely *hides* it from the view. Other table calculations, such as **Percent of Total**, will still operate on all the data in the cache. In this case, that allows the percent of total to be calculated for all departments, even though the table calculation filter is hiding one or more, as shown in the following screenshot:

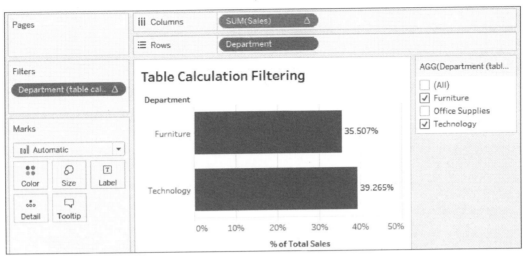

Figure 6.29: When a table calculation filter is used, all the aggregate
data is available in the cache for the % of Total Sales to be calculated for all departments

You might have noticed the ATTR function used. Remember that table calculations require aggregate arguments. ATTR (which is short for attribute) is a special aggregation that returns the value of a field if there is only a single value of that field present for a given level of detail or a * if there is more than one value.

To understand this, experiment with a view having both **Department** and **Category** on rows. Using the drop-down menu on the active field in the view, change **Category** to **Attribute**. It will display as * because there is more than one category for each department. Then, undo and change **Department** to **Attribute**. It will display the department name because there is only one department per category.

In this example, we've seen how to effectively use table calculations as filters when we need other table calculations to operate on all the data in the cache.

Summary

We've covered a lot of concepts surrounding table calculations in this chapter. You now have a foundation for using the simplicity of quick table calculations and leveraging the power of advanced table calculations. We've looked at the concepts of scope and direction as they apply to table calculations that operate relative to the row and column layout of the view. We've also considered the related concepts of addressing and partitioning as they relate to table calculations that have computations fixed to certain dimensions.

The practical examples we've covered barely scratch the surface of what is possible, but should give you an idea of what can be achieved. The kinds of problems that can be solved and the diversity of questions that can be answered are almost limitless.

We'll turn our attention to some lighter topics in the next couple of chapters, looking at formatting and design, but we'll certainly see another table calculation or two before we're finished!

7
Making Visualizations That Look Great and Work Well

Tableau applies many good visual practices by default, and, for quick analysis, you likely won't worry too much about changing many of these defaults. However, as you consider how to best communicate the data story you've uncovered, you'll want to consider how to leverage everything, from fonts and text, to colors and design, so that you can communicate well with your audience.

Tableau's formatting options give you quite a bit of flexibility. Fonts, titles, captions, colors, row and column banding, labels, shading, annotations, and much more, can all be customized to make your visualizations tell an impressive story.

This chapter will cover the following topics:

- Visualization considerations
- Leveraging formatting in Tableau
- Adding value to visualizations

As you think about why you should adjust a given visualization, there are several things to consider. We'll start with those considerations.

Visualization considerations

Tableau employs good practices for formatting and visualization from the time you start dropping fields on shelves. You'll find that the discrete palettes use colors that are easy to distinguish, the fonts are pleasant, the grid lines are faint where appropriate, and numbers and dates follow the default format settings defined in the metadata.

The default formatting is more than adequate for discovery and analysis. If your focus is analysis, you may not want to spend too much time fine-tuning the formatting until you are getting ready to share results. However, when you contemplate how you will communicate the data to others, you might consider how adjustments to the formatting can make a major difference to how well the data story is told.

 Sometimes, you will have certain formatting preferences in mind or a set of corporate guidelines that dictate font and color selections. In these cases, you might set formatting options in a blank workbook and save it as a template. This workbook file could be copied in the file system any time you wished to begin a new set of views and dashboards.

Here are some of the things you should consider:

- **Audience**: Who is the audience and what are the needs of the audience?

- **Goal**: Is the goal to evoke an emotional response or to lay out the facts for an impassioned decision? Are you highlighting an action that needs to be taken, or simply trying to generate interest in a topic?

- **Setting**: This is the environment in which the data story is communicated. Is it a formal business meeting where the format should reflect a high level of professionalism? Is it going to be shared on a blog informally?

- **Mode**: How will the visualizations be presented? You'll want to make sure rows, columns, fonts, and marks are large enough for a projector or compact enough for an iPad. If you are publishing to Tableau Server, Tableau Online, or Tableau Public, then did you select fonts that are safe for the web? Will you need to use the device designer to create different versions of a dashboard?

- **Mood**: Certain colors, fonts, and layouts can be used to set a mood. Does the data tell a story that should invoke a certain response from your audience? Is the data story somber or playful? The color red, for example, may connote danger, negative results, or indicate that an action is required. However, you'll need to be sensitive to your audience and the specific context. Colors have different meanings in different cultures and in different contexts. In some cultures, red might indicate joy or happiness. Also, red might not be a good choice to communicate negativity if it is the color of the corporate logo.

- **Consistency**: Generally, use the same fonts, colors, shapes, line thickness, and row-banding throughout all visualizations. This is especially true when they will be seen together on a dashboard or even used in the same workbook. You may also consider how to remain consistent throughout the organization without being too rigid.

These considerations will inform your design and formatting decisions. As with everything else you do with Tableau, think of design as an iterative process. Seek feedback from your intended audience often and adjust your practices as necessary to make sure your communication is as clear and effective as possible. The entire goal of formatting is to more effectively communicate the data.

Leveraging formatting in Tableau

We'll focus on worksheet-level formatting in this chapter, as we've already covered metadata in *Chapter 2, Connecting to Data in Tableau*, and we will cover dashboards and stories in *Chapter 8, Telling a Data Story with Dashboards*. However, it is beneficial to see the big picture of formatting in Tableau.

Tableau employs default formatting that includes default fonts, colors, shading, and alignment. Additionally, there are several levels of formatting you can customize, as shown in the following diagram:

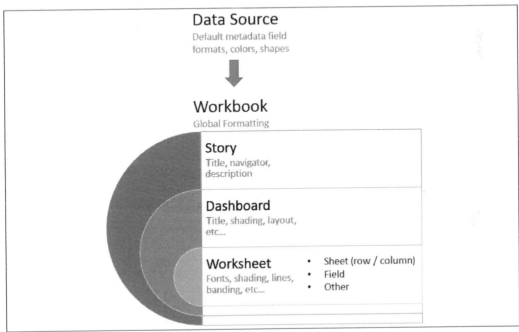

Figure 7.1: Levels of formatting in Tableau

Let's go into them in more detail:

- **Data source level**: We've already seen how you can set default formats for numeric and date fields. Other defaults, such as colors and shapes, can also be set using the **Default Properties** menu on the drop-down menu in the data pane.

- **Workbook level**: Various global formatting options may be set. From the menu, select **Format | Workbook**.

- **Story level**: Navigate to a story tab and select **Format | Story** (or **Story | Format**) to edit formatting for story-specific elements. These include options for customizing shading, title, navigator, and description.

- **Dashboard level**: Dashboard-specific elements can be formatted. When viewing a dashboard, select **Format | Dashboard** (or **Dashboard | Format**) to specify the formatting for dashboard titles, subtitles, shading, and text objects.

- **Worksheet level**: We'll consider the various options. The following types of formatting are available for a worksheet:

    - **Sheet formatting**: This formatting includes font, alignment, shading, borders, and lines. You may override the formatting for the entire sheet for row-and column-specific formatting.

    - **Field-level formatting**: This formatting includes fonts, alignment, shading, and number and date formats. This formatting is specific to how a field is displayed in the current view. The options you set at the field level override defaults set at a worksheet level. Number and date formats will also override the default field formatting.

    - **Additional formatting**: Additional formatting can be applied to titles, captions, tooltips, labels, annotations, reference lines, field labels, and more.

- **Rich-text formatting**: Titles, captions, annotations, labels, and tooltips all contain text that can be formatted with varying fonts, colors, and alignment. This formatting is specific to the individual text element.

Let's start by examining workbook-level formatting.

Workbook-level formatting

Tableau allows you to set certain formatting defaults at a workbook level. To view the options and make changes to the defaults, click **Format | Workbook....** The left pane will now show formatting options for the workbook:

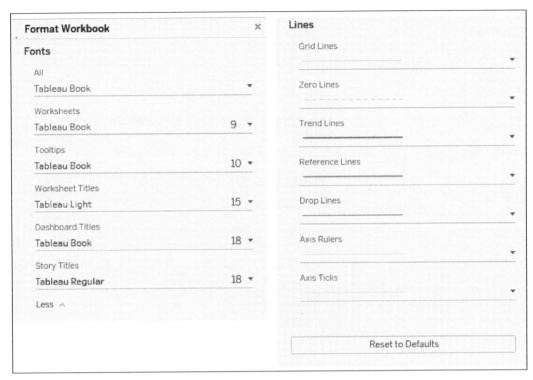

Figure 7.2: Workbook formatting options

The options include the ability to change default **Fonts**, which apply to various parts of a view or dashboard, and default **Lines**, which apply to the various types of lines used in visualizations. Notice also the **Reset to Defaults** button, should you wish to revert to the default formatting. Any changes here will impact the whole workbook.

At times, you'll want to apply formatting specific to a given sheet, and we'll consider that next.

Worksheet-level formatting

You've already seen how to edit metadata in previous chapters, and we'll cover dashboards and stories in detail in future chapters. So, we'll shift our attention to worksheet-level formatting.

Before we look at specifically how to adjust formatting, consider the following parts of a view related to formatting:

Formatting: Parts of the View

Department	Category	Consumer	Corporate	Home Office	Small Business	Grand Total
Furniture	Bookcases	92,626	262,085	79,404	73,381	507,496
	Chairs & Chairmats	305,381	407,724	212,830	238,651	1,164,586
	Office Furnishings	69,528	115,506	197,188	62,412	444,634
	Tables	228,934	363,979	287,507	181,502	1,061,922
	Total	696,469	1,149,294	776,929	555,946	3,178,638
Office Supplies	Appliances	63,813	167,941	124,757	100,225	456,736
	Binders and Binder Accessor..	103,625	225,160	148,472	161,326	638,583
	Envelopes	37,643	44,462	22,577	43,233	147,915
	Labels	3,713	7,929	5,411	6,393	23,446
	Paper	53,004	89,312	61,123	50,181	253,620
	Pens & Art Supplies	24,027	36,004	21,765	21,469	103,265
	Rubber Bands	1,710	2,197	2,294	2,469	8,670
	Scissors, Rulers and Trimme..	14,628	9,625	12,947	3,232	40,432
	Storage & Organization	121,719	154,918	179,151	129,929	585,717
	Total	423,882	737,548	578,497	518,457	2,258,384
Technology	Computer Peripherals	80,805	224,142	110,840	75,064	490,851
	Copiers and Fax	148,504	205,639	174,718	132,354	661,215
	Office Machines	260,011	516,513	245,019	197,112	1,218,655
	Telephones and Communicat..	225,571	436,295	282,962	199,456	1,144,284
	Total	714,891	1,382,589	813,539	603,986	3,515,005
Grand Total		1,835,242	3,269,431	2,168,965	1,678,389	8,952,027

Customer Segment

Figure 7.3: Parts of a view that can be formatted using worksheet-level formatting

This view consists of the following parts, which can be formatted:

1. **Field labels for rows**: Field labels can be formatted from the menu (**Format | Field Labels...**) or by right-clicking them in the view and selecting **Format....** Additionally, you can hide field labels from the menu (**Analysis | Table Layout** and then uncheck the option for showing field labels) or by right-clicking them in the view and selecting the option to hide. You can use the **Analysis | Table Layout** option on the top menu to show them again, if needed.

2. **Field labels for columns**: These have the same options as labels for rows, but they may be formatted or shown/hidden independently from the row-field labels.

3. **Row headers**: These will follow the formatting of headers in general, unless you specify different formatting for headers for rows only. Notice that subtotals and grand totals have headers. The subtotal and grand total headers are marked **a** and **b** respectively.

4. **Column headers**: These will follow the formatting of headers in general, unless you specify different formatting for headers for the columns only. Notice that subtotals and grand totals have headers. The grand total header marked in the preceding screenshot is a column header.

5. **Pane**: Many formatting options include the ability to format the pane differently than the headers.

6. **Grand totals (column) pane**: This is the pane for grand totals that can be formatted at a sheet or column level.

7. **Grand totals (row) pane**: This is the pane for grand totals that can be formatted at a sheet or row level.

Worksheet-level formatting is accomplished using the format window, which will appear on the left side, in place of the data pane.

To view the format window, select **Format** from the menu and then **Font...**, **Alignment...**, **Shading...**, **Borders...**, or **Lines...**:

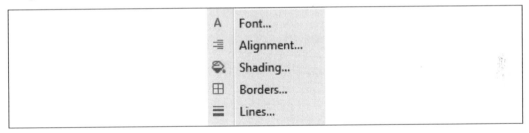

Figure 7.4: Formatting options for a worksheet

 You can also right-click nearly any element in the view and select **Format**. This will open the format window specific to the context of the element you selected. Just be sure to verify that the title of the format window matches what you expect. When you make a change, you should see the view update immediately to reflect your formatting. If you don't, you are likely working in the wrong tab of the formatting window, or you may have formatted something at a lower level (for example, **Rows**) that overrides changes made at a higher level (for example, **Sheet**).

You should now see the format window on the left, in this case, **Format Font**. It will look like this:

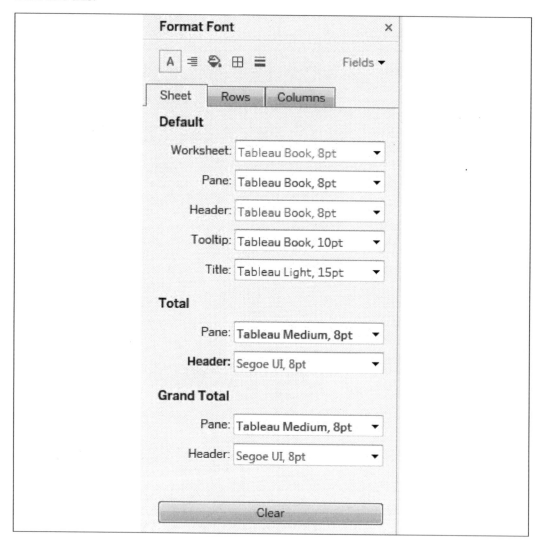

Figure 7.5: The Format Font pane

Notice these key aspects of the formatting window:

- The title of the window will give you the context for your formatting selections.
- The icons at the top match the selection options of the **Format** menu. This allows you to easily navigate through those options without returning to the menu each time.

- The three tabs, **Sheet**, **Rows**, and **Columns**, allow you to specify options at a sheet level and then override those options and defaults at a row and column level. For example, you could make the **Row** grand totals have different pane and header fonts than the **Column** grand totals (though this specific choice would likely be jarring and is not recommended!).

- The **Fields** dropdown in the upper-right corner allows you to fine-tune formatting at the field level.

- Any changes that you make will be previewed and result in a bold label to indicate that the formatting option has been changed from the default (notice how the font for **Header** under **Total** has been customized, resulting in the label text of **Header** being shown in bold).

The three options for clearing the format are as follows:

Clear Single Option: In the format window, right-click the label or control of any single option you have changed and select **Clear** from the pop-up menu.

Clear All Current Options: At the bottom of the format window, click the **Clear** button to clear all visible changes. This applies only to what you are currently seeing in the format window. For example, if you are viewing **Shading** on the **Rows** tab and click **Clear**, only the shading options on the **Rows** tab will be cleared.

Clear Sheet: From the menu, select **Worksheet | Clear | Formatting**. You can also use the dropdown from the **Clear** item on the toolbar. This clears all custom formatting on the current worksheet.

The other format options (such as alignment and shading) all work very similarly to the font option. There are only a few subtleties to mention:

- **Alignment** includes options for horizontal and vertical alignment, text direction, and text wrapping.

- **Shading** includes an option for row and column banding. The banding allows alternating patterns of shading that help to differentiate or group rows and columns. Light row banding is enabled by default for text tables, but it can be useful in other visualization types, such as horizontal bar charts as well. Row banding can be set to different levels that correspond to the number of discrete (blue) fields present on the **Rows** or **Columns** shelves.

- **Borders** refers to the borders drawn around cells, panes, and headers. It includes an option for row and column dividers. You can see in the view the dividers between the departments. By default, the level of the borders is set based on the next-to-last field in the rows or columns.

- **Lines** refers to lines that are drawn on visualizations using an axis. This includes grid lines, reference lines, zero lines, and axis rulers. You can access a more complete set of options for reference lines and drop lines from the **Format** option of the menu.

We've considered how to adjust formatting at the entire workbook level as well as for a given sheet. Let's turn our attention to formatting at the field level.

Field-level formatting

In the upper-right corner of the format window is a little drop-down menu labeled **Fields**. Selecting this drop-down menu gives you a list of fields in the current view, and selecting a field updates the format window with options appropriate for the field. Here, for example, is the window as it appears for the SUM(Sales) field:

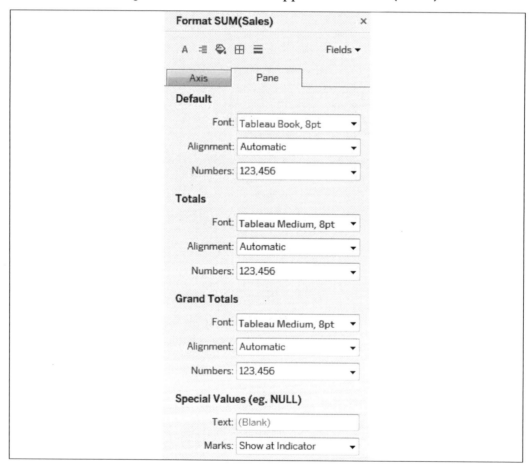

Figure 7.6: Format pane for field-level formatting

The title of the format window will alert you to the field you are formatting. Selecting an icon for **Font**, **Alignment**, and so on from the top-left corner of the window will switch back to sheet-level formatting. However, you can switch between the tabs of **Axis** and **Pane**. These two tabs allow you to have different formatting for a field when it is used in the header or as an axis label versus how it is formatted in the pane of the view. The options for fields include **Font**, **Alignment**, **Shading**, and **Number** and **Date** formats. The last two options will override any default metadata formats.

You'll notice special options for formatting certain types of fields. Numbers allow a wide range of formatting options and even include the ability to provide custom formatting, which we'll consider next.

Custom number formatting

When you alter the format of a number, you can select from several standard formats, as well as a custom format. The custom format allows you to enter a format string that Tableau will use to format the number. Your format string may use combinations of hash/pound (#), commas, negative signs, and parentheses, along with a literal string enclosed in quotation marks to indicate how the number should display.

The format string allows up to three entries, separated by semi-colons to represent positive, negative, and zero formats.

Here are some examples, assuming the positive number is 34,331.336 and the negative number is -8,156.7777:

Format String	Resulting Value
#;-#	34331 and -8157
#,###.##; (#,###.##)	34,331.34 and (8,156.78)
#,###.00000;-#,###.00000	34,331.33600 and -8,156.77770
"up "#,###;"down "#,###;"same"	up 34,331 and down 8,157
#,###"▲"; #,###"▼"	34,331▲ and 8,157▼

Figure 7.7: Examples of format strings and resulting values

You can replicate these examples and experiment with other format strings using the **Custom Number Formatting** view in the `Starter` or `Complete` workbooks:

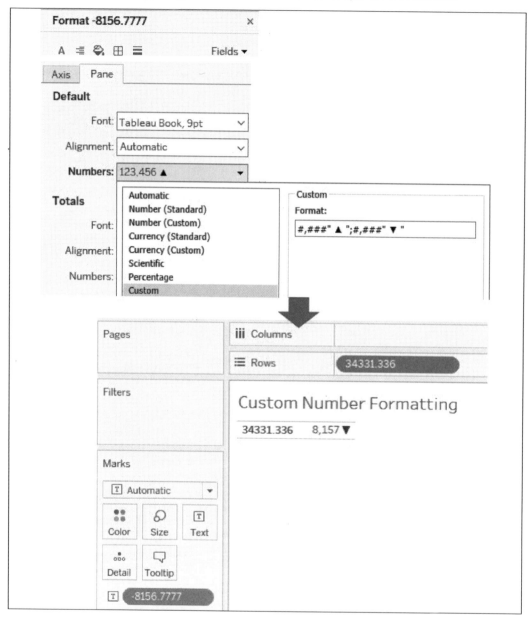

Figure 7.8: Experiment with format strings using the Custom Number Formatting view in the Chapter 7 workbook

Notice how Tableau rounds the display of the number based on the format string. Always be aware that numbers you see as text, labels, or headers may have been rounded due to the format.

Also observe how you can mix format characters such as the pound sign, commas, and decimal points with strings. The fourth example shown would provide a label where a value of zero would normally be displayed.

Finally, notice that the last example uses Unicode characters that give you a wide range of possibilities, such as displaying degrees or other units of measure. Unicode characters may be used throughout Tableau in text boxes, titles, field names and labels, aliases, and more!

 Selecting a predefined format that is close to what you want, and then switching to custom, will allow you to start with a custom format string that is close to your desired format.

Custom date formatting

In a similar way, you can define custom date formatting using a custom string. The following table illustrates some possible formatting of the date value of 11/08/2018, 1:30 PM based on various format strings:

Format String	Resulting Value
m/d/yyyy	11/8/2018
dd/mm/yyyy	08/11/2018
"The date is" m/d/yyyy	The date is 11/8/2018
mmm d, yyyy	Nov 8, 2018
mmmm dd yyyy	November 08 2018
mm/dd/yyyy h:mm AM/PM	11/08/2018 1:30PM
ttttt	1:30:28 PM
dddd, mmmm d, HH:MM:ss	Thursday, November 8, 13:30:28
ddd	Thu

Figure 7.9: Some possible date formatting examples

These are merely examples, and you may include as many literal strings as you'd like.

 For a complete list of custom date format string options, check out `https://onlinehelp.tableau.com/current/pro/desktop/en-us/dates_custom_date_formats.html`.

Notice how applying some custom date formatting improves the readability of the axis for a small timeline in this example:

Figure 7.10: The custom format string used here is mmmmm, which results in a single letter for the month

Custom number and date formats are fine when you have values that need to be formatted. But what if there is no value? That is, how can we format NULL values? Let's consider that next.

Null formatting

An additional aspect of formatting a field is specially formatting **Null** values. When formatting a field, select the **Pane** tab and locate the **Special Values** section, as shown in the following screenshot:

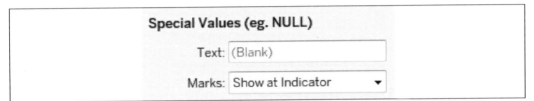

Figure 7.11: The Special Values options appear on the Format pane

Enter any text you would like to display in the pane (in the **Text** field) when the value of the field is null. You can also choose where marks should be displayed. The **Marks** drop-down menu gives multiple options that define where and how the marks for null values should be drawn when an axis is being used. You have the following options:

- **Show at Indicator** results in a small indicator with the number of null values in the lower right of the view. You can click the indicator for options to filter the null values or show them at the default value. You can right-click the indicator to hide it.

- **Show at Default Value** displays a mark at the default location (usually 0).

- **Hide (Connect Lines)** does not place a mark for null values but does connect lines between all non-null values.

- **Hide (Break Lines)** causes the line to break where there are gaps created by not showing the null values.

You can see these options in the following screenshots, with the location of two null values indicated by a gray band.

Show at Indicator reveals no marks in the gray band with the number of null values indicated in the lower-right corner:

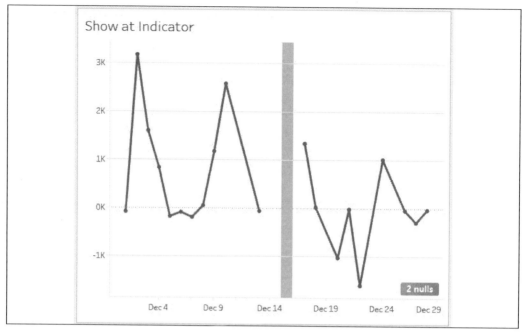

Figure 7.12: Show at Indicator

Show at Default Value places marks at 0 and connects the lines:

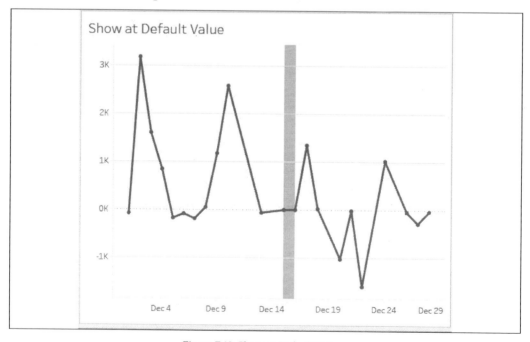

Figure 7.13: Show at Default Value

Hide (Connect Lines) removes marks for the missing values, but does connect the existing marks:

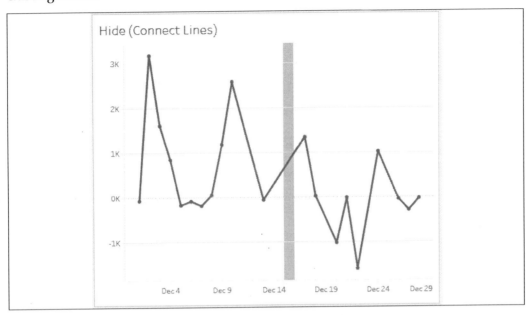

Figure 7.14: Hide (Connect Lines)

Hide (Break Lines) removes the marks for the missing values and does not connect the existing marks:

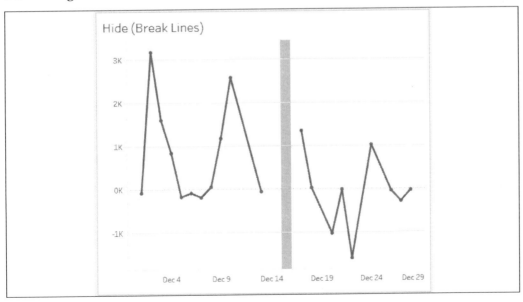

Figure 7.15: Hide (Break Lines)

Any of these options might have a good use but consider how each communicates the information. Connecting the lines might help communicate a movement over time but may also minimize the existence of missing data. Breaking the lines might help highlight missing values but might take away from the overall message. You'll need to decide which option best meets your goals based on the considerations mentioned at the beginning of this chapter.

You'll notice that the preceding line charts have little circle markers at the location of each mark drawn in the view. When the mark type is a line, clicking on the color shelf opens a menu that gives options for the markers. All mark types have standard options, such as color and transparency. Some mark types support additional options such as border and/or halo, as shown here:

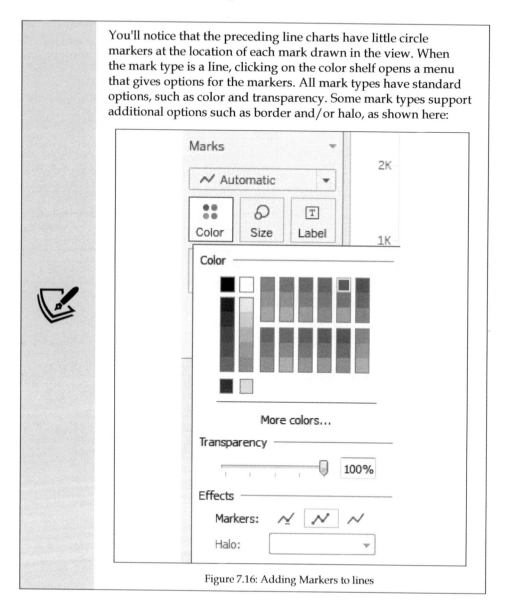

Figure 7.16: Adding Markers to lines

Knowing these options will help you as you think about how to communicate missing data, but always consider that another visualization type such as a bar chart might be even more effective in communicating missing values:

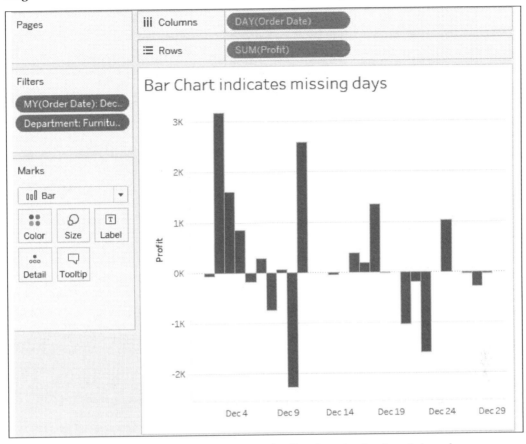

Figure 7.17: Bar charts are sometimes better than line charts for showing missing values

Knowing how to format null values gives you some options as you consider how to communicate the data. Let's take a look at a few additional options.

Additional formatting options

Additional formatting options can also be accessed from the formatting window. These options include the following:

- A myriad of options for **Reference Lines**
- Line and text options for **Drop Lines**
- Shading and border options for **Titles** and **Captions**

- Text, box, and line options for **Annotations**
- Font, shading, alignment, and separator options for **Field** labels
- Title and body options for **Legends**, **Quick Filters**, and **Parameters**
- **Cell** size and **Workbook** theme options

You'll find most of these relatively straightforward. A few options might not be as obvious:

- **Drop Lines**, which appear as lines drawn from the mark to the axis, can be enabled by right-clicking any blank area in the pane of the view with an axis and selecting **Drop Lines | Show Drop Lines**. Additional options can be accessed by using the same right-click menu and selecting **Edit Drop Lines**. Drop lines are only displayed in Tableau Desktop and Reader but are not currently available when a view is published to Tableau Server, Online, or Public.

- **Titles** and **Captions** can be shown or hidden for any view by selecting **Worksheet** from the menu and then selecting the desired options. In addition to standard formatting, which can be applied to titles and captions, the text of a title or caption can be edited and specifically formatted by double-clicking the title or caption, right-clicking the title or caption and selecting **Edit**, or by using the drop-down menu of the title or caption (or the drop-down menu of the view on a dashboard). The text of titles and captions can dynamically include the values of parameters, the values of any field in the view, and certain other data and worksheet-specific values.

- **Annotations** can be created by right-clicking a mark or space in the view, selecting **Annotate**, and then selecting one of the following three types of annotations:

  - **Mark** annotations are associated with a specific mark in the view. If that mark does not show (due to a filter or axis range), then neither will the annotation. Mark annotations can include a display of the values of any fields that define the mark or its location.

  - **Point** annotations are anchored to a specific point in the view. If the point is ever not visible in the view, the annotation will disappear. Point annotations can include a display of any field values that define the location of the point (for example, the coordinates of the axis).

- **Area** annotations are contained within a rectangular area. The text of all annotations can dynamically include the values of parameters, and certain other data and worksheet-specific values.

You can copy formatting from one worksheet to another (within the same workbook or across workbooks) by selecting **Copy Formatting** from the **Format** menu while viewing the source worksheet (or selecting the **Copy Formatting** option from the right-click menu on the source worksheet tab). Then, select **Paste Formatting** on the **Format** menu while viewing the target worksheet (or select the option from the right-click menu on the **Target** worksheet tab).

This option will apply any custom formatting present on the source sheet to the target. However, specific formatting applied during the editing of the text of titles, captions, labels, and tooltips is not copied to the target sheet.

We've now considered a lot of options for formatting the workbook, individual sheets, fields, numbers, dates, and null values. Now, let's consider how we can leverage some of these techniques to truly bring better understanding of the data.

Adding value to visualizations

Now that we've considered how formatting works in Tableau, let's look at some ways in which formatting can add value to a visualization.

When you apply custom formatting, always ask yourself what the formatting adds to the understanding of the data. Is it making the visualization clearer and easier to understand? Or is it just adding clutter and noise?

In general, try a minimalistic approach. Remove everything from the visualization that isn't necessary. Emphasize important values, text, and marks, while de-emphasizing those that are only providing support or context.

Consider the following visualization, all using default formatting:

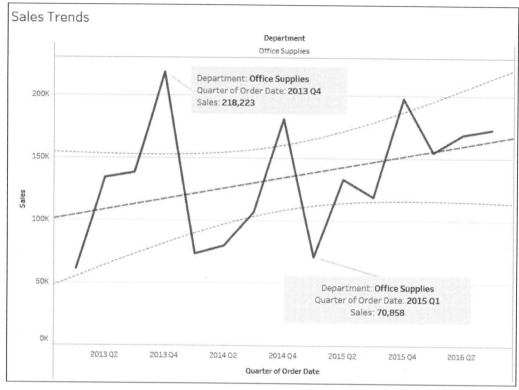

Figure 7.18: The default formatting is often great for data discovery and quick analysis but may be more cluttered than desired for clearly communicating and emphasizing the data story to others

The default format works fairly well, but compare that to this visualization:

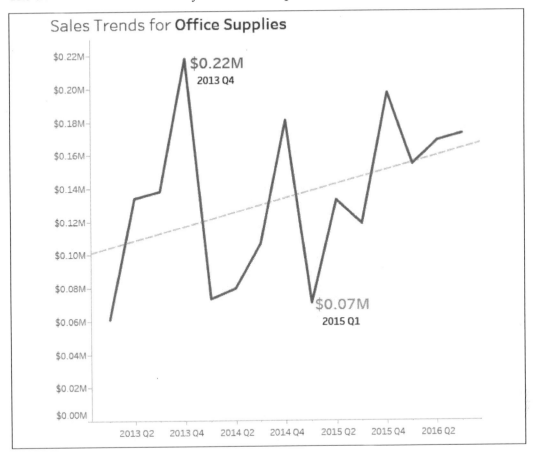

Figure 7.19: Formatting can make a visualization less cluttered and communicate the data more effectively

Both of the preceding diagrams show sales by the quarter, filtered to the **Office Supplies** department. The first view uses the default formatting. The second view has some formatting adjustments, including the following:

- **Title** has been adjusted to include the department name.

- **Sales** has been formatted to be shown using a custom currency with two decimal places and units of millions. This is true for the axis and the annotations. Often, a high level of precision can clutter a visualization. The initial view of the data gives us the trend and enough detail to understand the order of magnitude. Tooltips or additional views can be used to reveal detail and increase precision.

- The axis labels have been removed by right-clicking the axis, selecting **Edit Axis**, and then clearing the text. The title of the view clearly indicates that you are looking at Sales. The values alone reveal the second axis to be by the quarter. If there are multiple dates in the data, you might need to specify which one is in use. Depending on your goals, you might consider hiding the axes completely.

- The gridlines on **Rows** have been removed. Gridlines can add value to a view, especially in views where being able to determine values is of high importance. However, they can also clutter and distract. You'll need to decide, based on the view itself and the story you are trying to tell, whether gridlines are helpful.

- The trend line has been formatted to match the color of the line, though it is lighter and thinner, to de-emphasize it. Additionally, the confidence bands have been removed. You'll have to decide whether they add context or clutter based on your needs and audience.

- The lines, shading, and boxes have been removed from the annotations to reduce clutter.

- The size and color of the annotations have been altered to make them stand out. If the goal had been to simply highlight the minimum and maximum values on the line, labels might have been a better choice, as they can be set to display at only **Min/Max**. In this case, however, the lower number is actually the second-lowest point in the view.

- Axis rulers and ticks have been emphasized and colored to match the marks and reference line (axis rulers are available under the **Lines** option on the **Format** window).

Formatting can also be used to dramatically alter the appearance of a visualization. Consider the following chart:

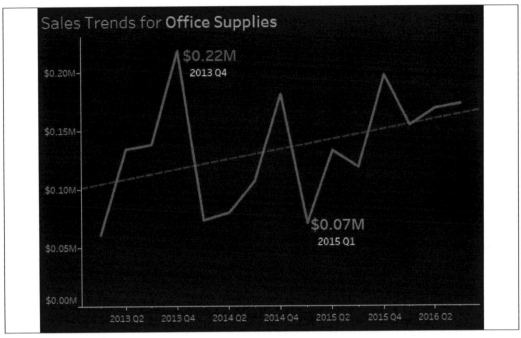

Figure 7.20: A dark background can be set by formatting the shading of a view

This visualization is nearly identical to the previous view. However, shading has been applied to the worksheet and the title. Additionally, fonts were lightened or darkened as needed to show up well on a dark background. Some find this format more pleasing, especially on mobile devices. If the view is to be embedded into a website with a dark theme, this formatting may be very desirable. However, you may find some text more difficult to read on a dark background. You'll want to consider your audience, the setting, and the mode of delivery as you consider whether such a format is the best for your situation.

Sequential color palettes (a single color gradient based on a continuous field) should be reversed when using a dark background. This is because the default of lighter (lower) to darker (higher) works well on a white background, where darker colors stand out and lighter colors fade into white. On a black background, lighter colors stand out more and darker colors fade into black. You'll find the reverse option when you edit a color palette using the drop-down menu on double-clicking the legend or right-clicking the legend selecting **Edit Colors...** and checking **Reversed**.

Tooltips

As they are not always visible, tooltips are an easily overlooked aspect of visualizations. However, they add a subtle professionalism. Consider the following default tooltip that displays when the end user hovers over one of the marks shown in the preceding screenshot:

Figure 7.21: Default tooltip

Compare it to this tooltip:

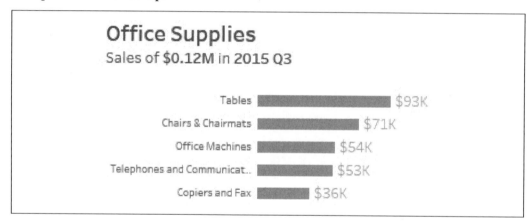

Figure 7.22: Customized tooltip

The tooltip was edited by clicking **Tooltip** on the **Marks** card, which brought up an editor allowing the rich editing of text in the tooltip:

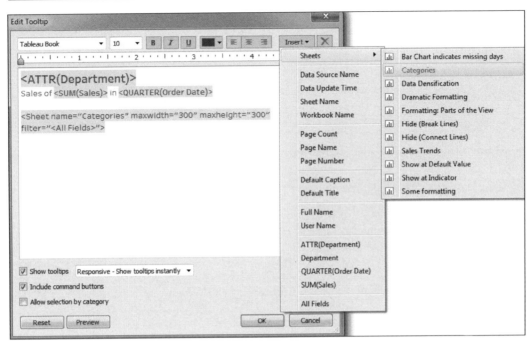

Figure 7.23: Tooltip editor

This editor is similar to those used for editing the text of labels, titles, captions, and annotations. You can input text and format it as desired. Additionally, the **Edit Tooltip** dialog has some additional functionality:

- The **Insert** drop-down menu in the upper-right corner allows you to insert sheets, fields, parameters, and other dynamic values. These special or dynamic text objects are enclosed as a tag in the text editor (for example, <SUM(Sales)>). We'll consider the special case of sheets in a moment.

- A checkbox option to **Show tooltips** and a drop-down menu to indicate the style of the tooltip (**Responsive - show tooltips instantly** or **On Hover**).

- A checkbox option to **Include command buttons**. This is the default, and you can observe the command buttons in the first, unedited tooltip in this section. The command buttons include options such as **Include**, **Exclude**, **Create Sets**, and so on. Many of these options are still available to the end user via a right-click, so removing them from the tooltip does not prevent the user from accessing them completely.

- A checkbox option to **Allow selection by category**. When enabled, this feature allows users to click the values of dimensions shown in the tooltip and thus select all marks associated with that value in the view.

 Consider unchecking **Show tooltips** for any view where they do not significantly and intentionally add value to the user experience.

Viz in Tooltip

Tableau allows you to embed visualizations in tooltips that are dynamically filtered as you hover over different marks. Often referred to as **Viz in Tooltip**, this greatly extends the interactivity available to end users, the ability to drill down to the details, and the ability to quickly see data in different ways.

In the preceding screenshot, the following tag was added to the tooltip by selecting **Insert | Sheets | Categories**:

```
<Sheet name="Categories" maxwidth="300" maxheight="300" filter="<All
Fields>">
```

This tag, which you may edit by directly editing the text, tells Tableau to show the visualization in the Categories sheet as part of the tooltip. The maximum width and height are set to 300 pixels by default. The filter indicates which field(s) act as a filter from the sheet to the Viz in Tooltip. By default, <All Fields> means that all dimensions in the view will act as filters. However, you may specify a list of fields to specifically filter by one or more dimensions that are present in the view (for example, <Department>, <Category>).

Notice the final view with the tooltip:

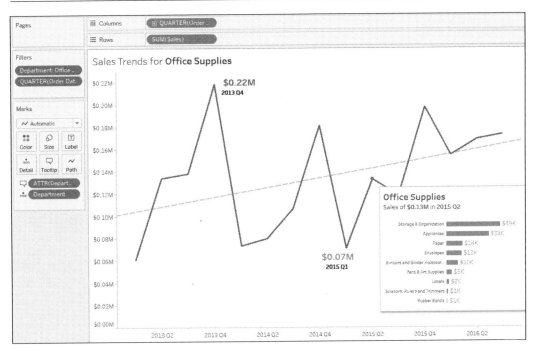

Figure 7.24: Viz in Tooltip

There are many possibilities with Viz in Tooltip. First, you can leverage the capability to drill down into details without using extra space on a dashboard and without navigating to a separate view. Second, you can show different aspects of the data (for example: geographic location as a tooltip for a time series). Finally, you might consider how to use Viz in Tooltip to allow the end user to see parts of the whole within a broader context.

There are a great many more valuable applications of this feature, but here are a few tips to wrap up our examination of Viz in Tooltip:

- You may have more than one Viz in a single tooltip.
- Setting the **Fit** option to **Entire View** for the sheet being used in a tooltip fits it to the maximum width and height.
- You may hide sheets used in tooltips by right-clicking the tab of the sheet and selecting **Hide**. To restore them, right-click the tab of the sheet being used in the tooltip and select **Unhide Sheets**.

Summary

The goal of formatting is to increase effective communication of the data at hand. Always consider the audience, setting, mode, mood, and consistency as you work through the iterative process of formatting. Look for formatting that adds value to your visualization and avoid useless clutter.

We covered quite a few options for formatting – from fonts, colors, lines, and more at the workbook level to formatting individual sheets and fields. We discussed how to customize formatting for numbers, dates, and null values and how to use these techniques to bring value to your visualizations.

With an understanding of how formatting works in Tableau, you'll have the ability to refine the visualizations that you created in discovery and analysis into incredibly effective communication of your data story.

In the next chapter, we'll look at how this all comes together on dashboards.

8

Telling a Data Story with Dashboards

In data discovery and analysis, you will likely create numerous data visualizations. Each of these visualizations gives you a snapshot of a story within the data. Each insight into the data answers a question or two. At times, the discovery and analysis phase is enough for you to make a key decision and the cycle is complete. In other cases, you will need to bring the snapshots together to communicate a complete and compelling story to your intended audience.

Tableau allows you to bring together related data visualizations into a single dashboard. This dashboard could be a static view of various aspects of the data or a fully interactive environment, allowing users to dynamically filter, drill down, and interact with the data visualizations.

In this chapter, we'll take a look at most of these concepts within the context of several in-depth examples, where we'll walk through the dashboard design process, step by step. As before, don't worry about memorizing lists of instructions. Instead, focus on understanding why and how the components and aspects of dashboards work.

This chapter will cover the following topics:

- Introduction to dashboards
- Designing dashboards in Tableau
- Designing for different displays and devices
- Interactivity with actions
- Stories

For the examples in this chapter, we'll return to the Superstore Sales sample data we used in the previous chapters. Go ahead and create a new workbook with a connection to that dataset, and we'll begin by introducing the key concepts of dashboards.

Introduction to dashboards

Before diving into some practical examples, let's take some time to understand what a dashboard is and why you might create one.

Dashboard definition

From a Tableau perspective, a **dashboard** is an arrangement of individual visualizations, along with other components, such as legends, filters, parameters, text, containers, images, extensions, buttons, and web objects, that are arranged on a single canvas. Ideally, the visualizations and components should work together to tell a complete and compelling data story. Dashboards are usually (but not always) interactive.

Dashboard objectives

The primary objective of a dashboard is to communicate data to a certain audience with an intended result. Often, we'll talk about *telling the data story*. That is, there is a narrative (or multiple narratives) contained within the data that can be communicated to others.

While you can tell a data story with a single visualization or even a series of complex dashboards, a single Tableau dashboard is the most common way to communicate a single story. Each dashboard seeks to tell a story by giving a clear picture of certain information. Before framing the story, you should understand what story the data tells. How you tell the story will depend on numerous factors, such as your audience, the way the audience will access the dashboard, and what response you want to elicit from your audience.

Stephen Few, one of the leading experts in the field of data visualization, defines a dashboard as *a visual display of the most important information that's needed to achieve one or more objectives, consolidated and arranged on a single screen so the information can be monitored at a glance.*

This definition is drawn from Few's paper *Dashboard Confusion*, which can be read here: `https://www.perceptualedge.com/articles/ie/dashboard_confusion.pdf`.

This definition is helpful to consider because it places some key boundaries around the data story and the way we will seek to tell it in Tableau. In general, your data story should follow these guidelines:

- The data story should focus on the most important information. Anything that does not communicate or support the main story should be excluded. You may wish to include that information in other dashboards.

- The data story that you tell must meet your key objectives. Your objectives may range from giving information to providing an interface for further exploration, to prompting your audience to act or make key decisions. Anything that doesn't support your objectives should be reserved for other dashboards.

- The data story should be easily accessible, and the main idea should be clear. Depending on your audience, you may wish to explicitly state your conclusions from the data, or you may want to guide your audience so that they can draw their own.

When you set out to build a dashboard, you'll want to carefully consider your objectives. Your discovery and analysis should have uncovered various insights into the data and its story. Now, it's your responsibility to package that discovery and analysis into a meaningful communication of the story to your particular audience in a way that meets your objectives and their needs. The way you handle this task is called your **approach**.

Dashboard approaches

There are numerous possible approaches to building dashboards based on your objectives. The following is by no means a comprehensive list:

- **Guided analysis**: You've done the analysis, made the discoveries, and thus have a deep understanding of the implications of the data story. Often, it can be helpful to design a dashboard that guides your audience through a similar process of making the discoveries for themselves, so the need to act is clear. For example, you may have discovered wasteful spending in the marketing department, but the team may not be ready to accept your results unless they can see how the data led you to that conclusion.

- **Exploratory**: Many times, you do not know what story the data will tell when the data is refreshed in the next hour, next week, or next year. What may not be a significant aspect of the story today might be a major decision point in the future. In these cases, your goal is to provide your audience with an analytical tool that gives them the ability to explore and interact with various aspects of the data on their own. For example, today, customer satisfaction is high across all regions. However, your dashboard needs to give your organization the ability to continually track satisfaction over time, dynamically filter by product and price, and observe any correlations with factors such as quality and delivery time.

- **Scorecard/Status snapshot**: There may be a wide agreement on **Key Performance Indicators (KPIs)** or metrics that indicate good versus poor performance. You don't need to guide the audience through discovery or force them to explore. They just need a high-level summary and the ability to drill down into details to quickly find and fix problems and reward success. For example, you may have a dashboard that simply shows how many support tickets are still unresolved. The manager can pull up the dashboard on a mobile device and immediately take action if necessary.

- **Narrative**: This type of dashboard emphasizes a story. There may be aspects of exploration, guided analysis, or performance indication, but primarily you are telling a single story from the data. For example, you may desire to tell the story of the spread of an invasive species of insect, including where it started, how quickly it spread, the results, and the efforts to contain it. Your dashboard should tell the story, using data, in a visual way.

We'll look at several in-depth examples to better understand a few of these different approaches and incorporate many of the skills we've covered in previous chapters. First, we'll introduce some key aspects of designing dashboards in Tableau.

Your dashboard may have a hybrid approach. For example, you might have an exploratory dashboard that prominently displays some KPIs. However, be careful to not overload a dashboard. Trying to meet more than one or two objectives with any single dashboard will likely result in an overwhelming mess.

Designing dashboards in Tableau

No matter your objective or approach, the practical task of designing a dashboard in Tableau will look similar each time. In this section, we will go through some fundamental concepts.

Objects

Dashboards are made up of objects that are arranged on a canvas. You'll see a list of objects that can be added to a dashboard in the left-hand pane of a dashboard:

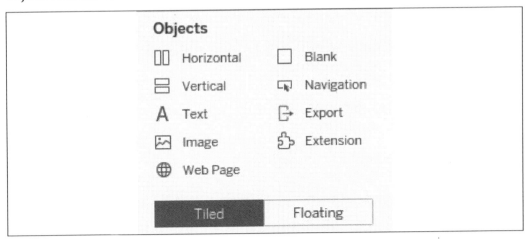

Figure 8.1: Objects available to add to a dashboard

The pane includes these objects:

- **Horizontal**: A layout container within which other objects will be arranged in a single row (horizontally).

- **Vertical**: A layout container within which other objects will be arranged in a single column (vertically).

- **Text**: An object that allows you to include richly formatted text in your dashboard.

- **Image**: An image (for example, .gif, .png, or .jpeg) that can be positioned and sized on your dashboard. Optionally, you may set a URL for navigation when a user clicks the image.

- **Web Page**: An object that allows you to embed web content in the dashboard. You may set the URL at design time. We'll also consider how to use actions to dynamically change the URL.

- **Blank**: A blank object that can be used as a placeholder or to provide spacing options.

- **Navigation**: A navigation button allows you to define user navigation to other sheets and dashboards in the workbook.

- **Export:** An export object allows you to create a link or button that gives the user an easy option to export the dashboard as an image, PDF, or PowerPoint.

- **Extension**: One of a growing number of tools developed by Tableau and third parties (or maybe even you!) that leverages the extensions API to provide extended functionality to dashboards. This could allow you to accomplish things such as gathering extensive usage data, dynamically updating parameters, incorporating visualizations from other platforms (such as D3), and much more.

In addition to the objects that you can add through the sidebar, there are other objects that may be applicable to a given dashboard:

- **Filters**: These will appear as controls for the end user so that they can select values to filter

- **Parameters**: Similar to filters, these will show up as controls for the end user to select a parameter option

- **Page controls**: These are controls that give the end user options for paging through the data and may be used to animate visualizations and dashboards

- **Legends**: These include color, size, and shape legends to help the end user understand various visualizations

- **Highlighters**: These allow the user to highlight various dimension values within views

- **Dashboard title**: A special text object that displays the name of the dashboard sheet by default

Tiled versus floating

An object is either tiled or floating. If it is a tiled object, it will snap into the dashboard or layout container where you drop it. If it is a floating object, it will float over the dashboard in layers. You can change the order of the layers for a floating object.

You'll notice the **Tiled** or **Floating** buttons directly beneath the **Objects** pallet in the preceding image. These buttons define the default setting for objects that you place on the dashboards, but you can change whether any given object is tiled or floating.

 Hold down the *Shift* key as you drag an object to quickly change it from tiled to floating, or from floating to tiled.

As you become experienced in designing dashboards, you'll likely develop a preference for designing using a predominately tiled approach or a predominately floating approach. (You can mix tiled and floating objects on any dashboard). Many designers find one design method or the other fits their style. Here are some considerations:

- **Precision**: Floating objects can be sized and positioned to exact pixel-perfection, while tiled objects will depend greatly upon their containers for position and size.

- **Speed**: Many designers find a tiled layout much faster to create as they don't have to worry about precision or layering.

- **Dynamic resizing**: Floating objects work well on a fixed-size dashboard, but a dashboard that dynamically resizes based on window size will shift floating objects, often into undesirable locations. Tiled objects move and resize more reliably (but not always perfectly!).

- **Flexibility**: Certain design techniques can be accomplished with one approach or the other. For example, transparent visualizations can be layered on top of background images using a floating technique. However, sheet swapping (which we'll consider in *Chapter 11, Dynamic Dashboards*) is often accomplished with a tiled approach.

- **Maintenance**: Changes to the layout of a floating dashboard might be harder and more tedious than doing so for tiled layouts.

Experiment with various design techniques and feel free to develop your own style!

Manipulating objects on the dashboard

You may wish to manipulate an object once it is part of a dashboard. Every object has certain controls that become visible when you select it:

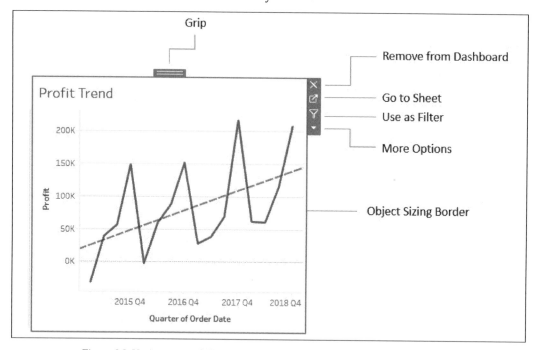

Figure 8.2: Various controls become accessible once you select a dashboard object

- **Grip**: Click and drag the grip to move the object.

- **Remove from Dashboard**: Click this to remove the object from the dashboard.

- **Go to Sheet**: To edit a single visualization on a dashboard, use this button to navigate to the individual sheet.

- **Use as Filter**: Clicking here will enable the view to be used as a filter. Selecting a mark in the view will now filter other views on the dashboard. We'll look at the specifics of filter actions later in this chapter and how you can have finer control over how a view can be used as a filter.

- **More Options**: This drop-down arrow reveals a host of options for the object, including control display options for parameters and filters; showing or hiding titles or captions on views; adding legends, parameters, and filters to the dashboard; formatting, layout, and size options; and more.

- **Object Sizing Border**: Hovering over the border will cause your cursor to change to a sizing cursor. You can drag the border to adjust the size of the object.

 You may notice different sizing behavior based on what type of container an object is inside and whether the object is tiled or floating.

In the first sections of this chapter, we have introduced the theoretical fundamentals of dashboards and some key elements of their design. Now, let's apply these concepts with a practical example.

A dashboard to understand profitability

Having covered some conceptual topics as well as practical matters related to dashboard design, we'll dive into an example.

Let's say you've been tasked with helping management find which items are the least profitable. Management feels that most of the least profitable items should be eliminated from their inventory. However, since you've done your analysis, you've discovered that certain items, while not profitable overall, have made a profit at times in various locations. Your primary objective is to give management the ability to quickly see an analysis of the least profitable items to identify whether an item has always been unprofitable, answering the question, "Is the least profitable item always unprofitable?" This example will combine aspects of a guided analytics dashboard and an exploratory tool.

Building the views

Use the Superstore Sales dataset and follow these steps to build the individual views that will form the basis of the dashboard:

1. Create a bar chart showing profit by category. Sort the categories in descending order by the sum of profit.

2. Add the **Department** field to **Filters** and show a filter. To accomplish this, use the drop-down menu of the **Department** field in the data pane and select **Show Filter**.

3. Name the sheet **Overall Profit by Category**:

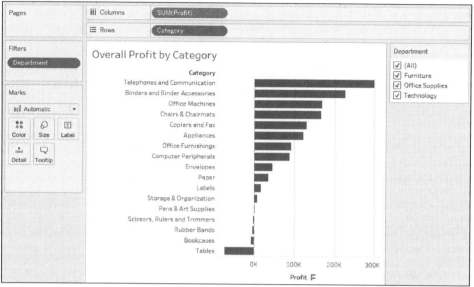

Figure 8.3: A bar chart showing the sum of profit by category with Department as a filter

4. Create another similar view showing profit by item. Sort the items in descending order by the sum of profit.

5. You'll notice that there are too many items to see at once. For your objectives on this dashboard, you can limit the items to only the top 10 least profitable ones. Add the **Item** field to the **Filters** shelf, select the **Top** tab, and adjust the settings to filter by field. Specify **Bottom 10** by Sum(Profit):

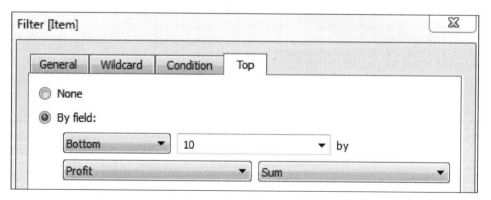

Figure 8.4: Use the Top tab to set the number of items to display

6. Rename the sheet **Top 10 Least Profitable Items**:

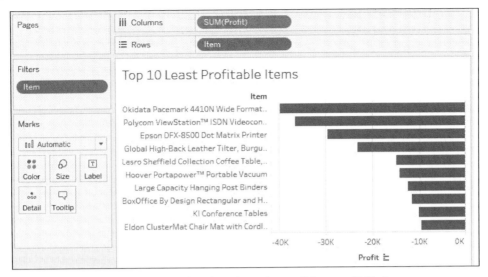

Figure 8.5: The resulting bar chart shows the top 10 least profitable items

7. Create another sheet that displays a filled map of profit by state. You can accomplish this rather quickly by double-clicking the **State** field in the data window and then dropping **Profit** on the **Color** shelf. (Note: if your regional settings are not US, you may need to use the **Edit Locations** option to set the country to the United States.)

8. Rename the sheet to **Profit by State**:

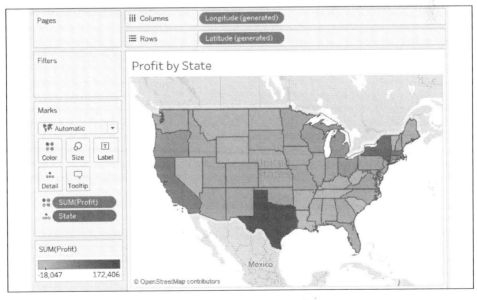

Figure 8.6: A filled map showing profit by state

9. Create one final sheet to show when profits were made or lost. Ensure that the **Order Date** field has been added as the **Quarter** date value and that it is continuous (green).

10. Add a linear trend line. To do this, switch to the **Analytics** tab of the left sidebar and drag **Trend Line** from **Model** to the view. Alternatively, right-click a blank area of the canvas of the view and select **Trend Lines | Show Trend Lines**.

11. Rename the sheet to **Profit Trend**:

Figure 8.7: A line chart showing the trend of profit by quarter

Now that you've created the views that will make up the dashboard, let's start to put the dashboard together!

Creating the dashboard framework

At this point, you have all of the necessary views to achieve the objectives for your dashboard. Now, all that remains is to arrange them and enable the interactivity that's required to effectively tell the story:

1. Create a new dashboard by clicking the **New Dashboard** tab to the right of all existing worksheet tabs or by selecting **Dashboard | New Dashboard** from the menu.

2. Rename the new dashboard `Is Least Profitable Always Unprofitable?`.

3. At the bottom of the left sidebar, check **Show dashboard title**.

4. Add the views to the dashboard by dragging them from the **Dashboard** pane of the left sidebar and dropping them into the dashboard canvas. Arrange them as follows:

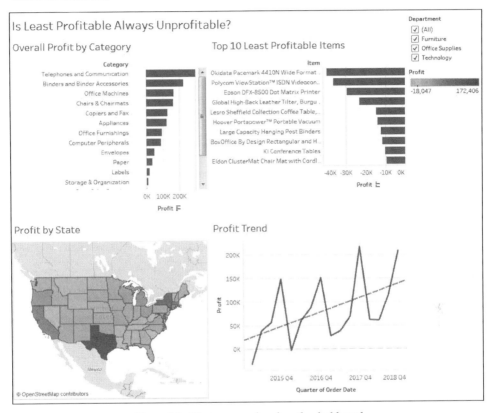

Figure 8.8: All views are placed on the dashboard

After adding views to the dashboard, you'll want to take some time to reposition and resize various elements and views.

5. Use the drop-down menu on the **Department** filter and change the control to **Single Value** (drop-down).

6. You'll notice that changing the value of the filter only changes the **Overall Profit by Category** view. You can adjust which views the filter applies to by using the drop-down menu. Using the drop-down menu, select **Apply to Worksheets | All Using This Data Source**.

Options for applying filters may be set using the drop-down on the filter control or on the field on the filters shelf in the view. The options include the following:

- **All Using Related Data Sources**: The filter will be applied to all data sources where the field used for filtering is related between data sources. Relationships may be edited from **Data | Edit Relationships** on the main menu.

- **All Using This Data Source**: The filter will be applied to any view using the data source as the primary data source.

- **Selected Worksheets...**: The filter will be applied to the worksheets you select.

- **Only This Worksheet**: The filter will be applied only to the current worksheet.

Now, let's get back to creating our dashboard framework.

7. From the left sidebar, drag and drop a text object above **Overall Profit by Category** and enter the following instructions:

   1. **Select a Department from the drop-down**
   2. **Select a category below**
   3. **Select an Item below**

8. Using the grip, move the **Department** filter immediately above the **Top 10 Least Profitable Items** view.

9. Size the text object to align the **Top 10** view with the overall view.

10. Move the **Profit** color legend below the **Profit by State** view.

11. Use the drop-down menu of **Overall Profit by Category** to **Fit | Entire View**. This will ensure that all of the categories are visible without the need for a scrollbar.

12. Additionally, fit **Top 10 Least Profitable Items** to **Entire View**.

At this point, your dashboard should look similar to the following:

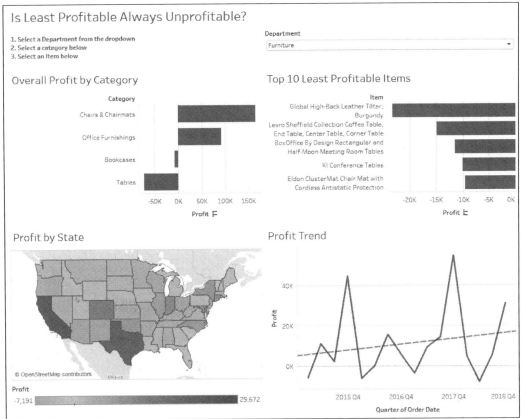

Figure 8.9: The polished dashboard with rearranged and resized objects

We now have a dashboard with all the views we want to include. As you've seen, it's easy to add views and objects and rearrange them as desired. Let's continue by examining how to drive a story with actions.

Implementing actions to guide the story

You now have a framework that will support the telling of the data story. Your audience will be able to locate the least profitable items within the context of a selected category. Then, the selection of an item will answer the question of whether it has always been unprofitable in every location. To enable this flow and meet your objectives, you'll often need to enable interactivity. In this case, we'll use actions. We'll conclude this example with some specific steps and then unpack the intricacies of actions later in the chapter:

1. Click the **Use as Filter** button on the **Overall Profit by Category** view. This will cause the view to be used as an interactive filter for the entire dashboard. That is, when the user selects a bar, all other views will be filtered based on the selection:

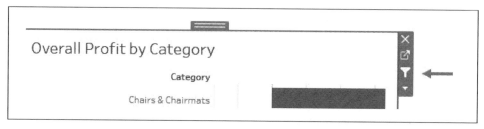

Figure 8.10: The Use As Filter control on the Profit by Category view

2. From the main menu, select **Dashboard | Actions**. You'll see a list containing one action named **Filter 1 (generated)**. This is the action that was created when you selected **Use as Filter** previously:

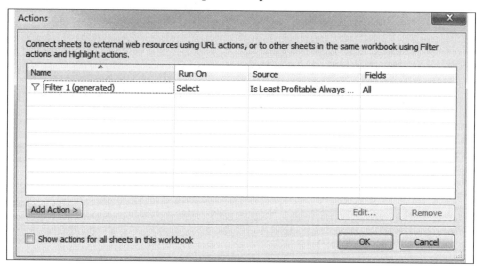

Figure 8.11: Filter 1 (generated) was created when the filter control was clicked

3. Click the **Add Action >** button and select **Filter**. The resulting dialog gives you options for selecting the source and target, as well as additional options for the action.

4. Here, we want an action that filters everything except the **Overall Profit by Category** view when the user selects an item. In the **Add Filter Action** dialog, set **Source Sheets** to **Top 10 Least Profitable Items**, and **Target Sheets** to **Profit by State** and **Profit Trend**. Make sure that the action is set to run on **Select**. Name the filter **Filter by Item**, and then click **OK** on this dialog. Do the same on the **Actions** dialog:

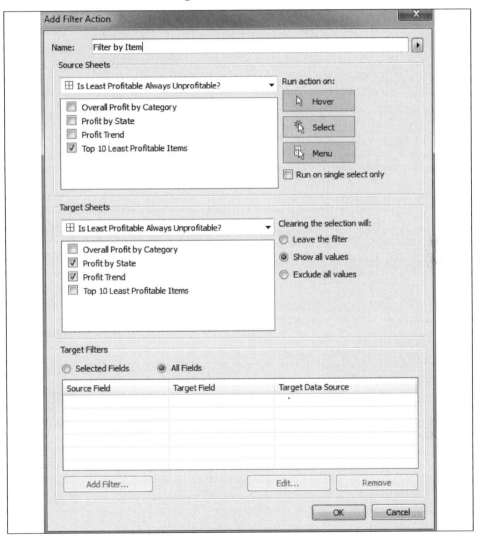

Figure 8.12: Setting options for the Filter by Item action

You now have three filters (two are actions) that drive the dashboard:

- Selecting a department from the drop-down will filter the entire dashboard (and actually all views in the workbook as you set it to filter every view using the data source)

- Selecting a category (clicking a bar or header) will filter the entire dashboard to that selection

- Selecting an item (clicking a bar or header) will filter the **Profit by State** and **Profit Trend** dashboards

> You can clear a selection in a view by clicking a blank area or by clicking the selected mark one more time. For example, if you click the bar for **Bookcases** to select it (and thus filter the rest of the dashboard), you may click the bar one more time to deselect it.

Experiment with the filters and actions to see how your dashboard functions.

Context filtering

You may have noticed that when you use the drop-down filter to select a single department or select a single category, you have fewer than 10 items in the Top 10 view. For example, selecting **Furniture** from the **Department** filter and clicking on the bar for **Tables** results in only three items being shown. This is because the **Top Item** filter is evaluated at the same time as the action filter. There are only three items with the category of **Tables** that are also in the **Top 10**.

What if you want to see the top 10 items within the category of **Tables**? You can accomplish this using context filters.

> **Context filters** are a special kind of filter in Tableau that are applied before other filters. Other filters are then applied within the context of the context filters. Conceptually, context filters result in a subset of data upon which other filters and calculations operate. In addition to **Top Filters**, **Computed Sets** and **Fixed Level of Detail** calculations are also computed within the context defined by context filters.

In this case, navigate to the **Top 10** sheet and add the **Department** filter and the newly added action **(Category)** filter to the context using the drop-down menu of the fields on the **Filters** shelf. Once added to the context, those fields will be gray on the filters shelf. Now, you will see the top 10 items within the context of the selected department and category:

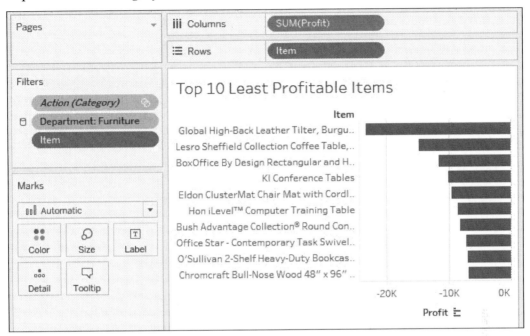

Figure 8.13: The 10 least profitable items will be within the context of the Action (Category) and Department filters

Notice that adding filters to the context causes the fields to be color-coded gray on the **Filters** shelf.

If you edit the action on the dashboard, the filter might be automatically updated and you may have to re-add it to the context.

Go ahead and step through the actions by selecting a couple of different categories and a couple of different items. Observe how the final dashboard meets your objectives by telling a story:

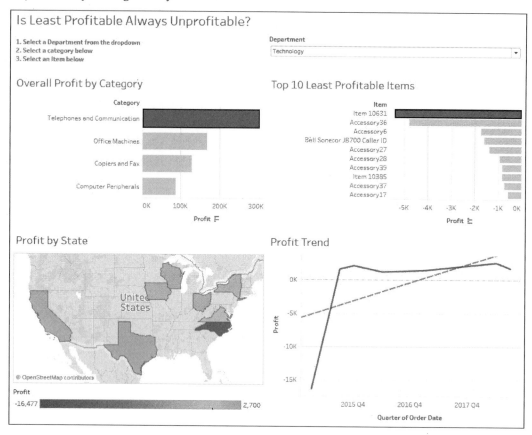

Figure 8.14: The final dashboard with filters triggered by selection

The user has selected **Technology** from the **Department** drop-down, **Telephones and Communications** from the **Category** list, and then **Item 10631**, which is the least profitable item within the category. This reveals the states where the item was sold (color-coded by profit) and a time series of profit for the item.

Should management remove item 10631 from the inventory? Not without first considering that the item only lost profit in one instance and that the trend is positive toward greater profitability. Granted, the original loss was a large loss, but this was also a long time ago and every subsequent sale of the item resulted in a gain. The results of your findings may lead to further analysis to determine what factors play a part in the profit and loss for the item and better decision making by management.

When you look at the `Chapter 08 Completed` workbook, you'll only see a tab at the bottom for the dashboard. The individual views have been hidden. Hiding tabs for sheets that are used in dashboards or stories is a great way to keep your workbook clean and guide your audience away from looking at sheets that are meant to be seen in the context of a dashboard or story. To hide a sheet, right-click the tab and select **Hide Sheet**. To unhide a sheet, navigate to the dashboard or story using the sheet, right-click the sheet in the left-hand side pane and uncheck **Hide Sheet**. Additionally, you can hide or unhide all sheets that are used in a dashboard by right-clicking the dashboard tab and selecting the appropriate option. Sheets that are used in tooltips may be hidden or unhidden in the same way.

You now have a fully interactive dashboard! You built the views, added them to the dashboard, and then created some meaningful calculations. Along the way, you learned about **top filters** and **context filters**. Now, let's consider how you might design dashboards for different displays and devices.

Designing for different displays and devices

When designing a dashboard, some of the first questions you'll often ask yourself are: *How will my audience view this dashboard? What kind of device will they use?* With the wide adoption of mobile devices, this latter question becomes very important because what looks great on a large flat-screen monitor doesn't always look great on a tablet or phone.

The top of the **Dashboard** tab on the left sidebar reveals a button to preview the dashboard on various devices, as well as a drop-down for **Size** options:

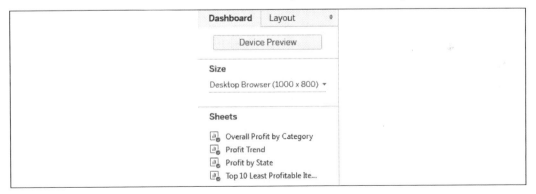

Figure 8.15: The Device Preview option allows you to design and preview your dashboard for other devices

Clicking the **Device Preview** button not only allows you to see how your dashboard will look with various device types (and even specific models) but also allows you to add a layout for each device type, which you can customize:

Figure 8.16: Customizable options for devices

You can not only see how your dashboard will appear on various devices and models but also how it will look based on the orientation of the device and whether the Tableau Mobile app is used (if available for the selected device).

Clicking the **Add Layout** button (that is, the **Add Tablet Layout** button in the preceding screenshot) will add a layout under the **Dashboard** tab on the left sidebar:

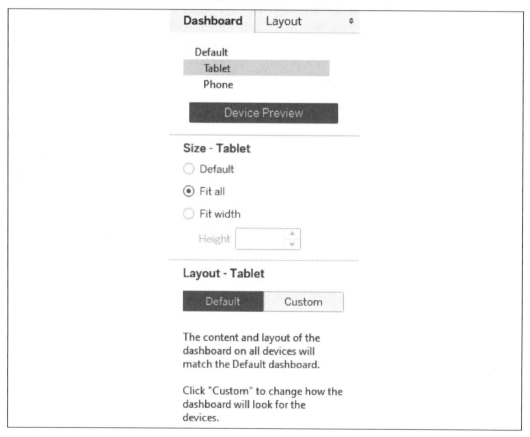

Figure 8.17: Each layout can be configured with various options

Each layout can have its own size and fit options, and the layout options allow you to switch from **Default** to **Custom**. This gives you the ability to rearrange the dashboard for any given layout. You may even remove views and objects for a certain layout. For example, you might simplify a dashboard to one or two views for a phone while leaving three or four in place for a desktop display.

The `Chapter 08 Completed` workbook contains an example of the profit analysis dashboard and has a couple of layout options. For example, here is that dashboard formatted for display on a phone in which the dashboard will fit according to the width of the phone and allow scrolling up and down:

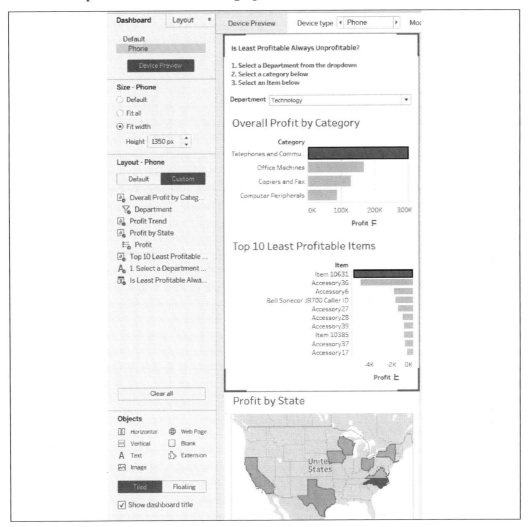

Figure 8.18: The phone layout of the dashboard

As you can see, the arrangement of the dashboard for the phone means that **Profit by State** and **Profit Trend** do not appear within the preview boundaries for a phone device. However, they are only a finger swipe away.

Interactivity with actions

In Tableau, an **action** is a user-initiated event that triggers a response from Tableau. You've seen a few examples of actions being used in dashboards already. We'll now consider some details of how actions work in Tableau.

Tableau supports six kinds of actions:

- **Filter actions**: The user's action causes one or more filters to be applied to one or more views.
- **Highlight actions**: The user's action causes specific marks and headers to be highlighted in one or more views.
- **URL actions**: The user's action causes a specific URL to be opened (either in a browser, a new tab, or in an embedded web object).
- **Go to Sheet**: The user's action causes navigation to a selected sheet or dashboard.
- **Parameter actions**: The user's action changes the value of a parameter. This allows the user to visually interact with parameters in new and exciting ways!
- **Set actions**: The user's action defines a set. Sets may be used in calculations, filters, and on shelves to define visual attributes of marks. This opens a lot of possibilities to allow complex and creative interactions.

Certain actions are automatically generated by Tableau based on shortcuts. For example, you can select **Use as Filter** from the drop-down menu of a view on a dashboard, which results in an automatically generated filter action. Enabling highlighting using the button on a discrete color legend or from the toolbar will automatically generate a highlight action:

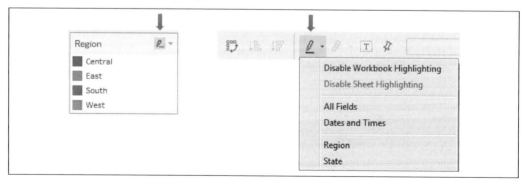

Figure 8.19: Options for enabling highlighting

You can also create or edit dashboard actions by selecting **Dashboard | Actions** from the menu. Let's consider the details of each type of action.

Filter actions

Filter actions are defined by one or more source sheets that pass one or more dimensional values as filters to target sheets upon an action. Remember that every mark on a sheet is defined by a unique intersection of dimensional values. When an action occurs involving one or more of those marks, the dimensional values that comprise the mark(s) can be passed as filters to one or more target sheets.

When you create or edit a filter action, you will see options like these:

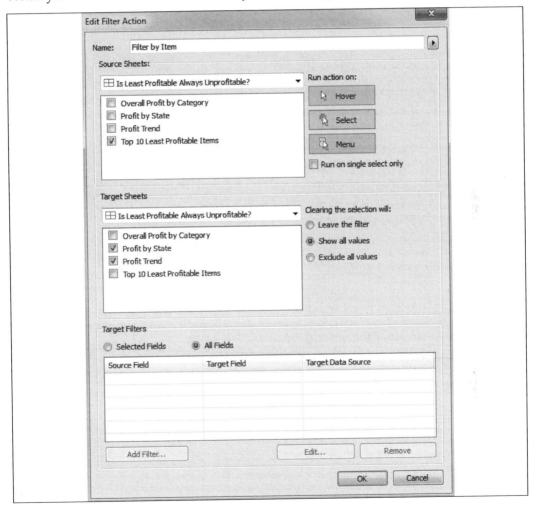

Figure 8.20: Options for filter actions

This screen allows you to do the following:

- Name the filter.

- Choose **Source** and **Target** sheets. The **Source** sheet is where the user will initiate the action (hover, selection, menu) and the **Target** sheet is where the response will be applied (filtering in this example, but also highlighting).

- Set the action that triggers the filter and whether the selection of multiple marks or only a single mark initiates the action.

- Choose what happens when the selection is cleared.

- Specify which dimensions are used to pass filter values to the **Target** sheet(s).

Try to name your actions using names that help you differentiate between multiple actions in the dashboard. Additionally, if your action is set to run on **Menu**, then the name you use will be shown as a link in the tooltip. Use the arrow to the right of the name to insert special field placeholders. These will be dynamically updated with the values of the fields for a mark when the user sees the menu option in a tooltip.

You may select as many source and target sheets as you desire. However, if you specify particular **Target filters** in the bottom section, the fields you select must be present in the source sheet (for example, on **Rows, Columns**, and **Detail**). You will receive a warning if a field is not available for one or more **Source** sheets and the action will not be triggered for those sheets. Most of the time, your source and target will be the same dashboard. Optionally, you can specify a different target sheet or dashboard, which will cause the action to navigate to the target in addition to filtering.

When filter actions are defined at the worksheet level (when viewing a worksheet, select **Worksheet | Actions** from the menu), a menu item for that action will appear as menu items for every mark on every sheet that uses the same data source. You can use this to quickly create navigation between worksheets and from dashboards to individual worksheets.

Filter actions can be set to occur on any one of three possible actions:

- **Hover**: The user moves the mouse cursor over a mark (or taps a mark on a mobile device).

- **Select**: The user clicks or taps a mark, and a rectangle/radial/lasso selects multiple marks by clicking and dragging a rectangle around them and clicks a header (in which case all marks for that header are selected). A user may deselect by clicking/tapping the already selected mark, clicking/tapping an empty space in the view, or by clicking/tapping the already selected header.

- **Menu**: The user selects the menu option for the action on the tooltip.

Consider the following example of a filter action that's triggered when a bar is selected in the source:

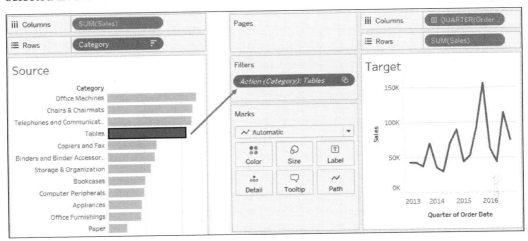

Figure 8.21: Clicking the bar for Tables passes Category as a filter to the Target sheet

Each bar mark in the source is defined by the **Category** dimension. When the bar for **Tables** is selected, a single filter is set on the target.

If the mark is defined by more than one dimension (for example, **Category** and **Region**), then the target sheet will still have a single filter with the combination of dimension values that had been selected.

In this example, the filter contains **Office Machines** and **West**, matching the dimensions that define the selected square:

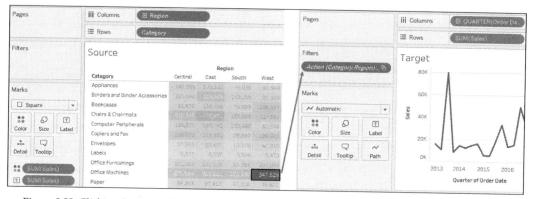

Figure 8.22: Clicking the square for the intersection of Office Machines and West passes both dimensional values as a single action filter to the target

By default, all dimensions present in the source view are used in a filter action. Optionally, you can specify which fields should be used. You can use the **Selected Fields** option in the **Edit Filter Actions** dialog to accomplish the following:

- Filter based on fewer dimensions. For example, if you only selected the **Region** field, then selecting the preceding square would only pass the West region as a filter to the target.

- Filter a target view using a different data source. The **Selected Fields** option allows you to map the source field to a target field (even if the target field has a different name, though the values must still match). For example, if the target used a data source where **East** was a possible value for a field named **Area**, you could map **Region** from the source to **Area** in the target.

Filter actions are very useful for narrowing focus, drilling into detail, and seeing different aspects of a selected dimension. You'll find yourself using them often. Let's consider another type of action: highlight actions.

Highlight actions

This type of action does not filter target sheets. Instead, **highlight actions** cause marks that are defined, at least in part, by the selected dimensional value(s) to be highlighted in the target sheets. The options for highlight actions are very similar to filter actions, with the same configuration options for source and target sheets, and which events are able to trigger the action.

Consider a dashboard with three views and a highlight action based on the **Region** field. When the action is triggered for the **East** region, all marks defined by **East** are highlighted. The dimension(s) that are used for the highlight must be present in all views where you want the highlighting to be applied. Both the map and scatter plot have **Region** on the *Detail* part of the *Marks* card:

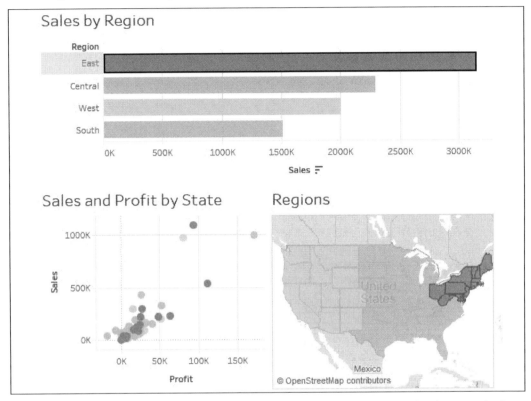

Figure 8.23: Clicking the bar for East has highlighted all other marks associated with that dimensional value

Highlighters (also called **data highlighters**) are shown as user controls (similar to filters and parameters) that cause highlighting based on user interaction. They can be applied to one or more views and will highlight the marks of the views. They do not create an action. To add highlighters, select any discrete (blue) field in the view and use the drop-down menu to click **Show Highlighter**. Alternatively, you can use the menu and select **Analysis | Highlighters**. On a dashboard, you can add a highlighter by using a view's drop-down menu and selecting **Highlighters**.

URL actions

URL actions allow you to dynamically generate a URL based on an action and open it within a web object in the dashboard or in a new browser window or tab. URL actions can be triggered by the same hover, menu, and select events as other actions. The name of the URL action differentiates it and will appear as the link when used as a menu.

The URL includes any hardcoded values you enter as well as placeholders that are accessible via the arrow to the right of the URL text box. These placeholders include fields and parameters. The values will be dynamically inserted into the URL string when the action is triggered based on the values for the fields that make up the selected mark(s) and current values for parameters.

If you have included a web object in the dashboard, the URL action will automatically use that as the target. Otherwise, the action opens a new browser window (using your default browser, when the dashboard is viewed in desktop or reader) or a new tab (when the dashboard is viewed in a web browser).

 Some web pages have different behaviors when viewed in iframes. The browser object does not use iframes in Tableau Desktop or Tableau Reader but does when the dashboard is published to Tableau Server, Tableau Online, or Tableau Public. You will want to test URL actions based on how your dashboards will be viewed by your audience.

You may specify a target for the URL action when you create or edit the URL action:

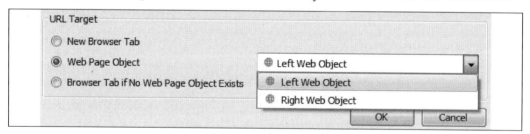

Figure 8.24: Options for a URL action

Options include **New Browser Tab**, **Web Page Object** (you may select which object if you have more than one on the dashboard), and **Browser Tab if No Web Page Object Exists**. If you have more than one web page object on the dashboard, you may wish to give them meaningful names to make selection easier.

To accomplish this, switch to the **Layout** tab on the left-hand side pane and expand **Item hierarchy** until you locate the objects you wish to rename. Right-click the object and select **Rename Dashboard Item...**:

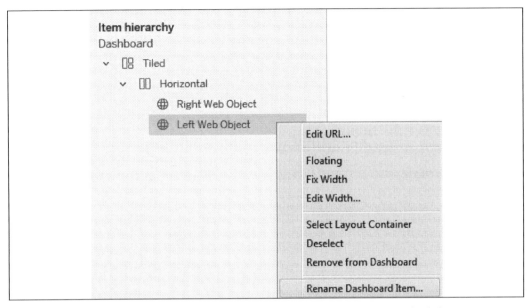

Figure 8.25: Dashboard objects can be renamed using the item hierarchy and the right-click context menu

After you have renamed the object, you will be able to more readily identify which one is the target of the URL action.

Next, we'll consider another type of action that accomplishes a specific result: navigation.

Go to Sheet actions

Go to Sheet actions (also called navigation actions) allow you to specify navigation to another dashboard or sheet in the workbook based on user interaction with one or more views. For example, clicking a bar in a bar chart might navigate to another dashboard. These are similar to filter actions that define another sheet as a target, but Go to Sheet actions do not set any filters.

Parameter actions

Parameter actions allow you to set the value of a parameter based on a user action. When you create a parameter action, you'll set options using a screen like this:

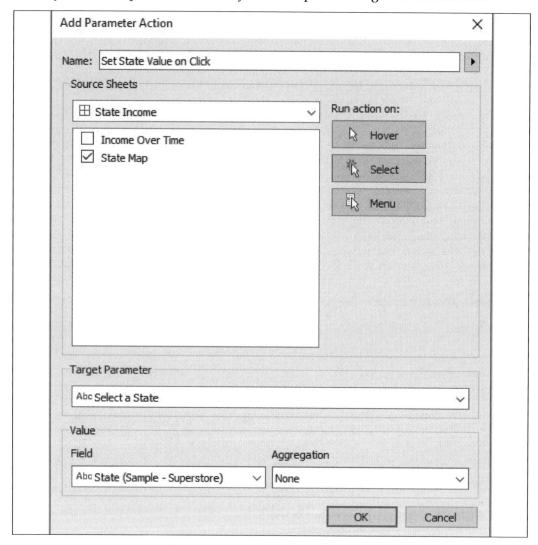

Figure 8.26: Options for a parameter action

As with other actions, you may select the sheets and user interactions (**Hover, Select, Menu**) that trigger the action. Additionally, you will set the target parameter and specify which field will set the value. You may use any field in the sheet and may also specify an aggregation for the field.

We saw in *Chapter 4, Starting an Adventure with Calculations and Parameters,* how parameters can be used to accomplish all kinds of results. You can use them in calculations, filters, and **Top N** sets, and you can use them to define reference lines and alter the visual aspects of any view. This opens a world of possibilities for driving an interactive experience using views and triggers.

Set actions

Set actions allow you to populate a set with one or more values for one or more dimensions. This is very powerful because sets can be used on any shelf to encode any visual element, can be leveraged in calculations, and can be used as filters. They can be used in all of these ways—and in different ways—in different views. This gives you incredible flexibility in what can be accomplished with set actions. We'll first take a moment to define sets more clearly and then look at an example of a set action.

Sets

A **set** in Tableau defines a collection of records from the data source. At a row-level, each record is either in or out of the set. There are two types of sets:

- Dynamic sets (sometimes called computed or calculated sets)
- Fixed sets

A **dynamic set** is computed for a single dimension based on a conditional calculation you define. As the data changes, the results of the condition may change and records may switch between in and out of the set.

For example, if you were to use the drop-down menu on **Customer Name** in the data pane and select **Create | Set**, then you could stipulate a condition that defines which records belong to the set:

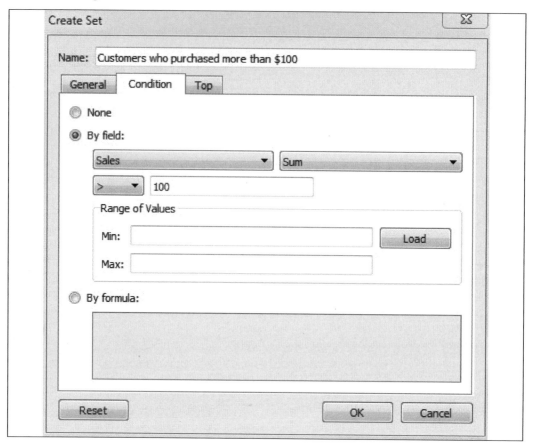

Figure 8.27: A dynamic set based on a condition

In this example, we've created a dynamic set named **Customers who purchased more than $100** with a condition that's set by the sum of sales being greater than **100**. You'll notice that there are also options for computing **By formula** or **Top** N. All of these conditions are going to be at an aggregate level (across the entire dataset or across the context if context filters are used) and then each record is evaluated as to whether it is in or out of the set. In this case, the total sales for each customer will be computed across the dataset and then each record will be counted in or out of the set based on whether the customer for that record has total sales greater than $100.

A **fixed set** is a list of values for one or more dimensions. If the values for a single record match the list defined by the set, then the record is in the set, and out otherwise. For example, you might create another set based on the **Customer Name** field, this time with the **General** tab:

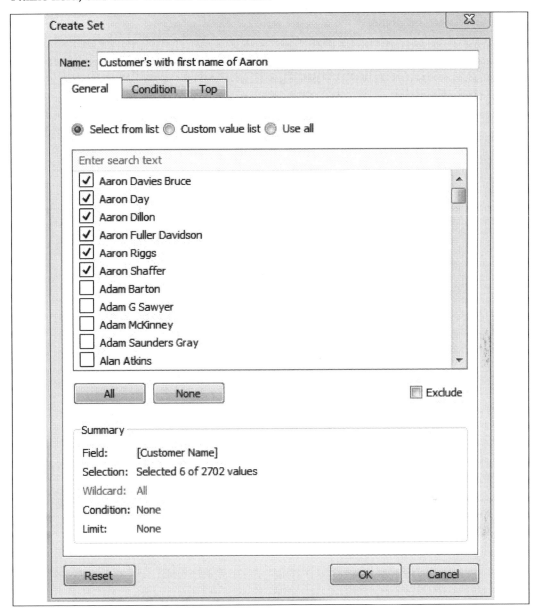

Figure 8.28: A static set based on the selection of members

Here, you can select individual values that will define what is in or out of the set. Note the option to exclude rather than include values. In this case, we've created a set named **Customers with first name of Aaron**. Any records that have a **Customer Name** value that matches one of the **6** values we selected will be in the set. All others will be out. Because this is a fixed set, the values are not ever calculated or recalculated. If records with a customer named Aaron Burr show up in the dataset next week, they will still be out of the set.

As we'll see in the following example, set actions operate on fixed sets.

A set action example

You'll find an example of a set action in the Chapter 08 Complete.twbx workbook in the dashboard named Sales by Region and Category (set actions), which looks like this:

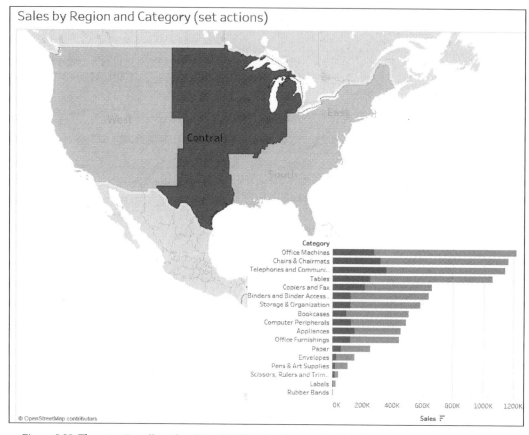

Figure 8.29: The set action allows brushing: highlighting the portion of the bars that belong to the selection

The dashboard consists of two views: a map and a bar chart. Selecting a region on the map triggers a set action that updates the bar chart. A filter action would filter the bar chart, causing the length of each bar to only show the value for the selected region. Here, however, the set action is used to show the portion of the overall bar that belongs to that region while still retaining the full length of the bar for all regions.

To replicate this interactivity, follow these steps:

1. Use the drop-down menu on the **Region** field under **Dimensions** on the data pane to select **Create | Set**. Name the set **Region Set**.

2. In the resulting **Create Set** dialog, under the **General** tab, check one or more values. This creates a fixed set. In this example, it does not matter which, if any, values you select because you'll configure the set action to update the values momentarily.

3. Create a bar chart of **Sales by Category**.

4. Drag **Region Set** from **Sets** on the data pane and drop it on **Color**:

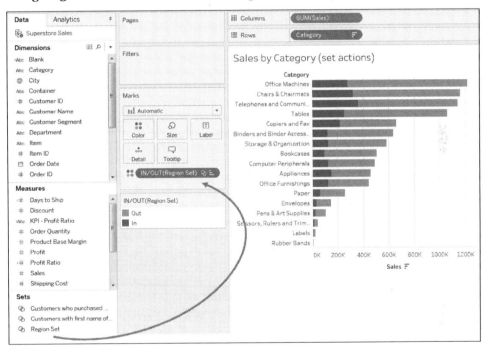

Figure 8.30: Drag and drop the set on Color to show the difference
between In and Out of the set

You may use a set on shelves, just as you would any other field. Notice how the set gives two values, that is, **In** and **Out**, which define two colors. You may wish to adjust the colors to emphasize **In**.

> You may use sets in calculated fields as well. For example, the code [Region Set] gives a Boolean true/false result for each record, indicating whether it is in the set.

Conclude the set action example by creating a region map, the dashboard, and implementing the set action:

5. Use the drop-down menu on **Region** to select **Geographic Role | Create from... | State**. This tells Tableau to treat **Region** as a geographic field based on its relationship with the geographic field **State**.

6. In a new, blank view, double-click the **Region** field to create the map view. Now that **Region** is recognized as a geographic field, Tableau will generate latitude, longitude, and the geometries that are necessary to render the shapes.

7. Add both the map and bar chart views to a single dashboard. You may position them however you'd like.

8. Add a set action by selecting **Dashboard | Actions** from the menu and then **Add Action | Change Set Values...** in the resulting dialog. The resulting dialog has many similar features to other action types:

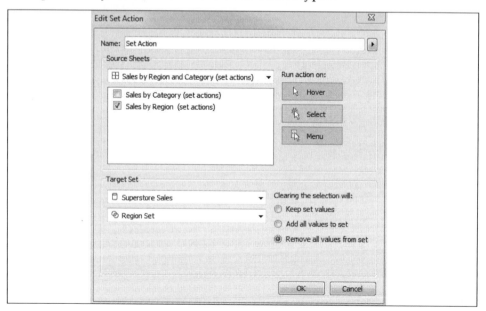

Figure 8.31: Options for the set action

You'll notice options to give the action values for **Name**; **Run action on: Hover**, **Select**, or **Menu**; and options for **Clearing the selection**. Just like other action types, you may also specify **Source** sheets that trigger the action. **Target Set** allows you to specify which data source and which fixed set in that data source will have values updated based on the action. In this case, we want to update **Region Set** when a selection is made on the **Sales by Region (set actions)** view. We'll elect to remove all values from the set when the selection is cleared.

Once you have created the preceding action, your dashboard should function very similarly to the example that was shown at the beginning of this section. Selecting a region on the map highlights the portion of the bars that correspond to that region. This technique is known as **brushing**, or **proportional brushing**.

This technique is only one of hundreds of the possible applications of set actions. Since sets can be used on any shelf and in calculations, updating the values via set actions opens up almost limitless possibilities for user interaction and analytics.

Having looked at the various kinds of actions, let's move on to consider another example of a different kind of dashboard.

A regional scorecard dashboard

Now, we'll consider another example dashboard that demonstrates slightly different objectives. Let's say everyone in the organization has agreed upon a KPI of profit ratio. Furthermore, there is consensus that the cut-off point between an acceptable and poor profit ratio is 15%, but management would like to have the option of adjusting the value dynamically to see whether other targets might be better.

Consider the following dashboard:

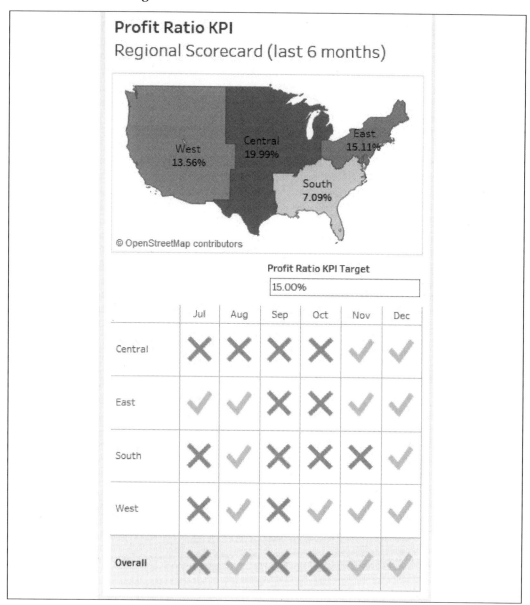

Figure 8.32: A simple profit KPI dashboard

This dashboard allows your audience to very quickly evaluate the performance of each region over the last six months. Executive management could very quickly pull this dashboard up on their mobile devices and take appropriate action as needed.

The dashboard provides interactivity with the KPI target parameter. Additional drill-down capability into other dashboards or views could be provided if desired. If this view were published on Tableau Server, it is not unreasonable to think that regional managers might subscribe to the view and receive a scheduled email containing an up-to-date image of this dashboard.

Let's consider how to create a similar dashboard:

1. Create a float type parameter named `Profit Ratio KPI Target` set to an initial .15, formatted as a percentage.

2. Create a calculation named `Profit Ratio` with the code `SUM([Profit]) / SUM([Sales])`. This is an aggregate calculation that will divide the profit total by the sum of sales at the level of detail defined in the view.

3. Create a second calculation named `KPI - Profit Ratio` with the following code:

   ```
   IF [Profit Ratio] >= [Profit Ratio KPI Target]
   THEN "Acceptable"
   ELSE "Poor"
   END
   ```

   This code will compare the profit ratio to the parameterized cut-off value. Anything equal to or above the cut-off point will get the value of `Acceptable`, and everything below will get the value of `Poor`.

4. Create a new sheet named **Region Scorecard**. The view consists of `Region` on **Rows**, `Order Date` as a discrete date part on **Columns**, and the `KPI - Profit Ratio` field on both shape and color. You'll observe that the shapes have been edited to use checkmarks and Xs, and that the color palette is using colorblind-safe blue and orange.

5. Add column grand totals using the **Analytics** pane and format the grand totals with a custom label of **Overall**, with bold font and light gray shading.

6. Add **Order Date** as a filter and set it to the top 6 by field (**Order Date** as **Min**). This will dynamically filter the view to the last six months:

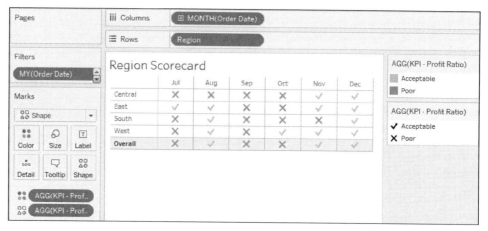

Figure 8.33: This view defines the Region scorecard showing Acceptable versus Poor results per region per month

7. Create another sheet named **Profit Ratio by Region**.

8. If you skipped the set actions example, use the drop-down menu on Region to select **Geographic Role | Create from... | State**. This tells Tableau to treat **Region** as a geographic field based on its relationship with the geographic field **State**.

9. Double-click the **Region** field in the data pane. Tableau will automatically generate a geographic visualization based on **Region**. We'll examine the creation of custom geographies in more detail in *Chapter 12, Exploring Mapping and Advanced Geospatial Features*.

10. Place **Profit Ratio** on **Color** and **Label**. You will also want to format **Profit Ratio** as a percentage. You may do so by formatting the field in this view specifically, or by setting the default number format for the field in the data pane (the latter is probably preferred as you will almost always want it to display as a percentage).

11. Additionally, add **Region** to **Label**. Rearrange the fields in the marks card to reorder the label or click the **Label** shelf to edit the label text directly.

12. Apply the same filter to this view as you did to the **Region Scorecard** view. You may wish to navigate to the **Region Scorecard** sheet and use the drop-down on **Order Date** on the **Filters** shelf to apply the existing filter to multiple sheets:

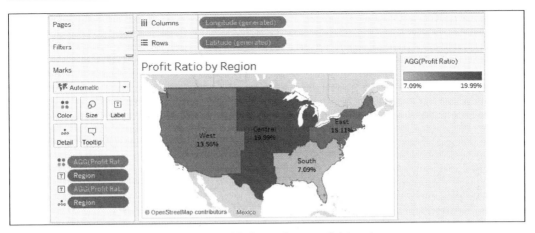

Figure 8.34: The filled map shows profit by region

Once both views have been created, you can arrange the views as a dashboard. The example in the Chapter 08 Complete workbook has a phone layout applied to it as seen here:

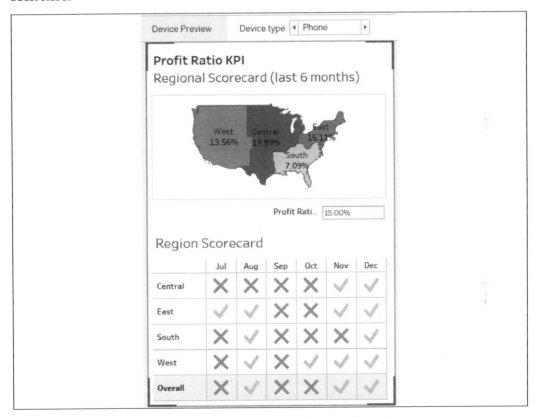

Figure 8.35: A phone layout for the KPI dashboard

Experiment with various layouts and positioning of the elements.

By default, all objects that are added to the dashboard are tiled. **Tiled** objects snap in place and appear beneath **floating** objects. Any object can be added to the dashboard as a floating object by switching the toggle under **New Objects** in the left window, or by holding *Shift* while dragging the objects to the dashboard.

Existing objects can be switched between floating and tiled by holding *Shift* while moving the object or using the drop-down caret menu. The drop-down caret menu also gives you options for adjusting the floating order of objects. Additionally, floating objects can be resized and positioned with pixel precision by selecting the floating object and using the positioning and sizing controls in the lower left.

You can mix tiled and floating elements, but many dashboard authors prefer to build dashboards that are composed entirely of one or the other. This ensures consistency between different layouts and sizes of screens (especially if the dashboard is set to an **Automatic** or **Range** sizing option).

This example illustrates a dashboard used for quick lookup and rapid decision making. What if we want to tell a more complex story and show progression of detail and maybe even present the data story in a specific order? Let's consider how to leverage a feature of Tableau designed specifically for that purpose.

Stories

The **stories** feature allows you to tell a story using interactive snapshots of dashboards and views. The snapshots become points in a story. This allows you to construct a guided narrative or even an entire presentation.

Let's consider an example in which story points might be useful. The executive managers are pleased with the **Regional Scorecard** dashboard you developed previously. Now, they want you to make a presentation to the board and highlight some specific issues for the South region. With minimal effort, you can take your simple scorecard, add a few additional views, and tell an entire story:

1. First, we'll build a couple of additional views. Create a simple geographic view named `ProfitRatio KPI by State`. Make this a filled map with the **KPI – Profit Ratio** field, defining color.

2. Add **Profit Ratio** to the **Detail** part of the **Marks** card so that it is available for later use:

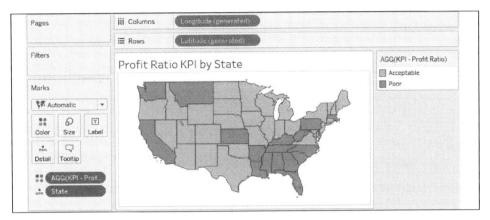

Figure 8.36: Profit Ratio KPI by State uses color encoding to show Acceptable versus Poor

3. Create one additional view named `Profit Ratio by Quarter`. Use **Order Date** as a continuous date value on **Columns** and **Profit Ratio** on **Rows**.

4. Set the mark type to bars. Add a reference line for the **Profit Ratio KPI Target** parameter value (you can right-click the **Profit Ratio** axis and set it to **Add Reference Line...**).

5. Add **KPI – Profit Ratio** to **Color**. You may also wish to click the **Color** shelf and add a border.

6. Go ahead and filter the view to the South region and use the drop-down menu to apply that filter to the **Profit Ratio KPI by State** view as well:

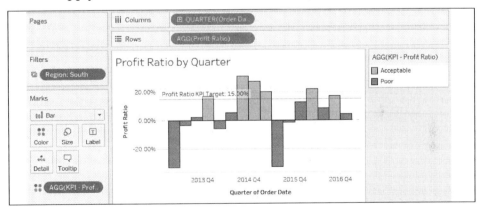

Figure 8.37: Profit Ratio by Quarter shows whether a given quarter was
Acceptable or Poor based on the target

7. Create a new dashboard with the two new views arranged in the same way as what's shown in the following screenshot. Add the **Profit Ratio KPI Target** parameter and **Region** filter if they do not show.

8. Use the drop-down on **Profit Ratio KPI by State** to use that view as a filter:

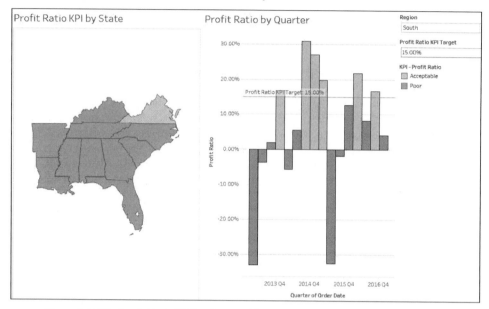

Figure 8.38: The Profit Ratio KPI by State and by Quarter views on the same dashboard

9. Create a new story by selecting **Story | New Story** from the menu, or by using the new story tab at the bottom next to the existing sheets:

The **Story** interface consists of a sidebar with all visible dashboards and views. At the top, you'll see the story title, which can be edited via a double-click. Each new point in the story will appear as a navigation box with text that can also be edited. Clicking on the box will give you access to the story point, where you can then add a single dashboard or view.

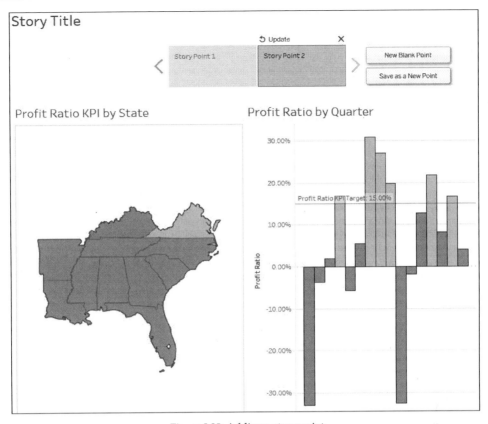

Figure 8.39: Adding a story point

You can create new story points using the **New Blank Point** button (for a new story point), the **Duplicate** button (which will create a duplicate snapshot of the currently selected story point), or the **Save as New Point** button (which will capture the current state of the dashboard as a new story point).

Clicking on a story point navigation box will bring up the snapshot of the view or dashboard for that story point. You may interact with the dashboard by doing such things as making selections, changing filters, changing parameter values, and adding annotations. Changing any aspect of the dashboard will present you with an option to update the existing story point to the current state of the dashboard. Alternatively, you can use the **Revert** button above the navigation box to return to the original state of the dashboard. Clicking **X** will remove the story point.

Each story point contains an entirely independent snapshot of a dashboard. Filter selections, parameter values, selections, and annotations will be remembered for a particular story point but will have no impact on other story points or any other sheet in the dashboard.

You may rearrange story points by dragging and dropping the navigation boxes.

We'll build the story by completing the following steps:

1. Give the story the title **South Region Analysis**.

2. Add the **Regional Scorecard** dashboard as the first story point. Select the **South** region in the map. Give the story point the following text: **The South Region has not performed well the last 6 months**:

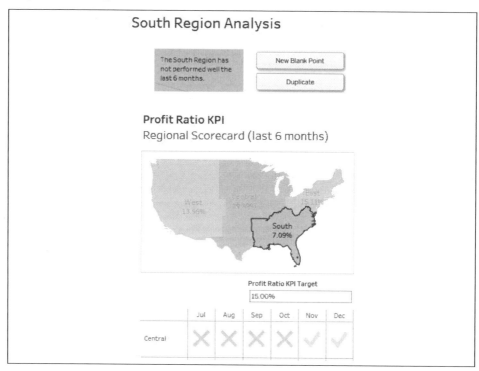

Figure 8.40: The first story point highlights performance in the South region

3. Click the **New Blank Point** button to create a new story point and add the **Profit Ratio Analysis** dashboard to the point.

4. Give this story point a caption of **Only one state has met the 15% target overall**.

5. Right-click **Virginia** on the map and select **Annotate | Mark**. Keep the state and profit ratio as part of the annotation:

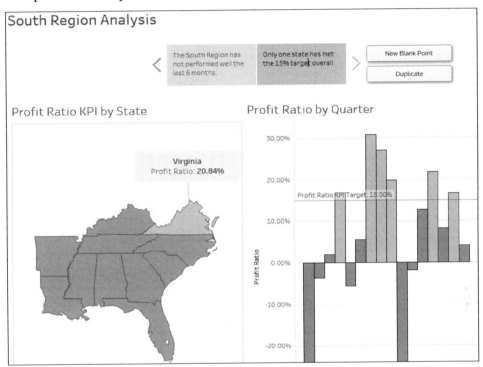

Figure 8.41: The second story point dives into the details

6. Click the **Duplicate** button to copy the current story point. Give this new story point a caption of **3 states would meet a goal of 10%**. Set **Profit Ratio KPI Target** to 10.00% and update the point.

7. Click the **Duplicate** button again and give the newly created point a caption of **Certain states have performed well historically**.

8. Right-click the annotation for Virginia, select **Remove** to delete it, and then add a similar annotation for **Louisiana**. Then, click **Louisiana** to select that state.

9. Make sure to click the **Update** button to capture the state of the dashboard.

In presentation mode, the buttons for adding, duplicating, updating, or removing story points are not shown. Your final story should look similar to this:

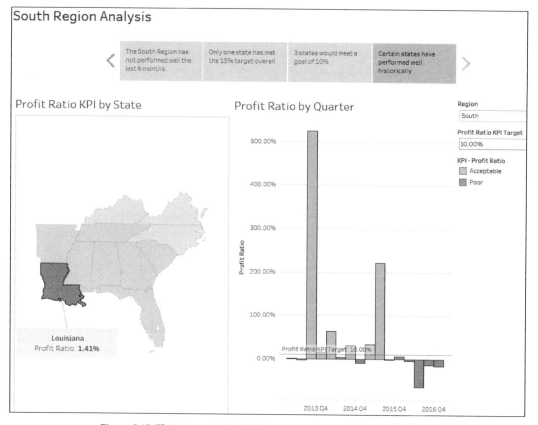

Figure 8.42: This story point highlights quarterly results for a single state

Take some time to walk through the presentation. Clicking navigation boxes will show that story point. You can fully interact with the dashboard in each story point. In this way, you can answer questions on the fly and dig into details, and then continue through the story.

 A great way to learn about dashboard techniques (and data visualization techniques in general) is to subscribe to *Viz of the Day* (http://www.tableau.com/public/community/viz-of-the-day). A new visualization, dashboard, or story is featured each day. When you see a design technique or visualization you want to understand, you can download the workbook and explore the various techniques that were used.

Summary

When you are ready to share your discovery and analysis, you will likely use dashboards to relate the story to your audience. The way in which you tell the story will depend on your objectives, as well as your audience and the mode of delivery. Using a combination of views, objects, parameters, filters, and legends, you can create an incredible framework for telling a data story. Tableau allows you to specifically design layouts for different devices to ensure that your audience has the best experience possible. By introducing actions and interactivity, you can invite your audience to participate in the story. Story points will allow you to bring together many snapshots of dashboards and views to craft and present entire narratives.

In the next chapter, we'll turn our attention to some deeper analysis involving trends, distributions, forecasting, and clustering.

9
Visual Analytics – Trends, Clustering, Distributions, and Forecasting

The rapid visual analysis that is possible using Tableau is incredibly useful for answering numerous questions and making key decisions. But it barely scratches the surface of the possible analysis. For example, a simple scatterplot can reveal outliers, but often, you want to understand the distribution or identify clusters of similar observations. A simple time series helps you to see the rise and fall of a measure over time, but often, you want to see the trend or make predictions for future values.

Tableau enables you to quickly enhance your data visualizations with statistical analysis. Built-in features such as trend models, clustering, distributions, and forecasting allow you to quickly add value to your visual analysis. Additionally, Tableau integrates with the R and Python platforms, which opens endless options for the manipulation and analysis of your data.

This chapter will cover the built-in statistical models and analysis, including the following topics:

- Trends
- Clustering
- Distributions
- Forecasting

We'll look at these concepts in the context of a few examples using some sample datasets. You can follow and reproduce these examples using the `Chapter 9` workbook.

When analyzing data that changes over time, understanding the overall nature of change is vitally important. Seeing and understanding trends is where we'll begin.

Trends

`World Population.xlsx` is included in the `Chapter 09` directory. It contains one record for each country for each year from **1960** to **2015**, measuring population. Using this dataset, let's take a look at the historical trends of various countries. Create a view similar to the one shown in the following screenshot, which shows the change in population over time for **Afghanistan** and **Australia**. You'll notice that **Country Name** has been filtered to include only **Afghanistan** and **Australia** and the field has additionally been added to the **Color** and **Label** shelves:

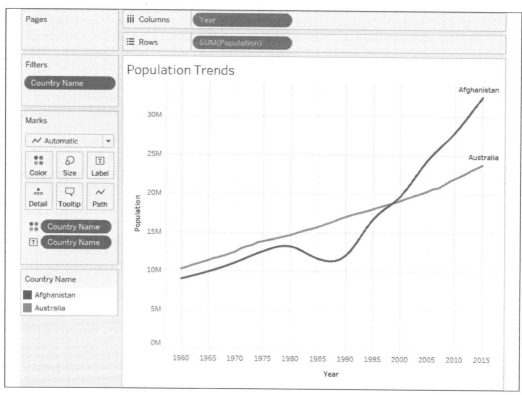

Figure 9.1: Population values for Afghanistan and Australia over time

From this visualization alone, you can make several interesting observations. The growth of the two countries' populations was fairly similar up to **1980**. At that point, the population of Afghanistan went into decline until **1988**, when it started to increase. At some point around **1996**, the population of Afghanistan exceeded that of Australia. The gap has grown wider ever since.

While we have a sense of the two trends, they become even more obvious when we see the trend lines. Tableau offers several ways of adding trend lines:

- From the menu, select **Analysis | Trend Lines | Show Trend Lines**.
- Right-click on an empty area in the pane of the view and select **Show Trend Lines**.
- Click on the **Analytics** tab on the left-hand sidebar to switch to the **Analytics** pane. Drag and drop **Trend Line** on the trend model of your choice (we'll use **Linear** in this example and discuss the others later in this chapter):

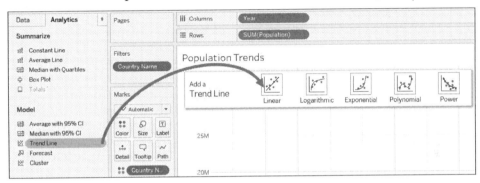

Figure 9.2: Adding a trend line to a view by dragging and dropping from the Analytics pane

Once you've added **Trend Line** to your view, you will see two trend lines: one for each country. We'll look at how we can customize the display shortly. For now, your view should look like this:

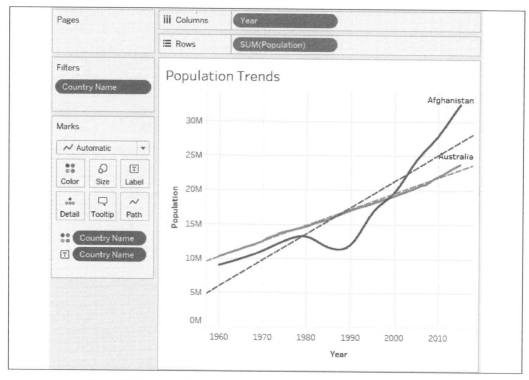

Figure 9.3: Each trend line shows the overall trend for the respective country

Trends are computed by Tableau after the query of the data source and are based on various elements in the view:

- **The two fields that define X and Y coordinates**: The fields on **Rows** and **Columns** that define the x and y axes describe coordinates, allowing Tableau to calculate various trend models. In order to show trend lines, you must use a continuous (green) field on both **Rows** and **Columns**. The only exception to this rule is that you may use a discrete (blue) **date** field. If you use a discrete **date** field to define headers, the other field must be a continuous field.

- **Additional fields that create multiple, distinct trend lines**: Discrete (blue) fields on the **Rows**, **Columns**, or **Color** shelves can be used as factors to split a single trend line into multiple, distinct trend lines.

- **The trend model selected**: We'll examine the differences in models in the next section, **Trend models**.

Observe in *Figure 9.3* that there are two trend lines. Since **Country Name** is a discrete (blue) field on **Color**, it defines a trend line per color by default.

Earlier, we observed that the population of Afghanistan increased and decreased within various historical periods. Note that the trend lines are calculated along the entire date range. What if we want to see different trend lines for those time periods?

One option is to simply select the marks in the view for the time period of interest. Tableau will, by default, calculate a trend line for the current selection. Here, for example, the points for Afghanistan from **1980** to **1988** have been selected and a new trend is displayed:

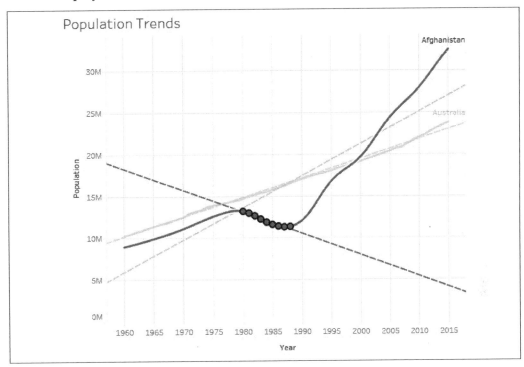

Figure 9.4: The default settings specify that trend lines will be drawn for selections

Another option is to instruct Tableau to draw distinct trend lines using a discrete field on **Rows**, **Columns**, or **Color**.

Go ahead and create a calculated field called **Period** that defines discrete values for the different historical periods using code like this:

```
IF [Year] <= 1979
   THEN "1960 to 1979"
ELSEIF [Year] <= 1988
   THEN "1980 to 1988"
ELSE "1988 to 2015"
END
```

When you place it on columns, you'll get a header for each time period, which breaks the lines and causes separate trends to be shown for each time period. You'll also observe that Tableau keeps the full date range in the axis for each period. You can set an independent range by right-clicking on one of the date axes, selecting **Edit Axis**, and then checking the option for **Independent axis range for each row or column**:

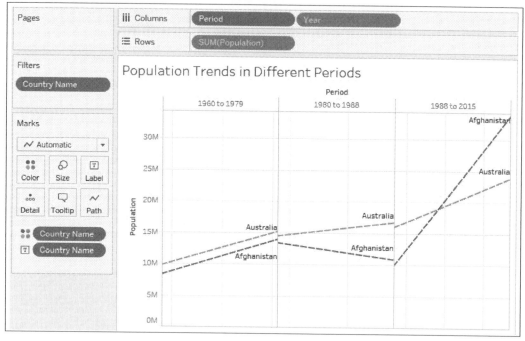

Figure 9.5: Here, the discrete dimension Period creates three separate time periods and a trend for each one

In this view, transparency has been applied to **Color** to help the trend lines stand out. Additionally, the axis for **Year** was hidden (by unchecking the **Show Header** option on the field). Now you can clearly see the difference in trends for different periods of time. Australia's trends only slightly change in each period. Afghanistan's trends vary considerably.

With an understanding of how to add trend lines to your visualization, let's dive a bit deeper to understand how to customize the trend lines and model.

Customizing trend lines

Let's examine another example that will allow us to consider various options for trend lines. Using the **Real Estate** data source, create a view like this one:

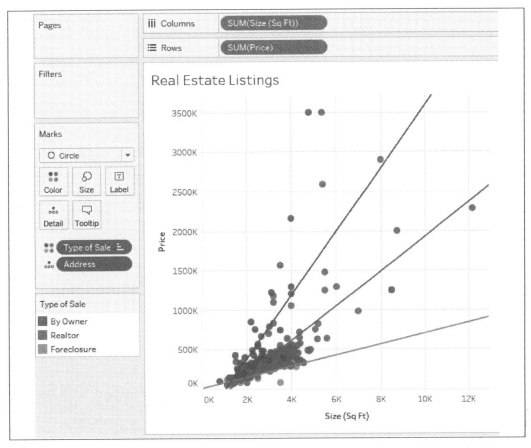

Figure 9.6: Trend lines on a scatterplot are often useful for better understanding correlation and outliers

Here, we've created a scatterplot with the sum of **Size (Sq Ft)** on **Columns** to define the *x* axis and the sum of **Price** on **Rows** to define the *y* axis. **Address** has been added to the **Detail** of the **Marks** card to define the level of aggregation. So, each mark on the scatterplot is a distinct address at a location defined by the size and price. **Type of Sale** has been placed on **Color**. Trend lines have been shown. As per Tableau's default settings, there are three: one trend line per color. The confidence bands have been hidden.

Assuming a good model, the trend lines demonstrate how much and how quickly **Price** is expected to rise in correlation with an increase in **Size** for each type of sale.

In this dataset, we have two fields, **Address** and **ID**, each of which defines a unique record. Adding one of those fields to the **Level of Detail** effectively disaggregates the data and allows us to plot a mark for each individual property. Sometimes, you may not have a dimension in the data that defines uniqueness. In those cases, you can disaggregate the data by unchecking **Aggregate Measures** from the **Analysis** menu.

Alternately, you can use the drop-down menu on each of the measure fields on rows and columns to change them from measures to dimensions while keeping them continuous. As dimensions, each individual value will define a mark. Keeping them continuous will retain the axes required for trend lines.

Let's consider some of the options available for trend lines. You can edit trend lines by using the menu and selecting **Analysis | Trend Lines | Edit Trend Lines...** or by right-clicking on a trend line and then selecting **Edit Trend Lines....** When you do, you'll see a dialog box like this:

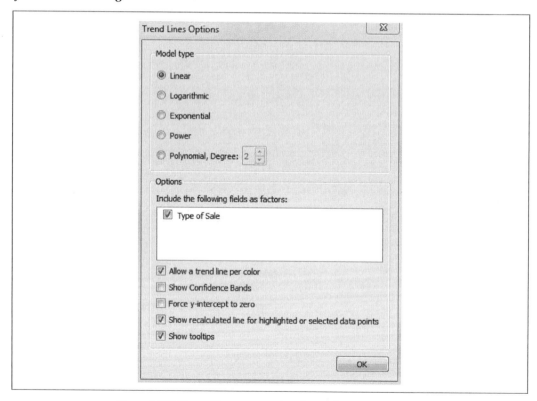

Figure 9.7: Tableau offers many options for configuring trend lines

Here, you have options for selecting a **Model type**; selecting applicable fields as factors in the model; allowing discrete colors to define distinct trend lines; showing **Confidence Bands**; forcing the y-intercept to zero; showing recalculated trends for selected marks; and showing **tooltips** for the trend line. We'll examine these options in further detail.

> You should only force the y-intercept to zero if you know that it must be zero. With this data, it is almost certainly not zero (that is, there are no houses in existence that are 0 square feet that are listed for $0).

For now, experiment with the options. Notice how either removing the **Type of Sale** field as a factor or unchecking the **Allow a trend line per color** option results in a single trend line.

You can also see the result of excluding a field as a factor in the following view where **Type of Sale** has been added to **Rows**:

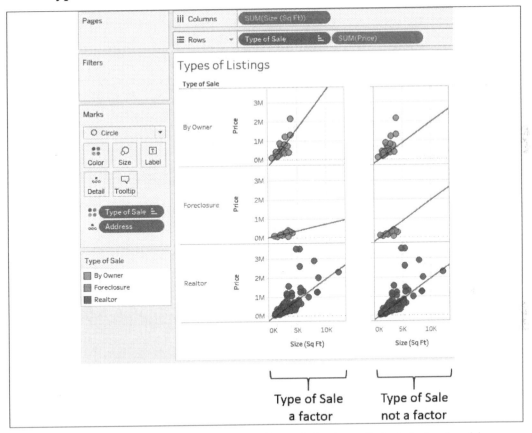

Figure 9.8: Including a field as a factor tells Tableau whether it contributes to the trend model

As represented in the left-hand portion of the preceding screenshot, **Type of Sale** is included as a factor. This results in a distinct trend line for each type of sale. When **Type of Sale** is excluded as a factor, the same trend line (which is the overall trend for all types) is drawn three times. This technique can be quite useful for comparing subsets of data to the overall trend.

Customizing the trend lines is only one aspect of using trends to understand the data. Also, of significant importance is the trend model itself, which we'll consider customizing in the next section.

Trend models

Let's return to the original view and stick with a single trend line as we consider the trend models that are available in Tableau. The following models can be selected from the **Trend Line Options** window.

Linear

We'd use a linear model if we assumed that, as **Size** increases, **Price** will increase at a constant rate. No matter how much **Size** increased, we'd expect **Price** to increase so that new data points fall close to the straight line:

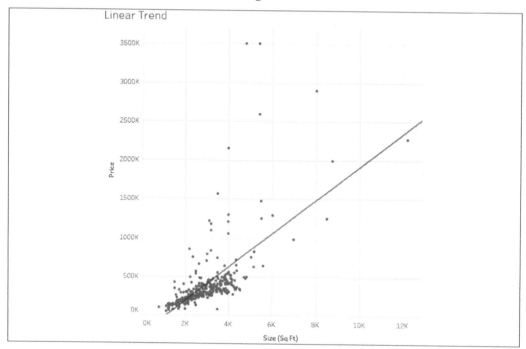

Figure 9.9: Linear trend

Logarithmic

We'd employ a logarithmic model if we expected the **law of diminishing returns** in effect — that is, the size can only increase so much before buyers will stop paying much more:

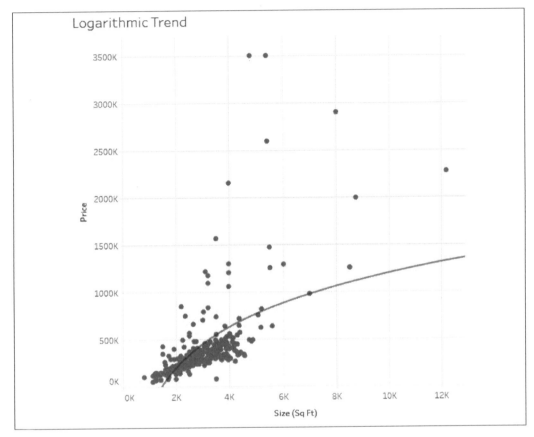

Figure 9.10: Logarithmic trend

Exponential

We'd use an exponential model to test the idea that each additional increase in size results in a dramatic (exponential!) increase in price:

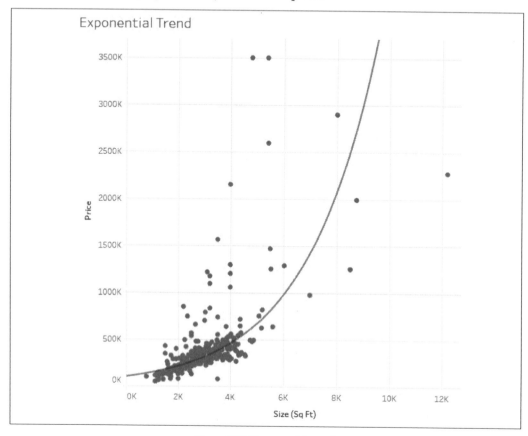

Figure 9.11: Exponential trend

Power

We'd employ a power trend model if we felt the relationship between size and price was non-linear and somewhere between a diminishing logarithmic trend and an explosive exponential trend. The curve would indicate that the price was a function of the size to a certain power. A power trend predicts certain events very well, such as the distance covered by the acceleration of a vehicle:

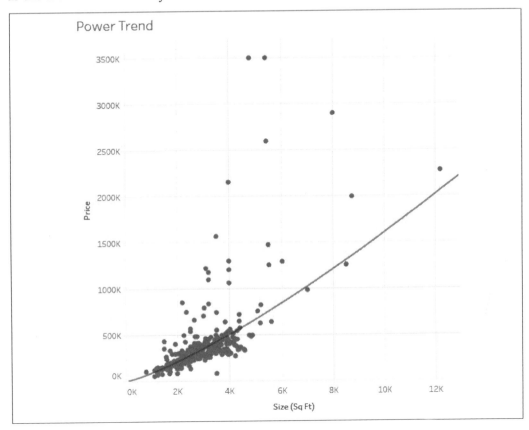

Figure 9.12: Power trend

Polynomial

We'd use this model if we felt the relationship between **Size** and **Price** was complex and followed more of an **S**-shaped curve where initially increasing the size dramatically increased the price but, at some point, the price leveled off. You can set the degree of the polynomial model anywhere from 2 to 8. The trend line shown here is a 3rd degree polynomial:

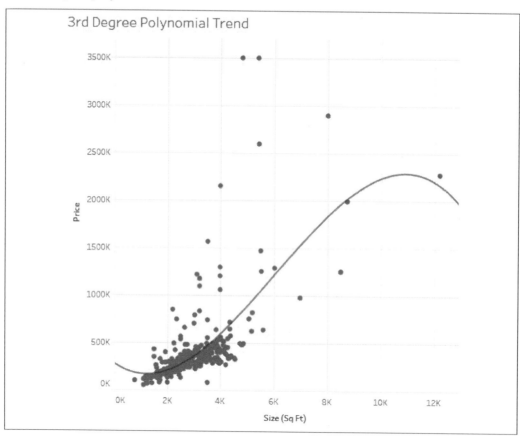

Figure 9.13: 3rd degree polynomial trend

You'll want to understand the basics of the trend models so that you can test and validate your assumptions of the data. Some of the trend models are clearly wrong for our data (though statistically still valid, it is highly unlikely that prices will exponentially increase). A mixture of common sense along with an ever-increasing understanding of statistics will help you as you progress through your journey.

You may also wish to analyze your models for accuracy, and we'll turn there next.

Analyzing trend models

It can be useful to observe trend lines, but often we want to understand whether the trend model we've selected is statistically meaningful. Fortunately, Tableau gives us some visibility into the trend models and calculations.

Simply hovering over a single trend line will reveal the formula as well as the **R-Squared** and **P-value** for that trend line:

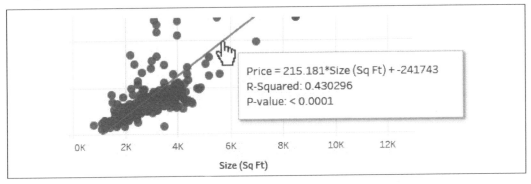

Figure 9.14: Tooltip displayed by hovering over the trend line

 A **P-value** is a statistical concept that describes the probability that the results of assuming no relationship between values (random chance) are at least as close as the results predicted by the trend model. A P-value of 5% (.05) would indicate a 5% chance of random chance describing the relationship between values at least as well as the trend model. This is why P-values of 5% or less are typically considered to indicate a significant trend model. A P-value higher than 5% often leads statisticians to question the correlation described by the trend model.

Additionally, you can see a much more detailed description of the trend model by selecting **Analysis | Trend Lines | Describe Trend Model...** from the menu or by using the similar menu from a right-click on the view's pane. When you view the trend model, you'll see the **Describe Trend Model** window:

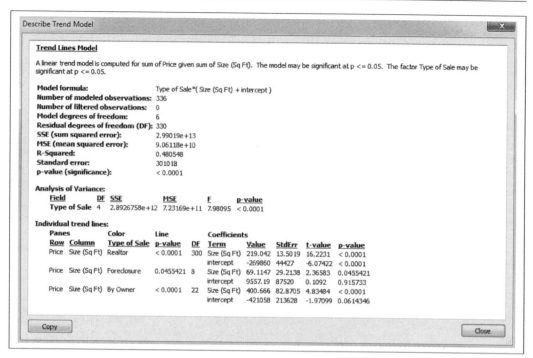

Figure 9.15: The Describe Trend Model window

You can also get a trend model description in the worksheet description, which is available from the **Worksheet** menu or by pressing *Ctrl + E*. The worksheet description includes quite a bit of other useful summary information about the current view.

The wealth of statistical information shown in the window includes a description of the trend model, the formula, the number of observations, and the **p-value** for the model as a whole and for each trend line. Note that, in the screenshot shown previously, the **Type** field was included as a factor that defined three trend lines. You may find that the p-value is different for different lines in a visualization (for example, the lines in *Figure 9.6*). At times, you may even observe that the model is statistically significant overall even though one or more trend lines may not be.

Additional summary statistical information can be displayed in Tableau Desktop for a given view by showing a summary. From the menu, select **Worksheet | Show Summary**. The information displayed in the summary can be expanded using the drop-down menu on the **Summary** card:

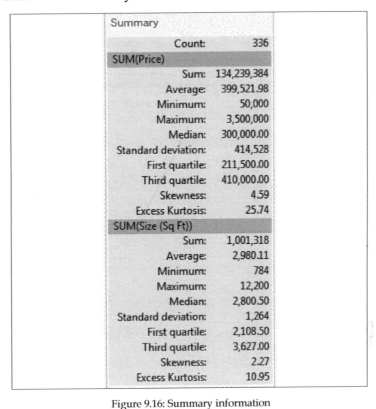

Summary	
Count:	336
SUM(Price)	
Sum:	134,239,384
Average:	399,521.98
Minimum:	50,000
Maximum:	3,500,000
Median:	300,000.00
Standard deviation:	414,528
First quartile:	211,500.00
Third quartile:	410,000.00
Skewness:	4.59
Excess Kurtosis:	25.74
SUM(Size (Sq Ft))	
Sum:	1,001,318
Average:	2,980.11
Minimum:	784
Maximum:	12,200
Median:	2,800.50
Standard deviation:	1,264
First quartile:	2,108.50
Third quartile:	3,627.00
Skewness:	2.27
Excess Kurtosis:	10.95

Figure 9.16: Summary information

The wealth of information available via tooltips and summaries will help you evaluate your trend models and understand the accuracy and details. But we can even go further, by exporting and analyzing statistical data for the trend models. We'll consider that next.

Exporting statistical model details

Tableau also gives you the ability to export data, including data related to trend models. This allows you to, more deeply—and even visually, analyze the trend model itself. Let's analyze the third-degree polynomial trend line of the real estate price and size scatterplot without any factors. To export data related to the current view, use the menu to select **Worksheet | Export | Data**. The data will be exported as a **Microsoft Access Database** (.mdb) file and you'll be prompted where to save the file.

 The ability to export data to **Access** is limited to a PC only. If you're using a Mac, you won't have the option. You may wish to skim this section, but don't worry that you aren't able to replicate the examples.

On the **Export Data to Access** screen, specify an access table name and select whether you wish to export data from the entire view or the current selection. You may also specify that Tableau should connect to the data. This will generate the data source and make it available with the specified name in the current workbook:

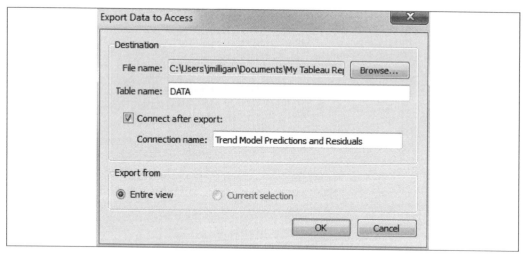

Figure 9.17: The Export Data to Access dialog box

The new data source connection will contain all the fields that were in the original view as well as additional fields related to the trend model. This allows us to build a view like the following, using the residuals and predictions:

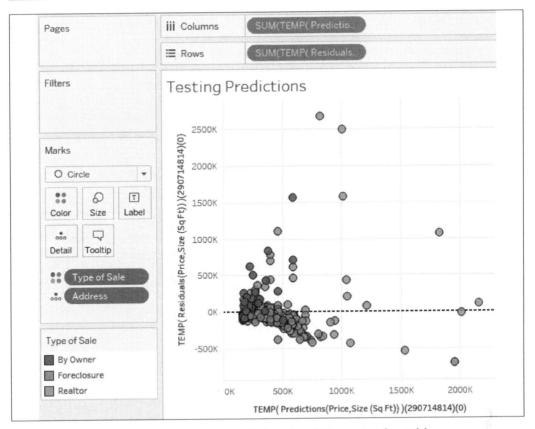

Figure 9.18: A view using residuals and predictions to test the model

A scatterplot of predictions (*x* axis) and residuals (*y* axis) allows you to visually see how far each mark was from the location predicted by the trend line. It also allows you to see whether residuals are distributed evenly on either side of zero. An uneven distribution would likely indicate problems with the trend model.

You can include this new view along with the original on a dashboard to explore the trend model visually. Use the highlight button on the toolbar to highlight the **Address** field:

Figure 9.19: The highlight button

With the highlight action defined, selecting marks in one view will allow you to see them in the other. You could extend this technique to export multiple trend models and dashboards to evaluate several trend models at the same time:

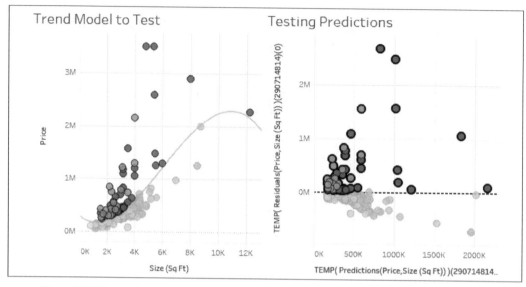

Figure 9.20: Placing the original view alongside the testing view allows you to see the relationship

Advanced statistics and more with R and Python

You can achieve even more sophisticated statistical analysis leveraging Tableau's ability to integrate with R or Python. **R** is an open source statistical analysis platform and programming language with which you can define advanced statistical models. **Python** is a high-level programming language that has quickly gained a wide following among data analysts and data scientists for its ease of use. It contains many capabilities for data cleansing as well as libraries of statistical functions.

 To use R or Python, you'll first need to install either an R server or TabPy (a Python API available from Tableau) and then configure Tableau to use an R server or TabPy. To learn more about installing and using R Server or TabPy, check out these resources:

R: https://www.tableau.com/solutions/r

Python: https://www.tableau.com/about/blog/2017/1/ building-advanced-analytics-applications-tabpy-64916

It's beyond the scope of this book to dive into the complexities of R and Python, but having an awareness of the capability will enable you to pursue the topic further.

Next, we'll take a look at Tableau's capability for identifying complex relationships within data using clustering.

Clustering

Tableau gives you the ability to quickly perform clustering analysis in your visualizations. This allows you to find groups, or **clusters**, of individual data points that are similar based on any number of your choosing. This can be useful in many different industries and fields of study, as in the following examples:

- Marketing may find it useful to determine groups of customers related to each other based on spending amounts, frequency of purchases, or times and days of orders.

- Patient care directors in hospitals may benefit from understanding groups of patients related to each other based on diagnoses, medication, length of stay, and the number of readmissions.

- Immunologists may search for related strains of bacteria based on drug resistance or genetic markers.

- Renewable energy consultants may like to pinpoint clusters of windmills based on energy production and then correlate that with geographic location.

 Tableau uses a standard **k-means clustering** algorithm that will yield consistent results every time the view is rendered. Tableau will automatically assign the number of clusters (k), but you have the option of adjusting the value as well as assigning any number of variables.

As we consider clustering, we'll turn once again to the real estate data to see whether we can find groupings of related houses on the market and then determine whether there's any geographic pattern based on the clusters we find.

Although you can add clusters to any visualization, we'll start with a scatterplot, because it already allows us to see the relationship between two variables. That will give us some insight into how clustering works, and then we can add additional variables to see how the clusters are redefined.

Beginning with the basic scatterplot of **Address** by **Size** and **Price**, switch to the **Analytics** pane and drag **Cluster** to the view:

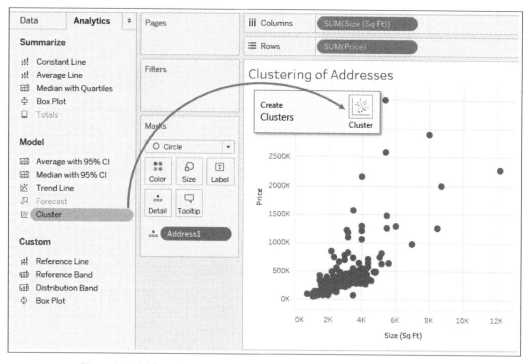

Figure 9.21: Adding clusters by dragging and dropping from the Analytics pane

When you drop **Cluster** onto the view, Tableau will generate a new **Clusters** field (automatically placed on **Color** here) and will display a **Clusters** window containing the fields used as **Variables** and an option to change the **Number of Clusters**. **Variables** will contain the measures already in the view by default:

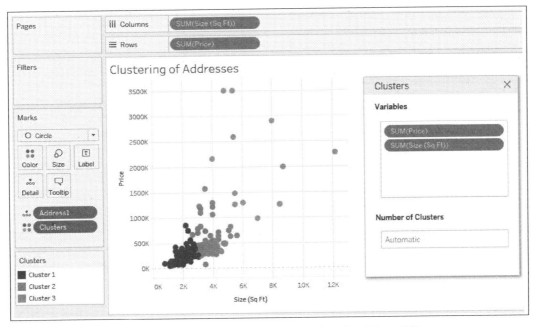

Figure 9.22: Clusters of individual addresses based on Price and Size

Variables are all the factors that the clustering algorithm uses to determine related data points. **Number of Clusters** determines into how many groups the data is partitioned. In the preceding view, you'll observe three clusters of houses:

- Those with a low price and a smaller size (blue)
- Those with an average price and size (orange)
- Those with a high price and a large size (gray)

Because the two variables used for the clusters are the same as those used for the scatterplot, it's relatively easy to see the boundaries of the clusters (you can imagine a couple of diagonal lines partitioning the data).

You can drag and drop nearly any field into and out of the **Variables** section (from the data pane or the view) to add and remove variables. The clusters will automatically update as you do so. Experiment by adding **Bedrooms** to the **Variables** list and observe that there's now some overlap between **Cluster 1** and **Cluster 2** because some larger homes only have two or three bedrooms while some smaller homes might have four or five. The number of bedrooms now helps define the clusters. Remove **Bedrooms** and note that the clusters are immediately updated again.

Once you have meaningful clusters, you can materialize the clusters as groups in the data source by dragging them from the view and dropping them into the **Data** pane:

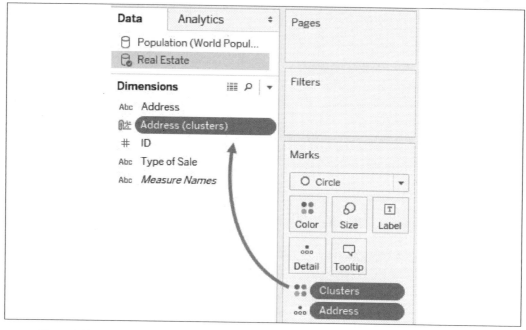

Figure 9.23: Materializing a cluster by dragging the Clusters field from the view to the Data pane

The cluster group will not be recalculated at render time. To recalculate the cluster group, use the dropdown on the field in the **Data** pane and select **Refit**.

Using a cluster group allows you to accomplish a lot, including the following:

- Cluster groups can be used across multiple visualizations and can be used in actions on dashboards.
- Cluster groups can be edited, and individual members moved between groups if desired.
- Cluster group names can be aliased, allowing more descriptive names than **Cluster 1** and **Cluster 2**.

- Cluster groups can be used in calculated fields, while clusters can't.

In the following example, a map of the properties has been color-coded by the **Address (clusters)** group in the previous view to help us to see whether there's any geographic correlation to the clusters based on price and size. While the clusters could have been created directly in this visualization, the group has some of the advantages mentioned:

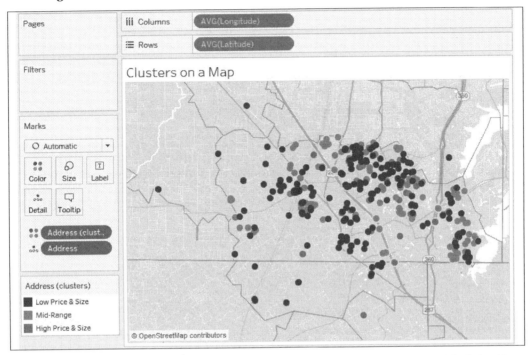

Figure 9.24: This view uses the clusters we identified to additionally understand any geospatial relationships

In the view here, each original cluster is now a group that has been aliased to give a better description of the cluster. You can use the drop-down menu for the group field in the data pane or, alternately, right-click the item in the color legend to edit aliases.

 There are a lot of options for editing how maps appear. You can adjust the layers that are shown on maps to help to provide additional context for the data you are plotting. From the top menu, select **Maps | Map Layers**. The layer options will show in the left-hand sidebar. The preceding map has had **Streets**, **Highways**, **County Borders**, and **Zip Code Borders** enabled to give each address a more precise context of location. The layers that are available to select will depend on the zoom level of the map.

In looking at the previous view, you do indeed find neighborhoods that are almost exclusively **Low Price & Size (Cluster 1)** and others that are almost exclusively **Mid-Range (Cluster 2)**. Consider how a real-estate investor might use such a visualization to look for a low-priced house in a mid-range neighborhood.

Distributions

Analyzing distributions can be quite useful. We've already seen that certain calculations are available for determining statistical information such as averages, percentiles, and standard deviations. Tableau also makes it easy to quickly visualize various distributions, including confidence intervals, percentages, percentiles, quantiles, and standard deviations.

You may add any of these visual analytic features using the **Analytics** pane (alternately, you can right-click an axis and select **Add Reference Line**). Just like reference lines and bands, distribution analytics can be applied within the scope of a table, pane, or cell. When you drag and drop the desired visual analytic, you'll have options for selecting the scope and the axis. In the following example, we've dragged and dropped **Distribution Band** from the **Analytics** pane onto the scope of **Pane** for the axis defined by Sum(Price):

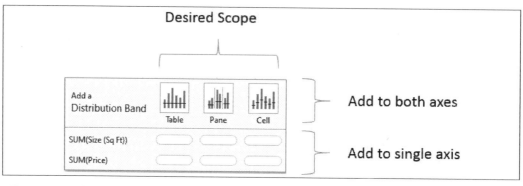

Figure 9.25: Defining the scope and axis as you add reference lines and distributions from the Analytics pane

Once you've selected the scope and axis, you'll be given options to change settings. You may also edit lines, bands, distributions, and box plots by right-clicking the analytic feature in the view or by right-clicking the axis or the reference lines themselves.

As an example, let's take the scatterplot of addresses by price and size with **Type of Sale** on **Columns** in addition to color:

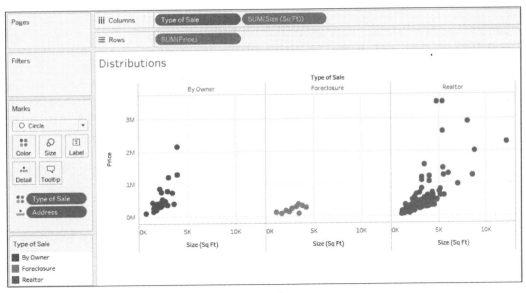

Figure 9.26: A scatterplot divided into three columns

Next, we drag and drop the **Distribution** band from the **Analytics** pane onto **Pane** only for the axis defined by **Price**. This brings up a dialog box to set the options:

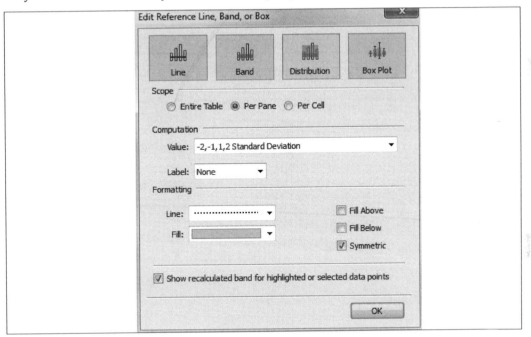

Figure 9.27: The dialog box for adding or editing lines, bands, distributions, or box plots

Each specific **Distribution** option specified in the **Value** drop-down menu under **Computation** has unique settings. **Confidence Interval**, for example, allows you to specify a percent value for the interval. **Standard Deviation** allows you to enter a comma-delimited list of values that describe how many standard deviations and at what intervals. The preceding settings reflect specifying standard deviations of **-2, -1, 1,** and **2**. After adjusting the label and formatting as shown in the preceding screenshot, you should see results like this:

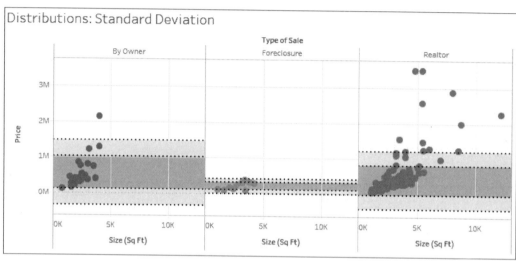

Figure 9.28: Two standard deviations of Price for each Type of Sale

Since you applied the standard deviations per pane, you get different bands for each type of sale. Each axis can support multiple distributions, reference lines, and bands. You could, for example, add an average line in the preceding view to help a viewer to understand the center of the standard deviations.

On a scatterplot, using a distribution for each axis can yield a very useful way to analyze outliers. Showing a single standard deviation for both **Area** and **Price** allows you to easily see properties that fall within norms for both, one, or neither (you might consider purchasing a house that was on the high end of size but within normal price limits!):

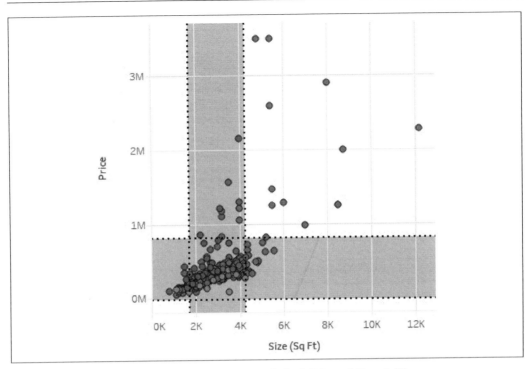

Figure 9.29: One standard deviation for both Price and Size of all houses

Forecasting

As we've seen, trend models make predictions. Given a good model, you expect additional data to follow the trend. When the trend is over time, you can get some idea of where future values may fall. However, predicting future values often requires a different type of model. Factors such as seasonality can make a difference not predicted by a trend alone. Tableau includes built-in forecasting models that can be used to predict and visualize future values.

To use forecasting, you'll need a view that includes a date field or enough date parts for Tableau to reconstruct a date (for example, a **Year** and a **Month** field). Tableau also allows forecasting based on integers instead of dates. You may drag and drop a forecast from the **Analytics** pane, select **Analytics** | **Forecast** | **Show Forecast** from the menu, or right-click on the view's pane and select the option from the context menu.

Here, for example, is the view of the population growth over time of Afghanistan and Australia with forecasts shown:

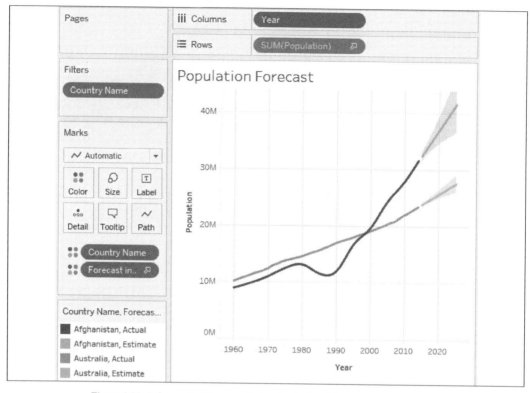

Figure 9.30: A forecast of the population for both Afghanistan and Australia

Note that, when you show the forecast, Tableau adds a forecast icon to the SUM(Population) field on **Rows** to indicate that the measure is being forecast. Additionally, Tableau adds a new special **Forecast indicator** field to **Color** so that forecast values are differentiated from actual values in the view.

 You can move the **Forecast indicator** field or even copy it (hold the *Ctrl* key while dragging and dropping) to other shelves to further customize your view.

When you edit the forecast by selecting **Analytics | Forecast | Forecast Options...** from the menu or use the right-click context menu on the view, you'll be presented with various options for customizing the trend model, like this:

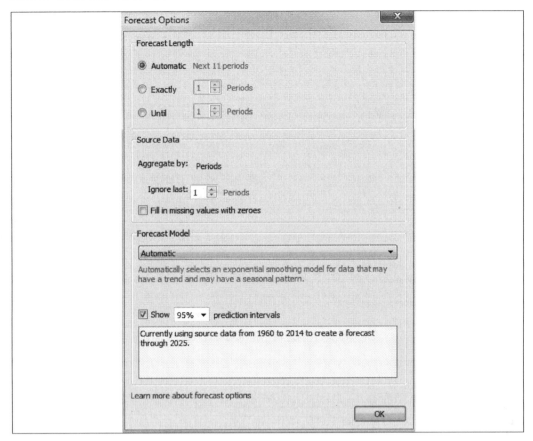

Figure 9.31: The Forecast Options dialog box

Here, you have options to set the length of the forecast, determine aggregations, customize the model, and set whether you wish to show prediction intervals. The forecast length is set to **Automatic** by default, but you can extend the forecast by a custom value.

The options under **Source Data** allow you to optionally specify a different grain of data for the model. For example, your view might show a measure by year, but you could allow Tableau to query the source data to retrieve values by month and use the finer grain to potentially achieve better forecasting results.

Tableau's ability to separately query the data source to obtain data at a finer grain for more precise results works well with relational data sources. However, **Online Analytical Processing (OLAP)** data sources aren't compatible with this approach, which is one reason why forecasting isn't available when working with cubes.

By default, the last value is excluded from the model. This is useful when you're working with data where the most recent time period is incomplete. For example, when records are added daily, the last (current) month isn't complete until the final records are added on the last day of the month. Prior to that last day, the incomplete time period might skew the model if it's not ignored.

The model itself can be set to automatic with or without seasonality, or can be customized to set options for seasonality and trend. To understand the options, consider the following view of **Sales** by **Month** from the Superstore sample data:

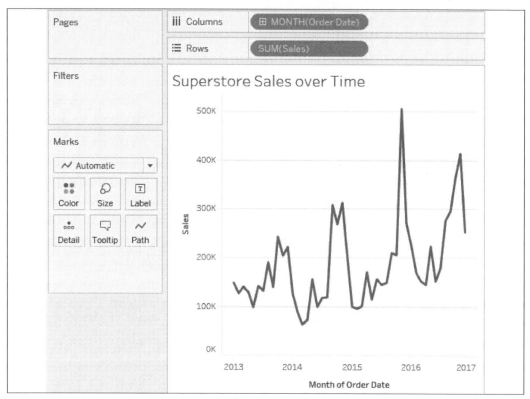

Figure 9.32: This time series shows a cyclical or seasonal pattern

The data displays a distinct cyclical or seasonal pattern. This is very typical for retail sales and other types of data. The following are the results of selecting various custom options:

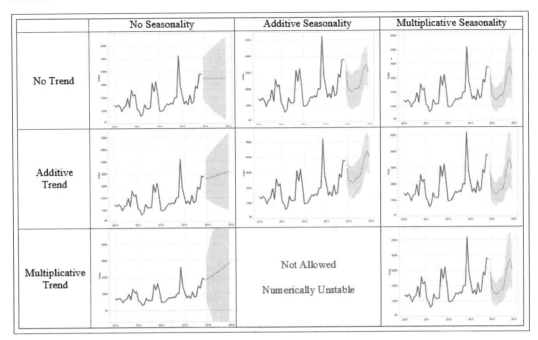

Figure 9.33: Selecting various forecast models will yield different results

Examining the differences above will help you understand the differences in the options. For example, note that no seasonality results in a straight line that does not fluctuate with seasons. Multiplicative trends result in sharper inclines and decreases, while multiplicative seasonality results in sharper variations.

Much like trends, forecast models and summary information can be accessed using the menu. Selecting **Analytics | Forecast | Describe Forecast** will display a window with tabs for both the summary and details concerning the model:

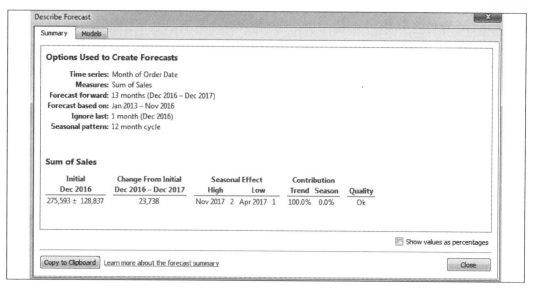

Figure 9.34: Tableau describes the forecast model

Clicking the **Learn more about the forecast summary** link at the bottom of the window will give you much more information on the forecast models used in Tableau.

 Forecast models are only enabled given a certain set of conditions. If the option is disabled, ensure that you're connected to a relational database and not OLAP, that you're not using table calculations, and that you have at least five data points.

Summary

Tableau provides an extensive set of features for adding value to your analysis. Trend lines allow you to more precisely identify outliers, determine which values fall within the predictions of certain models, and even make predictions of where measurements are expected. Tableau gives extensive visibility into the trend models and even allows you to export data containing trend model predictions and residuals. Clusters enable you to find groups of related data points based on various factors. Distributions are useful for understanding a spread of values across a dataset. Forecasting allows a complex model of trends and seasonality to predict future results. Having a good understanding of these tools will give you the ability to clarify and validate your initial visual analyses.

Next, we'll consider some advanced visualization types that will expand the horizons of what you are able to accomplish with Tableau and the way in which you communicate data to others!

10

Advanced Visualizations

We've explored many different types of visualizations and considered which types of questions they best answer. For example, bar charts aid in comparing values; line charts can show changes and trends over time; stacked bars and treemaps help us see part-to-whole relationships; box plots help us understand distributions and outliers. We've also seen how to enhance our understanding and data storytelling with calculations, annotations, formatting, and reference lines. With this knowledge as a foundation, we'll expand the possibilities of data analysis with some advanced visualizations.

These are only examples of Tableau's amazing flexibility and are meant to inspire you to think through new ways of seeing, understanding, and communicating your data. These are not designed as complex charts for the sake of complexity, but rather to spark creativity and interest to effectively communicate data.

We'll consider the following topics:

- Advanced visualizations – when and why to use them
- Slope charts and bump charts
- Waterfall charts
- Step lines and jump lines
- Spark lines
- Dumbbell charts
- Unit/symbol charts
- Marimekko charts
- Animated visualizations

Advanced visualizations – when and why to use them

The visualization types we've seen up to this point will answer many, if not most, of the questions you have about your data. If you are asking questions of *when?*, then a time series is the most likely solution. If you are asking *how much?*, a bar chart gives a good, quick result. But there are times when you'll ask questions that are better answered with a different type of visualization. For example, movement or flow might be best represented with a Sankey diagram. *How many?* might be best answered with a unit or symbol chart. Comparing changes in ranks or absolute values might be best accomplished with a slope or bump chart. The visualizations that follow are not what you will use as you first explore the data. But as you dive deeper into your analysis and want to know or communicate more, you might consider some of the options in this chapter.

Each of the visualizations in this chapter is created using the supplied Superstore data. Instead of providing step-by-step instructions, we'll point out specific advanced techniques used to create each chart type. The goal is not to memorize steps but to understand how to creatively leverage Tableau's features.

You can find completed examples in the Chapter 10 Complete workbook, or test your growing Tableau skills by building everything from scratch using the Chapter 10 Starter workbook.

Let's start our journey into advanced visualizations with slope and bump charts.

Slope charts and bump charts

A **slope chart** shows a change of values from one period or status to another. For example, here is a slope chart demonstrating the change in sales rank for each state in the **South** region from **2016** to **2017**:

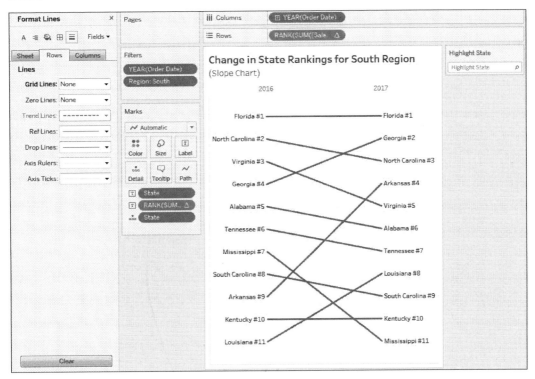

Figure 10.1: A slope chart is useful to compare the change of rank or absolute
values from one period or status to another

Here are some features and techniques used to create the preceding slope chart:

- The table calculation **Rank(SUM(Sales))** is computed by (addressed by)
  State, meaning that each state is ranked within the partition of a single year.

- **Grid Lines** and **Zero Lines** for **Rows** have been set to **None**.

- The axis has been reversed (right-click the axis and select **Edit**, then check the
  option to reverse). This allows rank **#1** to appear at the top and lower ranks
  to appear in descending order.

- The axis has been hidden (right-click the axis and uncheck **Show Header**).

- Labels have been edited (by clicking on **Label**) to show on both ends of the line, to center vertically, and to position the rank number next to the state name.

- The year column headers have been moved from the bottom of the view to the top (from the top menu, select **Analysis | Table Layout | Advanced** and uncheck the option to show the innermost level at the bottom).

- A **data highlighter** has been added (using the dropdown on the State field in the view, select **Show Highlighter**) to give the end user the ability to highlight one or more states.

Data highlighters give the user the ability to highlight marks in a view by selecting values from the drop-down list or by typing (any match on any part of a value will highlight the mark; so, for example, typing Carolina would highlight **North Carolina** and **South Carolina** in the preceding view). Data highlighters can be shown for any field you use as discrete (blue) in the view and will function across multiple views in a dashboard as long as that same field is used in those views.

Slope charts can use absolute values (for example, the actual values of **Sales**) or relative values (for example, the rank of **Sales**, as shown in this example). If you were to show more than two years to observe the change in rankings over multiple periods of time, the resulting visualization might be called a **Bump Chart** and look like this:

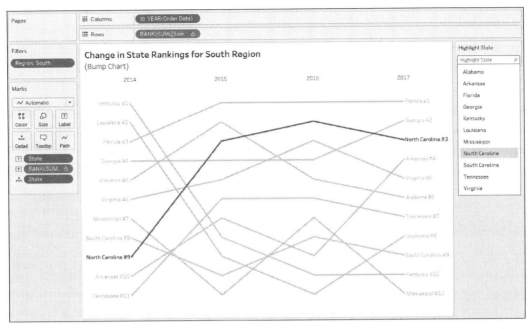

Figure 10.2: This bump chart shows the change in rank for each state over time and makes use of a highlighter

Slope charts are very useful when comparing ranks before and after or from one state to another. Bump charts extend this concept across more than two periods. Consider using either of these two charts when you want to understand the relative change in rank and make comparisons against that change.

Next, we'll consider a chart that helps us understand the build-up of parts to the whole.

Waterfall charts

A **waterfall chart** is useful when you want to show how parts successively build up to a whole. In the following screenshot, for example, a waterfall chart shows how profit builds up to a grand total across **Departments** and **Categories** of products. Sometimes profit is negative, so at that point, the waterfall chart takes a dip, while positive values build up toward the total:

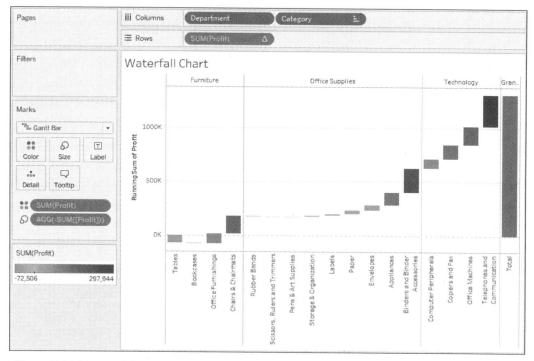

Figure 10.3: This waterfall chart shows how each Category adds (or subtracts) profit to build toward the total

Here are the features and techniques used to build the chart:

- The **SUM(Profit)** field on **Rows** is a **Running Total** table calculation (created using a **Quick Table Calculation** from the drop-down menu) and is computed across the table.

- **Row Grand Totals** have been added to the view (dragged and dropped from the **Analytics** pane).

- The mark type is set to **Gantt Bar** and an ad hoc calculation is used with code: **SUM(Profit)** for the size. This may seem a bit odd at first, but it causes the Gantt Bars to be drawn from the actual value and filled down when profit is positive or filled up when profit is negative.

- **Category** has been sorted by the sum of their profit in ascending order so that the waterfall chart builds slowly (or negatively) from left to right within each **Department**. You might want to experiment with the sort options to discover the impact on the presentation.

Waterfall charts will help you demonstrate a build-up or progression toward a total or whole value. Let's next consider step lines and jump lines to show discrete changes over time.

Step lines and jump lines

With a mark type of **Line**, click the **Path** shelf and you'll see three options for **Line Type**:

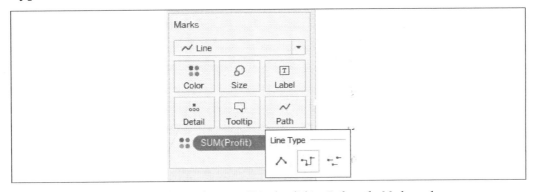

Figure 10.4: Change the type of Line by clicking Path on the Marks card

The three options are:

1. **Linear**: Use angled lines to emphasize movement or transition between values. This is the default and every example of a line chart in this book so far has made use of this line type.

2. **Step lines**: Remain connected but emphasize discrete steps of change. This is useful when you want to communicate that there is no transition between values or that the transition is a discrete step in value. For example, you might want to show the number of generators running over time. The change from 7 to 8 is a discrete change that might be best represented by a step line.

3. **Jump lines** are not connected; and when a value changes a new line starts. Jump lines are useful when you want to show values that indicate a certain state that may exist for a given period of time before jumping to another state. For example, you might wish to show the daily occupancy rate of a hotel over time. A jump line might help emphasize that each day is a new value.

In the following example, we've taken the build-up of profit that was previously demonstrated with a **waterfall chart** and used step lines to show each successive step of profit:

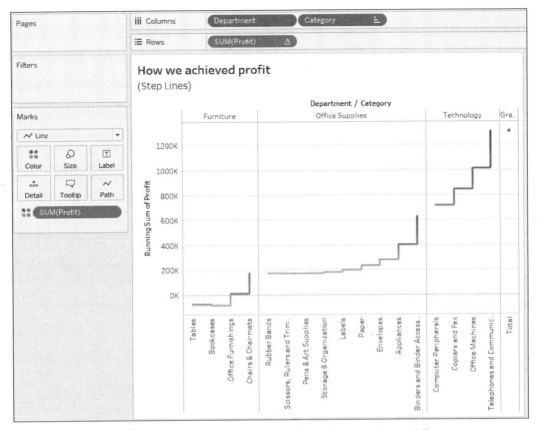

Figure 10.5: A step line chart emphasizes an abrupt change or discrete difference

Experiment with switching line types to see the visual impact and what each communicates about the data.

Sparklines

Sparklines are visualizations that use multiple small line graphs that are designed to be read and compared quickly. The goal of sparklines is to give a visualization that can be understood at a glance. You aren't trying to communicate exact values, but rather give the audience the ability to quickly understand trends, movements, and patterns.

Among various uses of this type of visualization, you may have seen sparklines used in financial publications to compare the movement of stock prices. Recall, that in *Chapter 1, Taking Off with Tableau*, we considered the initial start of a **Sparklines** visualization as we looked at iterations of line charts. Here is a far more developed example:

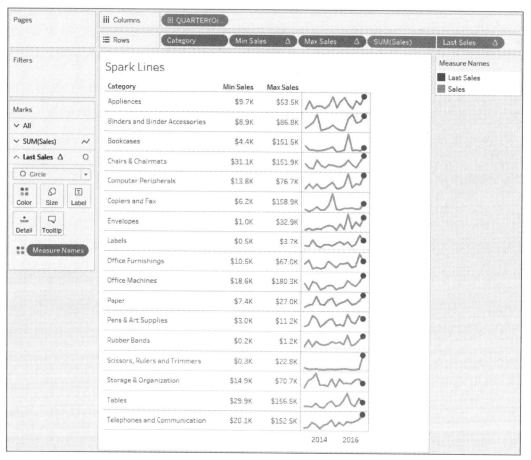

Figure 10.6: Spark Lines give you a quick glance at the "shape" of change over time across multiple categories

You can build a chart like this by following these steps:

1. Start with a simple view of **SUM(Sales)** by **Quarter** of **Order Date** (as a date value) with **Category** on **Rows**.

2. Create two calculated fields to show the minimum and maximum quarterly sales values for each category. **Min Sales** has the code `WINDOW_MIN(SUM(Sales))` and **Max Sales** has the code `WINDOW_MAX(SUM(Sales))`. Add both to **Rows** as discrete (blue) fields.

3. Place the calculation **Last Sales** with the code `IF LAST() == 0 THEN SUM([Sales]) END` on **Rows** and uses a synchronized dual axis with a circle mark type to emphasize the final value of sales for each timeline.

4. Edit the axis for **SUM(Sales)** to have independent axis ranges for each row or column and hide the axes. This allows the line movement to be emphasized. Remember: the goal is not to show the exact values, but to allow your audience to see the patterns and movement.

5. Hide grid lines for **Rows**.

6. Resize the view (compress the view horizontally and set to **Fit Height**). This allows the sparklines to fit into a small space, facilitating the quick understanding of patterns and movement.

Sparklines can be used with all kinds of time series to reveal overall big-picture trends and behaviors at a glance.

Dumbbell charts

A **dumbbell chart** is a variation of the circle plot that compares two values for each slice of data, emphasizing the distance between the two values.

Here, for example, is a chart showing the **Difference in Profit between East and West** regions for each **Category** of products:

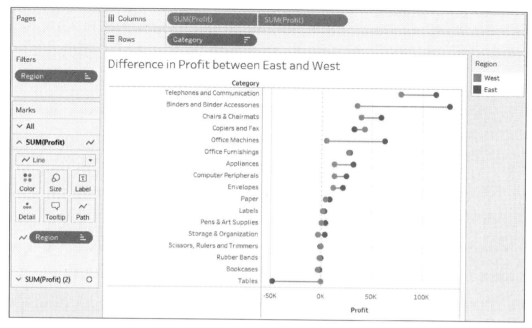

Figure 10.7: A dumbbell chart emphasizes the distance/difference between two values

This chart was built using the following features and techniques:

- A synchronized dual axis of **SUM(Profit)** has been used with one set to mark the type of **Circle** and the other set to **Line**.

- **Category** has been sorted by **Profit** descending (the sort sums profit for East and West).

- **Region** has been placed on the **Path** shelf for the line to tell Tableau to draw a line between the two **Regions**.

>
> The **Path** shelf is available for **Line** and **Polygon** mark types. When you place a field on the **Path** shelf, it tells Tableau the order to connect the points (following the sort order of the field placed on **Path**). Paths are often used with geographic visualizations to connect origins and destinations on routes but can be used with other visualization types. Tableau draws a single line between two values (in this case East and West).

- **Region** is placed on **Color** for the circle mark type.

Dumbbell charts are great at highlighting the disparity between values. Let's next consider how we can use unit/symbol charts to drive responses.

Unit/symbol charts

A **unit chart** can be used to show individual items, often using shapes or symbols to represent each individual. These charts can elicit a powerful emotional response because the representations of the data are less abstract and more easily identified as something real. For example, here is a chart showing how many customers had late shipments for each **Region**:

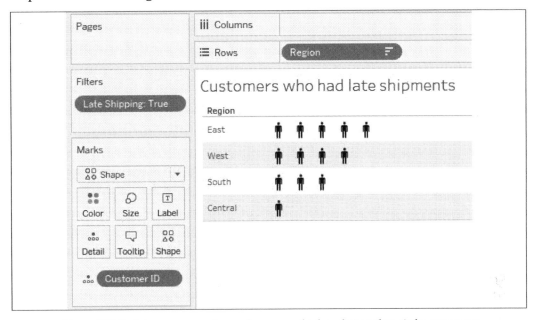

Figure 10.8: Each image represents a real person and is less abstract than circles or squares

The view was created with the following techniques:

- The view is filtered where **Late Shipping** is **True**. **Late Shipping** is a calculated field that determines if it took more than 14 days to ship an order. The code is as follows:

```
DATEDIFF('day', [Order Date], [Ship Date]) > 14
```

- **Region** has been sorted by the distinct count of **Customer ID** in descending order.

- **Customer ID** has been placed on **Detail** so that there is a mark for each distinct customer.

- The mark type has been changed to **Shape** and the shape has been changed to the included person shape in the **Gender** shape palette. To change shapes, click the **Shape** shelf and select the desired shape(s), as shown in the following screenshot:

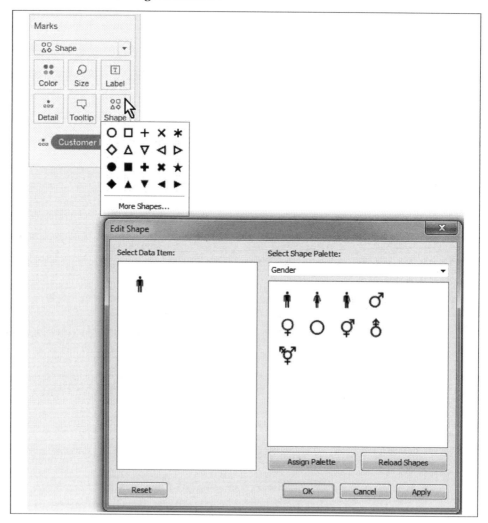

Figure 10.9: You can assign shapes to dimensional values using the Shape shelf

The preceding unit chart might elicit more of a response from regional managers than a standard bar chart when they are gently reminded that poor customer service impacts real people. Granted, the shapes are still abstract, but more closely represent an actual person. You could also consider labeling the mark with the customer name or using other techniques to further engage your audience.

Remember that normally in Tableau, a mark is drawn for each distinct intersection of dimensional values. So, it is rather difficult to draw, for example, 10 individual shapes for a single row of data that simply contains the value 10 for a field. This means that you will need to consider the shape of your data and include enough rows to draw the units you wish to represent.

Concrete shapes, in any type of visualization, can also dramatically reduce the amount of time it takes to comprehend the data. Contrast the amount of effort required to identify the departments in these two scatterplots:

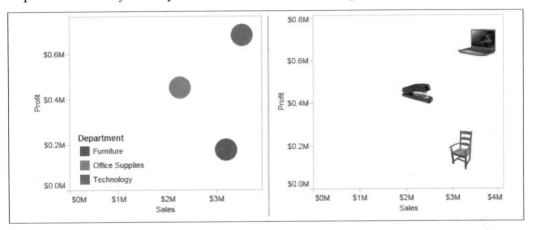

Figure 10.10: Notice the difference in "cognitive load" between the left chart and the right

Once you know the meaning of a shape, you no longer have to reference a legend. Placing a discrete field on the **Shape** shelf allows you to assign shapes to individual values of the field.

 Shapes are images located in the `My Tableau Repository\` `Shapes` directory. You can include your own custom shapes in subfolders of that directory by adding folders and image files.

Marimekko charts

A **Marimekko chart** (sometimes alternately called a **Mekko chart**) is similar to a vertically stacked bar chart, but additionally uses varying widths of bars to communicate additional information about the data. Here, for example, is a **Marimekko chart** showing the breakdown of sales by region and department.

The width of the bars communicates the total **Sales for Region**, while the height of each segment gives you the percentage of sales for the **Department** within the **Region**:

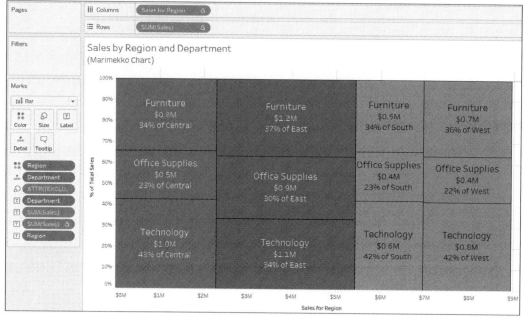

Figure 10.11: The amount of sales per Department is indicated by the height of each segment, while the width of each bar indicates the overall sales per Region

Creating Marimekko charts in Tableau leverages the ability to fix the width of bars according to the axis' units.

Clicking the **Size** shelf when a continuous (green) field is on **Columns** (thus defining a horizontal axis) and the mark type is set to **Bar** reveals options for a fixed size. You can manually enter a **Size** and **Alignment** or drop a field on the **Size** shelf to vary the width of the bars.

Here are the steps required to create this kind of visualization:

1. The mark type has been specifically set to **Bar**.

2. **Region** and **Department** have been placed on **Color** and **Detail**, respectively. They are the only dimensions in the view, so they define the view's **level of detail**.

3. **Sales** has been placed on **Rows** and a **Percent of Total** quick table calculation applied. The **Compute Using** (addressing) has been set to **Department** so that we get the percentage of sales for each department within the partition of the **Region**.

4. The calculated field **Sales for Region** calculates the x axis location for the right-side position of each bar. The code is as follows:

```
IF FIRST() = 0
    THEN MIN({EXCLUDE [Department] : SUM(Sales)})
ELSEIF LOOKUP(MIN([Region]), -1) <> MIN([Region])
    THEN PREVIOUS_VALUE(0) + MIN({EXCLUDE [Department] :
SUM(Sales)})
ELSE
    PREVIOUS_VALUE(0)
END
```

While this code may seem daunting at first, it follows a logical progression. Specifically, if this is the first bar segment, we'll want to know the sum of **Sales** for the entire region (which is why we exclude **Department** with an inline level of detail calculation). When the calculation moves to a new **Region**, we'll need to add the previous **Region** total to the new **Region** total. Otherwise, the calculation is for another segment in the same **Region**, so the regional total is the same as the previous segment. Notice again, the **Compute Using** option has been set to **Department** to enable the logical progression to work as expected.

Finally, a few additional adjustments were made to the view:

- The field on **Size** is an ad hoc level of detail calculation with the code `{EXCLUDE [Department] : SUM(Sales)}`. As we mentioned earlier, this excludes **Department** and allows us to get the sum of sales at a **Region** level. This means that each bar is sized according to the total sales for the given **Region**.

- Clicking on the **Size** shelf gives the option to set the alignment of the bars to Right. Since the preceding calculation gave the right position of the bar, we need to make certain the bars are drawn from that starting point.

- Various fields, such as **SUM(Sales)** as an absolute value and percentage, have been copied to the **Label** shelf so that each bar segment more clearly communicates meaning to the viewer.

To add labels to each **Region** column, you might consider creating a second view and placing both on a dashboard. Alternately, you might use annotations.

In addition to allowing you to create Marimekko charts, the ability to control the size of bars in axis units opens all kinds of possibilities for creating additional visualizations, such as complex cascade charts or stepped area charts. The techniques are like those used here. You may also leverage the sizing feature with **continuous bins** (use the drop-down menu to change a bin field in the view to continuous from discrete).

For a more comprehensive discussion of Marimekko charts, along with approaches that work with sparse data, see Jonathan Drummey's blog post at https://www.tableau.com/about/blog/2016/8/how-build-marimekko-chart-tableau-58153.

Animated visualizations

Previous versions of Tableau allowed rudimentary animation using the **Pages** shelf with playback controls. Tableau 2020.1 introduced true **Mark Animation**, which means marks smoothly transition when you apply filters, sorting, or page changes. Consider leveraging animation to extend your analytical potential in a couple of ways:

1. Turn it on while exploring and analyzing your data. This allows you to gain analytical insights you might otherwise miss, such as seeing how far and in which direction marks in a scatterplot move as a filter changes.

2. Use it strategically to enhance the data story. Animation can be used to capture interest, draw attention to important elements, or build suspense toward a conclusion.

We'll consider both approaches to animation in the following examples.

Enhancing analysis with animation

Consider the following bar chart, which shows the correlation of **Sales** and **Profit** for each **Department**:

Figure 10.12: Sales and profit per Department

Notice the **Region** filter. Change the filter selection a few times in the Chapter 10 workbook. You'll observe the standard behavior that occurs without animations: the circle marks are immediately redrawn at the new location determined by the filter. This works well, but there is a bit of a disconnect between filter settings. As you switch between regions, notice the mental difficulty in keeping track of where a mark was versus where it is with the new selection. Did one region's mark increase in profit? Did it decrease in sales?

Now, turn on animations for the view. To do this, use the menu to select **Format | Animations...** The **Animations** format pane will show on the left. Use it to turn **Animation** on for the **Selected Sheet**:

Figure 10.13: The Animations format pane gives various options
for workbook and individual sheet animation settings

Experiment with various duration settings and change the filter value. Notice how much easier it is to see the change in sales and profit from region to region. This gives you the ability to notice changes more easily. You'll start to gain insight, even without spending a lot of cognitive effort, into the magnitude and direction of change. Animations provide a path to this analytical insight.

Enhancing data storytelling with animation

Beyond providing analytical insight as you perform your data discovery and analysis, you can also leverage animation to more effectively drive interest and highlight decision points, opportunities, or risks in your data stories. As an example, consider this view in the Chapter 10 workbook:

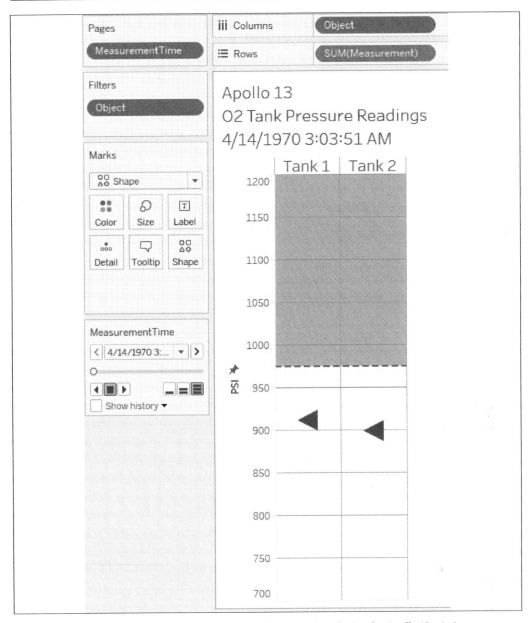

Figure 10.14: O2 Tank 1 and 2 pressure readings over time during the Apollo 13 mission

The view tells a part of the story of Apollo 13 and the disaster that crippled the spacecraft. It does this by making use of both the **Pages** shelf as well as smooth animation. Experiment with the animation speed and playback controls in the Chapter 10 workbook. Consider how animation can be used to heighten awareness, drive interest, or even create suspense.

When you use multiple views on a dashboard, each having the same combination of fields on the **Pages** shelf, you can synchronize the playback controls (using the caret drop-down menu on the playback controls) to create a fully animated dashboard.

Animations can be shared with other users of Tableau Desktop and are displayed on Tableau Server, Tableau Online, and Tableau Public.

Summary

We've covered a wide variety of advanced visualization types in this chapter! We've considered slope and bump charts that show changes in rank or value, step and jump lines that show discretely changing values, and unit charts that help materialize abstract concepts.

There is no way to cover every possible visualization type. Instead, the idea has been to demonstrate some of what can be accomplished and spark new ideas and creativity. As you experiment and iterate through new ways of looking at data, you'll become more confident in how to best communicate the stories contained in the data. Next, we'll return briefly to the topic of dashboards to see how some advanced techniques can make them truly dynamic.

11

Dynamic Dashboards

We've looked at dashboards previously, in *Chapter 8, Telling a Data Story with Dashboards,* and considered how to make them interactive using a variety of actions. Now we'll expand on that concept to consider how to create truly dynamic dashboards—dashboards where objects can be shown and hidden. This enables you to do all kinds of amazing things, such as allow the user to select which type of visualization to see or to dynamically hide or show controls that are relevant or desired.

We'll consider the following types of dynamic interactivity:

- Show/Hide buttons
- Sheet swapping
- Automatically showing and hiding controls

Let's start by considering how to show and hide content on dashboards using the Show/Hide buttons.

Show/Hide buttons

The Show/Hide buttons allow you to show and hide layout containers (and everything in them!). You'll find a couple of examples in the Chapter 11 Complete workbook. The Chapter 11 Starter workbook has the dashboards, but not the Show/Hide buttons or containers. The images used in the second example are also in the Chapter 11 directory.

To use the Show/Hide buttons, add a layout container to a dashboard as a **floating object** and then use the dropdown to select **Add Show/Hide Button**, as shown here in *Figure 11.1*:

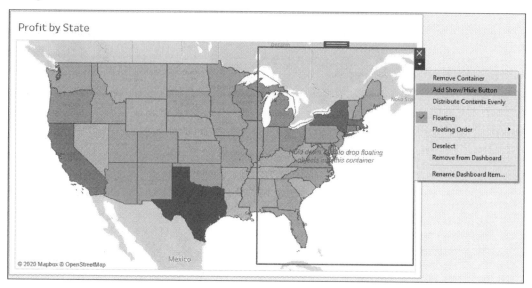

Figure 11.1: A dashboard with a single Map view and a floating layout container

On this dashboard, we've added a vertical layout container floating over the map. When we select **Add Show/Hide Button**, Tableau adds a small button to the dashboard:

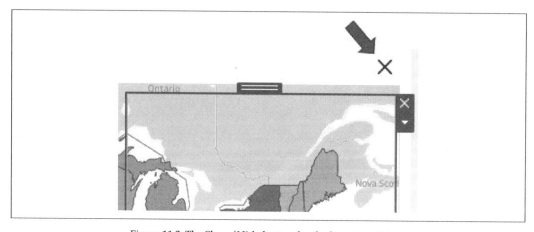

Figure 11.2: The Show/Hide button for the layout container

Each Show/Hide button can be applied to any single floating layout container on the dashboard.

Use the **Rename Dashboard Item...** option on the layout container dropdown to make it easy to identify which layout container is the target of a Show/Hide button.

You may edit the button's appearance and actions using the button's dropdown to select **Edit Button...**:

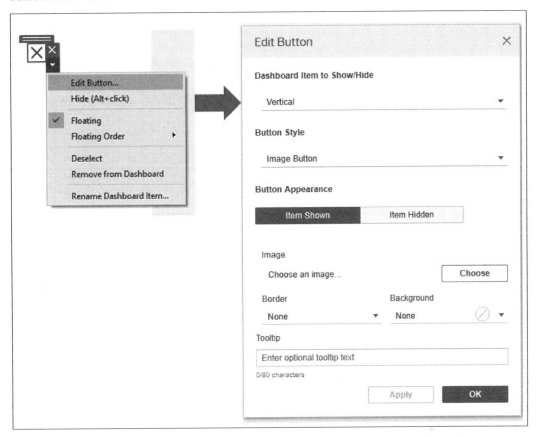

Figure 11.3: Selecting Edit Button... reveals many options for altering the button's behavior and appearance

In the resulting dialog box, you'll have options for selecting which layout container to show or hide, the style of the button (image or text), and which images or text to show when the container is shown or hidden.

In this example, the Show/Hide button uses the default **Image Button** style (as seen in *Figure 11.3*) and the layout container has been filled with a couple of filters and the map's legend.

You may include any dashboard objects in a container, including filters, legends, parameter and set controls, and even other views!

Additionally, the container has been given a border and a semi-transparent background so that the map is slightly visible beneath the container. This was accomplished by selecting the container and then using the **Layout** tab of the **Dashboard** pane, as shown here:

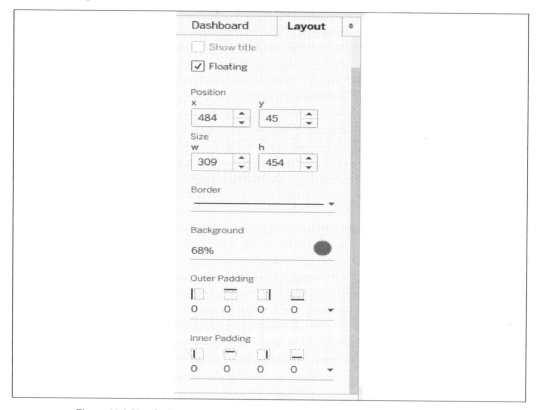

Figure 11.4: Use the Layout pane to adjust options for any selected dashboard object

The end result, demonstrated in the Chapter 11 workbook, is a dashboard with a Show/Hide button that makes it clear to the user that additional options can be shown or hidden:

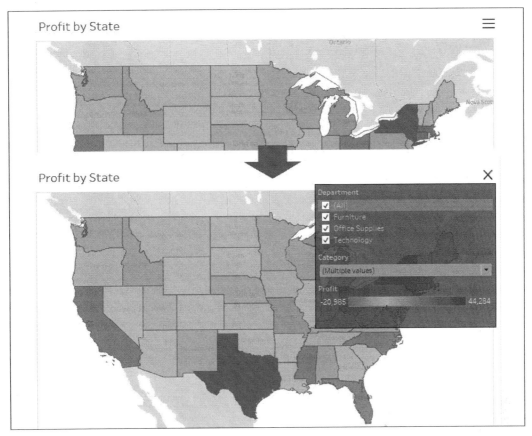

Figure 11.5: Here you can see the layout container's hidden and shown
states along with the changing image of the button

Use *Alt + Click* while in **Design Mode** to trigger the button action,
or switch to **Presentation Mode** where a single click will trigger
the button.

Show/Hide buttons give you a lot of flexibility in your dashboard design, from
optimizing space to simplifying the display, to removing filters and other clutter
from printed output.

Consider another example in the Chapter 11 Complete workbook that illustrates the possibility of showing and hiding instructions:

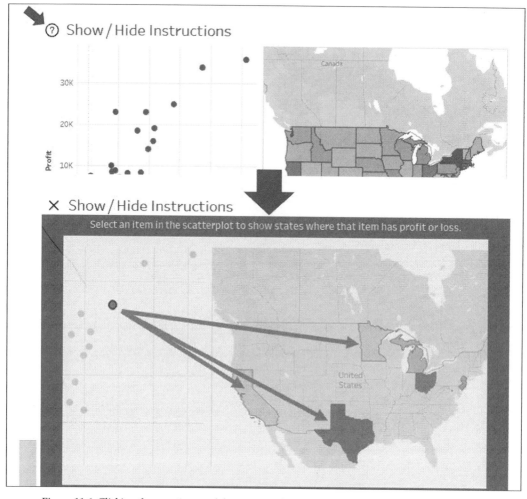

Figure 11.6: Clicking the question mark button reveals instructions for how to use the dashboard

In this case, the default button image has been replaced with a question mark icon. This is accomplished by editing the image as illustrated in *Figure 11.3* and changing the image (questionmark.png is included in the Chapter 11 directory.)

When the user clicks the button, a floating container appears over the top of the entire dashboard. It includes text as well as an annotated image to instruct the user on how to use the dashboard. In this simple example, it might be overkill to supply instructions in this way, when a simple text label would suffice.

However, as you build more complex dashboards or have detailed analyses that require explanation, this is a great way to give users additional instructions and detail that would otherwise clutter a dashboard.

> Consider also using Show/Hide buttons to allow user interactivity that you do not want to include in PDFs or printed pages of the dashboards. Filters and parameters are incredibly useful, but you don't always want them to show up in a polished output.

Let's move on to consider another method of dynamically showing, hiding, and even swapping out content on a dashboard.

Sheet swapping

Sheet swapping, sometimes also called **sheet selection**, is a technique in which views are dynamically shown and hidden on a dashboard, often with the appearance of swapping one view for another. The dynamic hiding and showing of views on a dashboard has an even broader application. When combined with floating objects and layout containers, this technique allows you to create rich and dynamic dashboards.

Let's start with some fundamental principles of sheet swapping.

Basic principles of sheet swapping

The basic principles are relatively simple. A view on a dashboard collapses when the following occur:

- At least one field is on rows or columns
- It is in a horizontal or vertical **layout container**
- It does not have a fixed height or width and the layout container is not set to distribute items equally
- A combination of filters or hiding prevents any marks from being rendered

Additionally, titles and captions do not collapse with the view. However, these can be hidden so that the view collapses entirely.

Next, we'll explore an example of how sheet swapping can be used in practice.

Using sheet swapping to change views on a dashboard

Let's consider a simple example with a view showing **Profit by Department and Category** with a **Department** quick filter. The dashboard has been formatted (from the menu, select **Format | Dashboard**) with gray shading to help us see the effect:

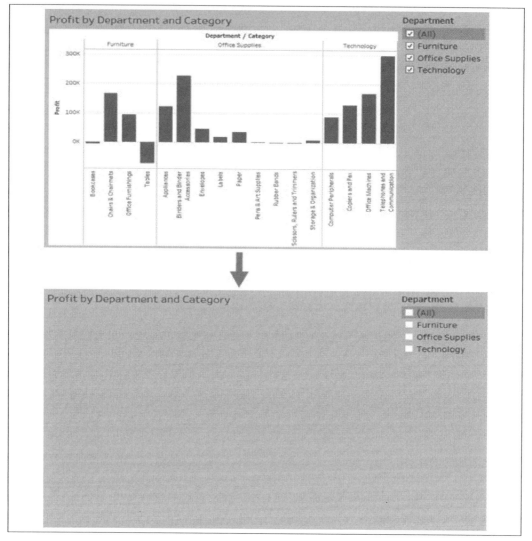

Figure 11.7: A demonstration of hiding a sheet in a dashboard

Observe how filtering out all departments results in the view collapsing. The title remains, but it could have been hidden.

In order to swap two different sheets, we simply take advantage of the collapsing behavior along with the properties of layout containers. We'll start by creating two different views filtered through a parameter and a calculated field. The parameter will allow us to determine which sheet is shown. Perform the following steps:

1. Create an integer parameter named Show Sheet with a list of **String** values set to **Bar Chart** and **Map**:

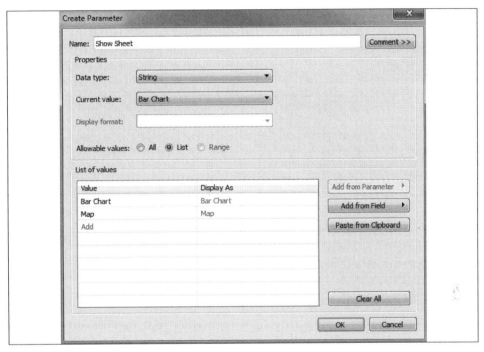

Figure 11.8: Creating a parameter to control which sheet is shown

2. Since we want to filter based on the parameter selection and the parameters cannot be directly added to the **Filters** shelf, instead we'll create a calculated field named Show Sheet Filter to return the selected value of the parameter. The code is simply [Show Sheet], which is the parameter name, which returns the current value of the parameter.

3. Create a new sheet named **Bar Chart**, similar to the **Profit by Department and Category** view shown in *Figure 11.7*.

4. Show the parameter control (right-click the parameter in the data window and select **Show Parameter Control**). Make sure the **Bar Chart** option is selected.

5. Add the Show Sheet Filter field to the **Filters** shelf and check **Bar Chart** to keep that value.

6. Create another sheet named **Map** that shows a filled map of states by profit:

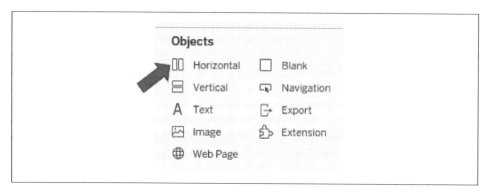

Figure 11.9: The Map view

7. Show the parameter on this view and change the selection to **Map**. Remember that parameter selections are universal to the worksheet. If you were to switch back to the **Bar Chart** view, it should no longer be showing any data because of the filter.

8. Add the Show Sheet Filter field to the **Filters** shelf and check **Map** as the value to keep.

9. Create a new dashboard named **Sheet Swap**.

10. Add a **Horizontal** layout container to the dashboard from the objects in the left window:

Figure 11.10: Insert a Horizontal layout container

> A **Vertical** layout container would work just as well in this case. The key is that a layout container will allow each view inside to expand to fill the container when the view is set to fit the entire view, or fit the width (for horizontal containers), or fit the height (for vertical containers). When one view collapses, the visible view will expand to fill the rest of the container.

11. Add each sheet to the layout container in the dashboard. The parameter control should be added automatically since it was visible in each view.

12. Using the drop-down menu on the **Bar Chart** view, ensure the view is set to fill the container (**Fit | Entire View**). You won't have to set the fill for the map because map visualizations automatically fill the container.

13. Hide the title for each view (right-click the title and select **Hide Title**).

You now have a dashboard where changing the parameter results in one view or the other being shown. When **Map** is selected, the filter results in no data for the bar chart, so it collapses and the map fills the container:

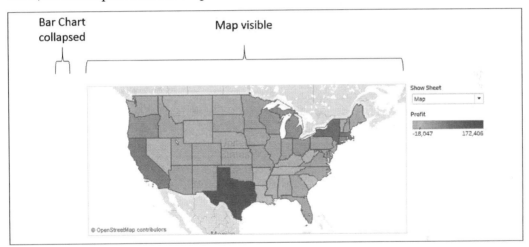

Figure 11.11: Map is visible while Bar Chart is collapsed

Alternately, when **Bar Chart** is selected, the map collapses due to the filter and the bar chart fills the container:

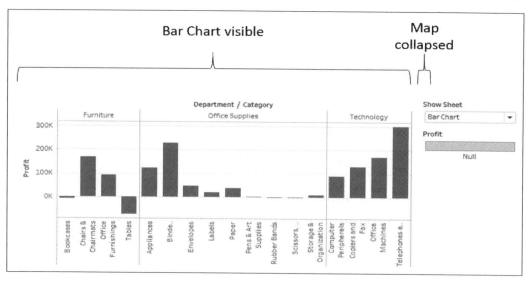

Figure 11.12: Bar Chart is visible while Map is collapsed

 The key to collapsing a view is to have a filter or set of filters that ensures no rows of data are shown. You do not have to use a parameter to control the filtering. You could use a regular filter or action filter to accomplish the same effect. This opens up all kinds of possibilities for dynamic behavior in dashboards.

Sheet swapping can lead to amazing effects on your dashboard. From allowing the user to select a type of visualization, to swapping out a view that works well for a small set of data, to a view that summarizes at a higher level for a larger set, consider using sheet swapping for a dynamic experience.

 In some cases, you might consider an alternative to sheet swapping, such as using a navigation button to navigate between different versions of the dashboard rather than trying to swap content in the same dashboard.

Sheet swapping allows you to swap views in a dashboard. What if the change in views makes certain legends, filters, or parameters no longer applicable and you wish to hide them? Let's consider some possibilities.

Automatically showing and hiding other controls

Views will collapse when all data is filtered out. However, other controls, such as quick filters, parameters, images, legends, and textboxes, will not collapse. You could use a Show/Hide button as we previously discussed, but often you'll want to show or hide these controls automatically as filters change, without forcing the user to take additional action.

Consider the simple example in the previous section. The color legend, which was automatically added to the dashboard by Tableau, applies to the map. But when the bar chart is shown, the legend is no longer applicable.

Fortunately, we can extend the technique we used in the previous section to expand a view to push items we want to show out from under a floating object and then collapse the view to allow the items we want to hide to return to a position under the floating object.

Let's extend the earlier sheet swapping example to see how to show and hide the color legend:

1. Create a new sheet named **Show/Hide Legend**. This view is only used to show and hide the color legend.

2. Create an ad hoc calculation by double-clicking on **Rows** and type MIN(1). We must have a field on rows or columns for the view to collapse, so we'll use this field to give us a single axis for **Rows** and a single axis for **Columns** without any other headers.

3. Duplicate the ad hoc calculation on **Columns**. You should now have a simple scatterplot with one mark.

4. As this is a helper sheet and not anything we want the user to see, we don't want it to show any marks or lines. Format the view using **Format | Lines** to remove **Grid Lines** from **Rows** and **Columns**, along with **Axis Rulers**. Additionally, hide the axes (right-click each axis or field and uncheck **Show Headers**). Also, set the color to full transparency to hide the mark.

5. We will want this view to show when the map option is selected, so show the parameter control and ensure it is set to **Map**, and then add the **Show Sheet Filter** to filters and check **Map**:

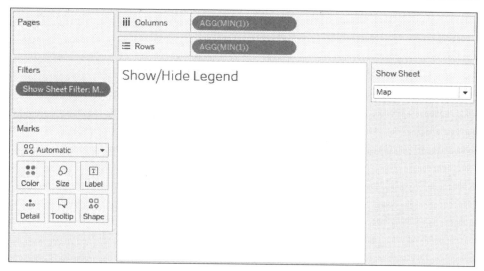

Figure 11.13: The Show/Hide Legend sheet with the Show Sheet Filter applied

6. On the **Sheet Swap** dashboard, add the **Show/Hide Legend** sheet to the layout container between the **Show Sheet** parameter dropdown and the color legend. Hide the title for the **Show/Hide Legend** sheet.

7. Ensure that **Map** is selected. The color legend should be pushed all the way to the bottom.

8. Add a layout container as a floating object. In terms of size and position, it should completely cover the area where the color legend used to be. It should cover the title of the **Show/Hide Legend** sheet but not the parameter dropdown.

 Objects and sheets can be added as floating objects by holding *Shift* while dragging, setting the **New Objects** option to **Floating,** or by using the drop-down menu on the object. You may also change the default behavior for new objects from tiled to floating in the **Dashboard** pane.

9. The layout container is transparent by default, but we want it to hide what is underneath. Format it using the drop-down menu and add white shading so it is indistinguishable from the background.

At this point, you have a dynamic dashboard in which the legend is shown when the map is shown and it is applicable, and hidden when the bar chart is visible. When **Map** is selected, the **Show/Hide Legend** sheet is shown and pushes the legend to the bottom of the **Layout Container**:

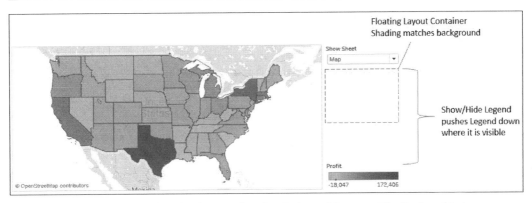

Figure 11.14: The Show/Hide Legend pushes the legend down past the floating object

When **Bar Chart** is selected, the **Show/Hide Legend** sheet collapses and the legend, which is no longer applicable to the view, falls under/hides behind the **Floating Layout Container**:

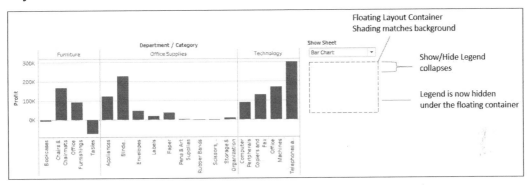

Figure 11.15: The Show/Hide Legend collapses, causing the legend to move under the floating object

There is no limit to how many variations of this technique you can use on a dashboard. You can have as many layers as you'd like. You can even use combinations of these techniques to push views and objects on and off the dashboard. The possibilities for creating a richly interactive user experience are incredible.

Summary

Creating truly dynamic dashboards give you incredible flexibility in your dashboard design. Show/Hide buttons give the end user the option to show or hide content on the dashboard. Sheet-swapping techniques allow you to swap out which views are shown and also automatically show or hide controls or other content.

The techniques covered in this chapter will enable you to accomplish all sorts of amazing interactivity, from hiding and showing controls, instructions, and explanations of business rules and analysis to allowing users to determine visualization types and swap views in and out.

Next, we'll turn our attention to exploring a certain kind of data using some advanced techniques: geospatial data!

12

Exploring Mapping and Advanced Geospatial Features

Up until now, we've seen examples of maps and geospatial visualizations that leverage some of the basic functionality of Tableau. In this chapter, we'll embark on a journey to uncover the vast range of mapping and geospatial features available. From levering the built-in geospatial database and supplementing it with additional data and spatial files, to using advanced geospatial functions, we'll explore what's possible with Tableau.

As we've done previously, this chapter will approach the concepts through some practical examples. These examples will span various industries, including real estate, transportation, and healthcare. As always, these examples are broadly applicable, and you'll discover many ways to leverage your data and uncover answers in the spatial patterns you'll find.

In this chapter, we'll cover the following topics:

- Overview of Tableau maps
- Rendering maps with Tableau
- Using geospatial data
- Leveraging spatial functions

- Creating custom territories
- Tableau mapping: tips and tricks
- Plotting data on background images

Overview of Tableau maps

Tableau contains an internal geographic database that allows it to recognize common geographic elements and render a mark at a specific latitude and longitude on a map. In many cases, such as with a country or state, Tableau also contains internal shapefiles that allow it to render the mark as a complex vector shape in the proper location. Tableau also leverages your specific geospatial data, such as latitude and longitude, shapefiles, and spatial objects. We'll consider some of those possibilities throughout this chapter. For now, we'll walk through some of the basics of how Tableau renders maps and some of the customizations and options available.

Rendering maps with Tableau

Consider the following screenshot (the Basic Map example in the Chapter 12 workbook), with certain elements numbered for reference:

Figure 12.1: A basic geospatial rendering in Tableau

The numbers indicate some of the important aspects of Tableau's ability to render maps:

1. A geographic field in the data is indicated with a globe icon. Fields that Tableau recognizes will have this icon by default. You may assign a geographic role to any field by using the menu and selecting **Geographic Role**.

2. The geographic field in the view (in this case, on **Detail**) is required to render the map.

3. If Tableau is able to match the geographic field with its internal database, the **Latitude (generated)** and **Longitude (generated)** fields placed on **Rows** and **Columns** along with the geographic field(s) on the **Marks** card will render a map.

4. Values that are not matched with Tableau's geographic database will result in an indicator that alerts you to the fact that there are unknown values.

You may right-click the unknown indicator to hide it, or click it for the following options:

- To edit locations (manually match location values to known values or latitude/longitude)

- Filter out unknown locations

- Plot at the default location (latitude and longitude of 0, a location that is sometimes humorously referred to as Null Island, located just off the west coast of Africa)

Tableau renders marks on the map similar to the way it would on a scatterplot (in fact, you might think of a map as a kind of scatterplot that employs some complex geometric transformations to project latitude and longitude). This means you can render circles, dots, and custom shapes on the map.

Under the marks, the map itself is a vector image retrieved from an online map service. We'll consider the details and how to customize the map layers and options next.

Customizing map layers

The map itself—the land and water, terrain, topography, streets, country and state borders, and more—are all part of a vector image that is retrieved from an online map service (an offline option is available).

Marks are then rendered on top of that image. You already know how to use data, calculations, and parameters to adjust how marks are rendered, but Tableau gives you a lot of control over how maps are rendered.

Use the menu to explore various options by selecting **Map | Background Maps**. Here, for example, is a **Dark Map**:

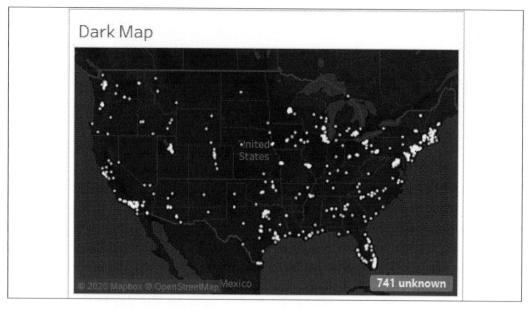

Figure 12.2: Dark Map is one of many options for map backgrounds

This map contains the exact same marks as the previous screenshot. It simply uses a different background. Other options include **Light**, **Streets**, **Satellite**, and more.

 If you will be using Tableau in an environment where the internet is not available (or publishing to a Tableau server that lacks an internet connection), select the **Offline** option. However, be aware that the offline version does not contain the detail or zoom levels available in the online options.

Additional layer options can be found by selecting **Map | Map Layers** from the menu. This opens a **Map Layers** pane that looks like this:

Figure 12.3: The Map Layers pane

The **Map Layers** pane gives you options for selecting a background, setting washout, selecting features to display, and setting a **Data Layer**. Various options may be disabled depending on the zoom level (for example, **Building Footprints** is not enabled unless you zoom in close enough on the map). **Data Layer** allows you to apply a filled map to the background based on various demographics. These demographics only appear as part of the image and are not interactive and the data is not exposed to either user interaction or calculation.

You may also use the menu options **Map | Background Maps | Manage Maps** to change which map service is used, allowing you to specify your own WMS server, a third party, or to use **Mapbox** maps. This allows you to customize the background layers of your map visualizations in any way you'd like.

The details of these capabilities are outside the scope of this book, however, you'll find excellent documentation from Tableau at https://help.tableau.com/current/pro/desktop/en-us/ maps_mapsources_wms.htm.

Customizing map options

Additionally, you can customize the map options available to end users. Notice the controls that appear when you hover over the map:

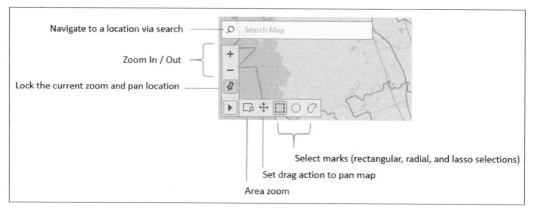

Figure 12.4 : Available controls when customizing a map

These controls allow you to search map, zoom in and out, pin the map to the current location, and use various types of selections.

 You can also use keyboard and mouse combinations to navigate the map. Use *Ctrl* + Mouse wheel or *Shift* + *Ctrl* + Mouse Click to zoom. Click and hold or *Shift* + Click to pan.

Additional options will appear when you select **Map | Map Options** from the top menu:

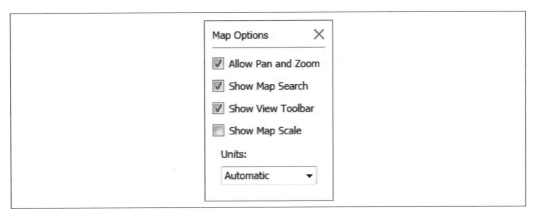

Figure 12.5: Map Options

These options give you the ability to set what map actions are allowed for the end user and whether to show a scale. Additionally, you can set the units displayed for the scale and **radial selections**. The options are **Automatic** (based on system configuration), **Metric** (meters and kilometers), and **U.S.** (feet and miles).

There are quite a few other geospatial capabilities packed into Tableau and we'll uncover some of them as we next explore how to leverage geospatial data.

Using geospatial data

We've seen that with any data source, Tableau supplies **Latitude (generated)** and **Longitude (generated)** fields based on any fields it matches with its internal geographic database. Fields such as country, state, zip code, MSA, and congressional district are contained in Tableau's internal geography. As Tableau continues to add geographic capabilities, you'll want to consult the documentation to determine specifics on what the internal database contains.

However, you can also leverage specific geospatial data in your visualizations. We'll consider ways to use data that enable geospatial visualizations, including the following:

- Including Latitude and Longitude as values in your data.
- Importing a .csv file containing definitions of Latitude and Longitude into Tableau's database.
- Leveraging Tableau's ability to connect to various spatial files or databases that natively support spatial objects.

We'll explore each of these options in the following section and then look at how to extend the data even further with geospatial functions in the next.

Including latitude and longitude in your data

Including latitude and longitude in your data gives you a lot of flexibility in your visualizations (and calculations). For example, while Tableau has built-in geocoding for countries, states, and zip codes, it does not provide geocoding at an address level. Supplying latitude or longitude in your data gives you the ability to precisely position marks on the map.

You'll find the following example in the Chapter 12 workbook using the Real Estate data source:

Figure 12.6: A map of houses for sale, sized by price

Here, each individual house could be mapped with a precise location and sized according to price. In order to help the viewer visually, the **Streets** background has been applied.

There are many free and commercial utilities that allow you to **geocode** addresses. That is, given an address, these tools will add latitude and longitude.

If you are not able to add the fields directly to your data source, you might consider using cross-database joins or data blending. Another alternative is to import latitude and longitude definitions directly into Tableau. We'll consider this option next.

Importing definitions into Tableau's geographic database

In order to import from the menu, select **Map | Geocoding | Import Custom Geocoding...** The import dialog contains a link to documentation describing the option in further detail:

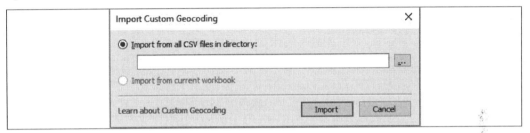

Figure 12.7: The Import Custom Geocoding dialog box

By importing a set of definitions, you can either:

- Add new geographic types
- Extend Tableau's built-in geographic types

Latitude and longitude define a single point. At times, you'll need to render shapes and lines with more geospatial complexity. For that, you'll want to consider some of the geospatial functions and spatial object support, which we'll look at next.

Leveraging spatial objects

Spatial objects define geographic areas that can be as simple as a point and as complex as multi-sided polygons. This allows you to render everything from custom trade areas to rivers, roads, and historic boundaries of counties and countries. Spatial objects can be stored in spatial files and are supported by some relational databases as well.

Tableau supports numerous spatial file formats, such as ESRI, MapInfo, KML, GeoJSON, and TopoJSON. Additionally, you may connect directly to ESRI databases as well as relational databases with geospatial support, such as ESRI or SQL Server. If you create an extract, the spatial objects will be included in the extract.

Many applications, such as Alteryx, Google Earth, and ArcGIS, can be used to generate spatial files. Spatial files are also readily available for download from numerous organizations. This gives you a lot of flexibility when it comes to geospatial analysis.

Here, for example, is a map of US railroads:

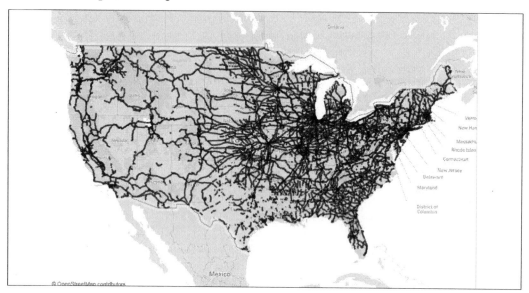

Figure 12.8: Map of US railroads

To replicate this example, download the shapefile from the United States' Census Bureau here: https://catalog.data.gov/dataset/tiger-line-shapefile-2015-nation-u-s-rails-national-shapefile.

Once you have downloaded and unzipped the files, connect to the tl_2015_us_rails.shp file. In the preview, you'll see records of data with ID fields and railway names. The **Geometry** field is the spatial object that defines the linear shape of the railroad segment:

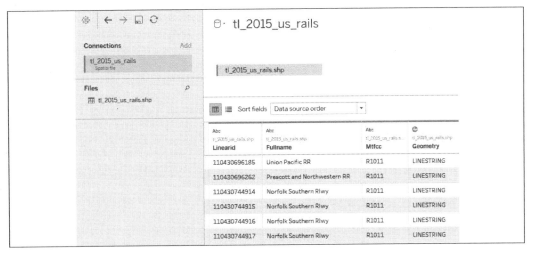

Figure 12.9: Map of US railroads preview

On a blank sheet, simply double-click the **Geometry** field. Tableau will include the geographic collection in the detail and introduce automatically generated latitude and longitude fields to complete the rendering. Experiment with including the ID field in the detail and with filtering based on **Fullname**.

 Consider using cross-database joins to supplement existing data with custom spatial data. Additionally, Tableau supports spatial joins, which allow you to bring together data that is only related spatially, even if no other relationships exist.

Next, we'll take a look at leveraging some spatial functions and even a spatial join or two to extend your analytics.

Leveraging spatial functions

Tableau continues to add native support for spatial functions. At the time of writing, Tableau supports the following functions:

- `Makeline()` returns a line spatial object given two points.
- `Makepoint()` returns a point spatial object given two coordinates.
- `Distance()` returns the distance between two points in the desired units of measurement.
- `Buffer()` creates a circle around a point with a radius of the given distance. You may specify the units of measurement.

We'll explore a few of these functions using the Hospital and Patients dataset in the Chapter 12 workbook. The dataset reimagines the real estate data as a hospital surrounded by patients, indicated in the following view by the difference in **Shape**, **Size**, and **Color**:

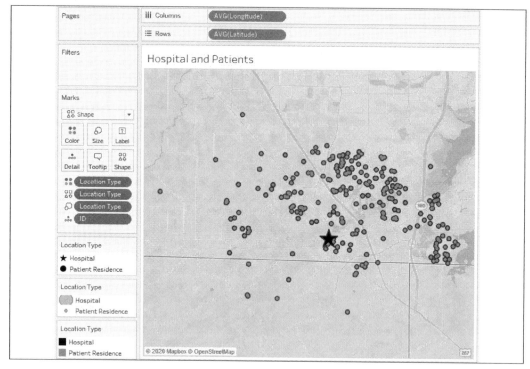

Figure 12.10: A hospital (represented by the star) surrounded by patients

There are numerous analytical questions we might ask. Let's focus on these:

- How far is each patient from the hospital?
- How many patients fall within a given radius?
- Which patients are outside the radius?

To start answering these questions, we'll create some calculated fields that give us the building blocks. In order to use multiple points in the same calculation, the latitude and longitude of the hospital will need to be included with each patient record. One way to achieve this is by using a couple of FIXED **Level of Detail (LOD)** expressions to return the values to each row.

We'll create a calculation called Hospital Latitude with the following code:

```
{FIXED : MIN(IF [Location Type] == "Hospital" THEN [Latitude] END)}
```

And a corresponding calculation called Hospital Longitude with the following code:

```
{FIXED : MIN(IF [Location Type] == "Hospital" THEN [Longitude] END)}
```

In each case, the latitude and longitude for the hospital is determined with the IF/THEN logic and returned as a row-level result by the FIXED LOD expression. This gives us the building blocks for a couple of additional calculations. We'll next consider a couple of examples, contained in the Chapter 12 workbook.

MAKELINE() and MAKEPOINT()

As we consider these two functions, we'll create a calculated field to draw a line between the hospital and each patient. We'll name our calculation Line and write this code:

```
MAKELINE(
    MAKEPOINT([Hospital Latitude], [Hospital Longitude]),
    MAKEPOINT([Latitude], [Longitude])
)
```

MAKELINE() requires two points, which can be created using the MAKEPOINT() function. That function requires a latitude and longitude. The first point is for the hospital and the second is the latitude and longitude for the patient.

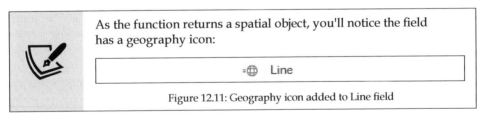

As the function returns a spatial object, you'll notice the field has a geography icon:

=⊕	Line

Figure 12.11: Geography icon added to Line field

On a new visualization, if you were to double-click the **Line** field, you'd immediately get a geographic visualization because that field defines a geospatial object. You'll notice the **COLLECT(Line)** field on **Detail**, and Tableau's **Longitude (generated)** and **Latitude (generated)** on **Columns** and **Rows**. The geospatial collection is drawn as a single object unless you split it apart by adding dimensions to the view.

In this case, each ID defines a separate line, so adding it to **Detail** on the **Marks** card splits the geospatial object into separate lines:

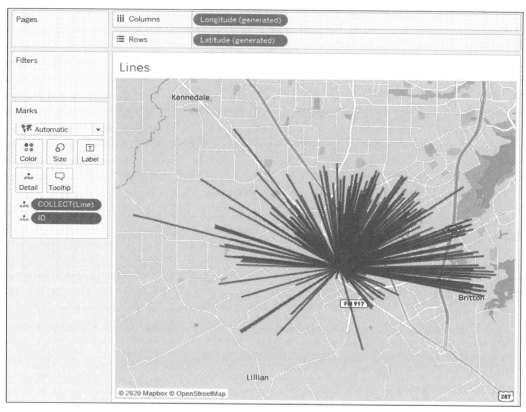

Figure 12.12: Each line originates at the hospital and is drawn to a patient

What if we wanted to know the distance covered by each line? We'll consider that next in an expanded example.

DISTANCE()

Distance can be a very important concept as we analyze our data. Knowing how far apart two geospatial points are can give us a lot of insight. The calculation itself is very similar to MAKELINE() and we might create a calculated field named Distance to the Hospital with the following code:

```
DISTANCE(
    MAKEPOINT([Hospital Latitude], [Hospital Longitude]),
    MAKEPOINT([Latitude], [Longitude]),
    'mi'
)
```

Similar to the MAKELINE() calculation, the DISTANCE() function requires a couple of points, but it also requires a unit of measurement. Here, we've specified miles using the argument 'mi', but we could have alternately used 'km' to specify kilometers.

We can place this calculation on **Tooltip** to see the distance covered by each line:

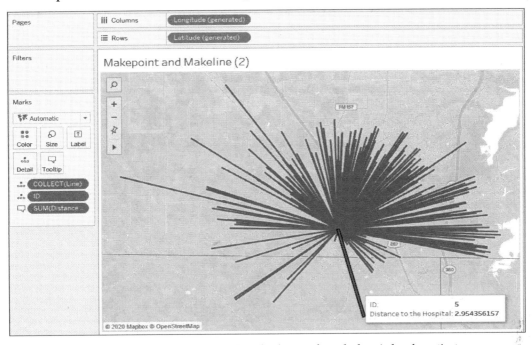

Figure 12.13: The tooltip now displays the distance from the hospital to the patient

This simple example could be greatly extended. Right now, we can tell that patient ID **5** is **2.954...** miles away from the hospital when we hover over the line. We could improve the display by rounding down the distance to 2 decimal places or looking up the patient's name. We could greatly increase the analytical usefulness by using the distance as a filter (to analyze patients that are over or under a certain threshold of distance) or using distance as a correlating factor in more complex analysis.

We can accomplish some of this visually with Buffer(), which we'll explore next!

BUFFER()

Buffer is similar to DISTANCE(), but the reverse. Rather than calculating a distance between two points, the BUFFER() function allows you to specify a point, a distance, and a unit of measurement to draw a circle with a radius of the specified distance around the point.

For example, you might want to visualize which patients fall within a 3-mile radius of the hospital. To do that, we'll create a calculated field named Hospital Radius, with the following code:

```
IF [Location Type] == "Hospital"
THEN BUFFER(MAKEPOINT([Latitude], [Longitude]), 3, 'mi')
END
```

This code first checks to make sure to perform the calculation only for the hospital record. The BUFFER() calculation itself uses the latitude and longitude to make a point and then specifies a 3-mile radius.

In order to visualize the radius along with the individual marks for each patient, we'll create a **dual-axis map**. A dual-axis map copies either the latitude or longitude fields on rows or columns and then uses the separate sections of the **Marks** card to render different geospatial objects. Here, for example, we'll plot the points for patients as circles and the radius using the **Automatic** mark type:

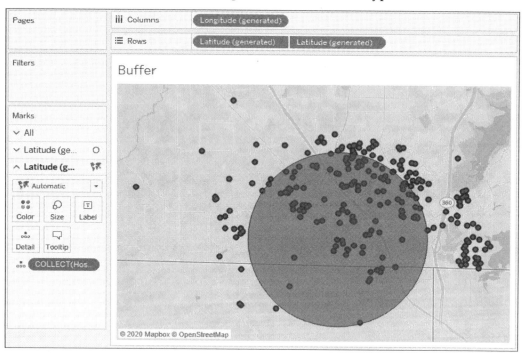

Figure 12.14: Patients who fall within a 3-mile radius of the hospital

Notice that we've used the generated **Latitude** and **Longitude** fields. These serve as placeholders for Tableau to visualize any spatial objects. On the first section of the **Marks** card, we include the **Latitude** and **Longitude** fields from the data. On the second, we included the **Hospital Radius** field. In both cases, the generated fields allow Tableau to use the geographic or spatial objects on the **Marks** card to define the visualization.

We've barely scratched the surface of what's possible with spatial functions. For example, you could parameterize the radius value to allow the end user to change the distance dynamically. You could use MAKEPOINT() and BUFFER() calculations as join calculations in your data source to bring together spatially related data. With this data, for example, you could **intersect join** the hospital record on BUFFER() to the patient records on MAKEPOINT() to specifically work with a dataset that includes or excludes patients within a certain radius. This greatly increases your analytic capabilities.

With a good understanding of the geospatial functions available, let's shift our focus just a bit to discuss another topic of interest: creating custom territories.

Creating custom territories

Custom territories are geographic areas or regions that you create (or that the data defines) as opposed to those that are built in (such as country or area code). Tableau gives you two options for creating custom territories: **ad hoc custom territories** and **field-defined custom territories**. We'll explore these next.

Ad hoc custom territories

You can create custom territories in an ad hoc way by selecting and grouping marks on a map. Simply select one or more marks, hover over one, and then use the **Group** icon. Alternately, right-click one of the marks to find the option. You can create custom territories by grouping by any dimension if you have latitude and longitude in the data or any geographic dimension if you are using Tableau's generated latitude and longitude.

Here, we'll consider an example using zip code:

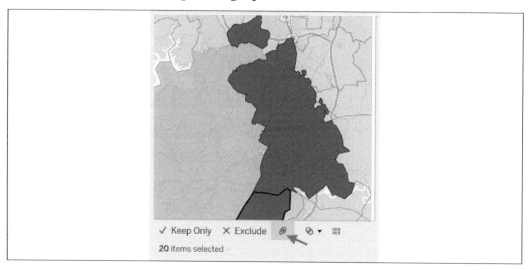

Figure 12.15: After selecting the filled regions to group as a new territory,
use the paperclip icon to create the group

You'll notice that Tableau creates a new field, Zip Code (group), in this example. The new field has a paperclip and globe icon in the data pane, indicating it is a group and a geographic field:

Custom Territories

Figure 12.16: A group and geographic field

Tableau automatically includes the group field on **Color**.

You may continue to select and group marks until you have all the custom territories you'd like. With zip code still part of the view level of detail, you will have a mark for each zip code (and any measure will be sliced by zip code). However, when you remove zip code from the view, leaving only the Zip Code (group) field, Tableau will draw the marks based on the new group:

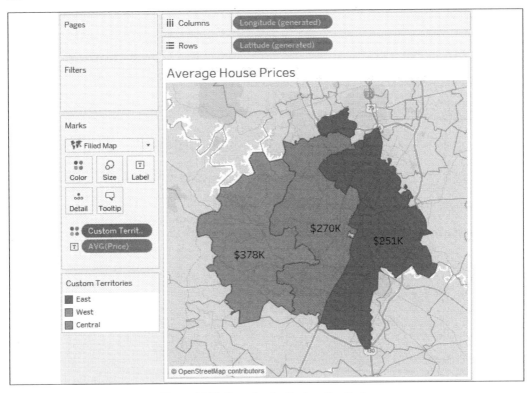

Figure 12.17: Grouping by Custom Territories

Here, the group field has been renamed `Custom Territories` and the group names have been aliased as `East`, `West`, and `Central`. We can see the average price of houses in each of the custom territories.

The details of these capabilities are outside the scope of this book, however, you'll find excellent documentation from Tableau at `https://help.tableau.com/current/pro/desktop/en-us/maps_mapsources_wms.htm`.

 With a filled map, Tableau will connect all contiguous areas and still include disconnected areas as part of selections and highlighting. With a symbol map, Tableau will draw the mark in the geographic center of all grouped areas.

Sometimes the data itself defines the territories. In that case, we won't need to manually create the territories. Instead, we'll use the technique described next.

Field-defined custom territories

Sometimes your data includes the definition of custom territories. For example, let's say your data had a field named **Region** that already grouped zip codes into various regions. That is, every zip code was contained in only one region. You might not want to take the time to select marks and group them manually.

Instead, you can tell Tableau the relationship already exists in the data. In this example, you'd use the drop-down menu of the **Region** field in the data pane and select **Geographic Role | Create From... | Zip Code**. **Region** is now a geographic field that defines custom territories:

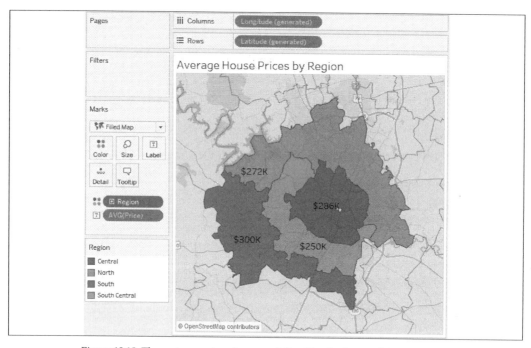

Figure 12.18: The custom regions here are defined by the Region field in the data

In this case, the regions have been defined by the **Region** field in the data. If the regions are redefined at a later date, Tableau will display the new regions (as long as the data is updated). Using field-defined custom regions gives us confidence that we won't need to manually update the definitions.

 Use ad hoc custom territories to perform quick analysis, but consider field-defined custom territories for long-term solutions because you can then redefine the territories in the data without manually editing any groups in the Tableau data source.

Tableau mapping – tips and tricks

There are a few other tips to consider when working with geographic visualizations:

Use the top menu to select **Map | Map Layers** for numerous options for what layers of background to show as part of the map.

- Other options for zooming include using the mouse wheel, double-clicking, *Shift + Alt* + click, and *Shift + Alt + Ctrl* + click.

- You can click and hold for a few seconds to switch to pan mode.

- You can show or hide the zoom controls and/or map search by right-clicking the map and selecting the appropriate option.

- Zoom controls can be shown on any visualization type that uses an axis.

- The pushpin on the zoom controls alternately returns the map to the best fit of visible data or locks the current zoom and location.

- You can create a **dual-axis map** by duplicating (*Ctrl* + drag/drop) either the **Longitude** on **Columns** or **Latitude** on **Rows** and then using the field's drop-down menu to select **Dual Axis**. You can use this technique to combine multiple mark types on a single map:

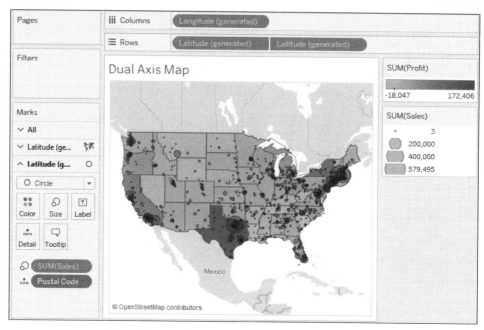

Figure 12.19: Dual Axis Map showing Profit at a state level
and Sales at a Postal Code level

You can use dual axes to display various levels of detail or to use different mark types. In this case, both are accomplished. The map leverages the dual axis to show **Profit** at a state level with a filled map and **Sales** at a **Postal Code** level with a circle:

- When using filled maps, consider setting **Washout** to **100%** in the **Map Layers** window for clean-looking maps. However, only filled shapes will show, so any missing states (or counties, countries, or others) will not be drawn:

Figure 12.20: Washed Out Map

- You can change the source of the background map image tiles using the menu and selecting **Map | Background Maps**. This allows you to choose between **None**, **Offline** (which is useful when you don't have an internet connection but is limited in the detail that can be shown), or **Tableau** (the default).

- Additionally, from the same menu option, you can specify **Map Services...** to use a WMS server or Mapbox.

Next, we'll conclude this chapter by exploring how plotting your data onto background images can further enhance data visualization and presentation.

Plotting data on background images

Background images allow you to plot data on top of any image. Consider the possibilities! You could plot ticket sales by seat on an image of a stadium, room occupancy on the floor plan of an office building, the number of errors per piece of equipment on a network diagram, or meteor impacts on the surface of the moon.

In this example, we'll plot the number of patients per month in various rooms in a hospital. We'll use two images of floorplans for the ground floor and the second floor of the hospital. The data source is located in the Chapter 12 directory and is named Hospital.xlsx. It consists of two tabs: one for patient counts and another for room locations based on the x/y coordinates mapped to the images. We'll shortly consider how that works. You can view the completed example in the Chapter 12 Complete. twbx workbook or start from scratch using Chapter 12 Starter.twbx.

To specify a background image, use the top menu to select **Map | Background Images** and then click the data source to which the image applies – in this example, Patient Activity (Hospital). On the **Background Images** screen, you can add one or more images.

Here, we'll start with Hospital - Ground Floor.png, located in the Chapter 12 directory:

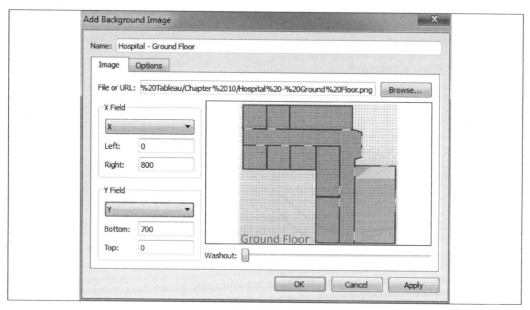

Figure 12.21: Add Background Image pane

You'll notice that we mapped the fields **X** and **Y** (from the **Locations** tab) and specified **Right** at **800** and **Bottom** at **700**. This is based on the size of the image in pixels.

You don't have to use pixels, but most of the time it makes it far easier to map the locations for the data. In this case, we have a tab of an Excel file with the locations already mapped to the **x** and **y** coordinates on the image (in pixels). With cross-database joins, you can create a simple text or Excel file containing mappings for your images and join them to an existing data source. You can map points manually (using a graphics application) or use one of many free online tools that allow you to quickly map coordinates on images.

We'll only want to show this blueprint for the ground floor, so switching to the **Options** tab, we'll ensure that the condition is set based on the data. We'll also make sure to check **Always Show Entire Image**:

Figure 12.22: Edit Background Image pane

Next, repeating the preceding steps, we'll add the second image (Hospital - 2nd Floor.png) to the data source, ensuring it only shows for 2nd Floor.

Once we have the images defined and mapped, we're ready to build a visualization. The basic idea is to build a scatterplot using the **X** and **Y** fields for axes. But we have to ensure that **X** and **Y** are not summed because if they are added together for multiple records, then we no longer have a correct mapping to pixel locations. There are a couple of options:

- Use **X** and **Y** as continuous dimensions.
- Use MIN, MAX, or AVG instead of SUM, and ensure that **Location** is used to define the view level of detail.
- Additionally, images are measured from 0 at the top to **Y** at the bottom, but scatterplots start with 0 at the bottom and values increase upward. So, initially, you may see your background images appear upside-down. To get around this, we'll edit the *y* axis (right-click and select **Edit Axis**) and check the option for **Reversed**.

We also need to ensure that the **Floor** field is used in the view. This is necessary to tell Tableau which image should be displayed. At this point, we should be able to get a visualization like this:

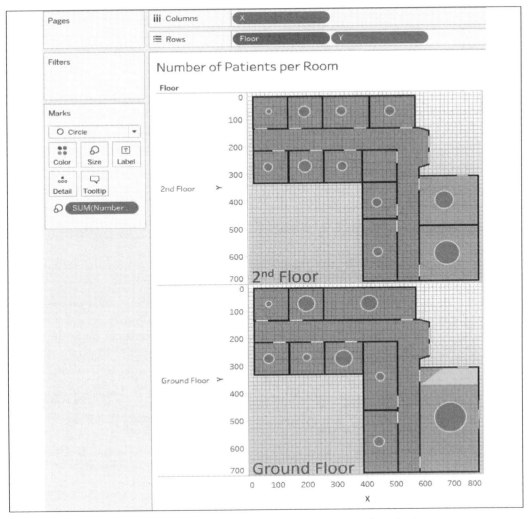

Figure 12.23: Plotting the number of patients per room on a floorplan image

Here, we've plotted circles with the size based on the number of patients in each room. We could clean up and modify the visualization in various ways:

- Hide the *x* and *y* axes (right-click the axis and uncheck **Show Header**)
- Hide the header for **Floor**, as the image already includes the label
- Add **Floor** to the **Filter** shelf so that the end user can choose to see one floor at a time

The ability to plot marks on background images opens a world of possibilities for communicating complex topics. Consider how you might show the number of hardware errors on a diagram of a computer network, the number of missed jump shots on a basketball court, or the distance between people in an office building. All of this, and more, is possible!

Summary

We've covered a lot of ground in this chapter! The basics of visualizing maps are straightforward, but there is a lot of power and possibility behind the scenes. From using your own geospatial data to leveraging geospatial objects and functions, you have a lot of analytical options. Creating custom territories and plotting data on background images expand your possibilities even further.

Next, we'll turn our attention to a brand new feature of Tableau 2020.2: Data Model! And we'll explore the difference between data model relationships, joins, blends, and see how all of them can be used to perform all kinds of valuable analysis!

13

Understanding the Tableau Data Model, Joins, and Blends

In this chapter, we'll gain a deeper understanding of how to model and structure data with Tableau. We've seen the **Data Source** screen in previous chapters and briefly explored how to drag and drop tables to form relationships. Now, we'll explore some of Tableau's more complex features to gain a good understanding of how Tableau allows you to relate multiple tables together, either logically or physically.

We'll start with a broad overview of Tableau's new data model and then examine some details of different types of joins and blends. The data model and blending apply primarily to Tableau Desktop (and Server), but pay special attention to the discussion of joins, as a good understanding of join types will aid you greatly when we discuss Tableau preparation in *Chapter 15, Taming Data with Tableau Prep.*

 The data model is only available in Tableau 2020.2 and later. If you are using an older version, the explanation of joins and blends will be directly applicable, while the explanation of the data model will serve as inspiration for you to upgrade!

In this chapter, we'll cover the following topics:

- Explanation of the sample data used in this chapter
- Exploring the Tableau data model
- Using joins
- Using blends
- When to use a data model, joins, or blends

We'll start by understanding the sample dataset included in the workbook for this chapter. This is so that you have a good foundation of knowledge before working through the examples.

Explanation of the sample data used in this chapter

For this chapter, we'll use a sample dataset of patient visits to the hospital. The data itself is contained in the Excel file `Hospital Visits.xlsx` in the `Learning Tableau\ Chapter 13` directory. The tabs of the Excel file represent tables of data, just as you might find in any relational database as multiple files, or simply as literal tabs in an Excel file! The relationship between those tables is illustrated here:

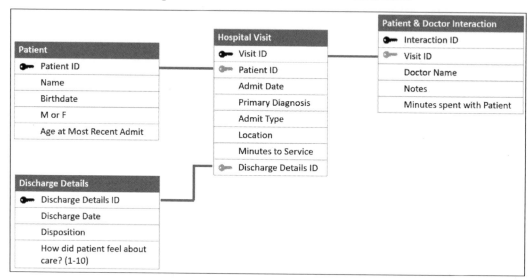

Figure 13.1: The four tabs of the Excel file illustrated as four tables with relationships

Excel does not explicitly define the relationships, but they are shown here as they might exist in a relational database using foreign key lookups. Here is a brief explanation of the tables and their relationships:

- **Hospital Visit**: This is the primary table that records the admission and diagnosis of a single patient on a single visit to the hospital. It contains attributes, such as **Admit Type** and **Location**, and a measure of **Minutes to Service**.

- **Patient**: This table contains additional information for a single patient, such as their **Name** and **Birthdate**, and a measure of their **Age at Most Recent Admit**.

- **Discharge Details**: This table gives additional information for the discharge of a patient, such as the **Discharge Date** and the **Disposition** (the condition under which they were discharged and where they went after being discharged). It also contains a measure **How did the patient feel about care? (1-10)** that ranks the patient's feelings about the level of care, with 1 being the lowest and 10 being the highest.

- **Patient & Doctor Interaction**: This table defines the interaction between a patient and a doctor during the visit. It includes the **Doctor Name**, **Notes**, and measures how long the doctor spent with the patient (**Minutes spent with Patient**).

The tables relate to each other in different ways. Here are some details:

- **Hospital Visit** to **Patient**: Each visit has a single patient, so **Hospital Visit** will always have a **Patient ID** field that points to a single record in the **Patient** table. We will also find additional patients in the **Patient** table who do not have recorded visits. Perhaps they are historical records from a legacy system or the patient's interaction with the hospital occurred in a manner other than a visit.

- **Hospital Visit** to **Discharge Details**: Each visit may have a single discharge, but some patients may still be in the hospital. In a well-designed data structure, we should be able to count on a record in the **Discharge Details** table that indicates "still in the hospital." In our Excel data, however, there may or may not be a **Discharge Details ID**, meaning there won't always be a matching **Discharge Details** record for every **Hospital Visit**.

- **Patient & Doctor Interaction** to **Hospital Visit**: Throughout the patient's visit, there may be one or more doctors who interact with a patient. It's also possible that no doctor records any interaction. So, we'll sometimes find multiple records in the **Patient & Doctor Interaction** that reference a single **Visit ID**, sometimes only a single record, and sometimes no records at all for a visit that exists in the **Hospital Visit** table.

With a solid grasp of the sample data source, let's turn our attention to how we might build a data model in Tableau.

Exploring the Tableau data model

You'll find the data model as a new feature in Tableau 2020.2 and later. Every data source will use the data model. Data sources created in previous versions will be updated to the data model but will be contained in a single object, so, functionally, they will work in the same way as the previous version.

Previous versions of Tableau allow you to leverage joining tables and blending data sources together, and we'll consider those options at the end of this chapter. For now, we'll look at creating a data model and understanding the paradigm.

Creating a data model

We've briefly looked at the **Data Source** screen in *Chapter 2, Connecting to Data in Tableau*. Now, we'll take a deeper look at the concepts behind the interface. Feel free to follow along with the following example in the Chapter 13 Starter.twb workbook, or examine the end results in Chapter 13 Complete.twbx.

We'll start by creating a connection to the Hospital Visits.xlsx file in the Chapter 13 directory. The **Data Source** screen will look like this upon first connecting to the file:

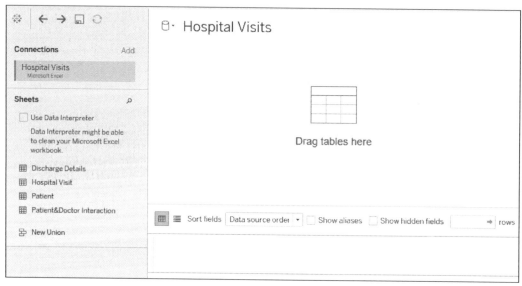

Figure 13.2: The Data Source screen lists the tabs in the Excel workbook and invites you to start a data model

We'll build the data model by dragging and dropping tables onto the canvas. We'll add all four tables. Tableau will suggest relationships for each new table added based on any matching field names and types. For our tables, we'll accept the default settings because the ID fields that indicate the correct relationship are identically named and typed.

The first table added is the root and forms the start of the data model. In this example, the order in which you add the tables won't matter, though you may notice a slightly different display depending on which table you start with. In the following screenshot, we've started with **Hospital Visit** (which is the primary table and, therefore, makes sense to be the root table) and then added all of the other tables:

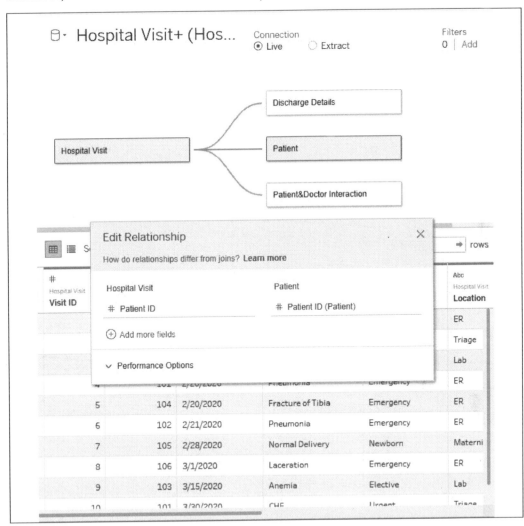

Figure 13.3: All tables have been added to the data model

You'll notice the **Edit Relationship** dialog box is open for the relationship between **Hospital Visit** and **Patient**. Tableau automatically created our relationships because the ID fields had the same name and type between both tables. If necessary, you could manually edit the relationships to change which fields define the relationship.

A **relationship** simply defines which fields connect the tables together. It does not define exactly how the tables relate to each other. We'll discuss the concepts of join types (for example, left join or inner join) later on in this chapter, but relationships are not restricted to a certain join type. Instead, Tableau will use the appropriate kind of join as well as the correct aggregations depending on which fields you use in your view. For the most part, you won't have to think about what Tableau is doing behind the scenes, but we'll examine some unique behaviors in the next section.

The ability to write calculations to define relationships is not available in 2020.2, but is a feature in 2020.3.

Also, notice the **Performance Options** drop-down menu in the relationship editor, as shown here:

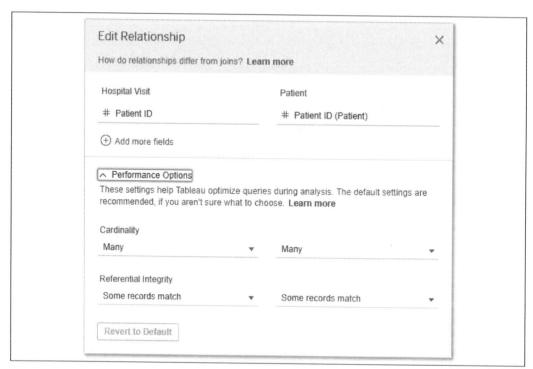

Figure 13.4: The Edit Relationship dialog box includes options to improve performance

These performance options allow Tableau to generate more efficient queries if the nature of the relationship is known. If you do not know the exact nature of the relationship, it is best to leave the options in their default settings as an incorrect setting can lead to incorrect results.

There are two basic concepts covered by the performance options:

- **Cardinality**: This term indicates how many records in one table could potentially relate to the records of another table. For example, we know that one visit matches to only one patient. However, we also know that many doctors could potentially interact with a patient during one visit.

- **Referential Integrity**: This term indicates whether we expect all records to find a match or whether some records could potentially be unmatched. For example, we know (from the preceding description) that there are patients in the **Patient** table that will not have a match in the **Hospital Visit** table. We also know that some patients will not have discharge records as they are still in the hospital.

If Tableau is able to determine constraints from a relational database, those constraints will be used. Otherwise, Tableau will set the defaults to **Many** and **Some records match**. For the examples in this chapter, we do know the precise nature of the relationships (they are described in the previous section), but we'll accept the performance defaults as the dataset is small enough that there won't be any perceptible performance gain in modifying them.

With our initial data model created, let's take a moment to explore the two layers of the data model paradigm.

Layers of the data model

A data model consists of two layers:

- The **logical layer**: A semantic layer made up of logical tables or objects that are related. Each logical table might be made up of one or more physical tables.

- The **physical layer**: A layer made up of the physical tables that come from the underlying data source. These tables may be joined or unioned together with conventional joins or unions or created from custom SQL statements.

Consider the following screenshot of a canvas containing our four tables:

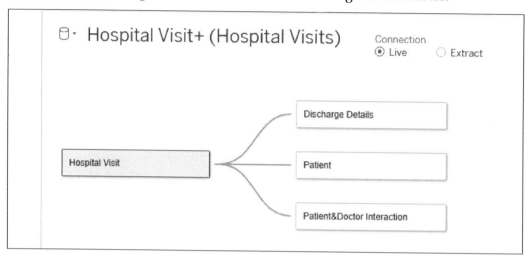

Figure 13.5: The logical layer of the data model

This initial canvas defines the **logical tables** of the data model. A logical table is a collection of data that defines a single structure or object that relates to other logical structures of data. Double-click on the **Hospital Visit** table on the canvas, and you'll see another layer beneath the logical layer:

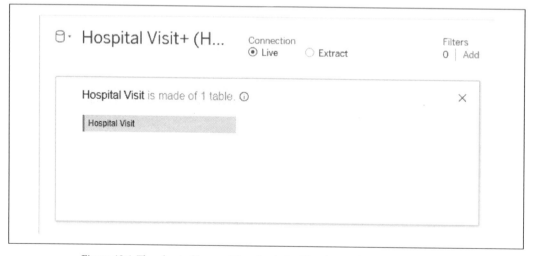

Figure 13.6: The physical layer of the physical tables that make up Hospital Visit

This is the physical layer for the logical **Hospital Visit** table. This physical layer is made up of physical tables of data—potentially unioned or joined together. In this case, we are informed that **Hospital Visit is made of 1 table**. So, in this case, the logical layer of **Hospital Visit** is identical to the physical layer underneath. In the *Using joins* section of this chapter, we'll explore examples of how we might extend the complexity of the physical layer with multiple tables while still treating the collection of tables as a single object.

Go ahead and close the physical layer of **Hospital Visit** with the **X** icon in the upper-right corner. Then navigate to the **Analysis** tab of the workbook for this chapter, and we'll explore how the data model works in practice.

Using the data model

For the most part, working with the data model will be relatively intuitive. If you've worked with previous Tableau versions, you'll notice some slight interface changes, and there are a few data model behaviors you should learn to expect. Once you are comfortable with them, your analysis will exceed expectations!

The new data pane interface

One thing you may notice is the difference in the **Data** pane, which will look something like this:

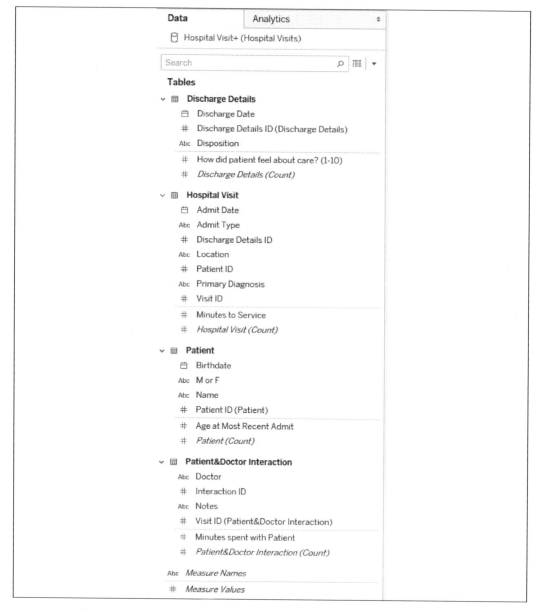

Figure 13.7: The Data pane is organized by logical tables and shows a separation of dimensions and measures per table

You'll notice that the **Data** pane is organized by logical tables, with fields belonging to each table. Measures and dimensions are separated by a thin line rather than appearing in different sections as they did previously. This makes it easier to find the fields relevant to your analysis and also helps you to understand the expected behavior of the data model. Also different from previous versions is that each logical table has its own `number of records` field that is named using the convention **Table Name (Count)**. You'll find the calculations you can add along with **Measure Names/Measure Values** at the bottom of the list of fields.

Following this overview of some of the UI changes, let's look at some behaviors you can expect from the data model.

Data model behaviors

In the **Analysis** tab of the `Starter` workbook, experiment with creating different visualizations. Especially note dimensions, what values are shown, and how measures are aggregated. We'll walk through a few examples to illustrate (which you can replicate in the `Starter` workbook or examine in the `Complete` workbook).

First, notice that dragging **Name** from the **Patient** table to **Rows** reveals 10 patients. It turns out that not all of these patients have hospital visits, but when we use one or more dimensions from the same logical table, we see the full domain of values in Tableau. That is, we see all the patients, whether or not they had visited the hospital. We can verify how many visits each patient had by adding the **Hospital Visit (Count)** field, resulting in the following view:

Figure 13.8: All patients are shown, even those with 0 visits

But if we add **Primary Diagnosis** to the table, notice that only 6 out of the 10 patients are shown:

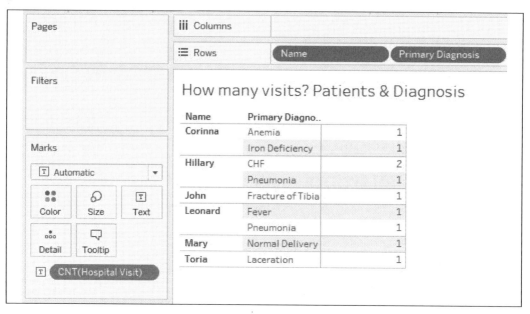

Figure 13.9: Only patients with visits are shown; most patients had a single visit with a given diagnosis, but one came in twice with the same diagnosis

This highlights another behavior: when you include dimensions from two or more tables, only matching values are shown. In essence, when you add **Name** and **Primary Diagnosis**, Tableau is showing you patients who exist in both the **Patient** and **Hospital Visit** tables. This is great if you want to focus on only patients who had visited the hospital.

But what if you truly want to see all patients and a diagnosis where applicable? To accomplish that, simply add a measure from the table of the field where you want to see the full domain. In this case, we could add either the **Age at Most Recent Admit** or **Patient (Count)** measures, as both come from the **Patient** table. Doing so results in the following view:

Figure 13.10: All patients are once again shown

Even though the **Age at Most Recent Admit** value is NULL for patients who have never been admitted, simply adding the measure to the view instructs Tableau to show all patients. This demonstrates a third behavior: including a measure from the same table as a dimension will force Tableau to show the full domain of values for that dimension.

Another basic principle of data model behavior is also displayed here. Notice that **Age at Most Recent Admit** is shown for each patient and each diagnosis. However, Tableau does not incorrectly duplicate the value in totals or subtotals. If you were to add subtotals for each patient in the **Age at Most Recent Admit** and **Count of Hospital Visit** columns, as has been done in the following view, you'll see that Tableau has the correct values:

Pages			

How old and how many visis?
with subtotals

Name	Primary Diagnosis	Age at Most Recent Admit	Count of Hospital Visit
Corinna	Anemia	41.00	1.00
	Iron Deficiency	41.00	1.00
	Total	41.00	2.00
Darrel	Null		0.00
	Total		0.00
Hillary	CHF	72.00	2.00
	Pneumonia	72.00	1.00
	Total	72.00	3.00
John	Fracture of Tibia	18.00	1.00
	Total	18.00	1.00
Leonard	Fever	22.00	1.00
	Pneumonia	22.00	1.00
	Total	22.00	2.00
Mary	Normal Delivery	30.00	1.00
	Total	30.00	1.00

Figure 13.11: Tableau calculates the subtotals correctly, even though traditional join behavior would have duplicated the values

This final behavior of the data model can be stated as: aggregates are calculated at the level of detail defined by the logical table of the measure. This is similar to how you might use a **Level of Detail (LOD)** expression to avoid a LOD duplication, but you didn't have to write the expression or break your flow of thought to solve the problem. The Tableau data model did the hard work for you!

Take some additional time to build out views and visualizations with the data model you've created. And review the following behaviors so you know what to expect and how to control the analysis you want to perform:

- When you use one or more dimensions from the same logical table, you'll see the full domain of values in Tableau
- When you include dimensions from two or more logical tables, only matching values are shown
- Including a measure from the same logical table as a dimension will force Tableau to show the full domain of values for that dimension (even when the previous behavior was in effect)
- Aggregates are calculated at the level of detail defined by the logical table of the measure

With just a bit of practice, you'll find that the behaviors feel natural, and you'll especially appreciate Tableau performing aggregations at the correct level of detail.

> When you first create a new data model, it is helpful to run through a couple of quick checks similar to the preceding examples. That will help you gain familiarity with the data model as well as help you validate that the relationships are working as you expect.

We'll now turn our focus to learn how to relate data in the physical layer using joins.

Using joins

A **join** at the physical level is a row-by-row matching of the data between tables. We'll look at some different types of joins and then consider how to leverage them in the physical layer of a data model.

Types of joins

In the physical layer, you may specify the following types of joins:

- **Inner**: Only records that match the join condition from both the table on the left and the table on the right will be kept. In the following example, only three matching rows are kept in the results:

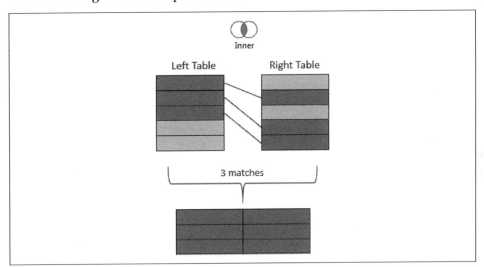

Figure 13.12: Inner join

- **Left**: All records from the table on the left will be kept. Matching records from the table on the right will have values in the resulting table, while unmatched records will contain NULL values for all fields from the table on the right. In the following example, the five rows from the left table are kept, with NULL results for any values in the right table that were not matched:

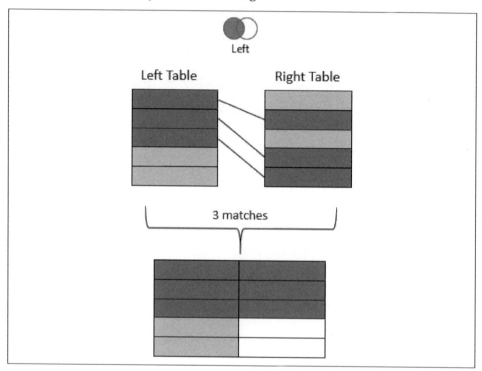

Figure 13.13: Left join

- **Right**: All records from the table on the right will be kept. Matching records from the table on the left will result in values, while unmatched records will contain NULL values for all fields from the table on the left. Not every data source supports a right join. If it is not supported, the option will be disabled. In the following example, the five rows from the right table are kept, with NULL results for any values from the left table that were not matched:

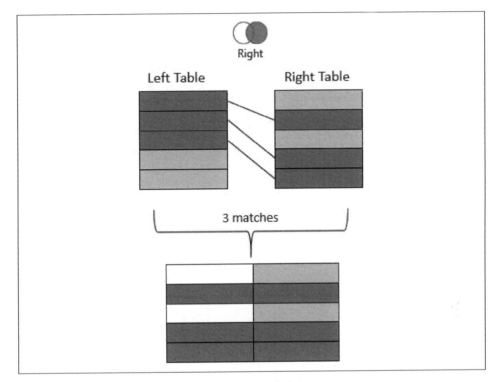

Figure 13.14: Right join

- **Full Outer**: All records from tables on both sides will be kept. Matching records will have values from the left and the right. Unmatched records will have NULL values where either the left or the right matching record was not found. Not every data source supports a full outer join. If it is not supported, the option will be disabled. In the following example, all rows are kept from both sides with NULL values where matches were not found:

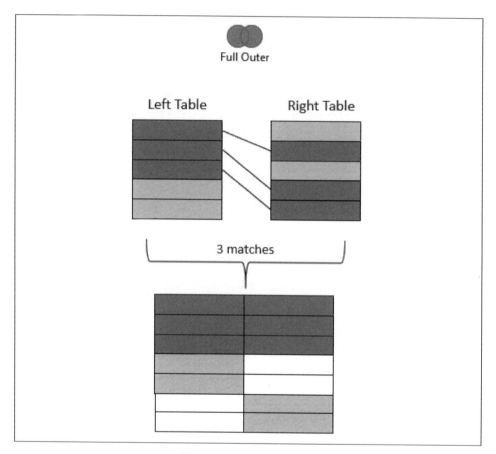

Figure 13.15: Full Outer join

- **Spatial**: This joins together records that match based on the **intersection** (overlap) of spatial objects (we discussed Tableau's spatial features in *Chapter 12, Exploring Mapping and Advanced Geospatial Features*). For example, a point based on the latitude and longitude might fall inside the complex shape defined by a shapefile. Records will be kept for any records where the spatial object in one table overlaps with the spatial object specified for the other:

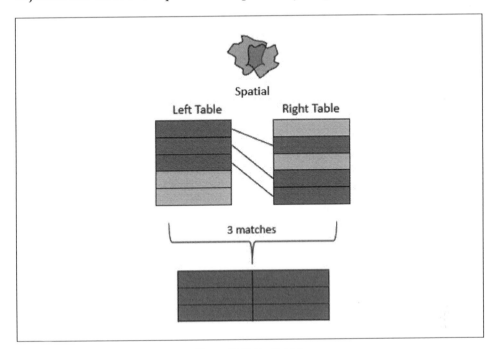

Figure 13.16: Spatial join

When you select spatial objects from the left and right tables, you'll need to specify **Intersects** as the operator between the fields to accomplish a spatial join, as shown in *Figure 13.17*:

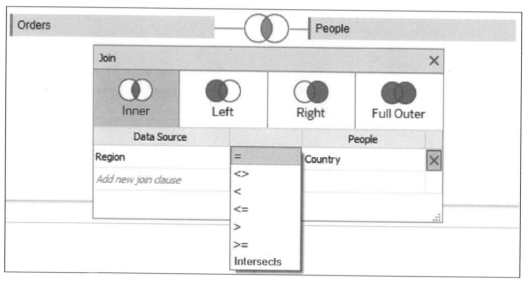

Figure 13.17: Assuming the two fields selected represent spatial objects, the Intersects option will be available

With a solid understanding of join types, let's consider how to use them in the physical layer of Tableau's data model.

Joining tables

Most databases have multiple tables of data that are related in some way. Additionally, you are able to join together tables of data across various data connections for many different data sources.

For our examples here, let's once again consider the tables in the hospital database, with a bit of simplification:

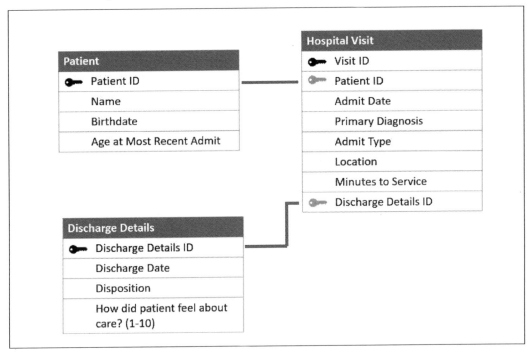

Figure 13.18: The primary Hospital Visit table with Patient and Discharge Details as they might exist in a relational database

Let's consider how we might build a data source using some joins in the physical layer. To follow along, create a new Excel data source in the Chapter 13 Starter. twbx workbook that references the Hospital Visits (Joins).xlsx file in the Chapter 13 directory. You may also examine the connection in the Chapter 13 Complete.twbx workbook.

Just as we did before, we'll start by dragging the **Hospital Visit** table onto the data source canvas such that we have a **Hospital Visit** object in the logical layer, like this:

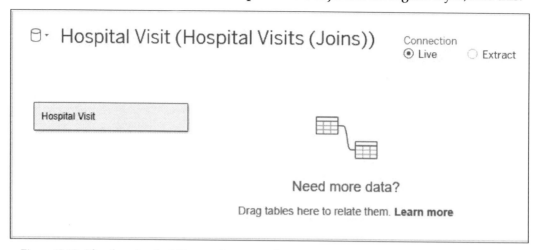

Figure 13.19: After dragging the table onto the canvas, the Hospital Visit object is created in the logical layer

At this point, the logical layer object simply contains a single physical table. But we'll extend that next. Double-click on the **Hospital Visit** object to expand the physical layer. It will look like this:

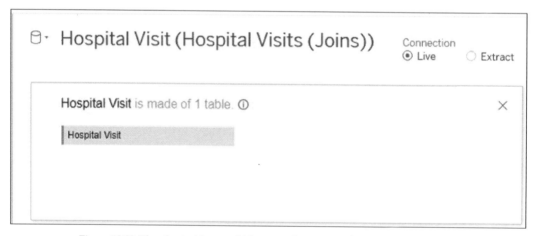

Figure 13.20: The physical layer, which currently consists of a single physical table

You can extend the physical model by adding additional tables. We'll do that here, by adding **Discharge Detail** and **Patient**. As we add them, Tableau will prompt you with a dialog box to adjust the details of the join. It will look like this:

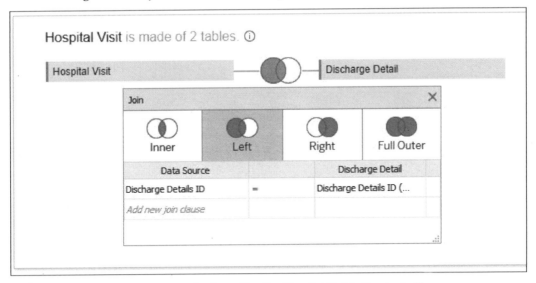

Figure 13.21: Joining Discharge Detail to Hospital Visit in the physical layer

The **Join** dialog allows you to specify the join type (**Inner, Left, Right,** or **Full Outer**) and to specify one or more fields on which to join. Between the fields, you may select which kind of operator joins the fields. The default is equality (=; the fields must be equal), but you may also select inequality (<>; the fields must not be equal), less than (<), less than or equal to (<=), greater than (>), or greater than or equal to (>=). The type of join and the field relationships that define the join will determine how many records are returned from the join. We'll take a look at the details in the next section.

 Typically, you'll want to start by dragging the primary table onto the physical layer canvas. In this case, **Hospital Visit** contains keys to join additional tables. Additional tables should be dragged and dropped after the primary table.

For now, accept the fields that Tableau automatically detects as shared between the tables (**Discharge Details ID** for **Discharge Details** and **Patient ID** for **Patient**). Change the join to **Discharge Details** to a left join. This means that all hospital visits will be included, even if there has not yet been a discharge. Leave **Patient** as an inner join. This will return only records that are shared between the tables so that only patients with visits will be retained.

Ultimately, the physical layer for **Hospital Visit** will look like this:

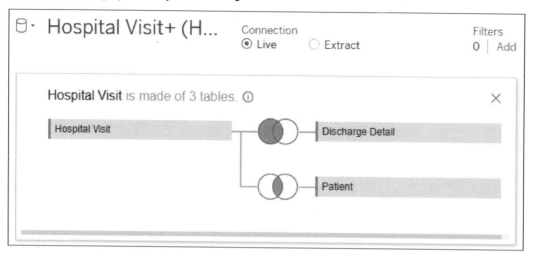

Figure 13.22: The physical layer is made up of three tables joined together

When you close the physical layer, you'll once again see the logical layer, which contains a single object: **Hospital Visit**. That object now contains a join icon, indicating that it is made up of joined physical tables. But it remains a single object in the logical layer of the data model and looks like this:

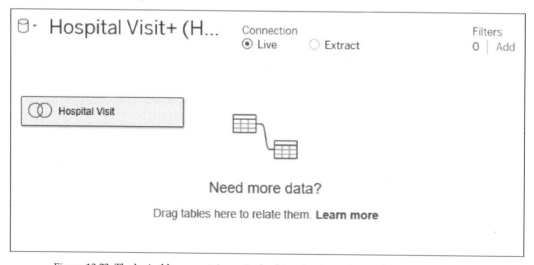

Figure 13.23: The logical layer contains a single object that is made up of three physical tables

All the joins create what you might think of as one flat table, which can be related together with other objects in the data model. Those objects, in turn, might each be made up of a single physical table or multiple physical tables joined together.

If you are following along with the example, rename this data source **Hospital Visits (Joins)**. We'll leverage this data source for one more example at the end of this chapter. In the meantime, let's consider a few additional details related to joins.

Other join considerations

We conclude this section with some further possibilities to leverage joins, as well as a caution regarding a potential problem that can arise from their use.

Join calculations

In the previous example, we noted that Tableau **joins** row-by-row based on fields in the data. You may come across cases where you need to join based on values that are not present in the data but can be derived from the existing data. For example, imagine that there is a **Patient Profile** table that would add significant value to your dataset. However, it lacks a **Patient ID** and only has **First Name** and **Last Name** fields.

To join this to our **Patient** table, we can use a **join calculation**. This is a calculation that exists only for the purpose of joining tables together. To create a join calculation, use the drop-down list of fields in the **Join** dialog box and select the final option, **Create Join Calculation**:

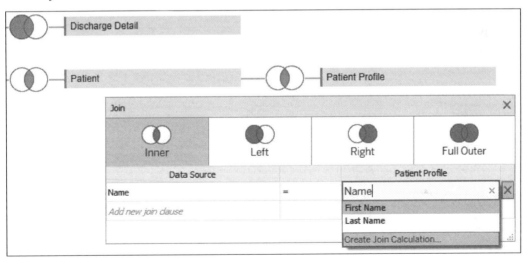

Figure 13.24: You can create a join calculation to aid in forming the correct joins

Selecting this option allows you to write row-level calculations that can be used in the join. For example, our join calculation might have code like [First Name] + " " + [Last Name] to return values that match with the **Name** field.

Try to avoid joining on text fields, especially in larger datasets for performance reasons. Joining on integers is far more efficient. Also, it is entirely possible for two separate people to share first and last names, so a real-world dataset that followed the structure in this example would be subject to false matches and errors.

You may also leverage the geospatial functions mentioned in *Chapter 12, Exploring Mapping and Advanced Geospatial Features*, to create a spatial join between two sources, even when one or both lack specific spatial objects on which to join. For example, if you have Latitude and Longitude, you might create a join calculation with the code MAKEPOINT([Latitude], [Longitude]) to find the intersection with another spatial object in another table.

Join calculations can also help when you are missing a field for a join. What if the data you want to join is in another database or file completely? In this scenario, we would consider cross-database joins.

Cross-database joins

With Tableau, you have the ability to join (at the row level) across multiple different data connections. Joining across different data connections is referred to as a **cross-database join**. For example, you can join SQL Server tables with text files or Excel files, or join tables in one database with tables in another, even if they are on a different server. This opens up all kinds of possibilities for supplementing your data or analyzing data from disparate sources.

Consider the hospital data. Though not part of the data included the Chapter 13 file set, it would not be uncommon for billing data to be in a separate system from patient care data. Let's say you had a file for patient billing that contained data you wanted to include in your analysis of hospital visits. You would be able to accomplish this by adding the text file as a data connection and then joining it to the existing tables, as follows:

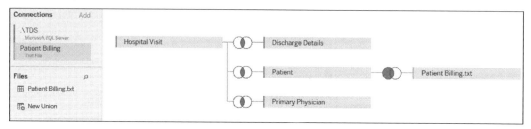

Figure 13.25: Joining tables or files based on separate data connections

You'll notice that the interface on the **Data Source** screen includes an **Add** link that allows you to add data connections to a data source. Clicking on each connection will allow you to drag and drop tables from that connection into the **Data Source** designer and specify the joins as you desire. Each data connection will be color-coded so that you can immediately identify the source of various tables in the designer.

You may also use multiple data sources in the logical layer.

Another consideration with joins is an unintentional error, which we'll consider next.

The unintentional duplication of data

Finally, we conclude with a warning about joins—if you are not careful, you could potentially end up with a few extra rows or many times the number of records than you were expecting. Let's consider a theoretical example:

Let's say you have a Visit table like this:

Visit ID	Patient Name	Doctor ID
1	Kirk	1
2	Picard	2
3	Sisko	3

And a Doctor table like this:

Doctor ID	Doctor Name
1	McCoy
2	Crusher
3	Bashir
2	Pulaski

Notice that the value 2 for Doctor ID occurs twice in the Doctor table. Joining the table on equality between the Doctor ID value will result in duplicate records, regardless of which join type is used. Such a join would result in the following dataset:

Visit ID	Patient Name	Doctor ID	Doctor Name
1	Kirk	1	McCoy
2	Picard	2	Crusher
3	Sisko	3	Bashir
2	Picard	2	Pulaski

This will greatly impact your analysis. For example, if you were counting the number of rows to determine how many patient visits had occurred, you'd overcount. There are times when you may want to intentionally create duplicate records to aid in analysis; however, often, this will appear as an unintentional error.

 In addition to the danger of unintentionally duplicating data and ending up with extra rows, there's also the possibility of losing rows where values you expected to match didn't match exactly. Get into the habit of verifying the row count of any data sources where you use joins.

A solid understanding of joins will not only help you as you leverage Tableau Desktop and Tableau Server, but it will also give you a solid foundation when we look at Tableau Prep in *Chapter 15, Taming Data with Tableau Prep*. For now, let's wrap up this chapter with a brief look at blends.

Using blends

Data blending allows you to use data from multiple data sources in the same view. Often, these sources may be of different types. For example, you can blend data from Oracle with data from Excel. You can blend Google Analytics data with a spatial file. Data blending also allows you to compare data at different levels of detail. Let's consider the basics and a simple example.

Data blending is done at an aggregate level and involves different queries sent to each data source, unlike joining, which is done at the row level and (conceptually) involves a single query to a single data source. A simple data blending process involves several steps, as shown in the following diagram:

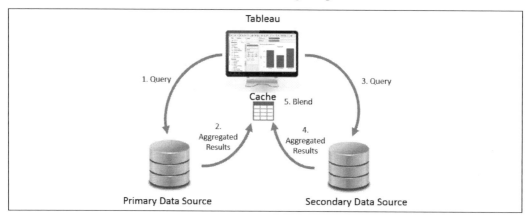

Figure 13.26: How Tableau accomplishes blending

We can see the following from the preceding diagram:

1. Tableau issues a query to the primary data source.

2. The underlying data engine returns aggregate results.

3. Tableau issues another query to the secondary data source. This query is filtered based on the set of values returned from the primary data source for dimensions that link the two data sources.

4. The underlying data engine returns aggregate results from the secondary data source.

5. The aggregated results from the primary data source and the aggregated results from the secondary data source are blended together in the cache.

It is important to note that data blending is different from joining. Joins are accomplished in a single query and results are matched row-by-row. Data blending occurs by issuing two separate queries and then blending together the aggregate results.

There can only be one primary source, but there can be as many secondary sources as you desire. *Steps 3 and 4* are repeated for each secondary source. When all aggregated results have been returned, Tableau matches the aggregated rows based on linking fields.

When you have more than one data source in a Tableau workbook, whichever source you use first in a view becomes the primary source for that view.

Blending is view-specific. You can have one data source as the primary in one view and the same data source as the secondary in another. Any data source can be used in a blend, but OLAP cubes, such as in SQL Server Analysis Services, must be used as the primary source.

In many ways, blending is similar to creating a data model with two or more objects. In many cases, the data model will give you exactly what you need without using blending. However, you have a lot more flexibility with blending because you can change which fields are related at a view level rather than at an object level.

Linking fields are dimensions that are used to match data blended between primary and secondary data sources. Linking fields define the level of detail for the secondary source. Linking fields are automatically assigned if fields match by name and type between data sources.

Otherwise, you can manually assign relationships between fields by selecting, from the menu, **Data | Edit Blend Relationships**, as follows:

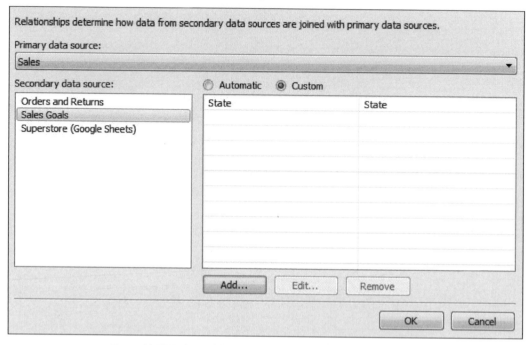

Figure 13.27: Defining blending relationships between data sources

The **Relationships** window will display the relationships recognized between different data sources. You can switch from **Automatic** to **Custom** to define your own linking fields.

Linking fields can be activated or deactivated to blend in a view. Linking fields used in the view will usually be active by default, while other fields will not. You can, however, change whether a linking field is active or not by clicking on the link icon next to a linking field in the data pane.

> Additionally, use the **Edit Data Relationships** screen to define the fields that will be used for **cross-data source filters**. When you use the drop-down menu of a field on **Filters** in a view, and select **Apply to Worksheets | All Using Related Data Sources**, the filter works across data sources.

Let's take this from the conceptual to the practical with an example.

A blending example

Let's look at a quick example of blending in action. Let's say you have the following table representing the service goals of various locations throughout the hospital when it comes to serving patients:

Location	Avg. Minutes to Service Goal
Inpatient Surgery	30
Outpatient Surgery	40
ICU	30
OBGYN	25
Lab	120

This data is contained in a simple text file, named `Location Goals.txt`, in the `Chapter 13` directory. Both the starter and complete workbooks already contain a data source defined for the file.

We'll start by creating a simple bar chart from the **Hospital Visit (Joins)** data source you created previously, showing the **Average Minutes to Service by Location** like so:

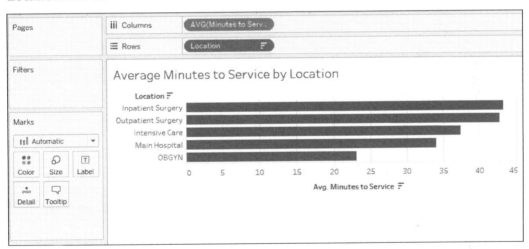

Figure 13.28: Average Minutes to Service by Location

Then, in the **Data** pane, we'll select the **Location Goals** data source. Observe the **Data** pane shown here:

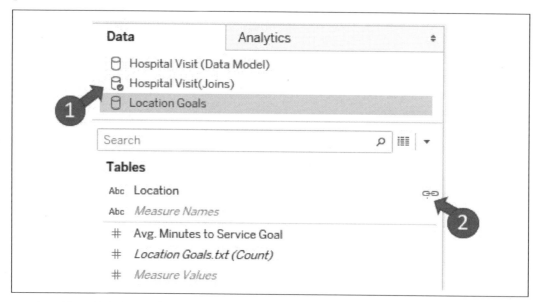

Figure 13.29: Hospital Visit (Joins) is shown as the Primary data source and Location in the Location Goals data source is indicated as a linking field

The blue checkmark on the **Hospital Visit (Joins)** data source (numbered **1** in *Figure 13.29*) indicates that the data source is primary. Tableau recognizes **Location** as a linking field and indicates that it is active with a connected link icon (numbered **2** in *Figure 13.29*). It is active because you have used **Location** from the primary data source in the current view. If you had not, Tableau would still show the link, but it would not be active by default. You may click on the link icon to switch from active to inactive or vice versa to control the level of detail at which aggregations are done in the secondary source.

For now, click on **Avg. Minutes to Service Goal** in the data pane and select **Bullet Graph** from **Show Me**, as indicated here:

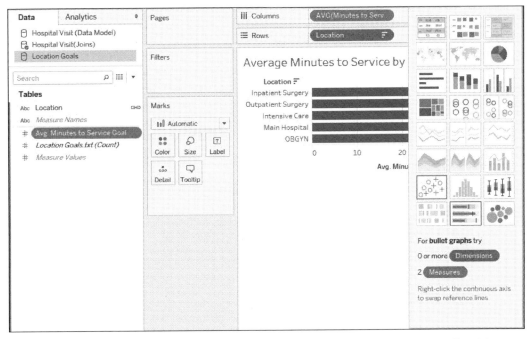

Figure 13.30: You may drag and drop fields from secondary sources into the view or use Show Me

You may have to right-click on the **Avg. Minutes to Service** axis in the view and select the **Swap Reference Line** fields to ensure the goal is the reference line and the bar is the actual metric. Your view should now look like this:

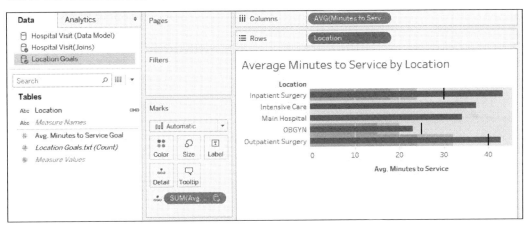

Figure 13.31: A view created from a primary source and a secondary source

Notice that both the **Hospital Visits (Joins)** data source and the **Location Goals** data source are used in this view. **Hospital Visit (Joins)** is the primary data source (indicated by a blue checkmark), while **Location Goals** is the secondary source (indicated by the orange checkmark). The **Avg. Minutes to Service Goal** field on **Detail** in the **Marks** card is secondary and also indicated by an icon with an orange checkmark.

You may also notice that **Main Hospital** and **Intensive Care** do not have goals indicated in the view. Recall that the primary data source is used to determine the full list of values shown in the view. **Main Hospital** is in the primary source but does not have a match in the secondary source. It is shown in the view, but it does not have a secondary source value.

Intensive Care also does not have a secondary value. This is because the corresponding value in the secondary source is **ICU**. Values must match exactly between the primary and secondary sources for a blend to find matches. However, blends do also take into account aliases.

An **alias** is an alternate value for a dimension value that will be used for display and data blending. Aliases for dimensions can be changed by right-clicking on row headers or using the menu on the field in the view or the data pane and selecting the **Aliases** option.

We can change the alias of a field by right-clicking on the row header in the view and using the **Edit Alias...** option, as shown here:

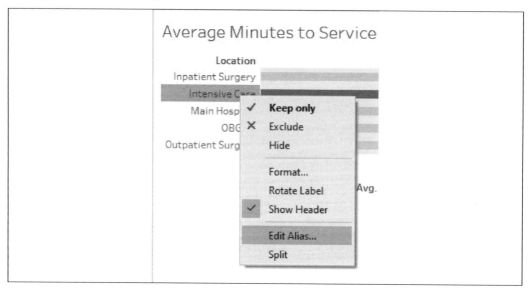

Figure 13.32: Using the Edit Alias... option

If we change the alias to **ICU**, a match is found in the secondary source and our view reflects the secondary value:

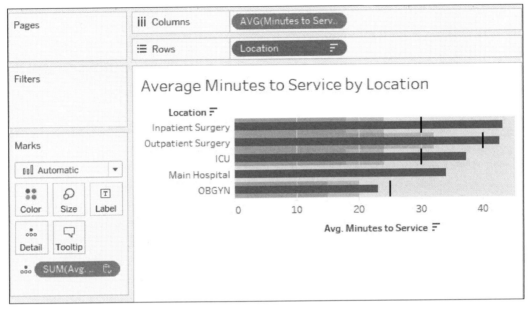

Figure 13.33: ICU now finds a match in the secondary source

A final value for **Location, Lab,** only occurs in the Location Goals.txt source and is, therefore, not shown in this view. If we were to create a new view and use **Location Goals** as the primary source, it would show.

We've covered quite a few options regarding how to relate data in this chapter. Let's just take a moment to consider when to use these different techniques.

When to use a data model, joins, or blends

In one sense, every data source you create using the latest versions of Tableau will use a data model. Even data sources using one physical table will have a corresponding object in the logical layer of a data model. But when should you relate tables using the data model, when should you join them together in the physical layer, and when should you employ blending?

Most of the time, there's no single right or wrong answer. However, here are some general guidelines to help you think through when it's appropriate to use a given approach.

In general, use a **data model** to relate tables:

- When joins would make correct aggregations impossible or require complex LOD expressions to get accurate results
- When joins would result in the duplication of data
- When you need flexibility in showing full domains of dimensions versus only values that match across relationships
- When you are uncertain of a data source and wouldn't know what type of join to use

In general, use **joins** at the physical level:

- When you must use an operator other than equality between fields
- When you want to do a spatial join
- When you want to specifically control the type of join used in your analysis
- When the performance of the data model is less efficient than it would be with the use of joins

In general, use **blending** when:

- You need to relate data sources that cannot be joined or related using a data model (such as OLAP cubes)
- You need flexibility to "fix" matching using aliases
- You need flexibility to adjust which fields define the relationship differently in different views

As you grow in confidence while using each of these approaches, you'll be able to better determine which makes sense in a given circumstance.

Summary

You now have several techniques to turn to when you need to relate tables of data together. The data model, a new feature in the latest versions of Tableau, gives a new paradigm for relating logical tables of data together. It introduces a few new behaviors when it comes to showing the full and partial domains of dimensional values, but it also greatly simplifies aggregations by taking into account the natural level of detail for the aggregation. In the physical layer, you have the option of joining together physical tables.

We covered the various types of joins and discussed possibilities for using join calculations and cross-database joins for ultimate flexibility. We briefly discussed how data blending works and saw a practical example. Finally, you examined a broad outline of when to turn to each approach. You now have a broad toolset to tackle data in different tables or even in different databases or files.

We'll expand that toolset quite a bit more in the next chapter as we look at Tableau Prep Builder. Tableau Prep gives you incredible power and sophistication, allowing you to bring together data from various sources, clean it, and structure it in any way you like!

14

Structuring Messy Data to Work Well in Tableau

So far, most of the examples we've looked at in this book assume that data is structured well and is fairly clean. Data in the real world isn't always so pretty. Maybe it's messy or it doesn't have a good structure. It may be missing values or have duplicate values, or it might have the wrong level of detail.

How can you deal with this type of messy data? In the previous chapter, we considered how Tableau's data model can be used to relate data in different tables. We will consider Tableau Prep Builder as a robust way to clean and structure data in the next chapter. Much of the information in this chapter will be an essential foundation for working with Tableau Prep.

For now, let's focus on some of the basic data structures that work well in Tableau and some of the additional techniques you can use to get data into those structures. We'll keep our discussion limited to native Tableau features in this chapter, but much of what you learn will apply to Tableau Prep in the next. By the end of this chapter, you'll have a solid foundation of understanding what constitutes a good data structure. Knowing which data structures work well with Tableau is key to understanding how you will be able to resolve certain issues.

In this chapter, we'll focus on some principles for structuring data to work well with Tableau, as well as some specific examples of how to address common data issues. This chapter will cover the following topics:

- Structuring data for Tableau
- The four basic data transformations
- Overview of advanced fixes for data problems

We'll start by discussing which data structures work well for Tableau.

Structuring data for Tableau

We've already seen that Tableau can connect to nearly any data source. Whether it's a built-in direct connection, **Open Database Connectivity (ODBC)**, or the use of the Tableau data extract API to generate an extract, no data is off limits. However, there are certain structures that make data easier to work with in Tableau.

There are two keys to ensure a good data structure that works well with Tableau:

- Every record of a source data connection should be at a meaningful level of detail
- Every measure contained in the source should match the level of detail of the data source or possibly be at a higher level of detail, but it should never be at a lower level of detail

For example, let's say you have a table of test scores with one record per classroom in a school. Within the record, you may have three measures: the average GPA for the classroom, the number of students in the class, and the average GPA of the school:

School	Classroom	Average GPA	Number of Students	Number of Students (School)
Pickaway Elementary	4th Grade	3.78	153	1,038
Pickaway Elementary	5th Grade	3.73	227	1,038
Pickaway Elementary	6th Grade	3.84	227	1,038
McCord Elementary	4th Grade	3.82	94	915
McCord Elementary	5th Grade	3.77	89	915
McCord Elementary	6th Grade	3.84	122	915

The first two measures (**Average GPA** and **Number of Students**) are at the same level of detail as the individual record of data (per classroom in the school). **Number of Students (School)** is at a higher level of detail (per school). As long as you are aware of this, you can do a careful analysis. However, you would have a data structure issue if you tried to store each student's GPA in the class record. If the data was structured in an attempt to store all of the students' GPAs per grade level (maybe with a column for each student or a single field containing a comma-separated list of student scores), we'd need to do some work to make the data more usable in Tableau.

Understanding the level of detail of the source (often referred to as **granularity**) is vital. Every time you connect to a data source, the very first question you should ask and answer is: what does a single record represent? If, for example, you were to drag and drop the `Number of Records` (or the `Table (Count)` field in Tableau 2020.2 and later) field into the view and observed 1,000 records, then you should be able to complete the statement, `I have 1,000 _____`. It could be 1,000 students, 1,000 test scores, or 1,000 schools. Having a good grasp of the granularity of the data will help you to avoid poor analysis and allow you to determine if you even have the data that's necessary for your analysis.

A quick way to find the level of detail of your data is to put the `Number of Records` (or the `Table (Count)` field in Tableau 2020.2 and later) field on the **Text** shelf, and then try different dimensions on the **Rows** shelf. When all of the rows display a 1, and the total that's displayed in the lower-left status bar equals the number of records in the data, then that dimension (or combination of dimensions) uniquely identifies a record and defines the lowest level of detail of your data.

With an understanding of the overarching principles regarding the granularity of data, let's move on and understand certain data structures that allow you to work seamlessly and efficiently in Tableau. Sometimes, it may be preferable to restructure the data at the source using tools such as `Alteryx` or Tableau Prep Builder. However, at times, restructuring the source data isn't possible or feasible. For example, you may not have write access to the database or it may be a cloud-based data source that has a predefined structure. We'll take a look at some options in Tableau for those cases. For now, let's consider what kinds of data structures work well with Tableau.

Well-structured data in Tableau

The two keys to a good structure, which we mentioned in the previous section, should result in a data structure where a single measure is contained in a single column. You may have multiple different measures, but any single measure should almost never be divided into multiple columns. Often, the difference is described as **wide data** versus **tall data**.

Wide data

Wide data is not typically a good structure for visual analysis in Tableau.

Wide data describes a structure in which a measure in a single row is spread over multiple columns. This data is often more **human-readable**. Wide data often results in fewer rows with more columns.

Here is an example of what wide data looks like in a table of population numbers:

Country Name	1960	1961	1962	1963	1964
Afghanistan	8,774,440	8,953,544	9,141,783	9,339,507	9,547,131
Australia	10,276,477	10,483,000	10,742,000	10,950,000	11,167,000

Notice that the level of detail for this table is a row for every country. However, the single measure (population) is not stored in a single column. This data is wide because it has a single measure (population) that is being divided into multiple columns (a column for each year). The wide table violates the second key to a good structure since the measure is at a lower level of detail than the individual record (per country per year, instead of just per country).

Tall data

Tall data is typically a good structure for visual analysis in Tableau.

Tall data describes a structure in which each distinct measure in a row is contained in a single column. Tall data often results in more rows and fewer columns.

Consider the following table, which represents the same data as earlier but in a tall structure:

Country Name	Year	Population
Afghanistan	1960	8,774,440
Afghanistan	1961	8,953,544

Afghanistan	1962	9,141,783
Afghanistan	1963	9,339,507
Afghanistan	1964	9,547,131
Australia	1960	10,276,477
Australia	1961	10,483,000
Australia	1962	10,742,000
Australia	1963	10,950,000
Australia	1964	11,167,000

Now, we have more rows (a row for each year for each country). Individual years are no longer separate columns and population measurements are no longer spread across those columns. Instead, one single column gives us a dimension of **Year** and another single column gives us a measure of **Population**. The number of rows has increased, while the number of columns has decreased. Now, the measure of population is at the same level of detail as the individual row, and so visual analysis in Tableau will be much easier.

Let's take a look at the difference this makes in practice.

Wide versus tall data in Tableau

You can easily see the difference between wide and tall data in Tableau. Here is what the **wide data** table looks like in the left **Data** window:

Figure 14.1: The wide data has a measure for every year

As we'd expect, Tableau treats each column in the table as a separate field. The wide structure of the data works against us. We end up with a separate measure for each year. If you wanted to plot a line graph of population per year, you would likely struggle. What dimension represents the date? What single measure can you use for the population?

This isn't to say that you can't use wide data in Tableau. For example, you might use **Measure Names/Measure Values** to plot all the **Year** measures in a single view, like this:

Figure 14.2: The wide data can still be used but in a complex and limited way

You'll notice that every **Year** field has been placed in the **Measure Values** shelf. The good news is that you can create visualizations from poorly structured data like this. The bad news is that views are often more difficult to create and certain advanced features may not be available.

The following limitations apply to the view in *Figure 14.2* based on the wide data structure:

- Because Tableau doesn't have a date dimension or integer, you cannot use forecasting
- Because Tableau doesn't have a date or continuous field in **Columns**, you cannot enable trend lines
- Because each measure is a separate field, you cannot use quick table calculations (such as running total, percent difference, and others)
- Determining things such as the average population across years will require a tedious custom calculation instead of simply changing the aggregation of a measure
- You don't have an axis for the date (just a series of headers for the measure names), so you won't be able to add reference lines

In contrast, the **tall data** looks like this in the **Data** pane:

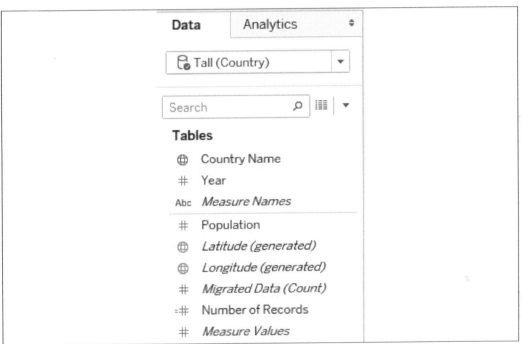

Figure 14.3: The tall data has a Year dimension and a single Population measure

This data source is much easier to work with. There's only one measure (**Population**) and a **Year** dimension to slice the measure. If you want a line chart of the population by year, you can simply drag and drop the **Population** and **Year** fields into **Columns** and **Rows**. Forecasting, trend lines, clustering, averages, standard deviations, and other advanced features will all work in the way you expect them to.

You can see that the resulting visualization is much easier to create in Tableau, using only three active fields:

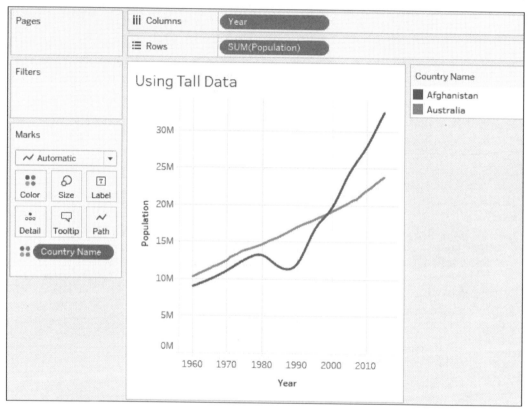

Figure 14.4: The view is much easier to create in Tableau with the tall data

Next, we'll consider a few other good structures for data that should work well with Tableau.

Star schemas (Data mart/Data warehouse)

Assuming they are well-designed, **star schema** data models work very well with Tableau because they have well-defined granularity, measures, and dimensions. Additionally, if they are implemented well, they can be extremely efficient to query. This allows for an ergonomic experience when using live connections in Tableau.

Star schemas are so named because they consist of a single fact table surrounded by related dimension tables, thus forming a star pattern. **Fact tables** contain measures at a meaningful granularity, while **dimension tables** contain attributes for various related entities. The following diagram illustrates a simple star schema with a single fact table (**Hospital Visit**) and three dimension tables (**Patient, Primary Physician,** and **Discharge Details**):

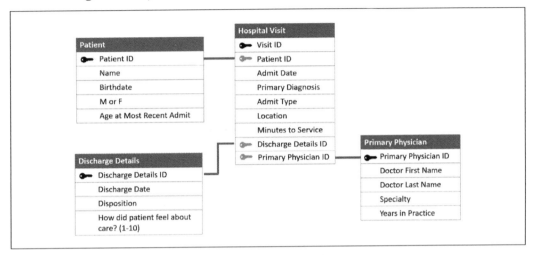

Figure 14.5: A simple star schema

Fact tables are joined to the related dimension using what is often called a **surrogate key** or **foreign key** that references a single dimension record. The fact table defines the level of granularity and contains measures. In this case, **Hospital Visit** has a granularity of one record for each visit. In this simple example, each visit is for one patient who saw one primary physician and was discharged. The **Hospital Visit** table explicitly stores a measure of Visit Duration and implicitly defines another measure of Number of Visits (as the row count).

Data modeling purists would point out that date values have been stored in the fact table (and even some of the dimensions). They would, instead, recommend having a date dimension table with extensive attributes for each date and only a surrogate (foreign) key stored in the fact table.

A date dimension can be very beneficial. However, Tableau's built-in date hierarchy and extensive date options make storing a date in the fact table, instead, a viable option. Consider using a date dimension if you need specific attributes of dates that are not available in Tableau (for example, which days are corporate holidays), have complex fiscal years, or if you need to support legacy BI reporting tools.

A well-designed star schema allows the use of **inner joins** since every surrogate key should reference a single dimension record. In cases where dimension values are not known or not applicable, special dimension records are used. For example, a hospital visit that is not yet complete (the patient is still in the hospital) may reference a special record in the **Discharge Details** table marked as Not yet discharged.

You've already worked with a similar structure of data in the previous chapter, where you experienced the differences of relating tables in the logical layer and the physical layer of the data model. Feel free to return to *Chapter 13, Understanding the Tableau Data Model, Joins, and Blends*, to review the concepts.

Well-implemented star schemas are particularly attractive for use in **live connections** because Tableau can improve performance by implementing join culling. **Join culling** is Tableau's elimination of unnecessary joins in queries, since it sends them to the data source engine.

For example, if you were to place the Physician Name on rows and the average of Visit Duration on columns to get a bar chart of average visit duration per physician, then joins to the **Treatment** and **Patient** tables may not be needed. Tableau will eliminate unnecessary joins as long as you are using a simple star schema with joins that are only from the central fact table and have referential integrity enabled in the source, or allow Tableau to assume referential integrity. For tables joined in the physical layer, select the data source connection from the data menu, or use the context menu from the data source connection and choose **Assume Referential Integrity**. For relationships in the logical layer of the data model, use the performance options for referential integrity for each applicable relationship.

Having considered some examples of good structures, let's turn our attention to some basic transformations that will help us to transform a poorly structured dataset to one with a good structure, which is easier to work with in Tableau.

The four basic data transformations

In this section, we'll give you an overview of some basic transformations that can fundamentally change the structure of your data. We'll start with an overview and then look at some practical examples.

Overview of transformations

In Tableau (and Tableau Prep), there are four basic data transformations. The following definitions broadly apply to most databases and data transformation tools, but there are some details and terminology that are Tableau-specific:

- **Pivots**: This indicates the transformation of columns to rows or rows to columns. The latter is possible in Tableau Prep only. The resulting dataset will be narrower and taller with fewer columns and more rows (columns to rows) or wider and shorter with more columns and fewer rows (rows to columns).

- **Unions**: This indicates the appending of rows from one table of data to another, with the matching columns **aligned** together. The resulting data structure is a single table containing rows from all unioned tables and columns that match between the original tables, along with unmatched columns containing NULL values for tables that did not have them.

- **Joins**: This indicates the row-by-row matching of two or more tables resulting in a data structure that includes columns from all tables. The number of rows is based on the type of join and how many matches are found.

- **Aggregations**: This indicates the **rolling up** of a table to a higher level of detail such that there will be a row for each unique set of values for all dimensions used for grouping, along with other values that are aggregated (such as a sum, min, max, or other aggregation).

In order to fully understand these definitions, we'll turn to some illustrations and practical examples.

Pivots (along with some simple data cleaning)

The Excel workbook World Population Data.xlsx, which is included in the Chapter 14 directory of the resources that are included with this book, is typical of many Excel documents. Here is what it looks like:

	A	B	C	D	E	F	G	H	I	J	K
1	**World Population Data**										
3		*This is sample data only.*									
4		*Accuracy and completeness is not guaranteed.*									
5											
6	**Country Name and Code**	**Indicator Name**	**Indicator Code**	1960	1961	1962	1963	1964	1965	1966	1967
7	Aruba (ABW)	Population, total	SP.POP.TOTL	54208	55435	56226	56697	57029	57360	57712	58049
8	Andorra (AND)	Population, total	SP.POP.TOTL	13414	14376	15376	16410	17470	18551	19646	20755
9	Afghanistan (AFG)	Population, total	SP.POP.TOTL	8774440	8953544	9141783	9339507	9547131	9765015	9990125	10221902
10	Angola (AGO)	Population, total	SP.POP.TOTL	4965988	5056688	5150076	5245015	5339893	5433841	5526653	5619643
11	Albania (ALB)	Population, total	SP.POP.TOTL	1608800	1659800	1711319	1762621	1814135	1864791	1914573	1965598
12	United Arab Emirates (ARE)	Population, total	SP.POP.TOTL	89608	97727	108774	121574	134411	146341	156890	167360
13	Argentina (ARG)	Population, total	SP.POP.TOTL	20623998	20959241	21295290	21630854	21963952	22293817	22618887	22941477
14	Armenia (ARM)	Population, total	SP.POP.TOTL	1867396	1934239	2002170	2070427	2138133	2204650	2269475	2332624
15	American Samoa (ASM)	Population, total	SP.POP.TOTL	20012	20478	21118	21883	22701	23518	24320	25116
16	Antigua and Barbuda (ATG)	Population, total	SP.POP.TOTL	54681	55403	56311	57368	58500	59653	60818	62002
17	Australia (AUS)	Population, total	SP.POP.TOTL	10276477	10483000	10742000	10950000	11167000	11388000	11651000	11799000
18	Austria (AUT)	Population, total	SP.POP.TOTL	7047539	7086299	7129864	7175811	7223801	7270889	7322066	7376998
19	Azerbaijan (AZE)	Population, total	SP.POP.TOTL	3897889	4030130	4167558	4307315	4445653	4579759	4708485	4832098

Figure 14.6: The World Population Data Excel file

Excel documents such as this are often more human-readable but contain multiple issues when used for data analysis in Tableau. The issues in this particular document include the following:

- Excessive headers (titles, notes, and formatting) that are not part of the data
- Merged cells
- Country name and code in a single column
- Columns that are likely unnecessary (**Indicator Name** and **Indicator Code**)
- The data is wide, that is, there is a column for each year, and the population measure is spread across these columns within a single record

When we initially connect to the Excel document in Tableau, the connection screen will look similar to *Figure 14.7*, as follows:

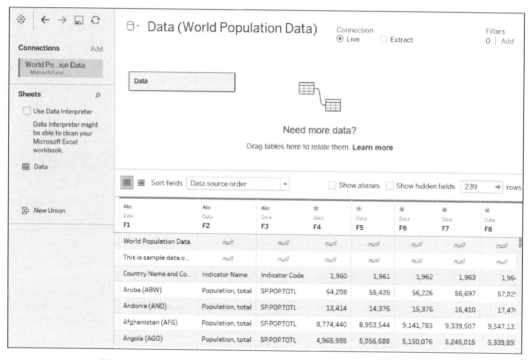

Figure 14.7: World Population Data.xlsx on Tableau's Data Source page

The data preview reveals some of the issues resulting from the poor structure:

- Since the column headers were not in the first Excel row, Tableau gave the defaults of **F1**, **F2**, and so on to each column

- The title **World Population Data** and the note about sample data were interpreted as values in the **F1** column
- The actual column headers are treated as a row of data (the third row)

Fortunately, these issues can be addressed in the connection window. First, we can correct many of the excessive header issues by turning on the **Tableau Data Interpreter**, a component that specifically identifies and resolves common structural issues in Excel or Google Sheets documents. When you check the **Use Data Interpreter** option, the data preview reveals much better results:

⊕ Data Country Name and ...	Abc Data Indicator Name	Abc Data Indicator Code	# Data 1960	# Data 1961	# Data 1962	# Data 1963	# Data 1964	# Data 1965
Aruba (ABW)	Population, total	SP.POP.TOTL	54,208	55,435	56,226	56,697	57,029	57,36C
Andorra (AND)	Population, total	SP.POP.TOTL	13,414	14,376	15,376	16,410	17,470	18,551
Afghanistan (AFG)	Population, total	SP.POP.TOTL	8,774,440	8,953,544	9,141,783	9,339,507	9,547,131	9,765,01£
Angola (AGO)	Population, total	SP.POP.TOTL	4,965,988	5,056,688	5,150,076	5,245,015	5,339,893	5,433,841
Albania (ALB)	Population, total	SP.POP.TOTL	1,608,800	1,659,800	1,711,319	1,762,621	1,814,135	1,864,791
United Arab Emirates (..	Population, total	SP.POP.TOTL	89,608	97,727	108,774	121,574	134,411	146,341

Figure 14.8: Tableau Data Interpreter fixes many of the common issues found
in Excel (and similar) data sources

Clicking on the **Review the results...** link that appears under the checkbox will cause Tableau to generate a new Excel document that is color-coded to indicate how the data interpreter parsed the Excel document. Use this feature to verify that Tableau has correctly interpreted the Excel document and retained the data you expected.

Observe the elimination of the excess headers and the correct names of the columns. However, a few additional issues will still need to be corrected.

First, we can hide the **Indicator Name** and **Indicator Code** columns if we feel they are not useful for our analysis. Clicking on the drop-down arrow on a column header reveals a menu of options.

Selecting **Hide** will remove the field from the connection and even prevent it from being stored in extracts:

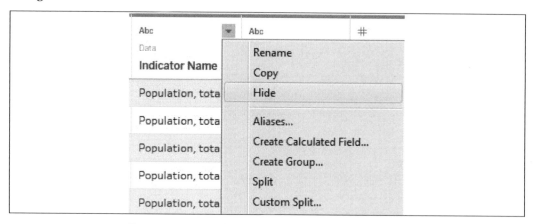

Figure 14.9: You can hide fields from the Data Source screen

Second, we can use the option on the same menu to split the **Country Name and Code** column into two columns so that we can work with the name and code separately. In this case, the **Split** option on the menu works well and Tableau perfectly splits the data, even removing the parentheses from around the code. In cases where the split option does not initially work, try the **Custom Split...** option. We'll also use the **Rename** option to rename the split fields from Country Name and Code - Split 1 and Country Name and Code - Split 2 to **Country Name** and **Country Code**, respectively. Then, we'll **Hide** the original Country Name and Code field.

At this point, most of the data structure issues have been remedied. However, you'll recognize that the data is in a **wide** format. We have already seen the issues that we'll run into:

Country Name	Country Code	Data 1961	Data 1962	Data 1963	Data 1964	Data 1965	Data 1966
Aruba	ABW	55,435	56,226	56,697	57,029	57,360	57,712
Andorra	AND	14,376	15,376	16,410	17,470	18,551	19,646
Afghanistan	AFG	8,953,544	9,141,783	9,339,507	9,547,131	9,765,015	9,990,125
Angola	AGO	5,056,688	5,150,076	5,245,015	5,339,893	5,433,841	5,526,653
Albania	ALB	1,659,800	1,711,319	1,762,621	1,814,135	1,864,791	1,914,573
United Arab Emirates	ARE	97,727	108,774	121,574	134,411	146,341	156,890

Figure 14.10: After some cleaning, the data is still in an undesirable wide structure

Our final step is to **pivot** the year columns. This means that we'll reshape the data in such a way that every country will have a row for every year. Select all the year columns by clicking on the **1960** column, scrolling to the far right, and holding *Shift* while clicking on the **2013** column. Finally, use the drop-down menu on any one of the year fields and select the **Pivot** option.

The result is two columns (**Pivot field names** and **Pivot field values**) in place of all the year columns. Rename the two new columns to **Year** and **Population**. Your dataset is now narrow and tall instead of wide and short.

Finally, notice that the icon on the **Year** column is recognized by Tableau as a text field. Clicking on the icon will allow you to change the data type directly. In this case, selecting **Date** will result in NULL values, but changing the data type to **Number (whole)** will give you integer values that will work well in most cases:

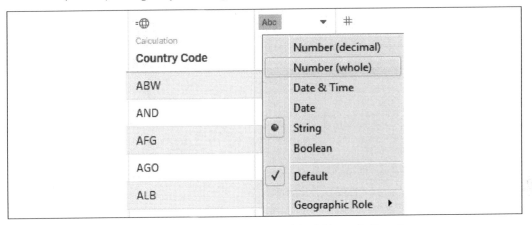

Figure 14.11: You can change the data types of the fields on the Data Source page

Alternatively, you could use the first drop-down menu in the Year field and select **Create Calculated Field....** This would allow you to create a calculated field name **Year (date)**, which parses the year string as a date with code such as DATE(DATEPARSE("yyyy", [Year])). This code will parse the string and then convert it into a simple date without a time. You can then hide the original **Year** field. You can hide any field, even if it is used in calculations, as long as it isn't used in a view. This leaves you with a very clean dataset.

The final cleaned, pivoted dataset is far easier to work with in Tableau than the original:

=⊕ Calculation Country Name	=⊕ Calculation Country Code	# Pivot Year	# Pivot Population
Aruba	ABW	1961	55,435
Andorra	AND	1961	14,376
Afghanistan	AFG	1961	8,953,544
Angola	AGO	1961	5,056,688
Albania	ALB	1961	1,659,800
United Arab Emirates	ARE	1961	97,727
Argentina	ARG	1961	20,959,241
Armenia	ARM	1961	1,934,239
American Samoa	ASM	1961	20,478
Antigua and Barbuda	ATG	1961	55,403
Australia	AUS	1961	10,483,000

Figure 14.12: The cleaned and pivoted dataset

The data interpreter, cleaning options, and ability to pivot data (columns to rows) in Tableau make working with many datasets far easier. Next, we'll take a look at unions.

Unions

Often, you may have multiple individual files or tables that, together, represent the entire set of data. For example, you might have a process that creates a new monthly data dump as a new text file in a certain directory. Or, you might have an Excel file where data for each department is contained in a separate sheet.

A **union** is a concatenation of data tables that brings together rows of each table into a single table. For example, consider the following three tables of data:

Originals:

Name	Occupation	Bank account balance
Luke	Farmer	$2,000
Leia	Princess	$50,000
Han	Smuggler	-$20,000

Prequels:

Name	Occupation	Bank account balance
Watto	Junk Dealer	$9,000
Darth Maul	Face Painter	$10,000
Jar Jar	Sith Lord	-$100,000

Sequels:

Name	Occupation	Bank account balance
Rey	Scavenger	$600
Poe	Pilot	$30,000
Kylo	Unemployed	$0

A union of these tables would give a single table containing the rows of each individual table:

Name	Occupation	Bank account balance
Luke	Farmer	$2,000
Leia	Princess	$50,000
Han	Smuggler	-$20,000
Watto	Junk Dealer	$9,000
Darth Maul	Face Painter	$10,000
Jar Jar	Sith Lord	-$100,000
Rey	Scavenger	$600
Poe	Pilot	$30,000
Kylo	Unemployed	$0

Tableau allows you to union together tables from file-based data sources, including the following:

- Text files (.csv, .txt, and other text file formats)
- Sheets (tabs) within Excel documents
- Subtables within an Excel sheet
- Multiple Excel documents
- Google Sheets
- Relational database tables

 Use the **Data Interpreter** feature to find subtables in Excel or Google Sheets. They will show up as additional tables of data in the left sidebar.

To create a union in Tableau, follow these steps:

1. Create a new data source from the menu, toolbar, or **Data Source** screen, starting with one of the files you wish to be part of the union. Then, drag any additional files into the **Drag table to union** drop zone just beneath the existing table on the canvas (in either the logical or physical layers; though, the union, technically, exists in the physical layer):

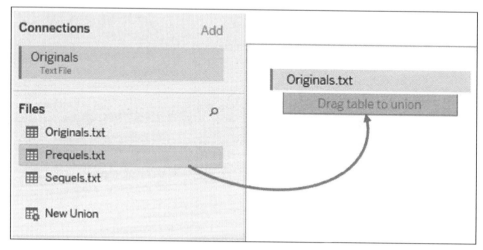

Figure 14.13: You may create unions by dragging and dropping tables or files directly under existing tables on the canvas

2. Once you've created a union, you can use the drop-down menu on the table in the designer to configure options for the union. Alternatively, you can drag the **New Union** object from the left sidebar into the designer to replace the existing table. This will reveal options to create and configure the union:

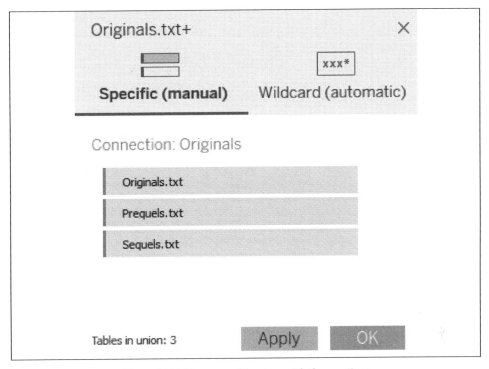

Figure 14.14: You may edit unions with these options

The **Specific (manual)** tab allows you to drag tables into and out of the union. The **Wildcard (automatic)** tab allows you to specify wildcards for filenames and sheets (for Excel and Google Sheets) that will automatically include files and sheets in the union based on a wildcard match.

 Use the **Wildcard (automatic)** feature if you anticipate additional files being added in the future. For example, if you have a specific directory where data files are dumped on a periodic basis, the wildcard feature will ensure that you don't have to manually edit the connection.

3. Once you have defined the union, you may use the resulting data source to visualize the data. Additionally, a union table may be joined with other tables in the designer window, giving you a lot of flexibility in working with data.

When you create a union, Tableau will include one or more new fields in your data source to help you to identify the file, sheet, and table where the data originated. **Path** will contain the file path (including the filename), **Sheet** will contain the sheet name (for Excel or Google Sheets), and **Table Name** will contain the subtable or text filename. You can use these fields to help you to identify data issues and also to extend your dataset as needed.

For example, if you had a directory of monthly data dump files, named 2020-01.txt, 2020-02.txt, 2020-03.txt, and so on, but no actual date field in the files, you could obtain the date using a calculated field with code such as the following:

```
DATEPARSE('yyyy-MM', [Table Name] )
```

In a union, Tableau will match the columns between tables by name. What happens when columns are not the same between tables or files? If you were to write a query to a database, you might expect a failed result as column names usually have to match exactly. However, Tableau allows you to union together files or tables with mismatched names.

> Columns that exist in one file/table but not in others will appear as part of the union table, but values will be NULL in files/tables where the column does not exist. For example, if one of the files contained a column named **Job** instead of **Occupation**, the final union table would contain a column named **Job** and another named **Occupation**, with NULL values where the column did not exist. You can merge the mismatched columns by selecting the columns and using the drop-down menu. This will coalesce (keep the first non-null of) the values per row of data in a single new column:

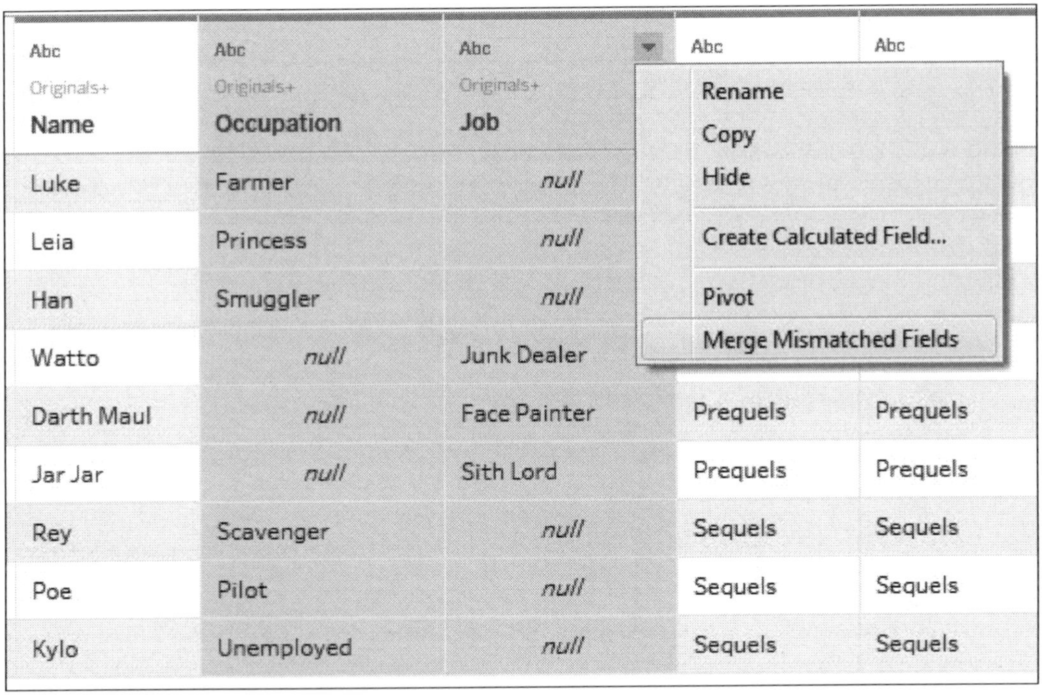

Figure 14.15: Use Merge Mismatched Fields to combine columns resulting from a union where the field names didn't match (this mismatch is not included in the example data)

You do not have to merge mismatched fields. At times, there will not be corresponding matches in all files or tables and that may be useful for your analysis.

Unions allow you to bring together multiple files or tables with relatively the same structure and **stack** them together so that you end up with all records from all tables/files. With pivots and unions explored, we've covered two of the four basic transformation types. We'll continue with an example of how joins can be used to restructure your data.

Joins

You'll recall that the concept of joins and the types of joins were previously discussed in *Chapter 13, Understanding the Tableau Data Model, Joins, and Blends*. While joins are quite useful in bringing together tables in the same database or even disparate data sources (data contained in different systems and formats), they can be used to solve other data issues too, such as reshaping data to make it easier to meet your objectives in Tableau.

 You can work through the following example in the `Chapter 14` workbook, but the server database data source is simulated with a text file (`Patient Visits.txt`).

Let's say you have a table in a server database (such as SQL Server or Oracle) that contains one row per hospital patient and includes the **Admit Date** and **Discharge Date** as separate columns for each patient:

Patient ID	Patient Name	Admit Date	Discharge Date
1	David	12/1/2018	12/20/2018
2	Solomon	12/3/2018	12/7/2018
3	Asa	12/5/2018	12/22/2018
4	Jehoshaphat	12/5/2018	12/6/2018
5	Joash	12/9/2018	12/16/2018
6	Amaziah	12/10/2018	12/14/2018
7	Uzziah	12/12/2018	12/24/2018
8	Jotham	12/16/2018	12/29/2018
9	Hezekiah	12/18/2018	12/22/2018
10	Josiah	12/22/2018	12/23/2018

While this data structure works well for certain kinds of analyses, you would find it difficult to use if you wanted to visualize the number of patients in the hospital day by day for the month of December.

For one, which date field do you use for the axis? Even if you pivoted the table so that you had all of the dates in one field, you would find that you have gaps in the data. **Sparse data**, that is, data in which records do not exist for certain values, is quite common in certain real-world data sources. Specifically, in this case, you have a single record for each **Admit** or **Discharge** date, but no records for the days in between.

Sometimes, it might be an option to restructure the data at the source, but if the database is locked down, you may not have that option. You could also use Tableau's ability to fill in gaps in the data (**data densification**) to solve the problem. However, that solution could be complex and, potentially, brittle or difficult to maintain.

An alternative is to use a join to create the rows for all dates. In this case, we'll leverage a cross-database join to bring in another source of data altogether. You might quickly create an Excel sheet with a list of dates you want to see, like this:

	A
1	Date
2	12/1/2018
3	12/2/2018
4	12/3/2018
5	12/4/2018
6	12/5/2018
7	12/6/2018
8	12/7/2018
9	12/8/2018
10	12/9/2018
26	12/25/2018
27	12/26/2018
28	12/27/2018
29	12/28/2018
30	12/29/2018
31	12/30/2018
32	12/31/2018

Figure 14.16: An Excel file containing only a comprehensive list of dates

The Excel file includes a record for each date. Our goal is to **cross join** (join every row from one table with every row in another) the data between the database table and the Excel table. With this accomplished, you will have a row for every patient for every date.

Joining every record in one dataset with every record in another dataset creates what is called a **Cartesian product**. The resulting dataset will have N1 * N2 rows (where N1 is the number of rows in the first dataset and N2 is the number of rows in the second). Take care in using this approach. It works well with smaller datasets. As you work with larger datasets, the Cartesian product may grow so large that this solution is untenable.

You'll often have specific fields in the various tables that will allow you to join the data together. In this case, however, we don't have any keys that define a join. The dates also do not give us a way to join all the data in a way that gives us the structure we want. To achieve the cross join, we'll use a join calculation. A **join calculation** allows you to write a special calculated field specifically for use in joins.

In this case, we'll select **Create Join Calculation...** for both tables and enter the single, hard-coded value, that is, 1, for both the left and right sides:

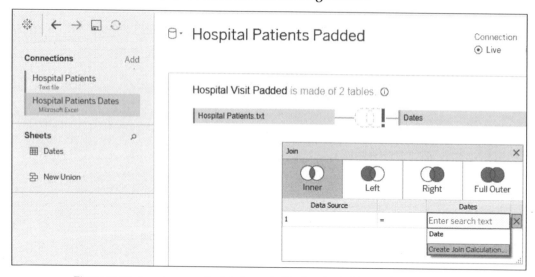

Figure 14.17: As we've seen, the join is created in the physical layer of the data model

Since 1 in every row on the left matches 1 in every row on the right, we get every row matching every row—a true cross join.

As an alternative, with many other server-based data sources, you can use **Custom SQL** as a data source. On the **Data Source** screen, with the **Patient Visits** table in the designer, you could use the top menu to select **Data | Convert to Custom SQL** to edit the SQL script that Tableau uses for the source. Alternatively, you can write your own custom SQL using the **New Custom SQL** object on the left sidebar.

The script in this alternative example has been modified to include 1 AS Join to create a field, called **Join**, with a value of 1 for every row (though, if you didn't do this in the script, you could simply use a join calculation). Fields defined in Custom SQL can also be used in joins:

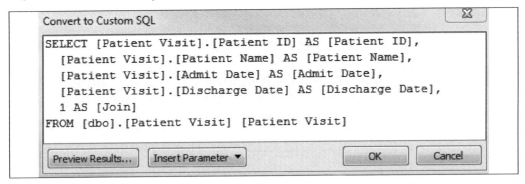

```
Convert to Custom SQL
SELECT [Patient Visit].[Patient ID] AS [Patient ID],
   [Patient Visit].[Patient Name] AS [Patient Name],
   [Patient Visit].[Admit Date] AS [Admit Date],
   [Patient Visit].[Discharge Date] AS [Discharge Date],
   1 AS [Join]
FROM [dbo].[Patient Visit] [Patient Visit]
```

Preview Results...   Insert Parameter ▼   OK   Cancel

Figure 14.18: A sample script that could be used to create a value on which to join

Based on the join calculation, our new cross-joined dataset contains a record for every patient for every date, and we can now create a quick calculation to see whether a patient should be counted as part of the hospital population on any given date. The calculated field, named **Patients in Hospital**, has the following code:

```
IF [Admit Date] <= [Date] AND [Discharge Date] >= [Date]
THEN 1
ELSE 0
END
```

This allows us to easily visualize the flow of patients, and even potentially perform advanced analytics based on averages, trends, and even forecasting:

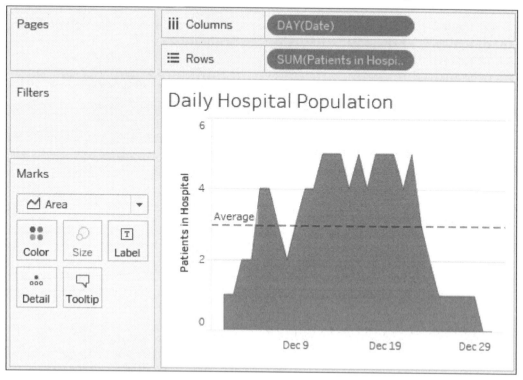

Figure 14.19: A visualization of the daily hospital population, made easy with some data restructuring

Ultimately, for a long-term solution, you might want to consider developing a server-based data source that gives the structure that's needed for the desired analysis. However, a join here allowed us to achieve the analysis without waiting on a long development cycle.

Having considered examples of pivots, unions, and joins, let's turn our focus to an example of the final major transformation type: aggregation.

Aggregation

Remember that the two keys to a good data structure are as follows:

- Having a level of detail that is meaningful
- Having measures that match the level of detail or that are possibly at higher levels of detail

Measures at lower levels tend to result in wide data and can make some analysis difficult or even impossible. Measures at higher levels of detail can, at times, be useful. As long as we are aware of how to handle them correctly, we can avoid some pitfalls.

Consider, for example, the following data (included as `Apartment Rent.xlsx` in the `Chapter 14` directory), which gives us a single record each month per apartment:

Apartment	Month	Rent Collected	Square Feet
A	Jan	$0	900
	Feb	$0	900
	Mar	$0	900
	Apr	$0	900
	May	$0	900
	Jun	$1,500	900
	Jul	$1,500	900
	Aug	$1,500	900
	Sep	$1,500	900
	Oct	$1,500	900
	Nov	$1,500	900
	Dec	$1,500	900
B	Jan	$1,200	750
	Feb	$1,200	750
	Mar	$1,200	750
	Apr	$1,200	750
	May	$1,200	750
	Jun	$1,200	750
	Jul	$0	750
	Aug	$0	750
	Sep	$0	750
	Oct	$0	750
	Nov	$0	750
	Dec	$0	750

Figure 14.20: The Apartment Rent data, which is poorly structured because the Square Feet measure is repeated for every month

The two measures are really at different levels of detail:

- **Rent Collected** matches the level of detail of the data where there is a record of how much rent was collected for each apartment for each month.

- **Square Feet**, on the other hand, does not change month to month. Rather, it is at the higher level of detail, of **Apartment** only.

 Tableau's data model would make this data very easy to work with if it was contained in two tables at the correct level of detail. If it was in a relational database where we could use a custom SQL statement to create a couple of tables at the right level of detail, we might consider that approach. In the next chapter, we'll consider how Tableau Prep could be used to easily solve this problem. For now, work through the details to gain some understanding of how to deal with aggregation issues if you are faced with a similar poor structure (and you'll gain an immense appreciation for what Tableau Prep and the Tableau data model can do!).

The difference in levels of detail can be observed when we remove the date from the view and look at everything at the **Apartment** level:

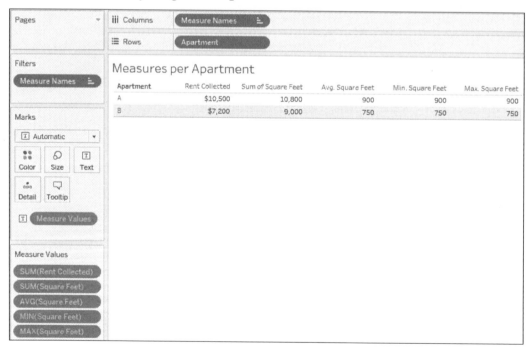

Figure 14.21: An illustration of how various aggregations might be right or wrong depending on the level of detail

Notice that the **SUM(Rent Collected)** makes perfect sense. You can add up the rent collected per month and get a meaningful result per apartment. However, you cannot Sum **Square Feet** and get a meaningful result per apartment. Other aggregations, such as average, minimum, and maximum, do give the right results per apartment.

However, imagine that you were asked to come up with the ratio of total rent collected to square feet per apartment. You know it will be an aggregate calculation because you have to sum the rent that's collected prior to dividing. But which of the following is the correct calculation?

- `SUM([Rent Collected])/SUM([Square Feet])`
- `SUM([Rent Collected])/AVG([Square Feet])`
- `SUM([Rent Collected])/MIN([Square Feet])`
- `SUM([Rent Collected])/MAX([Square Feet])`

The first one is obviously wrong. We've already seen that square feet should not be added each month. Any of the final three would be correct if we ensure that **Apartment** continues to define the level of detail of the view.

However, once we look at the view that has a different level of detail (for example, the total for all apartments or the monthly total for multiple apartments), the calculations don't work. To understand why, consider what happens when we turn on the column grand totals (from the menu, select **Analysis | Totals | Show Column Grand Totals**, or drag and drop **Totals** from the **Analytics** tab):

Apartment	Rent Collected	Sum of Square Feet	Avg. Square Feet	Min. Square Feet	Max. Square Feet
A	$10,500	10,800	900	900	900
B	$7,200	9,000	750	750	750
Grand Total	$17,700	19,800	825	750	900

Figure 14.22: None of the aggregations work to give us a grand total

The problem here is that the **Grand Total** line is at the level of detail of all apartments (for all months). What we really want as the **Grand Total** of square feet is 900 + 750 = 1,650. However, here, the sum of square feet is the addition of square feet for all apartments for all months. The average won't work. The minimum finds the value **750** as the smallest measure for all apartments in the data. Likewise, the maximum picks **900** as the single largest value. Therefore, none of the proposed calculations would work at any level of detail that does not include the individual apartment.

You can adjust how subtotals and grand totals are computed by clicking on the individual value and using the drop-down menu to select how the total is computed. Alternatively, right-click on the active measure field and select **Total Using**. You can change how all measures are totaled at once from the menu by selecting **Analysis | Totals | Total All Using**. Using this **two-pass total** technique could result in correct results in the preceding view, but it would not universally solve the problem. For example, if you wanted to show the price per square foot for each month, you'd have the same issue.

Fortunately, Tableau gives us the ability to work with different levels of detail in a view. Using **Level of Detail (LOD)** calculations, which we encountered in *Chapter 5, Leveraging Level of Detail Calculations*, we can calculate the square feet per apartment.

Here, we'll use a fixed LOD calculation to keep the level of detail fixed at the apartment level. We'll create a calculated field, named Square Feet per Apartment, with the following code:

```
{ INCLUDE [Apartment] : MIN([Square Feet]) }
```

The curly braces surround a LOD calculation and the keyword INCLUDE indicates that we want to include Apartment as part of the level of detail for the calculation, even if it is not included in the view level of detail. MIN is used in the preceding code, but MAX or AVG could have been used as well because all give the same result per apartment.

As you can see, the calculation returns the correct result in the view at the apartment level and at the grand total level, where Tableau includes **Apartment** to find **900** (the minimum for **A**) and **750** (the minimum for **B**) and then sums them to get **1,650**:

Apartment	Rent Collected	Square Feet per Apartment
A	$10,500	900
B	$7,200	750
Grand Total	$17,700	1,650

Figure 14.23: An LOD calculation gives us the correct result at all levels of detail

Now, we can use the LOD calculated field in another calculation to determine the desired results. We'll create a calculated field, named Rent Collected per Square Foot, with the following code:

```
SUM([Rent Collected])/SUM([Square Feet per Apartment])
```

When that field is added to the view and formatted to show decimals, the final outcome is correct:

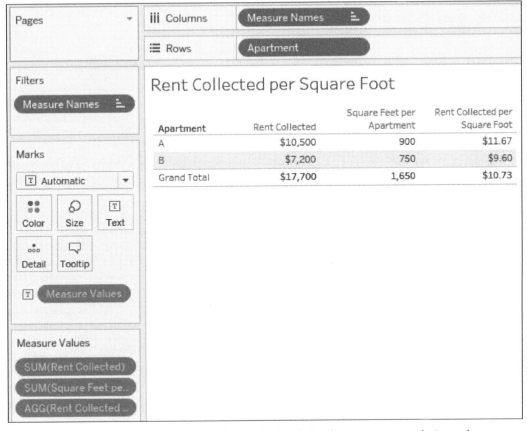

Figure 14.24: The LOD expression gives us the foundation for even more complexity, such as calculating the rent per area

Alternatively, instead of using INCLUDE, we could have used a FIXED level of detail, which is always performed at the level of detail of the dimension(s) following the FIXED keywords, regardless of what level of detail is defined in the view. This would have told Tableau to always calculate the minimum square feet per apartment, regardless of what dimensions define the view level of detail. While very useful, be aware that the FIXED LOD calculations are calculated for the entire context (either the entire dataset or the subset defined by the **context filters**). Using them without understanding this can yield unexpected results.

For now, we've learned how to handle some aggregation issues; however, in the next chapter, we'll explore how we can truly transform the data with aggregations to make problems like the previous exercise much easier. In the meantime, let's consider some alternative fixes for data problems.

Overview of advanced fixes for data problems

In addition to the techniques that we mentioned earlier in this chapter, there are some additional possibilities to deal with data structure issues. It is outside the scope of this book to develop these concepts fully. However, with some familiarity of these approaches, you can broaden your ability to deal with challenges as they arise:

- **Custom SQL**: It can be used in the data connection to resolve some data problems. Beyond giving a field for a cross-database join, as we saw earlier, custom SQL can be used to radically reshape the data that's retrieved from the source. Custom SQL is not an option for all data sources, but it is an option for many relational databases. Consider a custom SQL script that takes the wide table of country populations we mentioned earlier in this chapter and restructures it into a tall table:

```
SELECT [Country Name],[1960] AS Population, 1960 AS Year
FROM Countries

UNION ALL

SELECT [Country Name],[1961] AS Population, 1961 AS Year
FROM Countries

UNION ALL

SELECT [Country Name],[1962] AS Population, 1962 AS Year
FROM Countries
. . .
. . .
```

And so on. It might be a little tedious to set up, but it will make the data much easier to work with in Tableau! However, many data sources using complex custom SQL will need to be extracted for performance reasons.

- **Table calculations**: Table calculations can be used to solve a number of data challenges, from finding and eliminating duplicate records to working with multiple levels of detail. Since table calculations can work within partitions at higher levels of detail, you can use multiple table calculations and aggregate calculations together to mix levels of detail in a single view. A simple example of this is the **Percent of Total** table calculation, which compares an aggregate calculation at the level of detail in the view with a total at a higher level of detail.

- **Data blending**: Data blending can be used to solve numerous data structure issues. Because you can define the linking fields that are used, you can control the level of detail of the blend.

- **Data scaffolding**: Data scaffolding extends the concept of data blending. With this approach, you construct a scaffold of various dimensional values to use as a primary source and then blend them to one or more secondary sources. In this way, you can control the structure and granularity of the primary source while still being able to leverage data that's contained in the secondary sources.

- **Data model**: Data blending is useful when you need to control the level of the relationship per view. If the relationship is better defined, the data model will give you incredible power to relate tables that are at different levels of detail and have confidence that aggregations will work correctly.

Summary

Up until this chapter, we'd looked at data that was, for the most part, well-structured and easy to use. In this chapter, we considered what constitutes a good structure and ways to deal with poor data structures. A good structure consists of data that has a meaningful level of detail and that has measures that match that level of detail. When measures are spread across multiple columns, we get data that is wide instead of tall.

We also spent some time understanding the basic types of transformation: pivots, unions, joins, and aggregations. Understanding these will be fundamental to solving data structure issues.

You also got some practical experience in applying various techniques to deal with data that has the wrong shape or has measures at the wrong level of detail. Tableau gives us the power and flexibility to deal with some of these structural issues, but it is far preferable to fix a data structure at the source.

In the next chapter, we'll take a brief pause from looking at Tableau Desktop to consider Tableau Prep, another alternative to tackle challenging data!

15

Taming Data with Tableau Prep

We considered some options for structuring data in Tableau Desktop in the previous chapter. Many of the concepts around well-structured data will apply here as we now turn our attention to another product from Tableau: **Tableau Prep**. Tableau Prep extends the Tableau platform with robust options for cleaning and structuring data for analysis in Tableau. In the same way that Tableau Desktop provides a hands-on, visual experience for visualizing and analyzing data, Tableau Prep provides a hands-on, visual experience for cleaning and shaping data.

Tableau Prep is on an accelerated, monthly release cycle and while the platform continues to grow and expand, there is an underlying paradigm that sets a foundation for cleaning and shaping data. We'll cover a lot of ground in this chapter, but our goal is not to cover every possible feature—and indeed, we won't. Instead, we will seek to understand the underlying paradigm and flow of thought that will enable you to tackle a multitude of data challenges in Tableau Prep.

In this chapter, we'll work through a couple of practical examples as we explore the paradigm of Tableau Prep, understand the fundamental transformations, and see many of the features and functions of Tableau Prep.

We'll cover quite a few topics in this chapter, including the following:

- Getting ready to explore Tableau Prep
- Understanding the Tableau Prep Builder interface

- Flowing with the fundamental paradigm
  - Connecting to data
  - Cleaning the data
  - Calculations and aggregations in Tableau Prep
  - Filtering data in Tableau Prep
  - Transforming the data for analysis
- Options for automating flows

In this chapter, we'll use the term Tableau Prep broadly to speak of the entire platform that Tableau has developed for data prep and sometimes as shorthand for Tableau Prep Builder, the client application that's used to connect to data, create data flows, and define output. Where needed for clarity, we'll use these specific names:

- **Tableau Prep Builder**: The client application that's used to design data flows, run them locally, and publish them
- **Tableau Prep Conductor**: An add-on to Tableau Server that allows the scheduling and automation of published data flows

Let's start by understanding how to get started with Tableau Prep.

Getting ready to explore Tableau Prep

Tableau Prep Builder is available for Windows and Mac. If you do not currently have Tableau Prep Builder installed on your machine, please take a moment to download the application from https://www.tableau.com/products/prep/download. Licenses for Tableau Prep Builder are included with Tableau Creator licensing. If you do not currently have a license, you may trial the application for 14 days. Please speak with your Tableau representative to confirm licensing and trial periods.

The examples in this chapter use files located in the \Learning Tableau\Chapter 15 directory. Specific instructions will guide you on when and how to use the various files.

Once you've downloaded and installed Tableau Prep Builder, you will be able to launch the application. Once you do, you'll find a welcome screen that we'll detail as we cover the interface in the next section.

Understanding the Tableau Prep Builder interface

You'll find a lot of similarities in the interfaces of Tableau Prep Builder and Tableau Desktop. The home screen of Tableau Prep Builder will look similar to this:

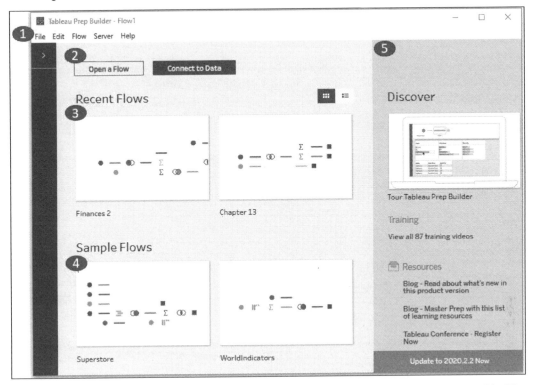

Figure 15.1: The Tableau Prep Builder welcome screen with numbering to identify key components of the UI

The following components have been numbered in *Figure 15.1*:

1. The menu includes options for opening files, editing and running flows, signing into Tableau Server, and various **Help** functions. Also notice the **Connections** Pane to the left, immediately beneath the **File** menu. It is collapsed initially, but will contain a list of data connections as you create them.

2. The two large buttons at the top give you the option to **Open a Flow**, which opens an existing Tableau Prep flow file, or **Connect to Data**, to start a new flow with an initial data connection. We'll define a flow in the next section. For now, think of a flow in terms of Tableau Prep's equivalent of a Tableau Desktop workbook.

3. **Recent Flows** shows the Tableau Prep data flows that you have recently saved. You may click on one of these to open the flow and edit or run it. A toggle button on the right allows you to switch between thumbnails and a list.

4. **Sample Flows** allows you to open some prebuilt examples.

5. The **Discover** pane gives you options for training and resources as you learn more about Tableau Prep. A notification to upgrade will also appear if there is a newer version available.

Once you have opened or started a new flow, the home screen will be replaced with a new interface, which will facilitate the designing and running of flows:

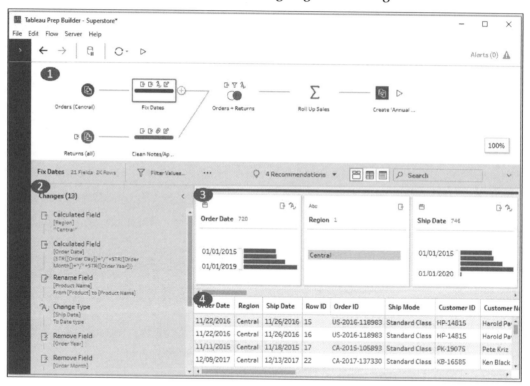

Figure 15.2: When designing a flow, you'll find an interface like this one. The major components are numbered and described as follows

This interface consists of the following, which are numbered in the preceding screenshot:

1. The flow pane, where you will logically build the flow of data with steps that will do anything from cleaning to calculation, to transformation and reshaping. Selecting any single step will reveal the interface on the bottom half of the screen. This interface will vary slightly, depending on the type of step you have selected.

2. The settings, or changes pane lists settings for the step and also a list of all changes that are made in the step, from calculations to renaming or removing fields, to changing data types or grouping values. You can click on individual changes to edit them or see how they alter the data.

3. The profile pane gives you a profile of each field in the data as it exists for the selected step. You can see the type and distribution of values for each field. Clicking on a field will highlight the lineage in the flow pane and clicking one or more values of a field will highlight the related values of other fields.

4. The data grid shows individual records of data as they exist in that step. Selecting a change in the changes grid will show the data based on changes up to and including the selected change. Selecting a value in the profile pane will filter the data grid to only show records containing that value. For example, selecting the first row of the Order Date field in the profile pane will filter the data grid to show only records represented by that bar. This allows you to explore the data, but doesn't alter the data until you perform a specific action that does result in a change.

You will also notice the toolbar that allows you to undo or redo actions, refresh data, or run the flow. Additionally, there will be other options or controls that appear based on the type of step or field that's selected. We'll consider those details as we dive into the paradigm of Tableau Prep, and a practical example later in the chapter.

Flowing with the fundamental paradigm

The overall paradigm of Tableau Prep is a hands-on, visual experience of discovering, cleaning, and shaping data through a flow. A flow (sometimes also called a data flow) is a logical series of steps and changes that are applied to data from input(s) to output(s).

Here is an example of what a flow looks like in the flow pane of Tableau Prep:

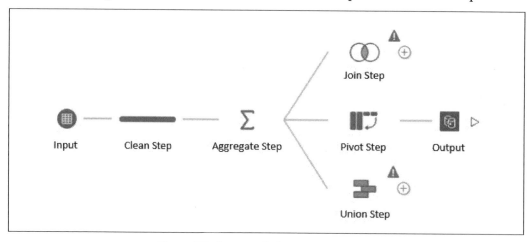

Figure 15.3: An example flow in Tableau Prep

Each of the individual components of the flow are called steps, which are connected by lines that indicate the logical flow of data from left to right. The lines are sometimes called connectors or branches of the flow. Notice that the **Aggregate Step** here has one line coming in from the left and three branches extending to the right. Any step can have multiple output branches that represent logical copies of the data at that point in the flow.

One important thing to notice is that four of the step types represent the four major transformations of data we discussed in *Chapter 14, Structuring Messy Data to Work Well in Tableau*. The step types of **Pivot**, **Union**, **Join**, and **Aggregate** exactly match those transformations, while the **Clean Step** allows various other operations involved in cleaning and calculating. You may wish to refresh your memory on the basic transformations in the previous chapter.

As we work through an example of a flow throughout this chapter, we'll examine each type of step more closely. For now, consider these preliminary definitions of the primary steps in Tableau Prep:

- **Input**: An input step starts the flow with data from a source such as a file, table, view, or custom SQL. It gives options for defining file delimiters, unions of multiple tables or files, and how much data to sample (for larger record sets).

- **Clean Step**: A clean step allows you to perform a wide variety of functions on the data, including calculations, filtering, adjusting data types, removing and merging fields, grouping and cleaning, and much more.

- **Aggregate Step**: An aggregate step allows you to aggregate values (for example, get MIN, MAX, SUM, AVG) at a level of detail you specify.

- **Join Step**: A join step allows you to bring together two branches of the flow and match data row by row based on the fields you select and the type of join.

- **Union Step**: A union step allows you to bring together two or more branches representing sets of data to be unioned together. You will have options for merging or removing mismatched fields.

Both the **Union Step** and **Join Step** in this example have an error icon, indicating that something has not been configured correctly in the flow. Hovering over the icon gives a tooltip description of the error. In this case, the error is due to only having one input connection, while both the union and join require at least two inputs. Often, selecting a step with an error icon may reveal details about the error in the changes pane or elsewhere in the configuration steps.

- **Pivot Step**: A pivot step allows you to transform columns of data into rows or rows of data into columns. You'll have options to select the type of pivot as well as the fields themselves. The term *transpose* is sometimes also used to describe this operation.

- **Output**: The output step defines the ultimate destination for the cleaned and transformed data. This could be a text file (.csv), extract (.hyper or .tde), or published extracted data source to Tableau Server. The ability to output to a database has been announced, although is not available at the time of writing. You'll have options to select the type of output, along with the path and filename or Tableau Server and project.

Right-clicking a step or connector reveals various options. You may also drag and drop steps onto other steps to reveal options such as joining or unioning the steps together. If you want to replace an early part of the flow to swap out an input step, you can right-click the connector and select **Remove**, and then drag the new input step over the desired next step in the flow to add it as the new input.

In addition to using the term *flow* to refer to the steps and connections that define the logical flow and transformation of the data, we'll also use the term flow to refer to the file that Tableau Prep uses to store the definition of the steps and changes of a flow. Tableau Prep flow files have the .tfl (unpackaged flow) or .tflx (packaged flow) extension.

The paradigm of Tableau Prep goes far beyond the features and capabilities of any single step. As you build and modify flows, you'll receive instant feedback so that you can see the impact of each step and change. This makes it relatively easy (and fun!) to iteratively discover your data and make the necessary changes.

> When you are building flows, adding steps, making changes, and interacting with data, you are in **design mode**. Tableau Prep uses a combination of the Hyper engine's cache, along with direct queries of the database, to provide near-instant feedback as you make changes. When you run a flow, you are using **batch mode** or **execution mode**. Tableau Prep will run optimized queries and operations that may be slightly different than the queries that are run in design mode.

We'll consider an example in the remainder of this chapter to aid in our discussion of the Tableau Prep paradigm and highlight some important features and considerations. The example will unfold organically, which will allow us to see how Tableau Prep gives you incredible flexibility to address data challenges as they arise and make changes as you discover new aspects of your data.

We'll put you in the role of an analyst at your organization, with the task of analyzing employee air travel. This will include ticket prices, airlines, and even a bit of geospatial analysis of the trips themselves. The data needs to be consolidated from multiple systems and will require some cleaning and shaping to enable the analysis.

To follow along, open Tableau Prep Builder, which will start on the home screen (there is not a starter flow for this chapter). The sample data is in the Chapter 15 directory, along with the Complete flow if you want to check your work. The Complete (clean) flow contains a sample of how a flow might be self-documented—it will not match screenshots precisely.

> When you open the Complete flow file, you'll likely receive errors and warnings that input paths and output paths are not valid. This is expected because your machine will almost certainly have a different drive and directory structure than the one on which the examples were prepared. You'll also run into this behavior when you share flow files with others. To resolve the issues, simply work through the connections in the **Connections** pane (expanded in *Figure 15.4*) on the left to reconnect to the files and set output steps to appropriate directories on your machine.

We'll start by connecting to some data!

Connecting to data

Connecting to data in Tableau Prep is very similar to connecting to data in Tableau Desktop. From the home screen, you may click either **Connect to Data** or the **+** button on the expanded **Connections** pane:

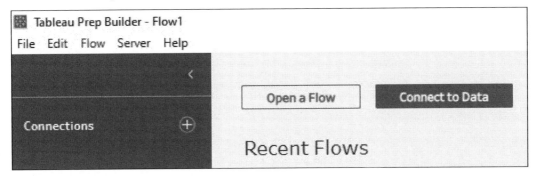

Figure 15.4: You can make a new data connection by clicking the + button or the Connect to Data button

Either UI element will bring up a list of data source types to select.

As with Tableau Desktop, for file-based data sources, you may drag the file from **Windows Explorer** or **Finder** onto the Tableau Prep window to quickly create a connection.

Tableau Prep supports dozens of file types and databases, and the list continues to grow. You'll recognize many of the same types of connection possibilities that exist in Tableau Desktop. However, at the time of writing this book, Tableau Prep does not support all the connections that are available in Tableau Desktop.

You may create as many connections as you like and the **Connections** pane will list each connection separately with any associated files, tables, views, and stored procedures, or other options that are applicable to that data source. You will be able to use any combination of data sources in the flow.

For now, let's start our example with the following steps:

1. Starting from the window shown in *Figure 15.4*, click **Connect to Data**.
2. From the expanded list of possible connections that appears, select **Microsoft Excel**.

3. You'll see a main table called **Employee Flights** and a sub-table named **Employee Flights Table 1**. Drag the **Employee Flights** table to the flow canvas. An input step will be created, giving you a preview of the data and other options. The input preview pane will initially look like this:

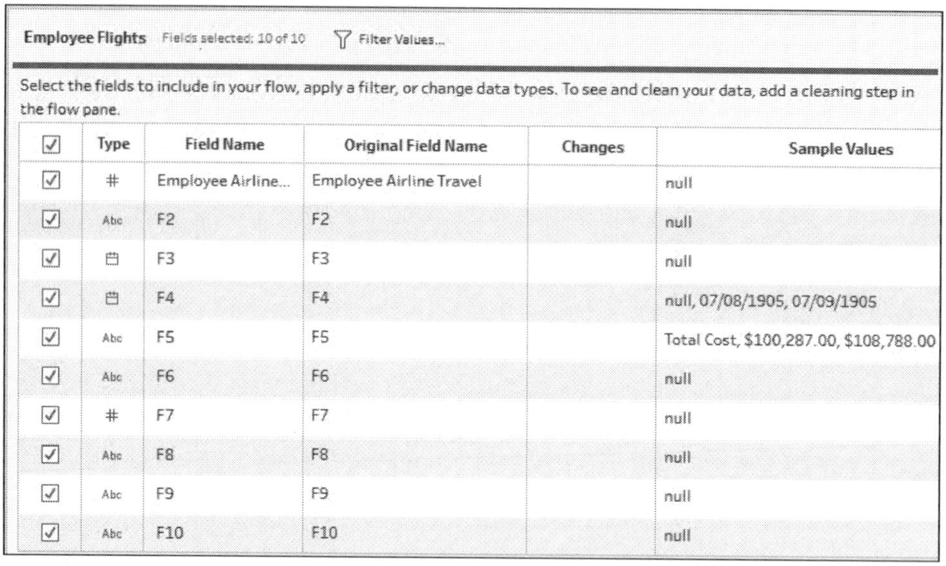

	Type	Field Name	Original Field Name	Changes	Sample Values
✓	#	Employee Airline...	Employee Airline Travel		null
✓	Abc	F2	F2		null
✓	📅	F3	F3		null
✓	📅	F4	F4		null, 07/08/1905, 07/09/1905
✓	Abc	F5	F5		Total Cost, $100,287.00, $108,788.00
✓	Abc	F6	F6		null
✓	#	F7	F7		null
✓	Abc	F8	F8		null
✓	Abc	F9	F9		null
✓	Abc	F10	F10		null

Employee Flights Fields selected: 10 of 10   ▽ Filter Values...

Select the fields to include in your flow, apply a filter, or change data types. To see and clean your data, add a cleaning step in the flow pane.

Figure 15.5: The input preview allows you to select input fields to
include in the flow, rename fields, and change data types

The input step displays a grid of fields and options for those fields. You'll notice that many of the fields in the **Employee Flights** table are named F2, F3, F4, and so on. This is due to the format of the Excel file, which has merged cells and a summary sub-table. Continue the exercise with the following steps:

4. Check the **Use Data Interpreter** option on the **Connections** pane and Tableau Prep will correctly parse the file as shown here:

Figure 15.6: The data interpreter parses the file to fix common issues such as
merged cells, empty headers, and sub-total lines

When you select an input step, Tableau Prep will display a grid of fields in the data. You may use the grid to uncheck any fields you do not wish to include, edit the **Type** of data by clicking the associated symbol (for example, change a string to a date), and edit the **Field Name** itself by double-clicking the field name value.

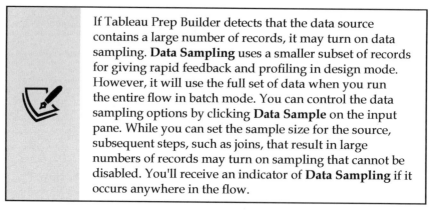

If Tableau Prep Builder detects that the data source contains a large number of records, it may turn on data sampling. **Data Sampling** uses a smaller subset of records for giving rapid feedback and profiling in design mode. However, it will use the full set of data when you run the entire flow in batch mode. You can control the data sampling options by clicking **Data Sample** on the input pane. While you can set the sample size for the source, subsequent steps, such as joins, that result in large numbers of records may turn on sampling that cannot be disabled. You'll receive an indicator of **Data Sampling** if it occurs anywhere in the flow.

5. Now, we'll continue to explore the data and fix some issues along the way. Click the + button that appears when you hover over the **Employee Flights** input step. This allows you to extend the flow by adding additional step types. In this case, we'll add a **Clean Step**. This will extend the flow by adding a clean step called **Clean 1**:

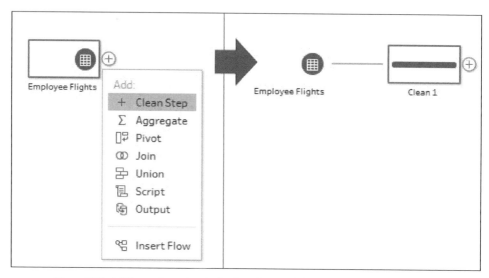

Figure 15.7: Adding a step extends the flow. Here, adding a clean step adds Clean 1

6. With the **Clean 1** step selected, take a moment to explore the data using the profile pane. Observe how selecting individual values for fields in the profile pane highlights portions of related values for other fields. This can give you great insight into your data, such as seeing the different price ranges based on Ticket Type:

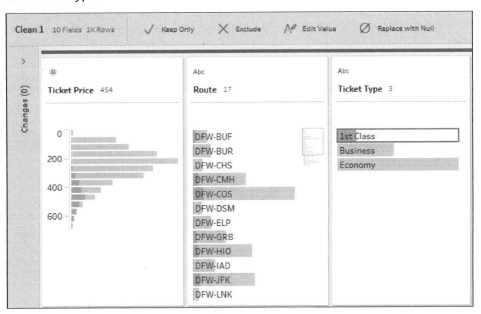

Figure 15.8: Selecting a value for a field in the profile pane highlights
which values (and what proportion of those values) relate to the selected value

Highlighting the bar segments across fields in the profile pane, which results from selecting a field value, is called brushing. You can also take action on selected values via the toolbar at the top of the profile pane or by right-clicking a field value. These actions include filtering, editing values, or replacing with NULL. However, before making any changes or cleaning any of the data, let's connect to some additional data.

It turns out that most of the airline ticket booking data is in one database that's represented by the Excel file, but another airline's booking data is stored in files that are periodically added to a directory. These files are in the \Learning Tableau\ Chapter 15\ directory. The files are named with the convention Southwest YYYY.csv (where YYYY represents the year).

We'll connect to all the existing files and ensure that we are prepared for additional future files:

1. Click the **+** icon on the **connections** pane to add a new connection to a **Text File**.

2. Navigate to the \Learning Tableau\Chapter 15\ directory and select any of the Southwest YYYY.csv files to start the connection. Looking at the **Input** settings, you should see that Tableau Prep correctly identifies the field separators, field names, and types:

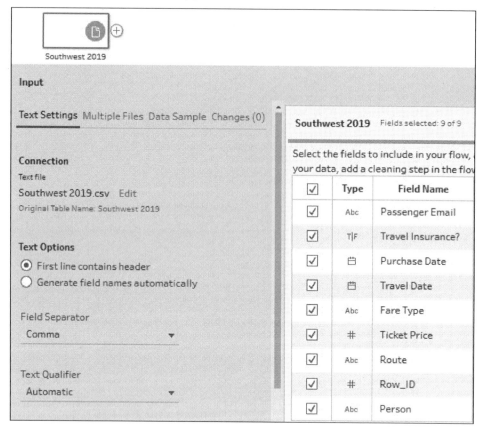

Figure 15.9: A text file includes options for headers, field separators, text qualifiers, character sets, and more. Notice also the tabs such as Multiple Files and Data Sample giving other options for the text input

3. In the **Input** pane, select the **Multiple Files** tab and switch from **Single table** to **Wildcard union**. Set **Matching Pattern** to Southwest* and click **Apply**. This tells Tableau Prep to union all of the text files in the directory that begin with Southwest together:

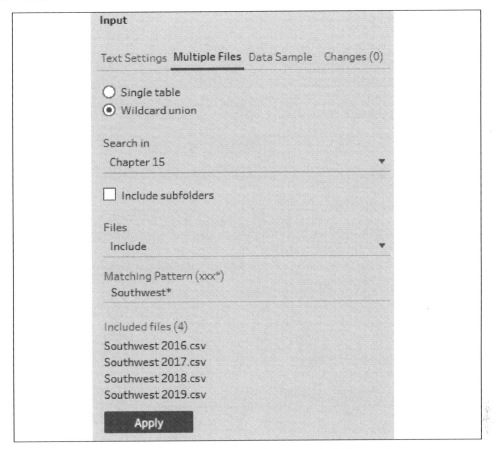

Figure 15.10: Using Matching Pattern tells Tableau Prep which files to union together.
That way, when Southwest 2020.txt and future files are dropped into the directory,
they will be automatically included

4. Use the **+** icon on the **Southwest** input step in the flow pane to add a new
    clean step. This step will be named **Clean 2** by default. Once again, explore
    the data, but don't take any action until you've brought the two sources
    together in the flow. You may notice a new field in the **Clean 2** step called
    File Paths, which indicates which file in the union is associated with each
    record.

With our input steps defined, let's move on to consider how to clean up some of the
data to get it ready for analysis.

Cleaning the data

The process of building out the flow is quite iterative, and you'll often make discoveries about the data that will aid you in cleaning and transforming it. We'll break this example into sections for the sake of reference, but don't let this detract from the idea that building a flow should be a flow of thought. The example is meant to be seamless!

We'll take a look at quite a few possibilities for prepping the data in this section, including merging and grouping. Let's start with seeing how to union together branches in the flow.

Unioning, merging mismatched fields, and removing unnecessary fields

We know that we want to bring together the booking data for all the airlines, so we'll union together the two paths in the flow:

1. Drag the **Clean 2** step onto the **Clean 1** step and drop it onto the **Union** box that appears. This will create a new **Union** step with input connections from both of the clean steps:

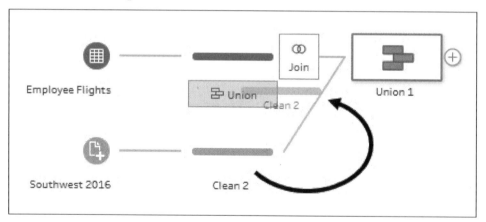

Figure 15.11: Dragging one step onto another in the flow reveals options for bringing the datasets together in the flow. Here, for example, there are options for creating a Union or Join

2. The **Union** pane that shows up when the **Union** step is selected will show you the mismatched fields, indicate the associated input, and give you options for removing or merging the fields. For example, Fare Type and Ticket Type are named differently between the Excel file and the text files, but in fact represent the same data. Hold down the *Ctrl* key and select both fields. Then, select **Merge Fields** from the toolbar at the top of the pane or from the right-click menu:

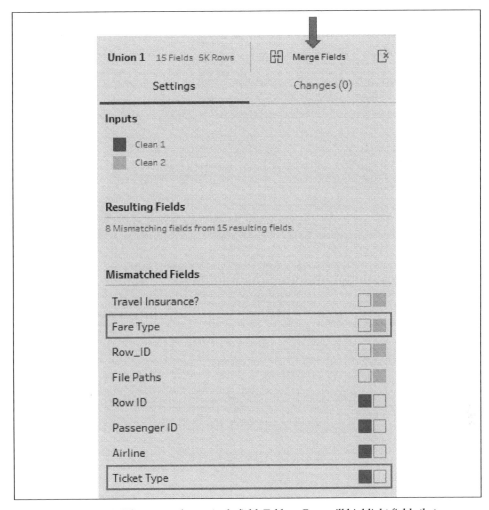

Figure 15.12: When you select a single field, Tableau Prep will highlight fields that
are potentially the same data. Selecting both reveals the Merge Fields option

3. Also, merge Row ID and Row_ID.

4. **File Paths** applies only to the Southwest files, which were unioned together
   in the **Input** step. While this auto-generated field can be very useful at times,
   it does not add anything to the data in this example. Select the field, then
   click the ellipses menu button and select **Remove Field**.

5. Similarly, Travel Insurance? and Passenger ID apply to only one of the
   inputs and will be of little use in our analysis. Remove those fields as well.

6. The single remaining mismatched field, `Airline`, is useful. Leave it for now and click the **+** icon on the **Union 1** step in the flow pane and extend the flow by selecting **Clean Step**. At this point, your flow should look like this:

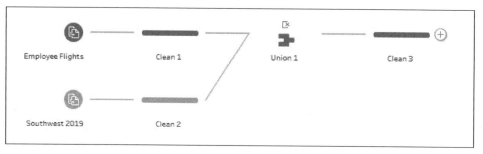

Figure 15.13: Your flow should look similar to this. You may notice some variation in the exact location of steps or color (you can change a step's color by right-clicking a step)

 There is an icon above the **Union 1** step in the flow, indicating changes that were made within this step. In this case, the changes are the removal of several of the fields. Each step with changes will have similar icons, which will reveal tooltip details when you hover over them and also allow you to interact with the changes. You can see a complete list of changes, edit them, reorder them, and remove them by clicking the step and opening the changes pane. Depending on the step type, this is available by either expanding it or selecting the changes tab.

Next, we'll continue building the flow and consider some options for grouping and cleaning.

Grouping and cleaning

Now, we'll spend some time cleaning up the data that came from both input sources. With the **Clean 3** step selected, use the profile pane to examine the data and continue our flow. The first two fields indicate some issues that need to be addressed:

Figure 15.14: Every null value in the Airline field comes from the Southwest files.
Fortunately, in this case, the source of the data indicates the airline

The Table Names field was generated by Tableau Prep as part of **Union 1** to indicate the source of the records. The Airline field came only from the Excel files (you can confirm this by selecting it in the profile pane and observing the highlighted path of the field in the flow pane). Click the **null** value for Airline and observe the brushing: this is proof that the null values in Airline all come from the Southwest files since those files did not contain a field to indicate the airline. We'll address the null values and do some additional cleanup:

1. Double-click the **null** value and then type Southwest to replace NULL with the value you know represents the correct airline. Tableau Prep will indicate that a **Group** and **Replace** operation has occurred with a paperclip icon.

2. We'll do an additional grouping to clean up the variations of **American**. Using the **Options** button on the Airline field, select **Group Values | Pronunciation**:

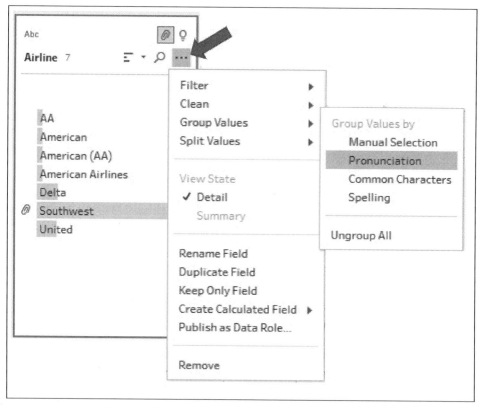

Figure 15.15: The ellipses button on a field will reveal a plethora of options,
from cleaning to filtering, to grouping, to creating calculations

Nearly all the variations are grouped into the **American** value. Only **AA**
remains.

3. In the **Group Values by Pronunciation** pane that has appeared, select the
    American Airlines group and manually add **AA** by checking it in the list that
    appears to the right:

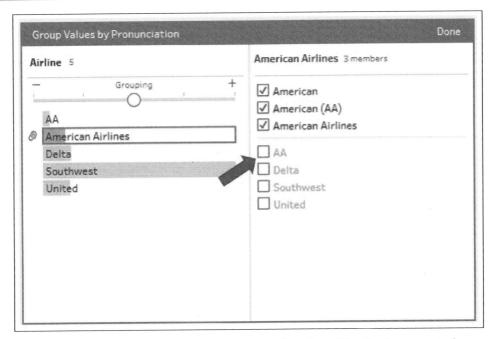

Figure 15.16: When grouping by pronunciation, you'll notice a slider allowing you control over the sensitivity of the grouping. You can also manually adjust groupings by selecting a field

4. Click **Done** on the **Group Values by Pronunciation** pane.

5. Next, select the Table Names field, which is no longer needed. Using either the toolbar option, the menu from a right-click for the field, or the options button, select **Remove Field.**

6. Some fields in the profile pane have a **Recommendations** icon (which resembles a lightbulb) in the upper-right corner. Click this icon on the Passenger Email field and then **Apply** the recommendation to assign a data role of **Email**:

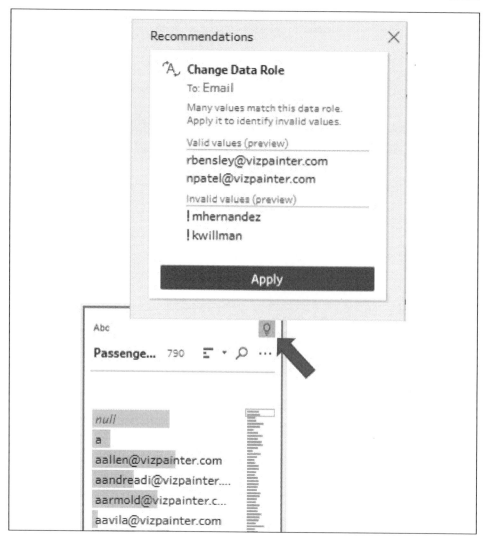

Figure 15.17: Recommendations will show when Tableau Prep has suggestions for cleaning a field

 Data Roles allow you to quickly identify valid or invalid values according to what pattern or domain of values is expected. Once you have assigned a data role, you may receive additional recommendations to either filter or replace invalid values.

After applying the recommendation, you'll see an indication in the profile pane for invalid values. As you continue following the example, we'll consider some options for quickly dealing with those invalid values.

7. Click the **Recommendations** button on the `Passenger Email` field again. You'll see two new options presented. **Apply** the option to **Group** and **Replace** invalid values with `null`:

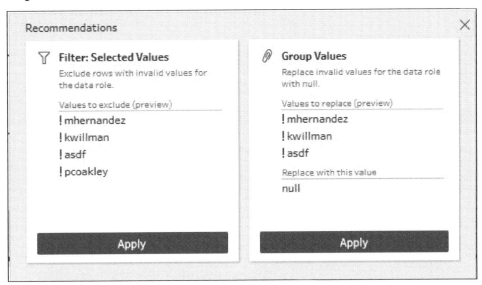

Figure 15.18: Here, Tableau Prep suggests either filtering out records with invalid values or replacing the invalid values with null. In this case, we don't want to filter out the entire record, but the invalid values themselves are useless and are best represented by null

8. Most of the remaining fields look fine, except for `Fare Type` (or possibly `Ticket Type`, depending on which name was kept when merging the fields previously). This field contains the values **1st Class** and **First Class**. Select both of these values by clicking each while holding down the *Ctrl* key and then **Group** them together with the **First Class** value. Two interface options for grouping the values are indicated here:

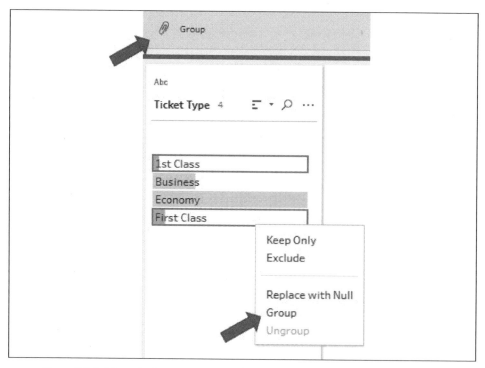

Figure 15.19: After selecting two or more values, you can group them together with the toolbar option or the right-click menu

9. At this point, we have a clean dataset that contains all our primary data. There's already a lot of analysis we could do. In fact, let's take a moment to preview the data. Right-click the **Clean 3** step and select **Preview in Tableau Desktop**:

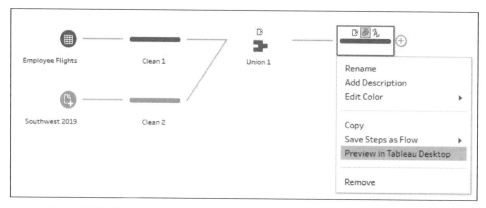

Figure 15.20: You may preview the data represented by any step in Tableau Desktop by selecting the option from the right-click menu for that step

A new data connection will be made and opened in Tableau Desktop. You can preview the data for any step in the flow. Take a few moments to explore the data in Tableau Desktop and then return to Tableau Prep. Now, we'll turn our attention to extending the dataset with some calculations, supplemental data, and a little restructuring.

Calculations and aggregations in Tableau Prep

Let's look at how to create calculations and some options for aggregations in Tableau Prep.

Row-level calculations

Calculations in Tableau Prep follow a syntax that's nearly identical to Tableau Desktop. However, you'll notice that only row-level and FIXED level of detail functions are available. This is because all calculations in Tableau Prep will apply to the row level. Aggregations are performed using an **Aggregate Step**, which we'll consider shortly.

Calculations and aggregations can greatly extend our analytic capabilities. In our current example, there is an opportunity to analyze the length of time between ticket purchase and actual travel. We may also want to mark each record with an indicator of how frequently a passenger travels overall. Let's dive into these calculations as we continue our example with the following steps:

1. We'll start with a calculation to determine the length of time between the purchasing of tickets and the day of travel. Select the **Clean 3** step and then click **Create Calculated Field**. Name the calculation **Days from Purchase to Travel** and enter DATEDIFF('day', [Purchase Date], [Travel Date]).

2. Examine the results in the profile pane. The new field should look like this:

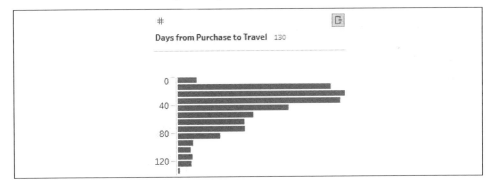

Figure 15.21: The calculated field shows up in the profile pane

The default view here (as in many cases with numeric fields) is a summary binned histogram. You can change the view to see its details by selecting the ellipses button in the upper right of the field and switching to **Detail**, which will show every value of the field:

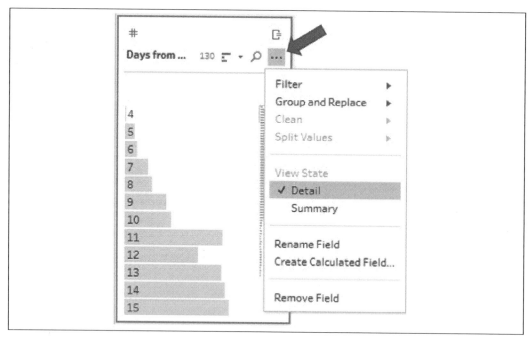

Figure 15.22: Numeric and date fields can be viewed in Summary or in Detail

The shape of the data that's indicated by the default summary histogram is close to what we might have expected with most people purchasing tickets closer (but not immediately prior) to the date of travel. There might be some opportunity for getting better deals by purchasing farther in advance, so identifying this pattern (and then exploring it more fully in Tableau Desktop) will be key for this kind of analysis.

Level of detail calculations

There are a few other types of analysis we may wish to pursue. Let's consider how we might create segments of passengers based on how often they travel.

We'll accomplish this using a FIXED **level of detail** (LOD) expression. We could create the calculation from scratch, matching the syntax we learned for Tableau Desktop to write the calculation like this:

```
{FIXED [Person] : COUNTD([Row_ID])}
```

The preceding calculation would count the distinct rows per person. Knowing that each row represents a trip, we could alternately use the code `{FIXED [Person] : SUM(1)}`, which would potentially be more performant, depending on the exact data source.

In this example, though, we'll leverage the interface to visually create the calculation:

1. Click the ellipses button on the `Person` field and select **Create Calculated Field | Fixed LOD**:

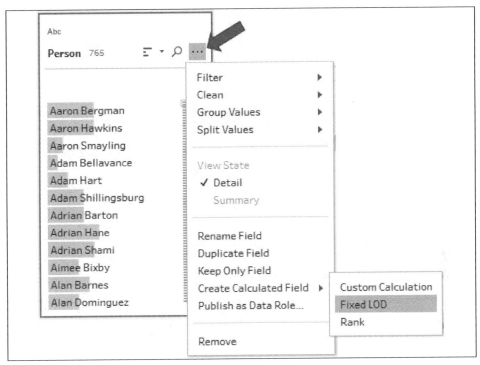

Figure 15.23: To create a Fixed LOD calculation, use the menu and select
Create Calculated Field | Fixed LOD

Notice also the options to create **Custom Calculation** (to write code) and **Rank** (to compute rank for the selected field).

2. This will bring up a **Fixed LOD** pane allowing us to configure the LOD expression. The **Group by** field is already set to `Person` (as we started the calculation from that field), but we'll need to configure **Compute using** to perform the distinct count of rows and rename the field as `Trips per Person`, as shown here:

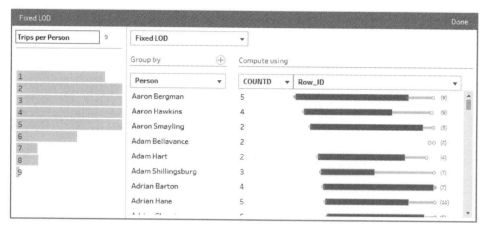

Figure 15.24: The Fixed LOD pane allows you to configure the LOD expression
visually and get instant visual feedback concerning results

3. Click **Done** when you have finished configuring the **Fixed LOD**.

4. We'll use the `Trips per Person` field to create segments of customers. We'll
   accomplish this with another calculated field, so click **Create Calculated
   Field…** to bring up the code editor. Name the field `Frequency Segment` and
   enter the following code:

```
IF [Trips per Person] <= 2 THEN "Rarely"
ELSEIF [Trips per Person] <= 5 THEN "Occasionally"
ELSE "Frequently"
END
```

The code uses the `Trips per Person` field in an `IF THEN ELSE` construction to create
three segments. You can visually see the correspondence between the fields in the
preview pane:

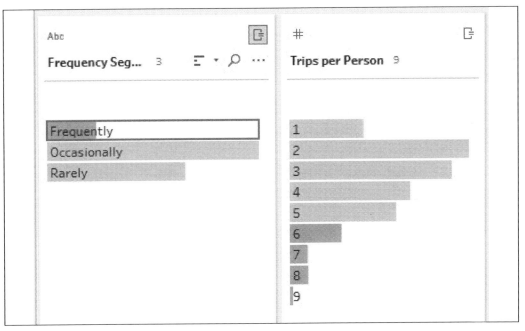

Figure 15.25: You can easily visualize how calculations relate to each other and other fields using the Profile pane

The Frequency Segment field can be used to accomplish all kinds of useful analysis. For example, you might want to understand whether frequent travelers typically get better ticket prices.

We've seen row-level and FIXED LOD calculations, and noted the option for **Rank**. Let's now turn our attention to aggregations.

Aggregations

Aggregations in Tableau Prep are accomplished using an aggregate step. We'll continue our flow with the idea that we want to better understand our frequency of travel segment:

1. Click the + symbol on **Clean 3** and add an **Aggregate** step. The new step will be named **Aggregate 1** by default:

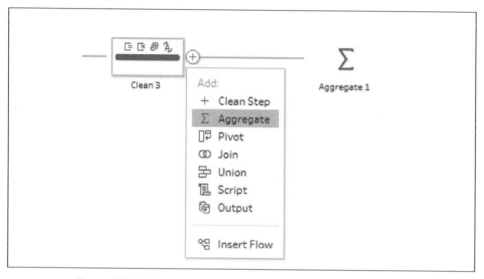

Figure 15.26: Adding an Aggregate step to the flow using the + symbol

2. Double-click the text **Aggregate 1** under the new step. This allows you to edit the name. Change the name from **Aggregate 1** to **Frequency Segment**.

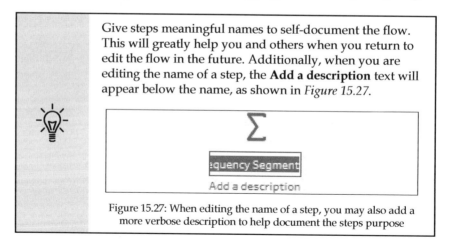

Give steps meaningful names to self-document the flow. This will greatly help you and others when you return to edit the flow in the future. Additionally, when you are editing the name of a step, the **Add a description** text will appear below the name, as shown in *Figure 15.27*.

Figure 15.27: When editing the name of a step, you may also add a more verbose description to help document the steps purpose

Selecting the aggregate step reveals a pane with options for grouping and aggregating fields in the flow:

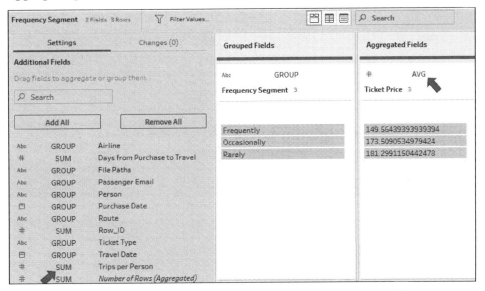

Figure 15.28: Adding an Aggregate step to the flow using the + symbol

You may drag and drop fields from the left to the **Grouped Fields** or **Aggregated Fields** sections and you may change the type of aggregation by clicking on the aggregation text (examples indicated by arrows in *Figure 15.28*: SUM next to Trips per Person or AVG above Ticket Price) and selecting a different aggregation from the resulting dropdown.

In *Figure 15.28*, notice that we've added **Frequency Segment** to the **GROUP** and Ticket Price to the **Aggregated Fields** as an AVG. Notice also the Number of Rows **(Aggregated)** that appears at the bottom of the list of fields on the left. This is a special field that's available in the aggregation step.

3. Conclude the example by clicking the **+** icon that appears when you hover over the **Frequency Segment** aggregate step and adding an **Output** step:

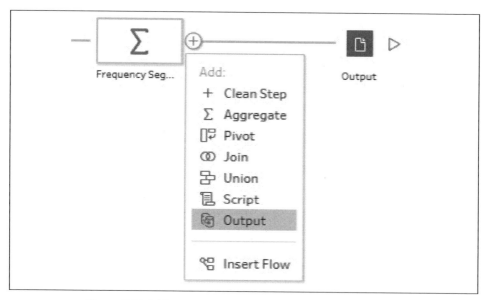

Figure 15.29 Adding an Output step to the flow using the + symbol

4. When you select the **Output** step, the **Output** pane shows options for saving the output and a preview of what the output will look like. In this case, we've configured the output to save to a **Comma Separated Values (.csv)** file named **Frequency Segment**:

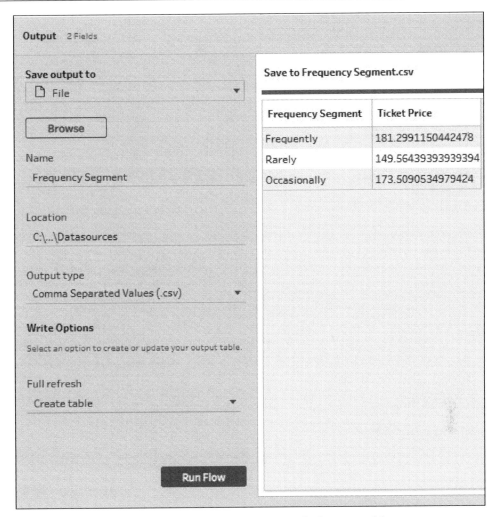

Figure 15.30: This output will contain exactly three rows of data

5. The **Output** pane also gives options for setting the output type, performing a full refresh of the data, or appending to existing data, and running the flow.

We'll extend our flow in the next few sections to additionally output detailed data. The detailed data as well as the output file of aggregate data gives us some nice options for leveraging Tableau's Data Model in Tableau Desktop to accomplish some complex analysis.

Let's continue by thinking about filtering data in Tableau Prep.

Filtering data in Tableau Prep

There are a couple of ways to filter data in Tableau Prep:

- Filter an input
- Filter within the flow

Filtering an input can be efficient because the query that's sent to the data source will return fewer records. To filter an input, select the input step and then click the **Filter Values...** button on the input pane:

	Type	Field Name	Original Field Name	Changes	Sample Values
✓	#	Row ID	Row ID		4,144, 9,102, 2,194
✓	Abc	Passenger Email	Passenger Email		ekiefer@vizpainter.com, abarton@vizpainter.com, achung@vizpainter.com
✓	📅	Purchase Date	Purchase Date		01/10/2019, 09/10/2017, 10/22/2018
✓	📅	Travel Date	Travel Date		02/06/2019, 11/12/2017, 12/17/2018

Employee Flights   Fields selected: 10 of 10   ▽ Filter Values...

Select the fields to include in your flow. If you make changes to the data, the data source will be queried again.

Figure 15.31: The Filter Values... option allows you to filter values on the input step. This could improve performance on large datasets or relational databases

The **Add Filter** dialog that pops up allows you to write a calculation with a Boolean (true/false) result. Only true values will be retained.

Filtering may also be done within a clean step anywhere in the flow. There are several ways to apply a filter:

- Select one or more values for a given field and then use the **Keep Only** or **Exclude** options.
- Use the **Option** button on a field to reveal multiple filter options based on the field type. For example, dates may be filtered by **Calculation...**, **Range of Dates**, **Relative Dates**, or **Null Values**:

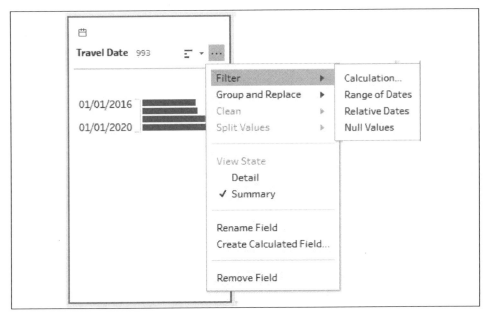

Figure 15.32: Filter options for a field include filtering by Calculation,
Range of Dates, and Relative Dates, and keeping or excluding Null Values

- Select a field and then **Filter Values** from the toolbar. Similar to the way filters work in the input pane, you will be prompted to write code that returns true for records you wish to keep. If, for example, you wanted to keep records for trips scheduled after January 1, 2016, you could write code such as the following:

```
[Travel Date] > MAKEDATE(2016, 1, 1)
```

While no filtering is required for the dataset in our example, you may wish to experiment with various filtering techniques.

At this point, your flow should look something like this:

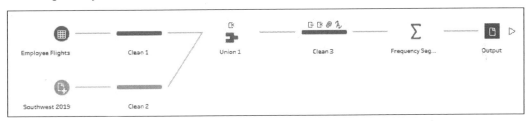

Figure 15.33: Your flow should look similar to this (exact placement and colors of steps may vary)

Let's conclude the Tableau Prep flow with some final transformations to make the data even easier to use in Tableau.

Transforming the data for analysis

Let's create a new branch in the flow to work once again with the detailed data. Click on the **Clean 3** step and examine the preview pane. In particular, consider the Route field:

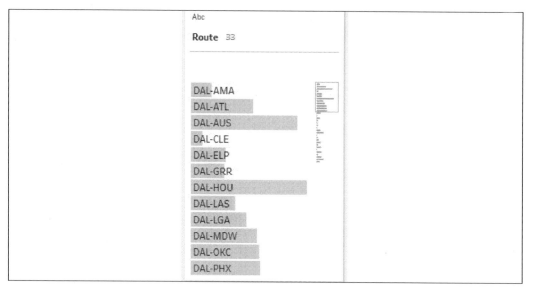

Figure 15.34: Route uses airport codes for origin and destination separated by a dash

Tableau Desktop (and Server) contain built-in geocoding for airport codes. But to accomplish our specific analysis goal (and open other possibilities for geospatial functions in Tableau Desktop), we'll supplement our data with our own geocoding. We'll also need to consider the shape of the data. Origins and destinations will be most useful split into separate fields, and if we want to connect them visually, we'll also want to consider splitting them into separate rows (a row for the origin and another row for the destination).

There are quite a few possibilities for visualizing this data. For example, we could keep origin and destination on the same row and use a dual-axis map. If we want to connect origins with destinations with a line, we could keep them in the same row of data and use Tableau's MAKELINE() function. The example you'll follow here will direct you to split the data into separate rows.

If you are following along, here are the steps we'll take:

1. Use the **+** button that appears when you hover over the **Clean 3** step. Use that to add a new clean step, which will be automatically named **Clean 4**:

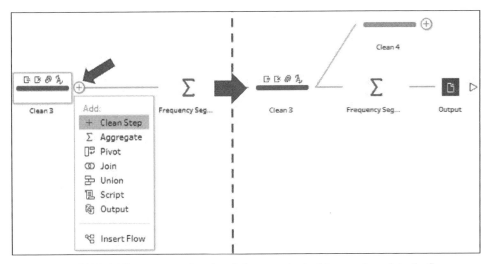

Figure 15.35: Adding to a step that already has an output adds a new branch to the flow

2. In the **Clean 4** step, use the ellipses button on the Route field and select **Split Values | Automatic Split**:

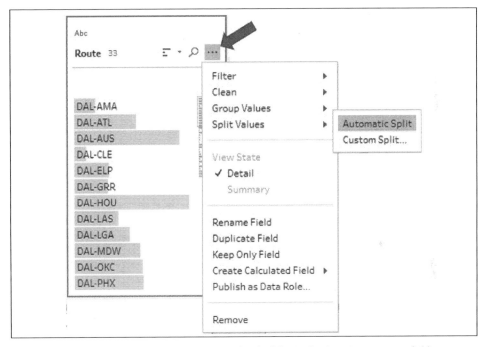

Figure 15.36: Split Values allows you to divide delimited strings into separate fields. Automatic Split attempts to determine the delimiter, while Custom Split… allows you greater options and flexibility

You'll now see two new fields added to the step:

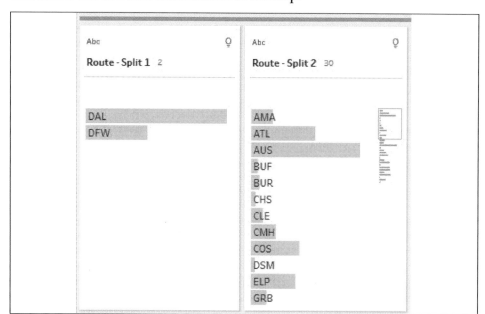

Figure 15.37: The results of the split will be new fields in the flow

3. **Route - Split 1** is the origin and **Route - Split 2** is the destination. Double-click the field name in the profile pane (or use the option from the ellipses button) to rename the fields to Origin and Destination.

4. Locate the US Airports.hyper file in the Chapter 15 directory. This file contains each Airport Code along with the Airport Name and Latitude and Longitude:

Abc	Abc	⊕	⊕	▾
Extract	Extract	Extract	Extract	
Airport Code	**Airport Name**	**Latitude**	**Longitude**	⌶
BTI	Barter Island LRRS Airport	70.1340	-143.582	
LUR	Cape Lisburne LRRS Airport	68.8751	-166.110	
PIZ	Point Lay LRRS Airport	69.7329	-163.005	
ITO	Hilo International Airport	19.7214	-155.048	
ORL	Orlando Executive Airport	28.5455	-81.333	

Figure 15.38: The hyper extract contains the data we'll need to supplement
the flow with our own geospatial data

5. Make a connection to this file in Tableau Prep. You may choose to drag and drop the file onto the Tableau Prep canvas or use the **Add Connection** button from the interface. Tableau will automatically insert an input step named **Extract (Extract.Extract)**. Feel free to change the name of the input step to **Airport Codes**:

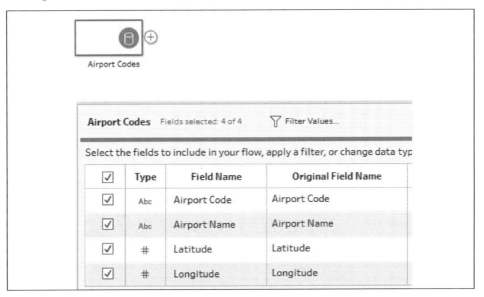

Figure 15.39: The input pane for the Airport Codes file

6. We'll want to join the **Airport Codes** into our flow to look up Latitude and Longitude, but before we do, we'll need to account for the fact that Origin and Destination in **Clean 4** are currently both on the same row of data. One option is to pivot the data. Use the **+** button on the **Clean 4** step to add a **Pivot** step:

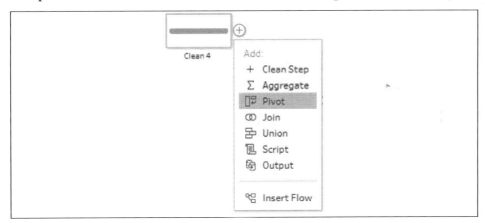

Figure 15.40: Adding a Pivot step from Clean 4

7. The pivot pane gives you options for transforming rows into columns or columns into rows. We'll keep the default option of **Columns to Rows**. Drag both the Origin and Destination fields into the **Pivot1 Values** area of the pane:

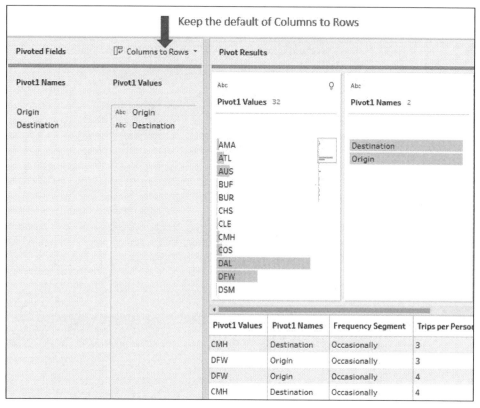

Figure 15.41: Pivot1 Names keeps values from the original column names, while Pivot1 Values contains the actual values from Origin and Destination

8. As a shortcut, instead of *steps 6* and *7*, you could have selected both the Origin and Destination fields in the **Clean 4** step, and selected **Pivot Columns to Rows**:

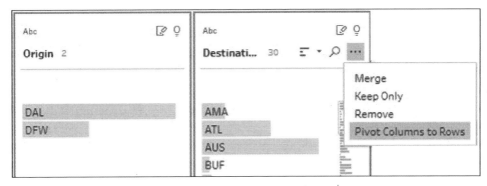

Figure 15.42: A shortcut for pivoting columns to rows

Continue with the following steps:

9. Double-click the text for **Pivot1 Values** and rename the field `Airport Code`. This field will contain all the airport codes for both the origin and destination records.

10. Double-click the text for **Pivot1 Names** and rename the field `Route Point`. This field will label each record as either an **Origin** or **Destination**.

   At this point, we have a dataset that contains a single record for each endpoint of the trip (either an origin or destination).

 Notice that the pivot resulted in duplicate data. What was once one row (origin and destination together) is now two rows. The record count has doubled, so we can no longer count the number of records to determine the number of trips. We also cannot SUM the cost of a ticket as it will double count the ticket. We'll need to use MIN/MAX/AVG or some kind of level of detail expression or filter to look at only origins or destinations. While many transformations allow us to accomplish certain goals, we have to be aware that they may introduce other complications.

The only location information we currently have in our main flow is the airport code. However, we already made a connection to `Airports.hyper` and renamed the input step as **Airport Codes**.

11. Locate the **Airport Codes** input step and drag it over the **Pivot** step. Drop it onto the **Join** area:

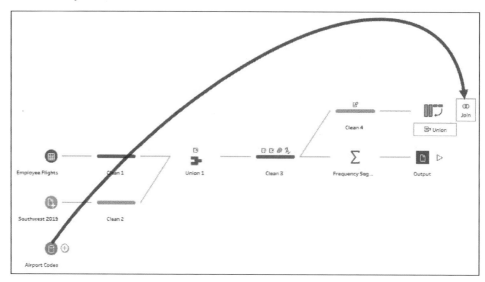

Figure 15.43: Dragging Airport Codes to the Join area of the Pivot step

After dropping the **Airport Codes** input step onto the **Join** area, a new join step will be created, named **Join 1**. Take a moment to examine the join pane:

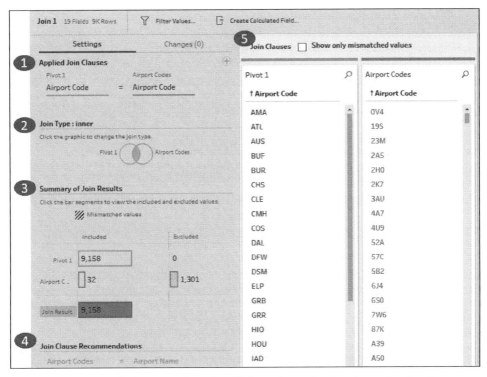

Figure 15.44: The join pane gives a lot of information and options for configuring the
join and understanding the results. Important sections of the interface are
numbered with descriptions below

You'll notice the following features in *Figure 15.44*:

1. **Applied Join Clauses**: Here, you have the option to add conditions to the join clause, deciding which fields should be used as keys to define the join. You may add as many clauses as you need.

2. **Join Type**: Here, you may define the type of join (inner, left, left inner, right, right inner, outer). Accomplish this by clicking sections of the Venn diagram.

3. **Summary of Join Results**: The bar chart here indicates how many records come from each input of the flow and how many matched or did not match. You may click a bar segment to see filtered results in the data grid.

4. **Join Clause Recommendations**: If applicable, Tableau Prep will display probable join clauses that you can add with a single click.

5. **Join Clauses**: Here, Tableau Prep displays the fields used in the join clauses and the corresponding values. Any unmatched values will have a red font color. You may edit values by double-clicking them. This enables you to fix individual mismatched values as needed.

We do not need to configure anything in this example. The default of an **Inner** join on the Airport Code fields works well. We can confirm that all 9,158 records from the **Pivot** step are kept. Only 32 records from the **Airport Codes** hyper file are actual matches (1,301 records didn't match). That is not concerning. It just means we had a lot of extra codes that could have possibly supplemented our data but weren't actually needed. Now, continuing from our previous example:

12. From **Join 1**, add a final output step and configure it to output to a .csv file named Airline Travel.csv.

13. Run the flow by using the run button at the top of the toolbar or by clicking the run button on the output step.

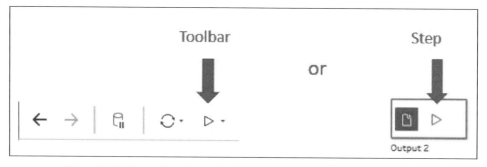

Figure 15.45: The toolbar allows you to run the flow for all outputs or a single output, while the button on the output step will run the flow only for that output

Your final flow will look something like this:

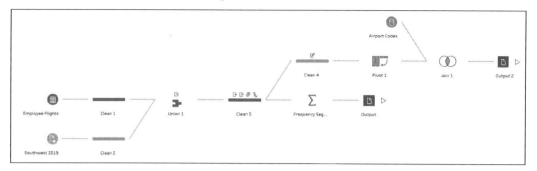

Figure 15.46: Your final flow will resemble this, but may be slightly different in appearance

The `Chapter 15 Complete (clean).tfl` file is a bit cleaned up with appropriate step labels and descriptions. As a good practice, try to rename your steps and include descriptions so that your flow is easier to understand. Here is how the cleaned version looks:

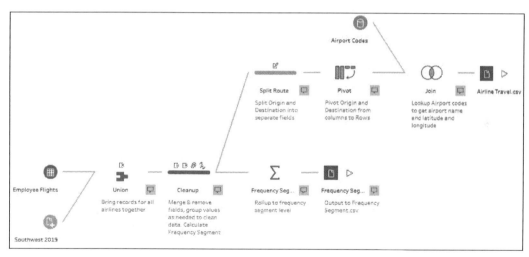

Figure 15.47: This flow is cleaned up and contains "self-documentation"

Once the flow has been executed, open the `Airline Travel.twb` workbook in the `\Learning Tableau\Chapter 15` directory to see how the data might be used and to explore it on your own:

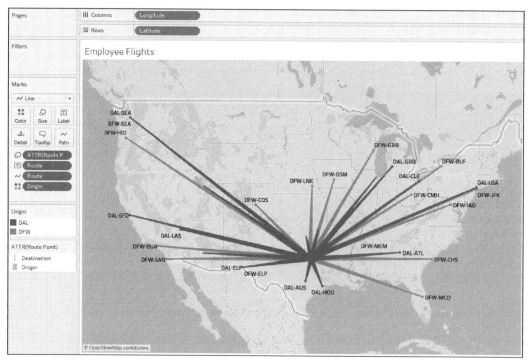

Figure 15.48: Exploring the data in the Airline Travel.twb workbook

 Unlike `.tde` or `.hyper` files, `.csv` files may be written to, even if they are open as a data source in Tableau Desktop. You will receive an error if you run a flow that attempts to overwrite a `.tde` or `.hyper` file that is in use. Additionally, you may rearrange the field order for a `.csv` file by dragging and dropping fields into the profile pane of a clean step prior to the output.

With our example concluded, let's wrap up by considering some options for automating Tableau Prep flows.

Options for automating flows

Tableau Prep Builder allows you to design and run flows using the application. Sometimes, data cleansing and prepping will be a one-time operation to support an ad hoc analysis. However, you will often want to run a flow subsequently to capture new or changed data and to cleanse and shape it according to the same pattern. In these cases, you'll want to consider some options for automating the flow:

- **Tableau Prep Builder** may be run via a command line. You may supply JSON files to define credentials for input or output data connections. This enables you to use scripting and scheduling utilities to run the flow without manually opening and running the Tableau Prep interface. Details on this option are available from Tableau Help: `https://onlinehelp.tableau.com/current/prep/en-us/prep_save_share.htm#refresh-output-files-from-the-command-line`.

- **Tableau Prep Conductor**, an add-on to Tableau Server, gives you the ability to publish entire flows from Tableau Prep Builder to Tableau Server and then either run them on demand or on a custom schedule. It also provides monitoring and troubleshooting capabilities.

Summary

Tableau Prep's innovative paradigm of hands-on data cleansing and shaping with instant feedback greatly extends the Tableau platform and gives you incredible control over your data. In this chapter, we considered the overall interface and how it allows you to iteratively and rapidly build out a logical flow to clean and shape data for the desired analysis or visualization.

Through a detailed, yet practical, example that was woven throughout this chapter, we explored every major transformation in Tableau Prep, from inputs to unions, joins, aggregates and pivots, to outputs. Along the way, we also examined other transformations and capabilities, including calculations, splits, merges, and the grouping of values. This gives you a foundation for molding and shaping data in any way you need.

In the next chapter, we'll conclude with some final thoughts on how you can leverage Tableau's platform to share your analysis and data stories!

16

Sharing Your Data Story

Throughout this book, we've focused on Tableau Desktop and learned how to visually explore and communicate data with visualizations and dashboards. Once you've made discoveries, designed insightful visualizations, and built stunning dashboards, you're ready to share your data stories.

Tableau enables you to share your work using a variety of methods. In this chapter, we'll take a look at the various ways to share visualizations and dashboards, along with what to consider when deciding how you will share your project.

Specifically, we'll look at the following topics:

- Presenting, printing, and exporting
- Sharing with users of Tableau Desktop and Tableau Reader
- Sharing with users of Tableau Server, Tableau Online, and Tableau Public

There are no examples to follow in this chapter, but it is highly recommended to read through the material for a solid understanding of the various options available for sharing your insights and discoveries.

Let's start with an overview of the presenting, printing and exporting processes.

Presenting, printing, and exporting

Tableau is primarily designed to build richly interactive visualizations and dashboards for consumption on a screen. Often, you will expect users to interact with your dashboards and visualizations. However, there are good options for presenting, printing, and exporting in a variety of formats.

Presenting

Tableau gives you multiple options for personally presenting your data story. You might walk your audience through a presentation of a single dashboard or view, or you might create an entire presentation. While there are multiple ways you might structure a presentation, consider the following options:

- Exporting to PowerPoint
- Presentation mode

Tableau Desktop and Server allow you to export directly to **PowerPoint**. In Tableau Desktop, select **File | Export as PowerPoint...**. After selecting a location and filename, Tableau will generate a PowerPoint file (.pptx), converting each tab in the Tableau workbook to a single slide in PowerPoint. Each slide will contain a static image of the views and dashboards as they exist at the time of the export. As each slide is simply a screenshot, there will be no dynamic interactivity following the export.

If you prefer a more dynamic presentation experience, consider using **Presentation mode**. This mode shows you all dashboards and views in full screen mode. It hides all toolbars, panes, and authoring objects. To activate presentation mode, select **Window** from the top menu or press *F7* or the option on the top toolbar. Press *F7* or the *Esc* key to exit presentation mode. While in presentation mode, you may still interact with dashboards and views using actions, highlighting, filtering, and other options. This enriches the presentation and gives you the ability to answer questions on the fly. When used with compelling dashboards and stories, presentation mode makes for an effective way to personally walk your audience through the data story.

 If you save a workbook by pressing *Ctrl + S* while in presentation mode, the workbook will be opened in presentation mode by default.

Printing

Tableau enables printing for individual visualizations, dashboards, and stories. From the **File** menu, you can select **Print** to send the currently active sheet in the workbook to the printer or the **Print to PDF** option to export to a PDF. Either option allows you to export the active sheet, selected sheets, or the entire workbook to a PDF. To select multiple sheets, hold the *Ctrl* key and click individual tabs.

When printing, you also have the option to **Show Selections**. When this option is checked, marks that have been interactively selected or highlighted on a view or dashboard will be printed as selected. Otherwise, marks will print as though no selections have been made. The map in the following dashboard has marks for the western half of the United States selected:

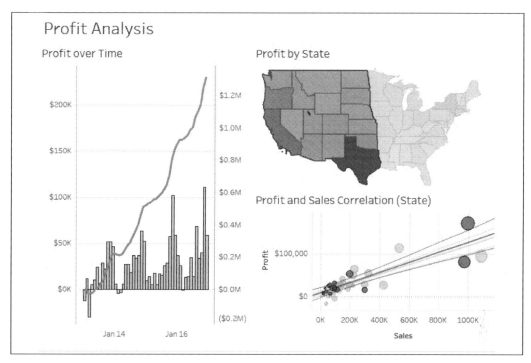

Figure 16.1: You can see states and circles that are selected in this screenshot.
You may optionally print views with selections

Here are some considerations, tips, and suggestions for printing:

- If a dashboard is being designed for printing, select a predefined paper size as the fixed size for the dashboard or use a custom size that matches the same aspect ratio.

- Use the **Page Setup** screen (available from the **File** menu) to define specific print options, such as what elements (legends, title, caption) will be included, the layout (including margins and centering), and how the view or dashboard should be scaled to match the paper size. The **Page Setup** options are specific to each view. Duplicating or copying a sheet will include any changes to the **Page Setup** settings:

If you are designing multiple sheets or dashboards for printing, consider creating one as a template, setting up all the desired print settings, and then duplicating it for each new sheet.

Figure 16.2: The Page Setup dialog contains options for layout and print scaling

- Fields used on the **Pages** shelf will define page breaks in printing (for individual sheets, but not dashboards or stories). The number of pages defined by the **Pages** shelf is not necessarily equivalent to the number of printed pages. This is because a single page defined by the **Pages** shelf might require more than one printed page.

- Each story point in a story will be printed on a new page.

- Printing the entire workbook can be an effective way to generate a single PDF document for distribution. Each visible sheet will be included in the PDF in the order of the tabs, from left to right. You may hide sheets to prevent inclusion in the PDF or reorder sheets to adjust the order of the resultant document. Consider also creating dashboards with images and text for title pages, table of contents, page numbers, and commentary. You might experiment with complete workbooks from previous chapters to see how various visual elements are retained or changed in the PDF conversion.

- Avoid scrollbars in dashboards as they will print as scrollbars, and anything outside the visible window will not be printed.

- You can also select multiple sheets in the workbook (hold the *Ctrl* key while clicking each tab) and then print only selected sheets.

 Sheets may be hidden if they are views that are used in one or more dashboards or tooltips, or if they are dashboards used in one or more stories. To hide a view, right-click the tab or thumbnail on the bottom strip or in the left-hand pane of the dashboard or story workspace and select **Hide Sheet**. To show a sheet, locate it in the left-hand pane of the dashboard or story workspace, right-click it, and uncheck **Hide Sheet.** You can also right-click a dashboard or story tab and hide or show all sheets used.

If you don't see a **Hide Sheet** option, this means this sheet is not used in any dashboard and can be deleted.

In addition to printing or outputting to PDF, we can also export data and images from views and dashboards. Let's see how!

Exporting

Tableau also makes it easy to export images of views, dashboards, and stories for use in documents, documentation, and even books like this one! Images may be exported as `.png`, `.emf`, `.jpg`, or `.bmp`. You may also copy an image to the clipboard to paste into other applications. You may also export the data as a cross-tab (Excel), a `.csv` file, or Microsoft Access database (on PC).

To copy an image or export images or data, use the menu options for **Worksheet**, **Dashboard**, or **Story**.

We'll consider using Tableau Server, Tableau Online, and Tableau Public in detail shortly. For now, let's consider some of the exporting features available on these platforms. When interacting with a view on Tableau Server, Online, or Public, you will see a toolbar unless you don't have the required permissions or the toolbar has been specifically disabled by a Tableau Server administrator:

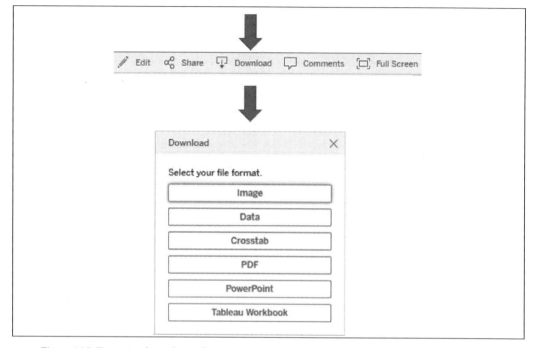

Figure 16.3: Exporting from the toolbar provides a similar experience for Server, Online, and Public

The **Download** option from the toolbar allows you to download an **Image**, **Data**, **Crosstab** (Excel), **PDF**, **PowerPoint**, or the **Tableau Workbook**. Images are exported in .png format and render the dashboard in its current state. Exporting a .pdf document will give the user many options, including layout, scaling, and whether to print the current dashboard, all sheets in the workbook, or all sheets in the current dashboard.

Exporting data or a crosstab will export for the active view in the dashboard; that is, if you click a view in the dashboard, it becomes active and you can export the data or crosstab for that particular view.

Other options exist for exporting from Tableau Server:

- Dashboards with **Export** buttons you may recall the **Export** button as one of the objects available to include on a dashboard. These can be configured to export the entire dashboard as a PDF, PowerPoint, or an image, and are a nice alternative to the toolbar option. This also allows for easy exporting from Tableau Desktop.

- **Tabcmd** gives you the ability to export data, images, or documents in a wide variety of formats via the command line or scripts.

- **REST API** gives you the ability to programmatically export data, images, or documents in a wide variety of formats.

- You may append the extension to the URL of a view hosted on Tableau Server or Online to view or download in the format defined by the link. For example, appending `.pdf` so that the URL would be something like `https://tableauserver/#/views/Dashboard/View.pdf` would render the view as a PDF document in the browser.

Beyond sharing image or document exports, most often you'll want to share fully interactive dashboards with others. Let's consider how you might accomplish this.

Sharing with users of Tableau Desktop and Tableau Reader

You may share workbooks with other users of Tableau Desktop and Tableau Reader. We'll consider the options and note some differences in the following sections.

Sharing with Tableau Desktop users

Sharing a workbook with other Tableau Desktop users is fairly straightforward, but there are a few things to consider.

One of the major considerations is whether you will be sharing a packaged workbook (`.twbx`) or an unpackaged workbook (`.twb`). Packaged workbooks are single files that contain the workbook (`.twb`), extracts (`.hyper`), file-based data sources that have not been extracted (`.xls`, `.xlsx`, `.txt`, `.cub`, `.mdb`, and others), custom images, and various other related files.

To share with users of Tableau Desktop, you have a variety of options:

- You may share either a packaged (`.twbx`) or unpackaged (`.twb`) workbook by simply sharing the file with another user who has the same or a newer version of Tableau Desktop.

> Workbook files will be updated when saved in a newer version of Tableau Desktop. You may receive errors or warnings when you open the workbook in an older version of Tableau. You will be prompted about updates when you first open the workbook and again when you attempt to save it. You may optionally export a workbook as a previous version from the **File** menu.

- If you share an unpackaged (`.twb`) workbook, then anyone else using it must be able to access any data sources, and any referenced images must be available to the user in the same directory where the original files were referenced. For example, if the workbook uses a live connection to an Excel (`.xlsx`) file on a network path and includes images on a dashboard located in `C:\Images`, then all users must be able to access the Excel file on the network path and have a local `C:\Images` directory with image files of the same name.

> Consider using a UNC (for example, `\\servername\ directory\file.xlsx`) path for common files if you use this approach.

Similarly, if you share a packaged workbook (`.twbx`) that uses live connections, anyone using the workbook must be able to access the live connection data source and have appropriate permissions.

Sharing with Tableau Reader users

Tableau Reader is a free application provided by Tableau Software that allows users to interact with visualizations, dashboards, and stories created in Tableau Desktop. Unlike Tableau Desktop, it does not allow for the authoring of visualizations or dashboards. However, all interactivity, such as filtering, drilldown, actions, and highlighting, is available to the end user.

Think of Tableau Reader as being similar to many PDF readers that allow you to read and navigate the document, but do not allow for authoring or saving changes.

To share with users of Tableau Reader, consider the following:

- Reader will only open packaged (.twbx) workbooks.
- The packaged workbook may not contain live connections to server or cloud-based data sources. Those connections must be extracted.

Be certain to take into consideration security and confidentiality concerns when sharing packaged workbooks (.twbx). Since packaged workbooks most often contain the data, you must be certain that the data is not sensitive. Even if the data is not shown on any view or dashboard, if it is a part of an extract or file packaged with the workbook, it is still accessible.

Reader and Desktop are good options but do require other users to have the application installed. You might also consider using Tableau Server, Online, or Public to share and collaborate with a wider audience.

Sharing with users of Tableau Server, Tableau Online, and Tableau Public

Tableau Server, **Tableau Online**, and **Tableau Public** are all variations on the same concept: hosting visualizations and dashboards on a server and allowing users to access them through a web browser.

The following table provides some of the similarities and differences between the products, but as details may change, please consult with a Tableau representative prior to making any purchasing decisions:

	Tableau Server	Tableau Online	Tableau Public
Description	A server application installed on one or more server machines that hosts views and dashboards created with Tableau Desktop.	A cloud-based service maintained by Tableau Software that hosts views and dashboards created with Tableau Desktop.	A cloud-based service maintained by Tableau Software that hosts views and dashboards created with Tableau Desktop or the free Tableau Public client.
Licensing cost	Yes	Yes	Free
Administration	Fully maintained, managed, and administered by the individual or organization that purchased the license.	Managed and maintained by Tableau Software with some options for project and user management by users.	Managed and maintained by Tableau Software.
Authoring and publishing	Users of Tableau Desktop may author and publish workbooks to Tableau Server. Web Authoring allows Tableau Server users the capability to edit and create visualizations and dashboards in a web browser.	Users of Tableau Desktop may author and publish workbooks to Tableau Online. Web Authoring allows Tableau Online users the capability to edit and create visualizations and dashboards in a web browser.	Users of Tableau Desktop or the free Tableau Public client can publish workbooks to Tableau Public. Future enhancements to allow online authoring have been announced.
Interaction	Licensed Tableau Server users may interact with hosted views. Views may also be embedded in intranet sites, SharePoint, and custom portals.	Licensed Tableau Online users may interact with hosted views. Views may also be embedded in intranet sites, SharePoint, and custom portals.	Everything is public-facing. Anyone may interact with hosted views. Views may be embedded in public websites and blogs.

	Tableau Server	**Tableau Online**	**Tableau Public**
Limitations	None.	Most data sources must be extracted before workbooks can be published. Most non-cloud-based data sources must have extracts refreshed using Tableau Desktop on a local machine or through the **Tableau Online Sync Client**.	All data must be extracted and each data source is limited to 15 million rows.
Security	The Tableau Server administrator may create sites, projects, and users and adjust permissions for each. Access to the underlying data can be restricted, and downloading of the workbook or data can be restricted.	The Tableau Server administrator may create projects and users and adjust permissions for each. Access to the underlying data can be restricted, and downloading of the workbook or data can be restricted.	By default, anyone may download and view data; however, access to these options may be restricted by the author.
Good uses	Internal dashboards and analytics and/or use across departments/divisions/clients through multi-tenant sites.	Internal dashboards and analytics, especially where most data sources are cloud-based. Sharing and collaboration with remote users.	Sharing visualizations and dashboards using embedded views on public-facing websites or blogs.

Publishing to Tableau Public

You may open workbooks and save to Tableau Public using either Tableau Desktop or the free Tableau Public client application. Please keep the following points in mind:

- In order to use Tableau Public, you will need to register an account.
- With Tableau Desktop and the proper permissions, you may save and open workbooks to and from Tableau Public using the **Server** menu and by selecting options under Tableau Public.

- With the free Tableau Public client, you may only save workbooks to and from the web.

 With these options, be aware that anyone in the world can view what you publish.

- Selecting the option to **Manage Workbooks** will open a browser so you can log in to your Tableau Public account and manage all your workbooks online.

- Workbooks saved to Tableau Public may contain any number of data source connections, but they must all be extracted and must not contain more than 15 million rows of extracted data each.

Consider using Tableau Public when you want to share your data story with the world!

Publishing to Tableau Server and Tableau Online

Publishing to Tableau Server and Tableau Online is a similar experience. To publish to Tableau Server or Tableau Online, from the menu select **Server | Publish Workbook**. If you are not signed in to a server, you will be prompted to sign in:

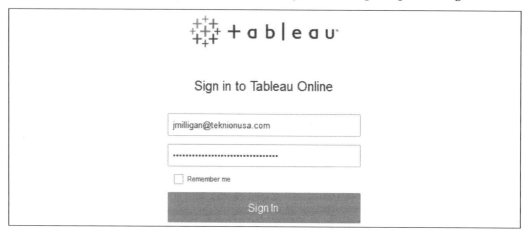

Figure 16.4: The sign-in screen for Tableau Online

You must have a user account with publish permissions for one or more projects. Enter the URL or IP address of the Tableau Server or the Tableau Online URL, your username, and password. Once signed in, you will be prompted to select a site, if you have access to more than one. Finally, you will see the publish screen:

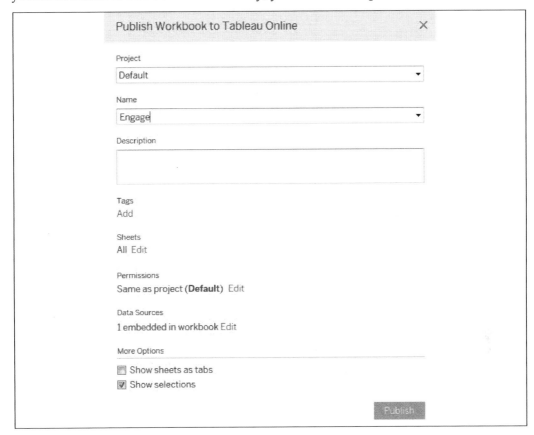

Figure 16.5: Publishing to Tableau Online

You have multiple options when you publish:

- Select the **Project** to which you wish to publish and **Name** your workbook. If a workbook has already been published with the same name as the selected project, you will be prompted to overwrite it.

- You may give the workbook a **Description** and use **Add Tags** to make searching for and finding your workbook easier.

- You may also specify which **Sheets** to include in the published workbook. Any sheets you check will be included; any you uncheck will not.

- You may edit user and group **Permissions** to define who has permission to view, interact with, and alter your workbook. By default, the project settings are used. Here is an example workbook with individual users and permissions:

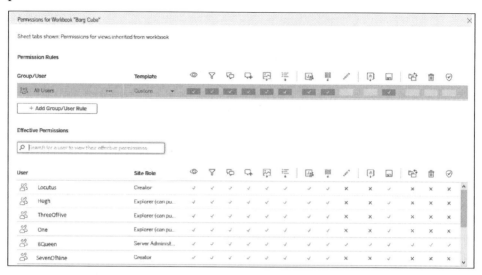

Figure 16.6: Tableau Server allows for a robust set of permissions. You can adjust individual and group permissions for viewing, filtering, commenting, editing, saving, and more

- You may edit properties for data sources. The options are described in detail in the next section.

- You also have the option to **Show Sheets as Tabs**. When checked, users on Tableau Server will be able to navigate between sheets using tabs similar to those shown at the bottom of Tableau Desktop. This option must be checked if you plan to have actions that navigate between views.

- **Show Selections** indicates that you wish any active selections of marks to be retained in the published views.

Editing data sources gives you options for authentication and scheduling:

- For each data connection used in the workbook, you may determine how database connections are authenticated. The options will depend on the data source as well as the configuration of Tableau Server. Various options include embedding a password, impersonating a user, or prompting a Tableau Server user for credentials.

- You may specify a schedule for Tableau Server to run refreshes of any data extracts.

Any live connections or extracted connections that will be refreshed on the server must define connections that work from the server. This means that all applicable database drivers must be installed on the server; all network, internet connections, and ports required for accessing database servers and cloud-based data must be open.

Additionally, any external files referenced by a workbook (for example, image files and non-extracted file-based data sources) that were not included when the workbook was published must be referenced using a location that is accessible by Tableau Server (for example, a network path with security settings allowing the Tableau Server process read access).

Once dashboards and views have been published to Tableau Server, you and other users with access will be able to interact with them. We'll consider the details next.

Interacting with Tableau Server

After a workbook is published to Tableau Server, other users will be able to view and interact with the visualizations and dashboards using a web browser. Once logged in to Tableau Server, they will be able to browse content for which they have appropriate permissions. These users will be able to use any features built into the dashboards, such as quick filters, parameters, actions, or drilldowns. Everything is rendered as HTML5, so the only requirement for the user to view and interact with views and dashboards is an HTML5-compatible web browser.

 The **Tableau Mobile** app, available for iOS and Android devices, can enhance the experience for mobile users. Use Tableau's device designer to target layouts for specific devices.

For the most part, interacting with a workbook on Server or Online is very similar to interacting with a workbook in Tableau Desktop or Reader. Quick filters, parameters, actions, and tooltips all look and behave similarly.

You will find some additional features:

- The side menu gives you various options related to managing and navigating Tableau Server.
- Below that, you'll find a breadcrumb trail informing you which workbook and view you are currently viewing.

- Beneath that, you'll find a toolbar that includes several features:

Figure 16.7: The Tableau Server toolbar

- **Undo** and **Redo** give you the ability to step backward and forward through interactions.

- **Revert** gives you the ability to undo all changes and revert to the original dashboard.

- **Refresh** reloads the dashboard and refreshes the data. However, this does not refresh any extracts of the data.

- **Pause** allows you to pause refreshing of the dashboard based on actions, filter selections, or parameter value changes until you have made all the changes you wish.

- **View** allows you to save the current state of the dashboard based on selections, filters, and parameter values so you can quickly return to it at a later point. You can also find your saved views here.

- **Alert** allows you to set up a conditional alert. When a mark in a view reaches a threshold you define, you will receive an alert through email. For example, you might have a line chart of profitability and expect an alert on a day when you meet an organizational goal. Or you might set an alert to receive notification when the count of errors indicated in the data exceeds 0.

- **Subscribe** allows you to schedule periodic emails of a screenshot of the dashboard. Administrators may also subscribe other users. You might want to consider this option to distribute daily performance reports, sales updates, inventory counts, or any other information you want to push out!

- **Edit** allows you to edit the dashboard. The interface is very similar to Tableau Desktop. The Tableau Administrator can enable or disable web editing per user or group and also control permissions for saving edited views.

- **Share** gives you options for sharing the workbook. These options include a URL you can distribute to other licensed users, as well as code for embedding the dashboard in a web page.

- The **Download** button allows you to download the data, images of the dashboard, the .pdf, or the workbook, as described earlier.

- **Comments** give you the ability to collaborate with other Tableau Server users by making comments on the view and responding to the comments of others.

- **Full Screen** allows you to view the dashboard or view in full screen mode.

- **Metrics** (not shown in *Figure 16.7*) give you the ability to define key numbers or indicators that you wish to track.

Now that we've explored some of Tableau Server's interactive capabilities, let's consider some further distribution options with Tableau Server and Tableau Online.

Additional distribution options using Tableau Server or Tableau Online

Both Tableau Server and Tableau Online provide several other options for sharing your views, dashboards, and data. Along with allowing users to log in to Tableau Server, you might consider the following options:

- Dashboards, views, and story points can be embedded in websites, portals, and SharePoint. Single-sign-on options exist to allow your website authentication to integrate seamlessly with Tableau Server.

- Tableau Server allows users to subscribe to views and dashboards and schedule email delivery. The email will contain an up-to-date image of the view and a link to the dashboard on Tableau Server.

- The **tabcmd** utility is provided with Tableau Server and may be installed on other machines. The utility provides the ability to automate many functions of Tableau Server, including export features, publishing, and user and security management. This opens up quite a few possibilities for automating delivery.

- The **REST API** allows programmatic interaction with Tableau Server. This gives you a wide range of options for exporting data, images, and documents and distributing to users as well as access to usage statistics, users, permissions, and more!

All these options greatly extend the flexibility of distributing data and visualizations to those in the organization who need them most!

Summary

Tableau is an amazing platform for exploring, prepping, and cleaning your data as you create useful and meaningful visualizations and dashboards to understand and communicate key insights. Throughout this book, we've considered how to connect to data—whether file-based, in an on-premises database, or in the cloud. You've worked through examples of exploring and prepping data to clean it and structure it for analysis. We've covered numerous types of visualization and how they can uncover deep analytical insights. The four main types of calculations were explored in depth, giving you the tools to extend the data, analysis, and user interactivity. You've built dashboards and told stories with the data. In this chapter, we considered how to share the results of all your work with others.

You now have a solid foundation. At its core, the Tableau platform is intuitive and easy to use. As you dive deeper, the simplicity becomes increasingly beautiful. As you discover new ways to understand your data, solve complex problems, ask new questions, and find new answers in your datasets, your new Tableau skills will help you uncover, interpret, and share new insights hidden in your data.

Other Books You May Enjoy

If you enjoyed this book, you may be interested in these other books by Packt:

Pandas 1.x Cookbook – Second Edition

Matt Harrison, Theodore Petrou

ISBN: 978-1-83921-310-6

- Master data exploration in pandas through dozens of practice problems
- Group, aggregate, transform, reshape, and filter data
- Merge data from different sources through pandas SQL-like operations
- Create visualizations via pandas hooks to matplotlib and seaborn
- Use pandas, time series functionality to perform powerful analyses
- Import, clean, and prepare real-world datasets for machine learning
- Create workflows for processing big data that doesn't fit in memory

Python Automation Cookbook – Second Edition

Jaime Buelta

ISBN: 978-1-80020-708-0

- Learn data wrangling with Python and Pandas for your data science and AI projects

- Automate tasks such as text classification, email filtering, and web scraping with Python

- Use Matplotlib to generate a variety of stunning graphs, charts, and maps

- Automate a range of report generation tasks, from sending SMS and email campaigns to creating templates, adding images in Word, and even encrypting PDFs

- Master web scraping and web crawling of popular file formats and directories with tools like Beautiful Soup

- Build cool projects such as a Telegram bot for your marketing campaign, a reader from a news RSS feed, and a machine learning model to classify emails to the correct department based on their content

- Create fire-and-forget automation tasks by writing cron jobs, log files, and regexes with Python scripting

Leave a review - let other readers know what you think

Please share your thoughts on this book with others by leaving a review on the site that you bought it from. If you purchased the book from Amazon, please leave us an honest review on this book's Amazon page. This is vital so that other potential readers can see and use your unbiased opinion to make purchasing decisions, we can understand what our customers think about our products, and our authors can see your feedback on the title that they have worked with Packt to create. It will only take a few minutes of your time, but is valuable to other potential customers, our authors, and Packt. Thank you!

Index

Printed by Amazon Italia Logistica S.r.l.
Torrazza Piemonte (TO), Italy

16183378R00332